Why Do I Have

Written by B. Annye Rothenberg, Ph.D.
Child/Parent Psychologist

Illustrated by David T. Wenzel

REDWOOD CITY, CALIFORNIA

DEDICATION

For all parents who do their best and still strive to do better.

And to my son, Bret, for his thoughtfulness and generosity, his listening and teaching, his informed advice, and his loving support. – B.A.R.

Library of Congress Cataloging-in-Publication Data

Rothenberg, B. Annye, 1940-
  Why do I have to? / written by B. Annye Rothenberg ; illustrated by David T. Wenzel. -- 1st ed.
    p. cm.
  ISBN 978-0-9790420-1-0 (pbk.)
1. Socialization--Juvenile literature. 2. Child development-- Juvenile literature.
3. Parental influences--Juvenile literature. 4. Expectation
(Psychology) in children--Juvenile literature. I. Wenzel, David, 1950- II. Title.
  HQ783.R665 2009
  649'.64--dc22

                    2008028425

Printed in China.   First printing January, 2009
10 9 8 7 6 5 4 3 2 1

Children's book in collaboration with
SuAnn and Kevin Kiser
Palo Alto, California

Parents' manual edited by
Caroline Grannan
San Francisco, California

Book design by
Cathleen O'Brien
San Francisco, California

REDWOOD CITY, CALIFORNIA

Published by
PERFECTING PARENTING PRESS
www.PerfectingParentingPress.com

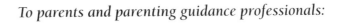

To parents and parenting guidance professionals:

• WHAT'S IN THIS BOOK FOR CHILDREN AND FOR PARENTS •

This second book in a series focuses on the ***constant challenge in child-rearing: getting your children to do what they're asked when they don't want to***. The ***first part*** of this book is a ***story that helps young children ages three through five*** understand why they need to listen and cooperate with their parents' rules. The ***second part is a comprehensive guidance section for parents*** (and their advisors, such as pediatricians and preschool teachers). This parenting manual will teach you to be a knowledgeable and consistent parent, and an effective limit-setter with your young children. Together, these two parts help you and your child understand each other's perspectives and your roles as parent and child.

The children's story shows what happens when Sophie, like many preschoolers, doesn't listen to her parents. Children learn that Sophie's parents make rules because they love and care about her. The story helps your preschooler accept your role as a limit-setter without seeing you as a barrier to freedom and fun.

Read the story to yourself first. Then read it to your child and talk about similar situations in your home. "What happens when we ask you to put your toys away?" "Why do we ask you to do that?" Connecting the book with real life helps children understand that rules teach important things they need to learn as they grow.

The Introduction and Section One of the Parents' Guidance Section help you to ***understand your young child***, to see why limits are hard for preschoolers to follow, and to decide what rules you and your spouse should set, and how. These two sections guide you to develop a comfortable child-rearing philosophy, good family values, and effective parenting practices. Section Two shows many ways to ***make it easier for your preschooler to cooperate and to feel understood*** during those oppositional years. Section Three explains ***reasonable and effective consequences***, and when and how to use them. The Guide includes real-life examples and ***concludes with a summary of practical guidelines***.

—Annye Rothenberg, Ph.D., Child/Parent Psychologist

❖ *For years, Dr. Annye Rothenberg has been a wise and treasured resource in our San Francisco Peninsula region to the many families she has counseled as well as to the guidance professionals whom she mentors.* ***Now she has written a second marvelous book in her current series, one that I highly recommend.*** *I am delighted that her wisdom and experience is being shared with a broader audience.*

— Mary Ann Carmack, MD, PhD; Chair, Department of Pediatrics, Palo Alto (CA) Medical Clinic

My favorite thing is playing. My least favorite thing is following rules. Mommy and Daddy have lots of rules. They always say, "Sophie, our rules show how much we love you." But how come if they love me, I can't just do what I want and not have rules?

While I was building with my blocks, Daddy came into the living room.

"Why aren't you at work, Daddy?" I asked.

"I'm staying home longer today because I worked so late last night," said Daddy. "I have some time to play with you before I go."

"Let's build a road," I said.

When we finished, I wanted to drive on our new road with my favorite ambulance, but I couldn't find it.

"Daddy," I said, "I don't know where my ambulance is."

"Sweetie," said Daddy, "what's the rule about toys?"

"I should always put my toys where they belong when I'm done playing," I said. "I forgot to."

Daddy helped me look for my ambulance. After a long time, we found it under my bed.

"Oh, good!" I said. "Now we can play again."

"I'm sorry, Sophie," said Daddy. "I don't have any more time right now. I have to go to work." He gave me a kiss goodbye. "I'll see you tonight."

I played by myself, but it wasn't as much fun as playing with Daddy.

"Sophie," said Mommy, "it's almost time to go shopping."

I like to go to the store, so I put all my toys away fast, including my favorite ambulance.

7

When we got home from shopping, Mommy said, "I have to make a phone call, Pumpkin. Could you please take the food out of the shopping bag and put it on the counter? That would be a big help."

When I took out the cheese, I saw it was white instead of orange. I had to tell Mommy right away. "Mommy, Mommy!" I said.

"Sophie, I'm talking on the phone," Mommy said. "I'll be done in a minute."

"But, Mommy," I said, "I have to tell you something important."

Mommy put her hand over the phone.

"What's so important, Honey?"

"Mommy," I said, "you didn't get the right cheese."

Mommy frowned at me and said, "The cheese is not important right now, Sophie. Please wait until I'm off the phone."

I don't like to wait.

When Mommy hung up the phone, she said, "Sophie, what's the rule when I'm on the phone?"

"I'm not supposed to interrupt you unless it's an emergency," I said, "because you can only hear one person at a time."

"That's exactly right," said Mommy.

"But, Mommy," I said, "when you're on the phone, I still need you."

"I know it's hard to wait, Honey," said Mommy. "I have an idea. Let's find something special for you to do when I'm on the phone."

We looked around, and Mommy found her old wallet and lots of pictures and cards and papers for me to put in it. Mommy showed me a special drawer nearby to keep the wallet in so I can play with it whenever Mommy or Daddy is on the phone. I liked that idea.

Soon it was time for lunch. We had grilled cheese sandwiches.

"Mmmm," I said. "This is really good."

"I'm glad you like it," said Mommy. "I bought this new kind of cheese especially for you."

"I thought cheese had to be orange to taste good," I said. Mommy laughed.

After lunch, Mommy said, "Do you want to bake some muffins with me? We could have them with supper. Daddy loves muffins and we can surprise him."

"Yes!" I shouted. "I love to bake."

Mommy and I made cranberry-orange muffins.
When the muffins were all baked, Mommy took
them out of the oven and put them on the counter.

"They're very, very hot," said Mommy. "So be sure not to touch them until they're cool. I'll let you know when they're ready. Now I have to do some laundry. You've been such a good helper. Do you want to help me with that too?"

"No," I said, "I want to watch the muffins."

"Watch, but don't touch," said Mommy.

I waited a long time for the muffins to cool — at least a whole minute. Then I thought, "Why do I have to wait until Mommy tells me the muffins are ready? They look ready now." I reached out and tried to pick up a muffin. "Ow!" I said. "Ow! Ow!" I jumped up and down and sucked on my burned fingers. They really hurt.

Mommy came running into the kitchen. "What happened?" she asked.

"I burned my fingers," I said.

Mommy ran cold water over my fingers and kissed me on the forehead. "Do you know why you got burned?" she asked.

"Because the muffins fooled me?" I said.

"No," said Mommy.

"Because I didn't follow your rule," I said.

Mommy nodded. "Rules have reasons," she said.

"I know," I sighed. "But sometimes I forget."

At dinner, I got to surprise Daddy.

"Look what I learned to make," I said, handing him a cranberry-orange muffin.

"These are delicious," said Daddy. "What else did you learn today?"

"I learned that rules are there to help me — so that I won't lose things or have bad manners or get hurt," I said. "I learned that you teach me the rules because you love me. But … "

"But what?" said Mommy.

"But I wish there was a rule that I could stay up and play instead of going to sleep."

"Then what would happen?" asked Daddy.

I thought for a moment. "I would probably be so tired that tomorrow wouldn't be any fun. That would not be a very good rule!"

Daddy and Mommy laughed.

"I know!" I said. "I just thought of a better rule. My own important rule!"

"What is it?" said Mommy.

"My rule is to always follow Mommy's and Daddy's rules."

Mommy and Daddy smiled.

After dinner, there was enough time for all of us to build a road and drive my ambulance.

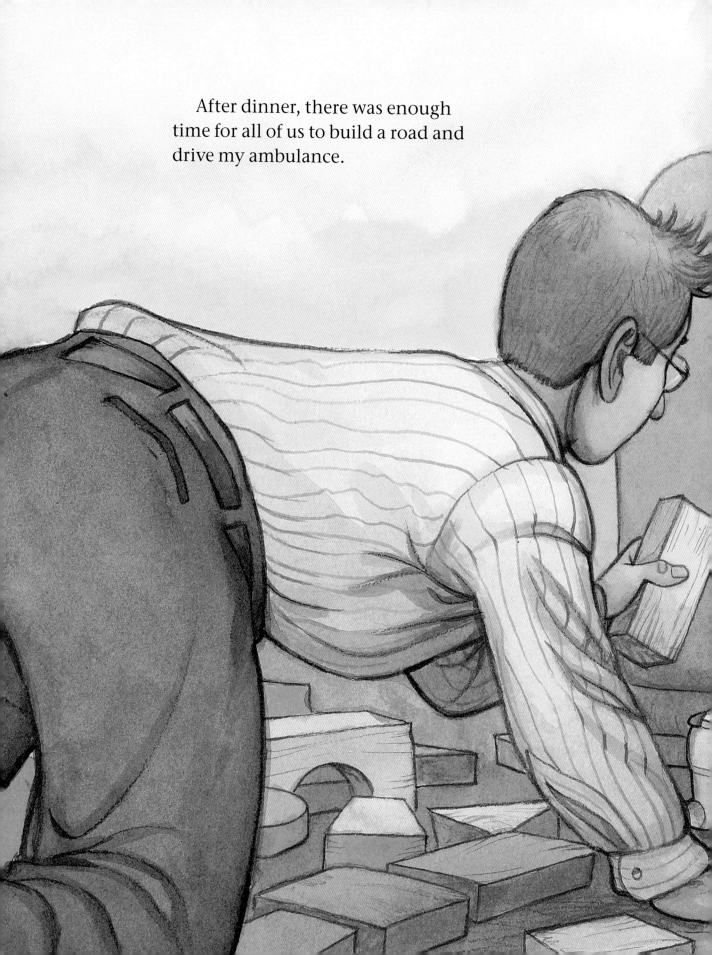

As soon as we finished, I made sure I put all my toys away.

Later, when Mommy was talking to Daddy, I did a puzzle and I didn't interrupt for a long time — two whole minutes at least!

At bedtime, Daddy kissed my sore fingers, and Mommy tucked me in.

When I fell asleep, I dreamed that I followed all the rules, and everyone was happy ... especially me!

A GUIDANCE SECTION FOR PARENTS
• INTRODUCTION •

Many parents are uncertain about what rules to have and frustrated about how to get their preschoolers to obey instead of ignoring, debating, negotiating, or refusing their parents' directions. Teaching children to do what they're told is an important part of parenting.

Preschoolers are playful, inquisitive, and eager learners. They delight, amaze, and fascinate us. They are also challenging because they think so differently than parents do. The preschool age is the hardest for most parents to understand.

INSIDE THE MIND OF A PRESCHOOLER

Preschoolers are oppositional, impulsive, self-centered, inflexible, and illogical — especially when upset. They have a narrower – often more literal – understanding of the meaning of words and figures of speech. Preschoolers can easily misunderstand a comment such as "I have to run downtown now." This happens a lot and is one of the reasons for misunderstandings between parents and young children.

It's easy for preschoolers to entrap themselves in defiance and disobedience, unable to think flexibly enough to avoid unpleasant outcomes. For example, when a parent tells a preschooler to pick up the toys he[1] stopped using an hour ago, the child may argue relentlessly that he isn't finished, that his hand is too tired, or that his 6-week-old baby sister took out the toys. The logic that whoever took them out must put them back doesn't seem compelling to him at this age. He becomes locked rigidly into refusing – almost regardless of what threat you use.

Many parents would impose time-out. But after time-out, a preschooler who's asked "Are you ready to pick up your toys now?" may say, "No, I like time-out." Preschoolers don't do well when backed into a corner. Parents who then threaten to give the toys away can be stumped by the retort, "I don't care. I don't like those toys anyway." The preschooler's natural oppositionality and rigidity have gotten him stuck.

Conflict escalates easily with preschoolers, making it difficult to stay "parental." In this guide, you'll learn effective ways to diminish conflicts and improve cooperation.

GETTING BEYOND "NO! I WON'T!"

Conflicts arise when parents tell their children to do something they don't want to do. When preschoolers resist our rules, we fear that they'll be even more defiant as teenagers. That can make us feel uncertain. But giving children free rein isn't an option. A parent must guide and teach children that rules are necessary and tolerable.

Children have different priorities and interests than their parents. While parents need to respect their children, children also need to learn to listen to their parents and do what's asked in a timely way – such as picking up their toys or going to bed. If, by respect, we mean we do what the other tells us, children need to respect parents to a much greater extent than parents need to respect children.

You need effective **strategies** for teaching your preschooler to do what you ask and building a lasting cooperative and respectful relationship with her. *Some of the most useful are: giving advance notice, making requests fun and/or interesting, giving reasons for them, showing compassion, helping her understand her own reactions, and, if needed, using consequences.*

These methods are part of **Respectful Age-Appropriate Direction**, which is explained in this guide book. This approach helps build a child's willingness to cooperate while fostering high self-esteem, a sense of responsibility, and empathy.

[1] To avoid the awkward use of "he/she," the sections in this guide will alternate between both.

• SECTION ONE •
DEFINING AND TEACHING THE RULES
Establishing Family Values

All families have to develop limits and rules that cover safety, respect, and routines and habits. It can be hard for parents to know which rules are age-appropriate, *and* in accord with their own family values, *and* within accepted community and cultural norms. The wide range of other families' rules and limits often adds to parents' uncertainty. To develop reasonable and achievable rules and limits, it helps to discuss with your spouse what values you both want to teach your child. These important conversations can be enjoyable, thoughtful, and insightful. Discussions of family values are generally low-conflict and tend to build the parenting partnership. Share what characteristics you'd like to see in your child by kindergarten, as a teen, even as an adult. Are you and your spouse modeling these traits? If not, are you willing to work on them? Talk about your goals for yourselves and your children in such areas as relating to others, making decisions, dealing with conflict, handling difficult emotions, working hard to succeed at a task, taking care of your bodies, handling money, using time, and caring for possessions

---

CASE STUDY:
FAMILY VALUES RE-EVALUATED

Nancy and Bill, parents of a four-year-old girl and a two-year-old boy, felt rudderless in their child-rearing. They began to discuss their floundering and to talk about values they shared for their children.

Nancy and Bill started to examine their own behavior. They wanted the children to eat nutritiously and exercise, but the family snacked on unhealthy foods, ate few vegetables or fruits, and didn't exercise regularly. Bill also realized that although he wanted his kids to be friendly, he wasn't very social himself after his typically stressful workdays. Nancy acknowledged that when she was busy with housework and the phone, the kids often watched three or four hours of TV a day.

Both parents were motivated to do the hard work of making changes to improve the family's quality of life and model better values. Bill looked for ways to reduce stress at work, and they made an effort to

---

socialize more. They began to serve healthier meals, and to take family walks and bike rides on weekends. Their improved social life as a couple allowed Nancy to cut back on conducting friendships by phone, so she could turn off the kids' TV and spend more time with them. Reducing TV helped the children become less moody, less wild, and more resourceful about finding things to do. As they worked on shared values and goals, the necessary rules and limits became clearer to the parents, and the children began to accept and incorporate them. Nancy and Bill agreed to use the children's birthdays and their anniversary to update their family goals and evaluate their children's progress.

PARENTING AS PARTNERS

Parents frequently disagree about the approaches to take to reach their common goals. We love our children so much – and are so deeply committed to helping them develop into well-functioning members of society – that *disagreements can be intense and uncompromising*.

The first book in this series – *Mommy and Daddy are Always Supposed to Say Yes ... Aren't They?* – addresses those issues in the section "When Mommy and Daddy Fail to Work as a Team."

RULES PRESCHOOLERS SHOULD LEARN

Parents need to learn reasonable expectations for their child at each age. You can do this by reading about child development; talking to teachers or your pediatrician; chatting with parents casually or at parenting classes; observing other children at the playground, on play dates, and at preschool; and taking care of other children. Knowing what to expect makes it easier to determine appropriate rules for your child's age.

It's valuable to use phrases with your young child such as "It's Mommy's and Daddy's job to teach you everything that a _____ -year-old needs to know." This concept helps reinforce that rule-making *is* a parent's job. Children should also be given reasons for new or changed rules: "We need to get dressed quickly today because..." And it's important to praise children for cooperating: "You picked up your toys so fast – that was great," or "That was so helpful." Parents need to determine effective methods for getting cooperation, such as making requests sound like fun. And the child needs to understand the consequences of not cooperating. Both will be addressed in detail later in this guide book.

The following are some suggested rules for preschoolers. *The first rule is that your child needs to pay attention when you speak to him.*

The second set of rules and limits involves safety. Parents are the most confident in enforcing limits in this area – rules like not touching a hot stove and not running into the street.

Third are rules and limits covering respect for other people and possessions. They include using "please" and "thank you," and speaking respectfully and kindly to parents, friends, and siblings. Preschoolers also need to learn to treat possessions – theirs and others' – appropriately: Don't scribble on walls, don't throw toys, and don't take others' things without asking.

Fourth are rules involving regular routines. Morning routines guide dressing, toothbrushing, and so on. Daytime routines dictate eating, playtime, TV, etc. Evening routines address preparing for bedtime, from putting away toys to how many stories. Routines provide the necessary predictability to children and decrease limit-testing.

Next are rules that cover necessary habits. These include table manners and good eating habits, toileting, and handwashing.

Last, parents need to encourage their child to *practice skills that prepare him for school:* speaking well and clearly, paying attention at read-aloud time, using scissors, learning the letter sounds, printing his name, and so forth.

These rules should teach a child the essential values to internalize as he grows up. Your rules and values help him to navigate life successfully. Rules help children eventually learn to get enough rest, manage their time, eat healthfully, limit impulse buying, play well with others, tackle unappealing tasks, and face challenges.

TOO STRICT, TOO LENIENT, OR JUST RIGHT?

Extreme rule-setting styles, whether too *strict* or too lenient, can lead to problems. Parents who are too **strict** don't give their children enough opportunity to understand their parents' reasoning. The children can feel overly controlled and may assume their thoughts and feelings are unimportant. When parents are too **lenient**, children assume they know best. Without appropriate expectations and guidance, children can lack motivation and direction, and expect to have a level of authority they're not ready for.

Try to keep your style of rulemaking fairly similar to that of other families you respect – neither much more strict nor much more lenient. If your family is extreme, your child may have trouble adjusting to unfamiliar levels of rules at school and elsewhere. The confusing differences can lead to misbehavior.

CASE STUDY:
WHEN FAMILY RULES DON'T LINE UP WITH KINDERGARTEN

Eileen and Tom loved their four-year-old's spirited nature. Ryan was hard to manage, but they were determined not to crush his spirit. They were also less routine-oriented and more spontaneous than most families they knew. When Ryan didn't cooperate with getting dressed in the morning, Eileen and Tom let him dawdle, even if he was late for preschool. When he ignored their requests that he pick up his toys or close the door on his way outside, they let it go. When he wanted extra time to play at bedtime, they felt his request was reasonable. When he didn't learn to print his name or draw because "it's too hard" and "it's no fun," they thought he'd learn in kindergarten.

Ryan's difficult adjustment to kindergarten lasted months longer than other children's. The teacher explained that children needed to arrive on time, but being rushed made Ryan angry. He didn't believe he had to obey the teacher unless he wanted to. He didn't want to put his papers away, push in his chair, or pick up his share of the toys. He found paper and pencil tasks too hard and called them "boring." In time, he became angry and frustrated that he lacked his classmates' writing and drawing skills.

Ryan disliked kindergarten and its rules and expectations. His teacher had trouble changing his attitude and behavior until his parents began to bring their rules and expectations into line with other families' and with the school's expectations.

It wasn't until April of his kindergarten year that Ryan stopped resisting and became less angry. Even then, he didn't enjoy school despite having a talented, experienced, and caring teacher.

DON'T GIVE CHILDREN TOO MUCH "SAY"

Knowing how much say or control to give your child is hard. Most parents believe a child's self-esteem is increased if she feels she has been heard. But young children don't have the judgment to make good decisions. Small decisions, like choosing between two acceptable shirts or pieces of fruit, give young children the right kind of practice in decision-making – although **when tired**, they may not be able to decide even between two choices. Small decisions can help your children cooperate more easily and begin to connect their choices with the outcomes – to see the link between cause and effect. **But parents need to resist giving children too much say too young.** A three-year-old who gets to choose the restaurant or decide the order of her parents' errands will likely become a four-year-old who expects to control more adult decisions – such as whether she has to go to preschool today or when she can have a play date. This demanding behavior frustrates and angers parents. *A child who has grown used to hearing yes will likely be angry when you say no.*

The decisions you give your child should affect only her. She shouldn't be choosing which shopping mall you'll go to with her. That gives her too much control, pressure, and responsibility.

Don't feel compelled to keep your child from "melting down" by saying yes too frequently. Parents who overindulge their children to avoid outbursts find the results disappointing. Young children who run the show often end up grumpy, unappreciative, and more demanding than ever.

Since children naturally want more say every day, you'll need to continuously monitor your child's age and judgment to recognize what choices are reasonable for her. For example, your preschooler can decide what she plays with or which stuffed animals to take to bed, but not when to pick up her toys nor how late to go to bed. Expect to offer increasing decision-making privileges little by little. By giving your child age-appropriate decisions, you can help her avoid becoming overly entitled, too self-centered, and less well-liked. A child who is not well-liked doesn't feel as good about herself.

As children mature, they can make more decisions. They can keep to agreements and take more responsibility for themselves. For example, older children can choose when they'll pick up their toys as long as it's done by dinnertime. This would not be possible for preschoolers. Older children can pick out their clothes. Preschoolers usually don't have the judgment to choose appropriate clothes for the season or the occasion.

BEING CONSISTENT

Children are more secure and confident when limits on their actions and behaviors are consistently enforced. However, it's much easier to make rules than to enforce them. Your child will check to see if you have good reasons behind your rules and if you'll cave in if he pushes your limits. He needs to know that you care enough to help him live up to your expectations. Make sure you stand behind your rules. Take an extra minute to think about whether you mean it before you say it. For example, you're not likely to carry out your threat to give away **all** his toys.

When you can't be consistent, it's helpful if your child knows that there is a good reason ("you don't have to close the screen door today because it's stuck").

If you cave in or make concessions frequently, your child will push your limits. This results in less respect for you and for authority in general. For example, Dad has repeatedly told Jake to get dressed if he wants to go to the hardware store. Although he wants to go, Jake dawdles. Finally, Dad says: "You'll have to stay home with Mommy, because I'm leaving now!" Jake cries and carries on, pleading, "I'll get dressed." Though angry, Dad helps Jake dress and takes him along. Dad has unfortunately proved that even after he says "that's it," he will still give in whenever Jake decides to cooperate. Why would Jake listen earlier if it's never too late to get what he wants? The more consistent you are, the easier it will be for your child to accept your limits, resulting in less negotiation, ignoring, and back-talking, now and in the future.

THE DETERMINED PRESCHOOLER'S AMAZING BAG OF TRICKS

Parents can be astonished, frustrated, and sometimes frightened at the powerful and provocative methods their young children use to get their way. Preschoolers refuse, argue, negotiate, and cover their ears. They have tantrums, screaming and crying, sometimes insisting they can't stop. They may hit, kick, spit at, bite, or pinch you, someone else, or themselves – or bang their heads. They may tell you that you're not their friend, you're mean, you're an awful parent and they want the garbage man to take you away. They might say you don't love them – or they don't love you – and even vow to run away and live with a new family. Some threaten to destroy your treasured possessions. Some preschoolers make themselves gag or even throw up. Some open the front door and shout that you're hurting them. Older preschoolers may even threaten to kill themselves.

The good news is that your preschooler won't use all these techniques. Children settle on some that seem effective. A child whose parents are visibly shaken and uncertain is likely to have more and stronger reactions. A child who is **innately** more persistent and strong-willed will work harder to get her way.

We shouldn't panic when our preschoolers use these powerful tools. Take a deep breath, understand why they're behaving this way, and explain the reason to them: "I think you're saying that because you're angry that we couldn't go to the park and you really want me to let you have your way. Here's a better way to tell me that." Use compassion if appropriate and consequences if necessary. Try not to become a marshmallow when she starts packing to go and find another family to live with — one that will always let her have her way.

EXPRESSING YOUR NEEDS

Healthy selfishness has an important place in parenting. *Learn to feel comfortable asserting your needs so that your child learns to respect them.* For example, if your child is being too loud by **your** standards, don't ignore or compromise with him. Tell him why what he's doing isn't OK and what his options are. Even when you play with your preschooler, you should teach him to take turns with you in deciding what to play rather than letting him be in charge. If he can get you – an adult – to do his bidding, he'll want to boss his peers, which can make it hard for him to play well with others.

The first book in this series — **Mommy and Daddy Are Always Supposed to Say Yes … Aren't They?** – helps parents understand how much choice and say to give preschoolers so they develop healthy self-esteem, without becoming more self-focused, **and** indulged, demanding, and angry when they don't get their way.

• SECTION TWO •
GAINING COOPERATION THROUGH *RESPECTFUL AGE-APPROPRIATE DIRECTION*

You can use **Respectful Age-Appropriate Direction** to help your child become more cooperative with your requests and learn the family rules. This section explains those methods.

YOUR PRESCHOOLER NEEDS TIME WITH YOU – BANK ON IT

Your preschooler needs some uninterrupted time with you, preferably every day, when you are not asking her to do something. She needs to know that you spend time with her because you like her company – time doing something you **both** enjoy. (TV doesn't count.) When this special time becomes part of your routine, your child will feel more connected to you and better about herself, and more willing to cooperate with you. Even ten minutes a day goes a long way. Spending time with your child is like putting money in the bank that you can draw on as needed. When there isn't enough one-on-one time, your child is more likely to resist your requests.

COOPERATION CAN BE FUN

Since preschoolers think very differently than older children, parents need to use "preschooler-friendly" methods to help gain their cooperation. *Some strategies that usually don't work well with preschoolers are:* repeating commands over and over, threatening punishment if they "do that again," lecturing, talking about "appropriate behavior," yelling, sticker charts, or extracting promises.

We need to find ways to make preschoolers want to say yes. Preschoolers – as we know – are more emotional and considerably less rational and logical than older children. Because they are so oppositional, they may automatically say no – even when "no" is to their disadvantage. It's important to make cooperating interesting and fun so they don't feel coerced. Convey enthusiasm. Instead of "it's bath time," try saying, "Let's poke holes in a paper cup to take into your bath." Making requests appealing rather than commanding and confrontational will help him see you as a guide rather than an oppressor. Parents can also mention the interesting activity that will begin right after the child puts away the toys or cleans up the spill. *"Making it fun"* makes preschoolers less likely to remain entrenched in a prolonged oppositional phase.

You don't need to invent a new idea or make it fun every time, but you should make your requests fun many times a day. It's hard to be creative and playful when rushed and stressed, but it's worth the effort. Come up with ideas when you're not rushed and hang notes on the refrigerator to remind yourself (for example, show your child that his striped shirt is whispering in your ear saying that it wants to go with its buddy, his blue pants). Playful ideas can become more natural when you see how they reduce stress for you and your child – especially when there's a lot of laughing. A carrot that tells your child, "I want to be in your tummy," or a marker that says, "Please don't leave me alone on the floor – put me in the box with my friends, the red and yellow markers," can make your request really amusing to a preschooler, and that encourages cooperation.

One Dad made a playful routine of bringing sunglasses into the bathroom at tooth-brushing time and putting them on with a flourish when 3½-year-old Jenny had brushed her teeth until they were "bright and dazzling." The sunglasses game transformed Jenny from a kicking, screaming toothbrush-fighter to an eager, giggling participant in the shared ritual. Preschoolers love repetition, so the identical routine went on every night for six months until Jenny grew out of needing it.

Adding fun and variety makes cooperating easier. *However, it's important not to use bribery – such as offering a new toy or a food treat – as a regular way to get cooperation.* You'll know when you're using bribery, because you won't feel good about making the offer. You don't want to start hearing your child say, "What am I going to get if I do it?" In contrast, there are no drawbacks to making it fun. *Preschoolers are grateful and happy when you make it easy for them to cooperate.* You'll need this technique less as he grows out of the oppositional stage – sometime about kindergarten age.

HOW WE PHRASE OUR REQUESTS FOR COOPERATION

When preschoolers get stuck in their refusals, parents often get frustrated and adamant. It doesn't help much to use authoritarian commands. Try to be a little more creative about "unsticking" your preschooler's rigidity. Instead of "Brush your teeth," try "My teeth and yours need brushing, so let's brush ours together."

Advance notice helps with cooperation. Try: "Pretty soon, it will be time to put away your toys so we can have dinner." Praise is also a powerful motivator. "You did a great job. You're awesome" – those are words a child loves to hear.

Many parents phrase requests for cooperation as if they were choices. In our current language pattern, we say, "Do you want to pick up your toys now?" instead of announcing, "It's almost time to pick up your toys." Or we tack on "OK?" – "Let's brush your teeth now, OK?" *Phrasing requests as questions confuses and frustrates literal-minded preschoolers*, making them think they have a choice. Choosing "no" and then being told to pick up toys anyway makes young children angry. Use statements, not questions, when you're not really offering a choice.

GENERAL TIPS TO MAKE COOPERATION EASIER

• *Slow down*— It helps if your child isn't rushed all the time. She needs some time every day to meander in her thoughts and play. If you expect preschoolers to be efficient, quick, or logical in all their tasks, they will usually become resistant.

• *Use humor* — Preschoolers get very intense and rigid when frustrated. This tends to trigger an identical reaction in parents, causing locked horns and a lot of emotions and exhaustion. Lightening up the situation with humor breaks the deadlock and the tension and models a successful way to deal with conflict. Be sure your child doesn't think you're making fun of her.

• *Use age as a motivator* — When a child cooperates readily or calms down quickly after an angry moment, say something like: "That's amazing – you did that just like you were 4 ½ years old, and you're only four."

• *Give reasons* — It's helpful if your preschooler learns that you have good reasons behind your rules. If she doesn't seem to be listening to your reasons, you can sometimes ask her if *she* knows why you have that rule. Your child is more likely to understand when she has to put into her own words what you've explained before, and you'll have another opportunity to praise her.

• *Use compassion* — Your compassion helps your preschooler feel understood *and* better understand herself. If she doesn't want to leave the park when it's time, you can say, "Of course you're mad. It's hard to stop when you're having so much fun."

• *Learn what works with your unique child* — Observe your child's reactions and try out different approaches to getting cooperation and using consequences. *Make sure you try an approach long enough to see if it's effective.*

REDIRECTING AND DISTRACTING

It's hard for your preschooler to stop what he's doing on command. It's important to present your request in a way that sounds interesting to him. For example: You find your son running his metal truck along the window. Instead of saying, "Austin, stop that," you're more likely to get cooperation if you say, "Austin, that could scratch the glass. Here's something we can do. Let's make a highway for your truck." Involve him in building the highway, perhaps between two long blocks on the kitchen floor. **This is redirecting, an important technique for getting cooperation from preschoolers.** Your child learns the reason behind the rule while finding another way to explore, learn, and have fun – and he also sees how happy you are with him. That's helping your child learn to cooperate, and also to think flexibly when he can't do what he wants.

If your child goes right back to doing what he shouldn't, either his idea was much more fun, your discipline style wasn't confident enough, or maybe he's just a very persistent child. In any case, remind him of other truck-playing options or engage him in a different activity. Tell him what will happen if he doesn't cooperate: "It would be sad if your truck were to go away, but children need to learn to do what grownups tell them." You might have to take the truck away and tell him you're getting grumpy because he's not listening. Then you could make a show of acting grumpy and unhelpful. He might need a time-out as well.

Distraction can be effective, **but to help your child learn to accept common frustrations and disappointments, you can't be afraid to say no when necessary.** When he's screaming that he's not going to pick up his toys, simply distracting him with "come make soup with me!" doesn't teach him that he has to do as you asked. If you skirt around conflict and avoid frustrating him, it's likely he will develop a lower frustration tolerance. There are many inevitable disappointments in daily life, even for a preschooler, such as those moments when he has to get in the car or can't have ice cream. We can help our preschoolers by getting them used to waiting rather than interrupting your phone call, by playing games that require taking turns, and by helping them express their frustration in words.

HELPING PRESCHOOLERS UNDERSTAND THEIR BEHAVIOR

It's not helpful to ask misbehaving preschoolers questions like "Why did you do that?" Most preschoolers aren't old enough to understand their reasons or how to articulate them, and don't want to get themselves into more trouble by answering you. Your preschooler will benefit most if you suggest possible reasons for her behavior: "I think you threw that block because when I said playtime was over, you didn't want to stop." Insights like this will make your child feel understood, and your explanation helps her understand her own behavior. It also encourages her to think about the real reason if your suggestion doesn't sound right.

It's important to suggest better options to your child. You could say, "Instead of throwing a block, Lily, try saying, 'I'm mad because I didn't have enough time to play'." Practice these phrases with her. You can teach her to say them forcefully so she'll experience some release of frustration and tension.

"Use your words" is too sophisticated a concept for many preschoolers. Instead, suggest what words. Of course, for misbehavior, there would typically also be additional consequences. (Section Three elaborates on consequences.)

Children experience emotional swings when things don't go their way. Their quick, dramatic mood changes can vary from happy and silly, to furious, sad, or anxious, to happy and calm again. This can drain parents while their child recovers quickly and moves on. The techniques in this section should be helpful when your child flatly refuses to cooperate.

WHEN YOUR PRESCHOOLER HAS A TANTRUM

Although tantrums are most common in toddlers (18 months to 2½ or three years), preschoolers still have tantrums. Frustration triggers tantrums. Preschoolers' tantrums are usually ignited by the limits you set: "No, you can't have a cookie" or "It's time to go." Tantrums may **also** be touched off by their inability to do something like getting the blocks to connect. We can guide preschoolers to find other ways to deal with these frustrations. Teach him to say, "I'm mad because I'm not done playing or "I need help – this is too hard." We can respond compassionately, telling him when he can get back to his toys or sympathizing when a task frustrates him.

Frustration can also be related to fatigue and hunger. Or it can come from a sense of being treated unfairly, not listened to, or spoken to harshly. And children who are not **used** to limits often have tantrums when you say no. As you consider these factors, you can begin to figure out ways to help your child diminish his tantrums' frequency and intensity.

When your child is having a tantrum, get him to a place in the house where he isn't the focus of attention. See if he can settle himself down in a few minutes. If the tantrum goes on and on, you could sit next to him and keep him company silently, perhaps stroking his arm. Trying to converse with him usually exacerbates things. Later, you can try teaching him some words to calm himself down, such as, "I'll be able to do it later."

If your child has frequent and long tantrums. you need to become a detective and a teacher. Like a detective, help him figure out what happened – and, like a teacher, show him skills to diminish the need for future tantrums. Parents sometimes have to consult with a pediatrician or mental health professional.

WHEN YOUR PRESCHOOLER HITS YOU

Preschoolers can quickly become emotional, and with that comes impulsiveness and irrationality. Many preschoolers hit their parents when they're frustrated and angry. **That needs to be stopped firmly – but not by our hitting them**. Take your child to time-out. After a preschooler hits, she has conflicting thoughts and feelings: She had the right to do it – no, she shouldn't have done it. You're mad at her – no, you love her. You'll abandon her – no, you would never leave her.

We need to figure out why she's hitting and make sure we're not hitting her or allowing others to do so. **When we spank or swat our kids, they are more likely to hit back**

when angry. *A child who is physically forced to comply – such as being wrestled into her clothes – is more likely to be physical toward us or others.*

We also need to teach better options. Suggest some phrases to use. And make sure she's getting enough exercise and sleep. We can help her to understand that she hit because she was frustrated, but that hitting is never OK. She needs to find a way to get back on your good side (with your help) – in addition to apologizing – because preschoolers misbehave more if they feel like "bad kids."

WHEN TO BE FLEXIBLE AND WHEN TO HOLD FIRM

Most parents hope they'll encourage cooperation by "giving" a little, perhaps helping the child pick up his toys although he was told to pick them up himself, or giving him dessert even though he didn't eat the agreed-upon bites of chicken and broccoli. Parents also hope to avoid preschoolers' outbursts by giving in partway. Yet if we continually compromise against our better judgment, we're setting the foundation for a continuing battleground.

We don't need to model rigidity, but when we bend a little, we should explain why. This provides room for some flexibility and allows children to have their voices heard without conveying that we are always open to negotiation. *Many parents joke that their child will be a "great lawyer" because of his debating and negotiating skills. But allowing our kids to argue constantly encourages them to become controlling and bossy, and stay self-centered.* It's generally important for parents to follow through on what they say, rather than sending confusing messages.

IT'S HARD BEING A PARENT

You may be thinking, "Why do I have to do all this? Why can't I just expect my child to do what I tell her?" *Preschoolers develop best when we guide them with age-appropriate understanding and tools.* Good parenting is hard work until you learn the tools of the trade. You'll need to update your parenting skills as your child grows. Being a thoughtful observer of your child helps enormously.

It's necessary to learn how to help your child through difficult periods, such as whiny, angry, demanding, or anxious stages. When our children have **continuing** behavior problems, rather than hope it's a stage, we need to work on figuring out why and how we can help them. It's not good for the child or the family to let a child continue to be annoying, sad, worried, etc. Your child needs you to become a skilled parent.

LEARNING FROM THE SITUATION

After a frustrating verbal and emotional pull-and-tug with your preschooler, you need to see if he learned what you wanted him to.

For example: Kristen needed to get out the door with her kids. She dressed her baby and sent three-year-old Jordan to get his shoes – twice. When Kristen noticed that Jordan still hadn't gotten the shoes, she said, "Jordan, I've asked you twice to get your shoes."

Jordan didn't look up and kept playing with his pony.

"Look at me," Kristen said. "Why haven't you gotten your shoes?"

"I don't know where they are," Jordan answered.

"You took them off last night in the kitchen," Kristen said. "Now please get them or we're not going to play at the park."

Jordan continued playing. Furious, Kristen took Jordan by the hand, walked him into the kitchen, got the shoes, and put them on Jordan. Then Kristen – who was eager to get out of the house herself – told her son: "I shouldn't take you to the park, but it's nice out. Next time you don't listen when I ask you to do something, I won't take you."

Ask yourself what Jordan learned from this scenario. He probably learned that when Mommy asks him to do something, he doesn't have to cooperate, because Mommy will give him many chances and will eventually do it herself. And Mommy will tell him he'll be punished but she doesn't mean it. *He's learning that he doesn't have to do what his Mother says. This is not a lesson you want to teach your child.*

• SECTION THREE •
WHEN ALL ELSE FAILS: ESTABLISHING CONSEQUENCES

Consequences are essential in child-rearing and an important part of the **Respectful Age-Appropriate Direction** approach.

THE PURPOSE OF CONSEQUENCES

Consequences help your child learn to do what you ask. They help her internalize your rules and requests – from picking up her toys, to going to bed, to using her manners. Preschoolers are naturally impulsive, so it can be hard for them to learn to comply. *Consequences should cause your child to hesitate before she repeats problem behavior and to begin to develop inner discipline.* You want her to eventually learn to do the right thing without your having to check on her constantly. If the consequences don't bother her, they're not *effective* consequences.

WHAT *NOT* TO USE AS CONSEQUENCES

Many kinds of consequences are recommended for preschoolers when they disobey or misbehave. There are some that are **no longer considered acceptable**: physical punishment (spanking, pinching, yanking, etc.), frightening children ("the bogey man will take you away," or locking them outside or in the dark) or humiliating them (making them stand facing the corner or asking them, "Why are you ruining our family?"). Instead, you can create boring, tedious, and therefore memorable consequences that will help your child think twice before repeating the misbehavior. Such consequences teach without the negative effects of fear and humiliation.

The most common but least effective technique is to repeat the request or rule without consequences: "Don't climb up on that table again" or "Go get your shoes. I'm not going to tell you again." Many things have to be taught using at least some consequences.

THINKING ABOUT CONSEQUENCES

It's wisest to have a variety of effective consequences thought out beforehand. Variety helps reinforce the lesson in multiple ways. Children can build up resistance to overused techniques.

It's impossible to anticipate every unexpected situation that calls for consequences on the spot. Developing your philosophy about what behavior is and isn't acceptable, and about what consequences are successful with your child *and* acceptable to you and our society, will help you react confidently, appropriately, and effectively.

EFFECTIVE CONSEQUENCES

Time-out is a common and useful consequence for young children. It's effective because young children don't want to be away from their parents. Time-outs are usually one minute per year of age (four-year-olds get four-minute time-outs). Your child should stay in his room with the door shut and may have toys to play with. (Doors can stay open for children who are going through a period of separation anxiety and can stay in their room.) Using the bedroom for time-out is unlikely to cause a preschooler to fear his room – unless you do something extreme like locking him in or keeping him there for very long periods. *The point of the time-out is that he can't be with the rest of the family nor have freedom of the house.* Many children will initially refuse to stay in their room. A parent can sit outside the door as a sentry, enforcing the time-out as well as letting him know where you are. Another way is to have the child sit on the couch, the stairs, or some other spot, but most children will test this limit by moving from spot to spot, aggravating the situation even more.

While in time-out, many young children will kick the door and throw toys. You can help your child by suggesting to the three-year-old something he can occupy himself with in his room, and by adding more time for kids four and older. With three-year-olds, you can place a three-minute hourglass "egg" timer – out of their reach but where they can see the sand falling. This gives them something to look at and a sense of how much time is left. A regular timer is fine for four and up. *Letting young children decide to come out of time-out when they think they can behave is not effective because it puts the child in charge of his own consequences.*

Children ages four and up often don't mind being in their room alone, so a second consequence is needed to help the older preschooler internalize rules. Using the time-out first conveys to the child that he needs to be on his own for a while because of his misbehavior, and the second consequence provides some memorable teaching.

SECOND CONSEQUENCES

The following are some "second half" or secondary consequences to help children four and older learn not to repeat the misbehavior. Many of these techniques can also be used with preschoolers as stand-alone consequences.

• *Losing a privilege* — Make television or a favorite toy off-limits for the rest of the day. Toys and other belongings that have been thrown or otherwise mishandled can be also put away for the rest of the day.

• *Out-of-time* — Let your child know that so much time has been spent trying to get her to cooperate that you are out of time. Tell her that there's no time left for a special project or outing because she spent that time not listening. Be sure to let her know when you **will** do that special outing so she doesn't get upset thinking she will never get to do it.

• *Redo and practice* — Have your child repeatedly practice doing what you asked her to do. For example, when she hasn't picked up her toys, warn her that if she doesn't, you'll have her pick them up along with another "mess" or two that you've made because "you need picking-up practice." With a child who often ignores you, let her know you'll be calling her name many times in the next half-hour and that she has to answer you. ("What, Mom?") Some of those times, you can say, "I didn't need you to do anything, but I need you to practice answering me when I call you." When your child is rude, have her tell you again in a kind way. *Without real practice, there isn't much change in a child's behavior. Practice results in better learning. Try three repetitions in a row.* Using Redo can decrease – even eliminate – the need to have "that" discussion after time-out: "Why are you in time-out? What are you going to do instead next time?" This discussion is generally lip-service, ending with promises, which are hard for preschoolers to keep.

• *Following meaningless directions* — Tell your child that she hasn't had a good listening day so she needs practice. Then have her follow several "meaningless" directions, such as "Put this paper on that corner of the table; put this cup right next to that door," etc. About four to eight in a row would be memorable enough.

• *Apology* — Have your child do something nice for you when her behavior makes you very angry, such as apologizing and drawing an apology picture, or bringing you something (such as a glass of ice water) to make up to you. Help her understand what you want – at least initially – by giving hints, or examples, if necessary. Some parents feel that an insincere apology would be meaningless. But a child needs to apologize even if she doesn't sincerely feel sorry. A child who is allowed to evade apologizing from the earliest years is likely to become unwilling to apologize and accept responsibility. Encourage your child to apologize in words, and, if necessary, in actions.

• *Empathy* — Older preschoolers can be asked to look at a situation from your perspective: "What does Mommy think about what just happened, and why does Mommy think that? What does Daddy feel about that and what does he want you to do to fix the problem?" These questions may be hard for your child to answer, but at least she will think about them, even if only briefly.

For these second or alternate consequences, make sure your older preschooler knows ahead of time that if she refuses, dawdles, etc., *she'll have to go back to time-out* and the same consequence will be waiting for her. If you change to another consequence, she's likely to think you're trying something else because you're not able to get her to comply. *Use consequences right away – after only one reminder. When parents repeat their requests several times before using consequences, this slows down a child's learning.*

AVOID AN ACCUSATORY "YOU" TONE

It puts a child on the defensive to say, "You haven't been listening to me" or "You took forever to clean up." It's more effective to say, "This hasn't been a good listening day" or "We need a lot of cleanup practice." If you use the "you" version, your child feels attacked, probably won't accept your correction, and often will verbally counterattack, requiring additional consequences. You'll get better results with a non-accusatory method of correction. Your child knows you mean him.

WHEN THE REACTION IS "I DON'T CARE!"

Many preschoolers will insist that the consequence doesn't bother them. They might say: "I don't care! I like time-out!" or "I didn't like that toy anyway!" Or at the end of a time-out they might say: "I'm not coming out of time-out because I like it here!" These comments are usually *bravado*. Preschoolers use many ways to preserve their autonomy and dignity. Holding your child to her word or even arguing would be a mistake in these situations. It's better to help her understand why she said what she did or to just let the statement go by, responding with a nonverbal gesture like a shrug. Ignoring your child is not recommended because it can teach her to ignore others.

THE PITFALLS OF USING ONLY REWARDS AND CONSEQUENCES TO GET YOUR CHILD TO BEHAVE

Many parents assume that rewards, such as a toy, and consequences, such as taking away dessert or TV, are the complete range of strategies necessary for dealing with a child who doesn't listen or otherwise misbehaves. But when parents rely entirely on these types of rewards and consequences, many children feel controlled but not understood, and feel resentful and emotionally more distant from the parents.

This type of parenting makes it harder for children to develop the desire and self-control to behave well. **Relying on payoffs and penalties doesn't encourage the child to develop a strong conscience and sense of morality.** For example, when the five-year-old sees that no one is watching, he may put his finger in the cake batter, even though the parent has explained why he shouldn't, or slip his teacher's marker into his pocket to bring home. Rewards and consequences are necessary in child-rearing – but not sufficient. It's more effective to use the range of tools explained in this guide, which help children to feel more understood, respected, and closer to their parents. Children gain a better understanding of the role, reasons, and needs of their parents, and they become more eager to please them. **It's very important that young children learn to behave in order to please their parents. By teen years and beyond, people behave to meet their own internalized expectations, which developed because they learned early on to please their parents.**

Rewards and consequences are effective, but the most successful rewards for young children involve spending time with their parents. The most useful consequences involve having the child practice better behavior. And the parent-child communication should include that little touch of guilt that is essential for good conscience development.

• CONCLUSION •

Limit-setting is critical in a child's development. Knowing what to expect helps children learn, over time, to behave acceptably and responsibly. Parents should base their essential rules on their values and those of their community, and on their child's age. It's useful to understand how preschoolers think and how to make it easier for them to listen – how to make it fun and interesting, as often as possible, for them to cooperate.

Respectful consequences hasten your young child's learning as she internalizes the rules and values of your family and society. When parents become respectful, age-appropriate limit-setters and develop effective consequences, it's easier for their children to cooperate. Parents enjoy their children and family life more when they feel self-assured and successful rather than frustrated, angry, and discouraged in their parenting. And their competence and satisfaction builds their children's confidence and skills – things all parents want for themselves and their children.

• GUIDELINES FOR GAINING COOPERATION AND TEACHING IMPORTANT RULES USING *RESPECTFUL AGE-APPROPRIATE DIRECTION* •

The following guidelines summarize how to develop family rules, get preschoolers to cooperate more easily, and use appropriate consequences that can help children internalize your family rules and values.

ONE: *Consider How Differently Preschoolers Think*

Preschoolers have a narrow and literal understanding of the world. They also tend to be oppositional, self-centered, impulsive, illogical, and rigid – especially when upset. This is the age at which many parents find their children's behavior hardest to understand.

TWO: *Work On The Rules And Limits You And Your Spouse Feel Will be Valuable for Your Preschooler*

Talk to your spouse about child-rearing values to determine what rules will help your family move toward those goals. Try to make sure your rules are in line with expectations and standards in your community, in your schools, and among the friends you respect. When your rules are among the strictest or the most permissive, your child's adjustment to her community will be harder. Step back and see if you and your spouse live by your own rules. For example, if you're teaching your child to clean up his toys and clothes but you leave your own things out, why should he pick his up?

THREE: *Don't Give Young Children Too Much Choice Or Say*

With too much decision-making power, preschoolers will begin to think they're in charge. For example, they may believe that they can help themselves to food whenever they want to, or decide the order of your errands. When you ask your children to listen, don't make it sound like a choice ("Do you want to pick up your toys now?" "How about getting ready for bed?").

FOUR: *Consider The Importance Of Consistency*

Does your child believe you mean what you tell her, or are your requests a starting point for negotiation, back-talking, and an exhausting battleground? Is your child learning that you **can't** comfortably and confidently say no? Do you give concessions? ("You can't have three cookies, but you can have two now and one later").

Don't go into shock or panic and don't give in when your preschooler uses powerful techniques to get what she wants, such as hitting you, telling you "you're not the boss of me," or telling you she's going to live with a new family that will let her do what she wants.

FIVE: *Don't Rush Your Preschooler All the Time, And Give Advance Notice*

Preschoolers need some time every day when they can do things at their own speed. Preschoolers are easily distracted and often go from one thing to another in a manner that looks inefficient to an adult. They need freedom to be without time pressure sometimes. Give advance notice when possible: "You have time to finish that puzzle and then we need to leave. If we go soon, we'll have time to stop and watch the train go by."

SIX: *Learn Some Playful And Humorous Techniques For Gaining Cooperation*

To be effective and less confrontational and argumentative, make it fun, captivating, and motivating for your preschooler to follow your requests. For example, when you want him to get dressed, tell him that the red shirt is a good friend of his blue pants and the friends want to be together. Or explain that he has to leave the park soon because his dog Patches is waiting to play with him at home.

• GUIDELINES FOR GAINING COOPERATION AND TEACHING IMPORTANT RULES USING *RESPECTFUL AGE-APPROPRIATE DIRECTION* •

SEVEN: *Encourage Empathy*

Make sure you express your needs. Preschool children learn to be less self-centered and more empathetic when we express our feelings and needs. We should tell them how what they said or did affected us, and why we're reacting the way we are ... in a way that actually affects them.

EIGHT: *Use Redirection*

If your child is disappointed and stuck about what to do when her friend can't come over, say: "Let's go outside and water the plants. They look so dry and thirsty." Redirection can help your child move past the upset. However, parents need to help their children build some tolerance for frustration rather than believing they should keep frustration out of the child's life.

NINE: *Be Willing To Explain The Reasons Behind Your Rules*

This is especially important for new or changed rules. This is respectful to your preschooler and lets him understand that you have his best interests at heart. However, children should learn to do what you ask them to more than vice versa. (*Parents and children* **are not** *each others' peers.*)

TEN: *Help Your Child Understand Her Feelings And Misbehavior*

This is best done by using compassion and interpretation: "Of course you're sad and frustrated. You wanted Morgan to come over and play. But if you keep hitting your toy puppy, it might break."

ELEVEN: *Become Skilled At Figuring Out What Your Child Learned About Your Rules And Limits From A Situation*

For example, you wanted him to pick up the paper scraps from his craft project and he refused, with numerous excuses. You send him to time-out. Furious, he says you're mean and he's not your friend. You try to convince him that you're not mean and that you love him, but before you know it, you're emotionally exhausted and you've cleaned up the mess. What has he learned? He learned that he can argue and negotiate and doesn't have to cooperate with your requests. Try to figure out what you might have done differently.

TWELVE: *Develop A Repertoire Of Consequences That Are Effective With Your Child*

Don't expect that telling her over and over what she should have done will be enough. Effective consequences should cause your child to hesitate before repeating the problem behavior and eventually to stop herself altogether. Consequences can include time-out or removal of privileges, along with a repertoire of others (see Section Three) so your child doesn't become immune to the same ones used over and over. But use them enough to be sure of their effectiveness. Don't change your strategies before you have a chance to see if they work. Apply consequences early, after only one reminder, to hasten your child's learning. Remember, consequences should not be enjoyable to children, but also should **not** be humiliating, physical, or frightening. Learn the techniques in this guide so that material rewards and punishments are not your only tools and strategies.

B. ANNYE ROTHENBERG, Ph.D., *author*, has been a child/parent psychologist and a specialist in child rearing and development of young children for more than 25 years. Her parenting psychology practice is in Emerald Hills, California. She is also an adjunct clinical assistant professor of pediatrics at Stanford University School of Medicine and frequently consults to pediatricians and teachers. Dr. Rothenberg was the founder/director of the Child Rearing parenting program in Palo Alto, California, and is the author of the award-winning book *Parentmaking* and other parenting education books for parenting guidance professionals. Her first book in this series is *Mommy and Daddy Are Always Supposed to Say Yes … Aren't They?* (2007). She is the mother of one son.

DAVID T. WENZEL, *illustrator*, has been creating children's books for over 25 years. His work covers a vast area of subject matter, and he has gained recognition for visualizing the fantastic creatures in J.R.R. Tolkien's *The Hobbit* and the carefree adventures of *Rudolph The Red Nosed Reindeer*. Other titles include Max Lucado's *A Hat for Ivan* and Eileen Spinelli's *Baby Loves You So Much*, plus many more. David works in watercolor or colored inks on Waterford watercolor paper. He is married, has two sons, and lives in Connecticut.

ACKNOWLEDGMENTS

The author thanks *SuAnn* and *Kevin Kiser* for their outstanding critique and collaboration on the Children's Story, and *Caroline Grannan* and *Sharon Barela* for their terrific editing of the Parents' Guide. *Cathleen O'Brien* has done a remarkable job on book design. Many, many thanks to *Michael Vezo* of Westcom Associates, who has been most generous in his contribution to the quality of the printing. The valuable critiques by the focus groups at the *Joan Bourriague Preschool* in Los Altos and *St. Joseph's Preschool* in Atherton, both in California, were very helpful and much appreciated. Gratitude is also expressed for the very thoughtful reviews by the following pediatricians, all of whom are parents of preschoolers: *Aimee Blaustein, M.D., Lloyd Brown, M.D., Robin Drucker, M.D.*, and *Kim Jones, M.D.*

*"This book shows Dr. Rothenberg's strength and skills in understanding the preschool child and her parents. It has a very good story to read to children. The parent guide is terrific and **will save you reading a mountain of other parenting books.**"*
—Marcia Schwartz, PhD, Psychologist and parent of young children, San Mateo, CA

*"Finally, some **effective, true and tested parenting tools in a concise book perfect for busy parents!** It allowed us to improve cooperation from our children and bring back the fun into our parenting."* —Béatrice and Claude Boselli, parents of three children (ages 3, 5 and 7)

*"**Why Do I Have To?** is more than a how-to book. Dr. Rothenberg uses her extensive background of working with families to share the complexities of the preschool child while providing **so many jewels of information for parents and for parent educators.**"* —Mary Kay Stranik, MS; Family Program Consultant, Minneapolis, MN

*"**Dr. Rothenberg's unique understanding of children and parents has led to these very special books.** The charming story will help children develop a better understanding of rules and build their cooperation and responsibility. This wonderful book also includes guidelines that give parents the tools needed for positive child-rearing. **I recommend these books not only to parents, but to anyone who works with children.**"*
—Karina Garcia-Barbera, PhD; Director, Beresford Montessori Schools, San Mateo and Redwood City, CA

*"At last, a book that is easy to read, understand and implement on helping preschoolers cooperate. **You can expect the results to be successful.**"*
—Julie M. Soto, MS; Director, Parent Education/Early Learning, Bellevue Community College, Bellevue, WA

*"We have used the creative strategies in this book to get our five-year-old back on track with her friends and family, and for that we are eternally grateful. **Having this tool in our home library has been an important key to our family's happiness.**"* —Brooke and Glen Kernick, parents of two children (ages 5 and 7)

*"This attractive book provides **an entertaining story for children and valuable insights for parents.** Preschool teachers will also find this very useful."*
—Karen DeBord, PhD; Professor, Child Development, North Carolina State University, Raleigh, NC

*"Using many examples of everyday parent-child emotional upheavals, Annye Rothenberg shows us how to transform times of irritation to times of opportunity for problem-solving. **This book is a great resource for preschoolers, their parents, and preschool teachers.**"*
—Sandi Snider, Director, Ladera Community Church Preschool, Portola Valley, CA

*"Dr. Rothenberg has given us a new way to understand and interpret the behavior of our preschool daughter. The parenting recommendations are clear and effective. Our daughter is more cooperative and happier, and is thriving. **And our family is growing closer as a result.** Thank you!"*
—Janet and James Wong, parents of two children (ages 1½ and 4)

*"This book is particularly valuable because Dr. Rothenberg not only helps us understand what overarching principles should guide consistent decision-making by parents; she also couples these with **specific strategies for improving a child's cooperation.** Readers will gain valuable insights into what strategies do and don't work well with preschoolers – and why."*
—Mary Ann Carmack, MD, PhD; Chair, Department of Pediatrics, Palo Alto (CA) Medical Clinic

RAND McNALLY

ANSWER ATLAS

Featuring maps from *Goode's World Atlas*

With Special Question-and-Answer Section

**Vice President and General Manager,
Rand McNally Map and Atlas Publishing**
Jayne L. Fenton

Executive Editor
Jon M. Leverenz

Editors
Brett R. Gover
Ann T. Natunewicz

Marketing
Kendra L. Ensor
David M. Collins
JoEllen A. Klein

Art Direction
John C. Nelson

Design
Donna M. McGrath

Cover Design
Brian C. Doherty

Design Production
DePinto Graphic Design

Cartographic Direction
V. Patrick Healy

Cartographic Staff
Robert K. Argersinger
Lynn Jasmer
Patty A. Porter
James A. Purvis
L. Charlene Smith
Stephen F. Steiner
James Wooden
David C. Zapenski

Research
Susan K. Hudson

Continental Thematic Maps
Thomas F. Vitacco
Marzee L. Eckhoff
Gwynn A. Lloyd
Robert L. Merrill
David R. Simmons
Ashley James Snyder
Barbara Benstead-Strassheim
Dara L. Thompson

Continental Introductions
Ryan Ver Berkmoes

Production Coordination
James E. Hernandez

Photo Research
Feldman and Associates, Inc.

Photograph Credits:

Comstock: front cover (r)

FPG International: © Jim Cummins, front cover (b); © Mark Scott, front cover (t)

H. Armstrong Roberts: © R. Kord, 7, 11 (b); © Zefa, 100; © M. Schneiders, 108; © Smith/Zefa, 150 (b)

© Randall Hyman: 101

© Wolfgang Kaehler: 135

Odyssey Chicago: © R. Frerck, 152

Tony Stone Images: © K. Wood, 9 (t); © Mark Segal, 68; © David Frazier, 69; © Jacques Jangoux, 98 (t); © John Warden, 98 (b); © Owen Franken, 110; © John Lamb, 122 (t); © Yann Layma, 134; © Paul Chelsey, 153

Information Credits:

Volcano data, pages 9, 12, and 16: Tom Simkin, Smithsonian Institution Global Volcanism Program

Earthquake data, page 17: Paula Dunbar, National Geophysical Data Center, National Oceanic and Atmospheric Administration

Australia information, page 18: Australian Tourist Commission

Much of the information on the destruction of the Amazonian rain forest, page 101, was provided by Fred Engel of the Center for Earth and Planetary Science, National Air and Space Museum, Smithsonian Institution, Washington, D.C.

Answer Atlas

Copyright © 1996 by Rand McNally and Company

Published and printed in the United States of America

Library of Congress Catalog Number: 96-068293

ISBN: 0-528-83872-5

Table of Contents

Using the Atlas

Maps and Atlases

Today, satellite images (Figure 1) and aerial photography show us the face of the Earth in precise detail. It is hard to imagine how difficult it once was to ascertain what our planet looked like—even small parts of it. Yet from earliest history we have evidence of humans trying to depict the world through maps and charts.

Figure 1

Twenty-five hundred years ago, on a tiny clay tablet the size of a hand, the Babylonians inscribed the earth as a flat disk (Figure 2) with Babylon at the center. The section of the Cantino map of 1502 (Figure 3) is an example of a portolan chart used by mariners to chart the newly discovered Americas. Handsome and useful maps have been produced by many cultures. The Mexican map (Figure 4) drawn in 1583 marks hills with wavy lines and roads with footprints between parallel lines. The methods and materials used to create these maps were dependent upon the technology available, and their accuracy suffered considerably. The maps in this atlas show the detail and accuracy that cartographers are now able to achieve. They benefit from our ever-increasing technology, including satellite imagery and computer-assisted cartography.

Figure 2

In 1589, Gerardus Mercator used the word "atlas" to describe a collection of maps. Atlases have become a unique and indispensable reference for graphically defining the world and answering the question "Where?" Only on a map can the countries, cities, roads, rivers, and lakes covering a vast area be simultaneously viewed in their relative locations. Routes between places can be traced, trips planned,

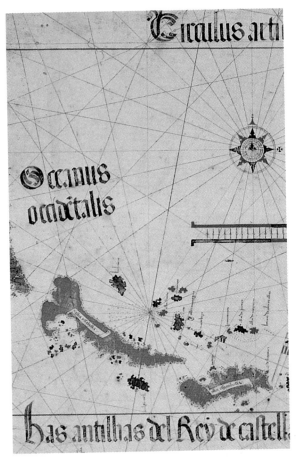

Figure 3

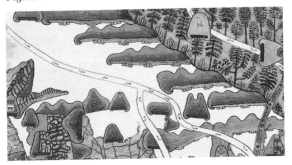

Figure 4

boundaries of neighboring states and countries examined, distances between places measured, the meandering of rivers and streams and the sizes of lakes visualized, and remote places imagined.

Getting the Information

An atlas can be used for many purposes, from planning a trip to finding hot spots in the news and supplementing world knowledge. To realize the potential of an atlas, the user must be able to:

1) Find places on the maps
2) Measure distances
3) Determine directions
4) Understand map symbols

Finding Places

One of the most common and important tasks facilitated by an atlas is finding the location of a place in the world. A river's name in a book, a city mentioned in the news, or a potential vacation spot may prompt your need to know where the place is located. The illustrations and text below explain how to find Lagos, Nigeria.

1) Look up the place-name in the index at the back of the atlas. Lagos, Nigeria can be found in the map on page 128, and it can be located on the map by its latitude and longitude, expressed in degrees: 7 North Latitude, 3 East Longitude (Figure 5).

La Fayette, In., U.S. 40N	87W	**90**
Lafayette, La., U.S. 30N	92W	**95**
Laghouat, Alg. 34N	3 E	**128**
Lagos, Nig. 7N	3 E	**128**
La Grande, Or., U.S. 45N	118W	**82**
LaGrange, Ga., U.S. 33N	85W	**92**
Lahore, Pak. 32N	74 E	**143**
Lahti, Fin. 61N	26 E	**116**

Figure 5

2) Turn to the map of Northern Africa on page 128. Note that the latitude appears in the right and left margins of the map, and the longitude in the upper and lower margins.

3) To find Lagos on the map, place your left index finger on the left margin at 7 degrees (between 5 and 10); and your right index finger in the top margin at 3 degrees East (between 0 and 5). Move your left finger across the map and your right finger down the map. Your fingers will meet in the area in which Lagos is located (Figure 6).

Figure 6

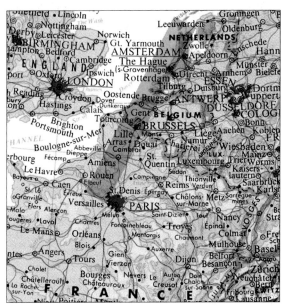

Figure 7

Measuring Distances

In planning trips, determining the distances between two places is essential, and an atlas can help in travel preparation. For instance, to determine the approximate distance between Paris, France and Amsterdam, Netherlands, follow these three steps:

1) Lay a slip of paper on the map on page 117 so that its edge touches the two cities. Adjust the paper so only one corner touches Paris. Mark the paper directly at the spot where Amsterdam is located (Figure 7).

2) Place the paper along the scale of miles beneath the map. Position the corner at 0 and line up the edge of the paper along the scale. The pencil mark on the paper indicates Amsterdam is between 250 and 300 miles from Paris (Figure 8).

3) To find the exact distance, make a second pencil mark at the 250-mile point of the scale. Then slide the paper to the left so that this second mark is lined up with 0 on the scale (Figure 9). The Amsterdam mark now falls at the third 10-mile point on the scale. This means that the Paris and Amsterdam are approximately 250 plus 30—or 280—miles apart.

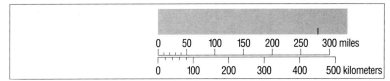

Figure 8

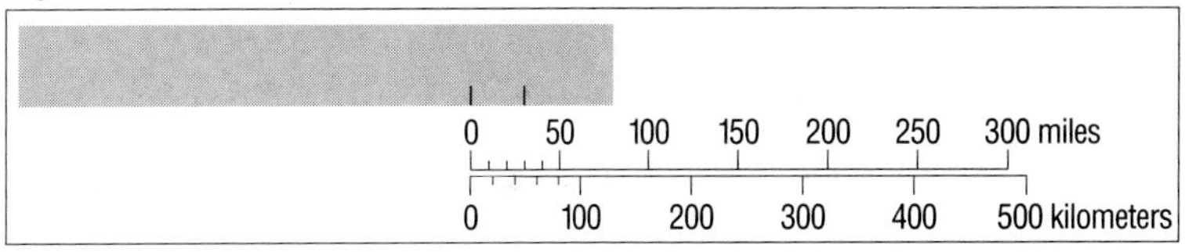

Figure 9

Determining Directions

Most of the maps in the atlas are drawn so that when oriented for normal reading, north is at the top of the map, south is at the bottom, west is at the left, and east is at the right. Most maps have a series of lines drawn across them—the lines of latitude and longitude. Lines of latitude, or parallels of latitude, are drawn east and west. Lines of longitude, or meridians of longitude, are drawn north and south (Figure 10, at bottom of page).

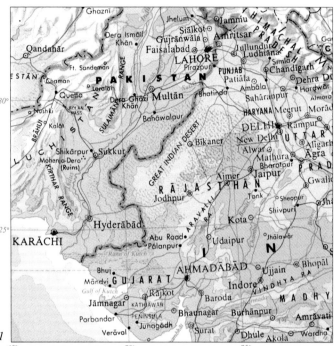

Figure 11

Parallels and meridians appear as either curved or straight lines. For example, in the section of the map of Southwestern Asia (Figure 11), from page 143, the parallels of latitude appear as curved lines. The meridians of longitude are curved vertical lines.

Latitude and longitude lines help locate places on maps. Parallels of latitude are numbered in degrees north and south of the Equator. Meridians of longitude are numbered in degrees east and west of a line called the Prime Meridian, running through Greenwich, England, near London. Any place on Earth can be located by the latitude and longitude lines running through it.

To determine directions or locations on the map, you must use the parallels and meridians. For example, suppose you want to know which is farther north, Karachi, Pakistan or Delhi, India. The map in Figure 11 shows that Karachi is south of the 25° parallel of latitude and that Delhi is north of it. Therefore Delhi is farther north than Karachi. By looking at the meridians of longitude, you can determine which city is farther east. Karachi is approximately 2° east of the 65° meridian, and Delhi is about 2° east of the 75° meridian. Delhi is farther east than Karachi.

Understanding Map Symbols

In a very real sense, every map is a symbol representing the world or part of it. It is a reduced representation of the Earth: each of the world's features—cities, rivers, etc.—is represented by a symbol. Map symbols may take the form of points, such as dots or squares (often used for cities, capital cities, or points of interest) or lines (roads, railroads, rivers). Symbols may also occupy an area, showing extent of coverage (terrain, forests, deserts). They seldom look like the feature they represent and therefore must be identified and interpreted. For instance, some of the maps in this atlas define political units by a colored line depicting their boundaries. Neither the colors nor the boundary lines are actually found on the surface of the Earth, but because countries and states are such important political components of the world, strong symbols are used to represent them. The Legend on page 51 of this atlas identifies the symbols used on the maps.

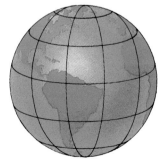

Figure 10

The Answer Section

Questions and Answers

World Superlatives, Facts, and Rankings

Questions and Answers

North America

Q What is the difference between "Central America" and "Middle America"?

A The term "Central America" refers to the North American countries which lie south of Mexico and north of Colombia: Belize, Guatemala, Honduras, El Salvador, Nicaragua, Costa Rica, and Panama. The Caribbean islands are not considered part of Central America. "Middle America" is comprised of Central America as well as Mexico and all of the Caribbean islands.

Q What is the largest U.S. city east of Reno, Nevada and west of Chicago?

Los Angeles, California

A Surprisingly, the answer is Los Angeles. Although Los Angeles is located on the Pacific Coast, it actually lies slightly farther east than Reno. The coast, which forms the western edge of the U.S., curves dramatically eastward below Cape Mendocino in northern California. San Diego, at the southern end of California's coast, is approximately as far east as the eastern borders of Washington and Oregon. (*Refer to map on pages 74-75.*)

Q Which is the southernmost U.S. state? The northernmost? The westernmost? The easternmost?

A Hawaii is the southernmost state; Alaska is both the westernmost and the northernmost. The question of which state is the easternmost is a bit problematic. Generally, Maine is considered to be the easternmost, since it extends farther east than any other state along the Atlantic seaboard. However, Alaska is technically the easternmost state, since the Aleutian Islands cross the 180° longitude line which divides the globe into eastern and western hemispheres. These islands sit at the eastern edge of the eastern hemisphere.

Q How many national flags have flown over Texas?

A Six. Spain (1682-1821), France (1685-1686), Mexico (1821-1836), the Republic of Texas (1836-1845), the United States (1845-1861), the Confederate States of America (from 1861 until the state was re-admitted to the Union in 1870), and the United States again (1870 through the present). Texas is the only U.S. state to have existed as an independent country.

Q What is the oldest city in the United States to be founded by Europeans?

A St. Augustine, Florida. Spanish explorer Juan Ponce de León, searching for the Fountain of Youth, landed nearby and claimed the area for Spain in 1513. The French established a colony on the site in 1564, but it was destroyed in 1565 by the Spanish, who then founded the present city. The oldest U.S. state capital is Santa Fe, New Mexico, which was founded in 1609, also by the Spanish.

Q What is Papiamento?

A Papiamento is a language which blends Dutch, Spanish, Portuguese, English, and Indian words. It is the principal language of Aruba and other islands in the Dutch Caribbean, and is spoken by an estimated 200,000 people.

Q If you were on a ship sailing from the Atlantic Ocean to the Pacific Ocean, in which direction would you be traveling as you passed through the Panama Canal?

A Southeast. The Pacific lies west of the Atlantic, and it would seem that a ship passing through the canal from the Atlantic would be sailing west. However, because of the twisting shape of the Isthmus of Panama, the canal's Pacific end lies south and east of its Atlantic end. (*Refer to inset map on page 96.*)

Q Into what body of water does the Colorado River empty?

A Currently, it doesn't empty into any body of water. Until recently, the river flowed into the Gulf of California. As the populations of water-poor Arizona and California have soared, more and more water has been drawn from the river for farms, industry, and homes. Today the Colorado is barely a trickle when it crosses the border into Mexico, and it disappears in the desert before it reaches the Gulf of California.

Q What is Canada's smallest province? Its largest?

A Prince Edward Island is Canada's smallest province, at 2,185 square miles (5,660 sq km). Canada's largest province is Quebec, which covers 594,860 square miles (1,540,680 sq km). The Northwest Territories represent the country's largest administrative division, spreading over an area of 1,322,910 square miles (3,426,320 sq km). If the Northwest Territories were an independent country, it would be larger than all but six of the world's countries: Russia, Canada, China, Brazil, the United States, and Australia.

Q What is the Continental Divide?

A An imaginary line running down the backbone of North America. Except for those which empty into the Great Basin and other basins, rivers to the west of this line flow into the Pacific Ocean, including its bays and gulfs; rivers to the east flow into the Atlantic or Arctic oceans, including their bays and gulfs. From northwest Canada south to New Mexico, the Divide runs along the crest of the Rocky Mountains, and in northern Mexico it follows the ridge of the Sierra Madre Occidental. All continents except frozen Antarctica have "divides."

Q Is Niagara Falls the highest waterfall in the world?

A Not even close. Niagara Falls' maximum drop of 167 feet (51 m) is surpassed by at least 22 waterfalls in North America alone. The highest waterfall in the world is Angel Falls in Venezuela, which spills 3,212 feet (979 m) from a flat mountain plateau. However, Niagara Falls ranks first in a different category: more than 210,000 cubic feet of water cascade over its edge each second, an amount nearly double that of any other waterfall.

Niagara Falls actually consists of two separate waterfalls: American Falls, at left, and Canadian (Horseshoe) Falls.

Q What did ships do before the Panama Canal was built?

A Before the canal opened, ships traveling between New York and San Francisco would sail 13,000 miles

(21,000 km) around the entire continent of South America. When the canal opened in 1914, this journey was shortened to 5,200 miles (8,400 km). However, the canal is now too narrow for many of today's largest ocean-going vessels, so they must once again sail around South America to reach their destination. A project to widen the canal began in 1992.

Gatun Lake,
Panama Canal

Q What is the largest inland body of water in Central America?

A Lake Nicaragua, which has a surface area of 3,150 square miles (8,158 sq km). Its only outlet is the San Juan River, which flows into the Caribbean Sea. Lying in a lowland region called the Nicaragua Depression, the lake was once part of the sea but became separated when the land began to rise. The freshwater lake is home to many species of fish usually found only in salt water, including sharks, tuna, and swordfish.

Q Why does Minnesota have so many lakes?

A During the height of the most recent Ice Age, glaciers moved southward from the Arctic regions to cover Canada and much of the northern U.S., including Minnesota. As they advanced, the glaciers scoured the landscape, gouging out countless depressions. When the Earth's climate grew warmer, the glaciers began to melt and retreat, and the depressions filled with meltwater to become lakes. Although Minnesota bills itself as the "Land of 10,000 Lakes," it actually has more than 15,000 lakes. Other areas of the world which experienced extreme glaciation, including parts of Europe and Siberia, also contain many lakes.

Q What is the most popular U.S. national park?

A Great Smoky Mountains National Park. Covering over 521,500 acres (211,200 hectares) in eastern Tennessee, the park receives approximately 9.1 million visitors each year. Arizona's Grand Canyon National Park has the second-highest visitor count: it receives around 4.6 million people annually.

Q What two U.S. states share borders with the most other states?

A Missouri and Tennessee, which each border eight other states. Missouri borders Iowa, Illinois, Kentucky, Tennessee, Arkansas, Oklahoma, Kansas, and Nebraska. Tennessee borders Kentucky, Virginia, North Carolina, Georgia, Alabama, Mississippi, Arkansas, and Missouri.

Q How many U.S. states border only one other state?

A One: Maine, which borders only New Hampshire. Two states, Alaska and Hawaii, border no others.

Q What is the one place in North America where you can see both the Atlantic Ocean and the Pacific Ocean?

A Irazú, a volcano in central Costa Rica. From its summit, both the Atlantic and Pacific oceans can be seen on a clear day.

Q Where is the Yucatan Peninsula?

A This thumb of land juts off of southeastern Mexico, separating the Gulf of Mexico from the Caribbean Sea. Yucatan was the center of the Maya civilization from about the first century B.C. through the tenth century A.D. Extensive Mayan ruins can be found at Chichén Itzá, Kabah, Mayapán, Tulum, and Uxmal. Near the town of Chicxulub at the northern tip of the peninsula, there is evidence of an enormous crater which is thought to be the point of impact of a meteorite 65 million years ago. The impact would have sent so much dust into the atmosphere that the sun's rays would have been blocked for months or perhaps years, lowering temperatures globally and possibly causing the extinction of the dinosaurs.

Q What is the oldest capital city in the Americas?

A Mexico City. The city originated as Tenochtitlán, the capital of the Aztecs, founded in the mid-1300s. By the early 1500s, the city had a population of perhaps 150,000, which was not only greater than any other city in the Americas but also greater than any European city at the time. In 1521, after a three-month siege, Spanish invaders under Hernán Cortés captured Tenochtitlán, razed the entire city, and founded Mexico City upon its ruins.

Q What is the most densely populated country in North America?

A El Salvador, which has a density of 650 people per square mile (251 per sq km). The U.S. ranks eighth, with 69 people per square mile (27 per sq km). Canada, the continent's largest country, is by far the least densely populated: it averages only 7.3 people per square mile (2.8 per sq km).

Q What is the largest island in Caribbean Sea?

A Cuba, the world's 15th-largest island. It has a land area of 42,800 square miles (110,800 sq km). The second-largest Caribbean island is Hispaniola, which covers 29,400 square miles (76,200 sq km) and contains the countries of Haiti and the Dominican Republic. Jamaica, measuring 4,200 square miles (11,000 sq km), is the third-largest Caribbean island.

Q How many U.S. states have volcanoes that have been active in this century?

A Four. Alaska has the most: 34 of its volcanoes, most of which are located on the Alaska Peninsula and the Aleutian Islands, have erupted since 1900. The other states with documented eruptions in this century are: Hawaii (3), Washington (1), and California (1).

Caldera and lava lake of Kilauea, on the island of Hawaii

Q What is the only Caribbean island with large oil reserves?

A Trinidad. The island's economy is based on oil, which accounts for about 80% of its exports. As a result of oil wealth, Trinidadians enjoy a higher standard of living than the people of most other Caribbean countries.

Q Which U.S. state has the highest average elevation?

A Colorado, with an average elevation of 6,800 feet (2,074 m) above sea level. However, the four highest peaks in the U.S. are found not in Colorado but in Alaska.

Questions and Answers

South America

What is Latin America?

The term "Latin America" designates the parts of North and South America which were settled by Spanish and Portuguese colonists and still retain a Hispanic character. These include Mexico, Cuba, Puerto Rico, the Dominican Republic, some of the smaller islands in the West Indies, all of Central America except for Belize, and all of South America except for Guyana, Suriname, and French Guiana.

If you flew due south from Chicago, which South American country would you fly over first?

You wouldn't fly over any South American countries. A straight line drawn south from Chicago passes through the Gulf of Mexico, Central America, and the Pacific Ocean. Point Parinas, Peru, the westernmost point of mainland South America, is about 500 miles (800 km) east of this line. The Galapagos Islands, which belong to Ecuador, lie about 75 miles (120 km) west of the line.

What percentage of the world's coffee beans come from South America?

South America currently produces approximately 45% of the world's coffee beans. Brazil leads the continent, producing just under one-quarter of the world total. Another 16% are grown in Colombia. Coffee plants require hot, moist climates, and they yield the most flavorful beans when cultivated at elevations between 3,000 and 6,000 feet (900 and 1800 m). South America's principal coffee-growing regions are found in the Brazilian and Guiana Highlands, and in the valleys and foothills of the Andes.

Giant Galapagos turtle

What scientist made the Galapagos Islands famous?

Charles Darwin, who visited the islands during his 1831-1836 expedition on the H.M.S. *Beagle.* Darwin's observations of how various animal species had adapted to life on the islands contributed to his ground-breaking theory of evolution, which he presented in the 1859 book *On the Origin of Species.*

Where are the Falkland Islands?

In the Atlantic Ocean, about 275 miles (440 km) off the east coast of Argentina. The Falklands are a dependency of the United Kingdom, and nearly all of the residents are English-speakers of British descent. Argentina, which has asserted claims to the Falklands since 1816, invaded and occupied the islands in 1982. The U.K. sent a large task force that defeated the Argentineans in a war lasting less than a month.

What South American country is the longest when measured from north to south?

Brazil. The country measures 2,725 miles (4,395 km) north to south, which is the approximate distance from New York City to Reno, Nevada. The second-longest country is Chile, with a length of 2,647 miles (4,270 km). In contrast to its great length, Chile measures only 235 miles (380 km) east to west at its widest point.

What was discovered in Venezuela's Lake Maracaibo in 1914?

Oil. Maracaibo sits above one of the world's largest oil fields, and today the lake's surface is a thicket of oil derricks. Wealth from oil exportation has helped to make Venezuela one of the richest countries in Latin America.

What is Patagonia?

Patagonia is a wind-swept plateau region occupying the southern third of South America, east of the Andes. The plateau receives little precipitation, and its only végetation is scrubby grasses and thorny desert shrubs. The name "Patagonia" probably comes from the Grand Patagon, a dog-headed monster in a European romance called *Primaleon of Greece.* In 1592, the crew members of the ship *Desire* were attacked by a war-party of Tehuelche Indians wearing dog masks.

What South American city is the world's highest national capital?

La Paz, Bolivia. The city sprawls across the floor of a deep canyon high in the Andes, at an elevation of 12,000 feet (19,350 km)—approximately the same height as the summit of Japan's Mt. Fuji. The canyon walls protect the city from the bitterly cold winds that whip across the surrounding plateau. Visitors from lower elevations often suffer from altitude sickness for several days until their bodies adjust to the thin, oxygen-poor air.

What is the southernmost city in the world?

Ushuaia, Argentina, on the island of Tierra del Fuego. This city of 29,452 people lies at 54°48' south latitude, less than 700 miles (1,100 km) from Antarctica. The world's southernmost city with a population greater than 100,000 is Punta Arenas, Chile, located 150 miles (240 km) northwest of Ushuaia.

How many South American countries are named for famous people or cities?

Three. Bolivia was named for Simón Bolívar, the revolutionary who helped to liberate much of northern South America from Spanish rule. Colombia takes its name from the explorer Christopher Columbus, who "discovered" South America in 1498 and sailed along the coast of present-day Colombia in 1502. The name "Venezuela" is Spanish for "Little Venice." When European explorers reached Lake Maracaibo in 1499, they found villages built on pilings over the shallow waters, which reminded them of Venice, Italy.

Why is South America sometimes referred to as "the hollow continent"?

South America earned this nickname because most of its people live on or near the coasts; the interior is sparsely populated. Sixteen of the 20 largest metropolitan areas lie within 200 miles (320 km) of the coast. The continent's uneven population distribution has both a historical and a geographical explanation. Beginning in the 16th century, European colonists settled in the coastal regions from which raw materials were shipped back to Europe. The Amazon rain forest—hot, humid, and nearly impenetrable in places—has discouraged settlement of the northern half of the continent, and the Andes present a formidable barrier to eastward expansion from the Pacific coast. *(Refer to population map on page 99.)*

Q How many of South America's 20 longest rivers empty into the Pacific Ocean?

A None. South America's continental divide runs along the crest of the Andes at the continent's western edge. In most places the divide lies within 200 miles (320 km) of the Pacific coast. Rivers originating west of the divide have only a short distance to travel before reaching the Pacific. Rivers flowing east from the divide have nearly the whole expanse of the continent to cross before emptying into the Atlantic.

Q What South American city was the capital of the Inca empire?

Cathedral and rooftops in Cusco

A Cusco, Peru. The city was built by the Incas in the fourteenth century and served as their capital for 200 years until it was destroyed by Francisco Pizarro in 1533. Today, Cusco thrives as a major tourist attraction. Many of its houses and buildings are constructed on foundations of stone first cut by the Incas. Lying about 50 miles (80 km) northwest of Cusco is Machu Picchu, a well-preserved mountaintop Inca city, which was rediscovered in 1911.

Q What stretch of ocean off the South American coast is considered one of the most treacherous to ships?

A The Drake Passage. Approximately 500 miles (1,800 km) wide, this strait separates Cape Horn—at the southern tip of South America—from the South Shetland Islands which lie just north of Antarctica. First traversed in 1615, the passage was part of a major trade route between the Atlantic and Pacific oceans until 1914, when the Panama Canal opened. Frigid temperatures, rough waters, and high winds make the passage treacherous for all vessels but especially for the sailing ships of centuries past. Because the passage is so perilous, many ships avoid it by cutting through the Strait of Magellan to the north. However, this strait has its own dangers: it is narrow and twisting, and has been the site of numerous major shipwrecks.

Q Where is the Land of Fire?

A At the southern tip of South America. Tierra del Fuego, Spanish for "Land of Fire," is a group of islands lying south of the Strait of Magellan. When Portuguese explorer Ferdinand Magellan arrived in 1520, he named the islands after observing the native inhabitants carrying torches. The largest island, also called Tierra del Fuego, accounts for two-thirds of the land area of the island group. The eastern third of the islands belong to Argentina, and the rest belong to Chile.

Q What are the Nazca Lines?

A The Nazca Lines are gigantic drawings that were etched into Peru's desert floor by the Nazca people between 500 B.C. and A.D. 500. Scattered across 200 square miles (520 sq km), they form the world's largest display of art. The drawings fall into two categories: animal motifs and geometric patterns of crisscrossing straight lines. They were made by scraping away the top layer of red gravel to reveal the yellow sand below it. Archaeologists still disagree about the purpose of the Nazca Lines, but some theories hold that the lines formed ancient highways or were used as a giant calendar.

Q What is "El Niño"?

A El Niño is a seasonal ocean current that flows south along the Pacific coast of South America. The current takes its name—which is Spanish for "the Child"—from its usual arrival during the Christmas season. In normal years, when El Niño reaches northern Peru, southeasterly trade winds push its warm surface waters westward across the Pacific, away from the coast. Every four or five years, these trade winds weaken, allowing El Niño to travel farther south along the coast, raising local water temperatures by several degrees. This warmer water kills plankton and fish, crippling the fishing industry. Increased evaporation leads to excessive rainfall over parts of South America. The change in El Niño's normal flow pattern affects other ocean currents which often leads to dramatic climatic changes around the world.

Q How many of the Earth's species are found in the Amazon rain forest?

A Most of the Amazon basin has not been fully explored, and therefore most of its plant and animal species have not yet been catalogued. However, scientists estimate that the Amazon rain forest, which covers less than 5% of the Earth's total land area, contains almost one-half of the planet's animal and plant species. One in ten of the most common medicines we use today comes from rain forest plants, and scientists believe that cures for many diseases, such as cancer, might be derived from plant species not yet discovered.

Q Where in South America could you find places in which no rainfall has ever been recorded?

A The Atacama Desert in northern Chile. This barren land of sand, rocks, borax lakes and saline deposits is one of the driest regions in the world. In parts of the desert, no rainfall has ever been recorded, and the city of Arica, at the northern edge, endured more than 14 consecutive years of drought from October 1903 through January 1918.

Q What South American possession lies farthest from the mainland?

A Easter Island, situated 2,300 miles (3,700 km) west of Chile in the Pacific Ocean. This small volcanic island was discovered on Easter Sunday in 1722, and was annexed by Chile in 1888. Although it belongs to Chile, geographically Easter Island is considered to be part of Oceania, not South America. It is best known for its strange monuments: scattered over the island are more than 600 huge stone faces, the earliest dating back more than 1,500 years.

Ancient statues, Easter Island

Q Where are the pampas?

A These flat, grassy plains—which are much like the prairies of North America—are found in the temperate regions of southern South America, east of the Andes. The largest such plain, known simply as the Pampa, covers much of central and northern Argentina, and extends into Uruguay. Since the 1550s, when European colonists introduced cattle to the Pampa, livestock raising has been a thriving industry. For many people, gauchos, or Argentinean cowboys, are the enduring symbol of the Pampa, although in the last century farming has superseded cattle ranching in economic importance.

Questions and Answers

Europe

Where is the Black Forest?

In southwestern Germany, between the Rhine and Neckar rivers. The Black Forest, or *Schwarzwald* in German, is a mountainous region that takes its name from the dark coniferous trees that cover its slopes. Its fertile valleys provide good pastureland and produce grapes for wine, and its trees supply the lumber and woodworking industries, as well as toy and cuckoo clock manufacturers. The region's scenic beauty, winter sports facilities, and mineral springs attract many tourists each year.

How many national capitals are located on the Danube River?

Four. The capital cities of Bratislava (Slovakia), Budapest (Hungary), Belgrade (Yugoslavia), and Vienna (Austria) are all found along the banks of the Danube. Five other capitals are located on tributaries of the Danube: Bucharest (Romania), Sofia (Bulgaria), Ljubljana (Slovenia), Zagreb (Croatia), and Sarajevo (Bosnia & Herzegovina).

Old Town of Zagreb, Croatia

What is killing the forests of Northern Europe?

Acid rain. In the atmosphere, airborne pollutants—especially sulfur and nitrogen dioxides from automobile and industrial emissions—adhere to water droplets, and then fall back to Earth as acidified rain, snow, or hail. This precipitation poisons plant and animal life, erodes buildings, and contaminates soil and drinking water. As a result of acid rain, as many as one-half of the trees in Germany's Black Forest and Switzerland's central alpine region are dead or dying. At least 4,000 lakes in Sweden are so acidic that no fish survive in them. To combat acid rain, the countries of the European Union recently agreed to significantly reduce nitrogen oxide and sulfur dioxide emissions.

What independent countries were once part of the U.S.S.R.?

When the Union of Soviet Socialist Republics (U.S.S.R.) broke up in 1991, its 15 republics all became independent countries: Armenia, Azerbaijan, Belarus, Estonia, Georgia, Kazakhstan, Krygyzstan, Latvia, Lithuania, Moldova, Russia, Tajikistan, Turkmenistan, Ukraine, and Uzbekistan.

How many times has the name of St. Petersburg, Russia, changed in this century?

Three times. St. Petersburg was founded in 1703 by Peter the Great. In 1914, its name was changed to Petrograd, Russian for "Peter's City," and then in 1924 it was changed again, this time to Leningrad, in honor of Vladimir Lenin, the founder of Russian Communism. In 1991, following the collapse of Communist rule, the city name was changed back to St. Petersburg. Older citizens joke about being born in St. Petersburg, attending school in Petrograd, working in Leningrad, and growing old in St. Petersburg—all while living in the same place.

What independent countries were once part of Yugoslavia?

Prior to 1991, Yugoslavia was comprised of six republics: Bosnia and Herzegovina, Croatia, Macedonia, Montenegro, Serbia, and Slovenia. In 1991-92, four of the six republics—Croatia, Slovenia, Macedonia, and Bosnia and Herzegovina—declared their independence. Yugoslavia now comprises only two republics, Serbia and Montenegro.

What is the Chunnel?

"Chunnel" is a nickname for the English Channel Tunnel, which connects England and France via rail under the English Channel. There are actually three separate tunnels: two for trains and a parallel service tunnel. The tunnels run for 31 miles between Coquelles, France, and Folkestone, England, at an average depth of 150 feet (46 m) below the seafloor. Work on the tunnels began in 1987, and the first trains crossed under the Channel in 1994.

Where is "Europe's Grand Canyon"?

Along the Verdon River in the Provence region of southeastern France. The Verdon has carved a deep, narrow gorge, known as the Grand Cañon du Verdon, through the limestone plateau between the town of Castellane and the artificial Lac de Ste-Croix. The gorge stretches for 13 miles (21 km) and reaches a depth of 3,170 feet (965 m). It is considered one of the natural wonders of Europe.

What is the only volcano on the European mainland that has erupted in the 20th century?

Mt. Vesuvius (Vesuvio), located in southern Italy nine miles (15 km) east of Naples. It has been active through much of the century, with significant eruptions in 1906, 1929, and 1944. Two thousand years ago, most Romans did not recognize Vesuvius as a volcano, and numerous farming communities thrived on the fertile land around its base. Then, in August of A.D. 79, the volcano exploded in a mighty eruption, burying the cities of Pompeii, Herculaneum, and Stabiae under cinders, ash, and mud, and killing more than 3,500 people.

How many European countries fall partially within the Arctic Circle?

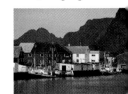

Four: Finland, Norway, Russia, and Sweden. Technically, a fifth country could be added to this list: Iceland's mainland ends just short of the Arctic Circle, but one of the country's islands, Grimsey, straddles the line, its northern half sitting within the Circle.

The historic Henningsvc Port in the Lofoten Islar of Norway, north of the Arctic Circle

Where is Waterloo, site of Napoleon's famous defeat?

Today, Waterloo is a suburb of Brussels, Belgium, although at the time of the battle—June 18, 1815—it lay 12 miles (19 km) away from the city, which was then much smaller. At Waterloo, the troops of French emperor Napoleon I were defeated by British forces under the command of the Duke of Wellington and Prussian forces led by Gebhard Blücher. The French defeat ended the Napoleonic Wars, which had begun in 1803.

Is Venice, Italy, really sinking?

Yes, although at a much slower rate than earlier in the century. The city, which dates back to the 4th century A.D., is built on 118 small islands in a lagoon at the top of the Adriatic Sea. Its buildings sit on foundations of wooden pilings driven deep into the underlying sand, silt and clay. Originally the buildings were safely above high tide level, but over the course of 15 centuries, natural compaction of the sub-soil caused the city to sink more than 30 inches (76 cm). Earlier this century, groundwater was pumped out of the subsoil to satisfy water needs on the mainland. This proved disastrous for Venice: the city quickly sank another five inches (13 cm) at a time when the sea level was rising by four inches (10 cm). The pumping was stopped, and Venice's sinking has slowed to its earlier "natural" rate. Unfortunately, the foundations of many buildings have been severely damaged by high water.

Gondola and canal, Venice

Which independent European countries are smaller than Rhode Island, the smallest U.S. state?

Seven independent European countries cover a smaller area than Rhode Island's 1,545 square miles (4,002 sq km): Vatican City, Monaco, San Marino, Liechtenstein, Malta, Andorra, and Luxembourg.

How many official languages are recognized in Switzerland?

Four: German, French, Italian, and Romansch. German is the most widely spoken language: 65% of the Swiss speak a dialect known as *Schwyzerdütsch*, or Swiss German. French is spoken by 18% of the population, Italian by 10%, and Romansch by only 1%.

Why is Ukraine called "the breadbasket of Europe"?

Ukraine's topography—flat plains, or "steppes," cover most of the country—and extremely fertile soils combine to make it one of the world's most outstanding agricultural areas. In 1994, the country produced almost 36 million tons (33 metric tons) of grain. Major crops include wheat, rye, barley, corn, potatoes, sunflower seeds, sugar beets, and cotton. Ukraine also has thriving dairy and livestock industries, as well as many food-processing plants.

If the Caspian Sea is a *sea*, then how can it be the world's largest *lake*?

Actually, it is both a sea *and* a lake. The word "sea" is used most often to designate specific regions of the oceans that are more or less surrounded by land; however, it can also apply to inland bodies of water, especially if they are large and/or salty. The Caspian Sea is both large and salty, so it is called a sea. "Lake" is a general term for inland bodies of water of substantial size. The Caspian Sea lies inland and has a surface area of 143,240 square miles (370,990 sq km), so it is also considered to be a lake. Other "sea-lakes" in the world include the Aral Sea, the Dead Sea, the Sea of Galilee, and California's Salton Sea.

Where is Transylvania?

In northwestern Romania. The region is bounded by the Carpathian Mountains in the north and east, the Transylvanian Alps in the south, and by Romania's borders with Hungary and Yugoslavia in the west. A high plateau, averaging 1,000 to 1,600 feet (300 to 500 m) in elevation, covers much of Transylvania. In Bram Stoker's 1897 novel *Dracula*, Transylvania is the home of the blood-sucking Count. Stoker based the story on local vampire legends, many of which persist today: in some parts of eastern Europe, peasants still wear garlic necklaces and hang garlic wreaths from their doors to ward off vampire spirits.

What countries contain parts of the Carpathian Mountains?

Five: the Czech Republic, Slovakia, Poland, Ukraine, and Romania. Curving for more than 900 miles (1,450 km) along the north and east sides of the Danube plain in central and eastern Europe, the Carpathians roughly form a half-circle connecting the Alps and the Balkans. The mountain system consists of two main parts: the Northern Carpathians, which include the Beskid and the Tatra ranges, and the Southern Carpathians, also called the Transylvanian Alps. The Carpathians' highest peak is Gerlachovský štít in Slovakia, which rises to 8,711 feet (2,655 m).

Where is Lapland?

In northern Scandinavia. Lapland is home to the Lapps, a nomadic people who have traditionally engaged in hunting, fishing, and reindeer-herding. When the Finns arrived in the southern part of present-day Finland 2,000 years ago, they found the Lapps already settled there. Over the years, the Lapps have been pushed north, and their territory has expanded to cover parts of northern Norway, Sweden, Finland, and northwestern Russia. Today, there are approximately 42,000 Lapps, most of whom work in a variety of farming, construction, and service fields. The Finnish government has made many efforts to protect the Lapps' language, called Sami, and culture.

What European country has a shorter coastline than any other maritime country in the world?

Monaco, whose Mediterranean coastline is a mere three-and-a-half miles (5.6 km) long. Another European country, Bosnia and Herzegovina, ranks second in this category: its coast on the Adriatic Sea between Croatia and Yugoslavia is only 13 miles (21 km) long. In third place is Slovenia, whose Adriatic coast is 29 miles (47 km) long.

Harbor and coastline, Monaco

What European city is the largest city in the world north of the Arctic Circle?

Murmansk, Russia, a city of 472,900 people located on the Kola Gulf of the Barents Sea. Although Murmansk lies approximately 150 miles north of the Arctic Circle, its harbor remains ice-free throughout the year due to the moderating effect of a warm ocean current called the North Atlantic Drift. While there are thousands of cities and towns north of the Arctic Circle, there are none at all south of the Antarctic Circle at the opposite end of the world.

Questions and Answers

Africa

What is the East African Rift System?

This term refers to a series of rift valleys running through East Africa from Mozambique to the southern end of the Red Sea. These valleys are part of the Great Rift Valley, a 4,000-mile (6,430-km)-long depression that also includes the Red Sea, the Dead Sea, and the rest of the Jordan Valley. The East African Rift System marks the line along which geological forces are splitting East Africa off from the rest of the continent. Eventually, everything east of the Rift System—including all or part of present-day Mozambique, Tanzania, Rwanda, Burundi, Uganda, Kenya, Ethiopia, Djibouti, and Somalia—will be a huge island off of Africa's eastern coast. Madagascar was attached to the African mainland before similar forces split it off into an island 175 million years ago.

What is the Serengeti?

Located in northern Tanzania, east of Lake Victoria and west of Kilimanjaro, the Serengeti is a vast plain of grassland, acacia bushes, forest, and rocky outcrops. Serengeti National Park, established in 1951, covers an area of the plain about the size of Connecticut. The park is home to one of the last great concentrations of African wildlife, including antelope, buffalo, cheetahs, elephants, gazelles, giraffes, hyenas, leopards, lions, black rhinoceroses, wildebeests and zebras. Tourists from all over the world visit the park to observe the wildlife and to witness the large-scale animal migrations that occur in May and June.

Giraffes on the Serengeti

How has the Aswan High Dam affected the Nile Valley ?

Before the dam was built in 1971, floodwaters inundated the Nile Valley each fall, depositing fresh, fertile silt across the valley floor. This annual replenishment of the soil helped agriculture to thrive in the valley for thousands of years. The dam ended the annual floods, and now much of the Nile's water-borne silt settles to the bottom of Lake Nassar, the enormous artificial lake behind the dam. Water evaporating from the lake's surface has increased the regional humidity, which has accelerated the decay of many of the valley's great tombs and monuments. On the positive side, the dam supplies more than 25% of Egypt's hydro-electric power, and desert irrigation projects using water from Lake Nassar have created 900,000 new acres of arable land.

What is remarkable about the delta of the Okavango River?

It is the largest inland delta in the world. The Okavango originates in the mountains of central Angola and flows 1,000 miles (1,600 km) to the northwest corner of Botswana, where it spills over the Gomare fault and fans out into a swampy delta covering 4,000 square miles (10,350 sq km). Meandering through a myriad of shallow channels, the waters of the Okavango quickly evaporate. The small amount that eventually emerges from the southeastern end of the delta represents less than 5% of the river's pre-delta flow.

What African country was previously known as Upper Volta?

Burkina Faso. The Volta River's three upper branches—the Volta Blanche (White Volta), Volta Rouge (Red Volta), and Volta Noire (Black Volta)—all originate within the country, hence the earlier name. Burkina Faso, the Mossi-dialect name adopted in 1984, translates roughly as "Country of Honest Men."

What are the most important crops grown in Africa?

Woman in sorghum fields, Bema

Africa is the world's leading producer of cocoa beans (55% of the world total) and cassava roots (45% of the world total). It is also a major producer of grain and millet sorghum (27%), coffee (20%), peanuts (20%), palm oil (14%), tea (12%), and olive oil (12%).

What object found along the banks of the Orange River in 1867 changed the course of South African history?

A 21-carat diamond. The discovery of this gem near Hopetown precipitated a huge diamond rush, and thousands of people from all over the continent and the world raced to southern Africa. The town of Kimberley, site of the famous open mine known as the Big Hole, became the diamond capital of the world. Between 1871 and 1914, more than 14 million carats of diamonds were removed from the mine, which eventually reached a depth of 4,000 feet (1,220 m) and a width of one mile (1.6 km).

What is Cabinda?

A coastal province of Angola that lies north of the Congo River and is separated from the rest of the country by a 19-mile (31-km)-wide corridor belonging to Zaire. Most of Cabinda's 2,807 square miles (7,270 sq km) are covered by tropical forest. Offshore lie rich oil fields which produce one million barrels annually.

What African country was founded in 1847 by freed American slaves?

Liberia, whose name comes from the Latin word *liber*, meaning "free." It is the only country in sub-Saharan Africa that has never been ruled by a colonial power. Liberia's capital city, Monrovia, was named for James Monroe, the fifth U.S. president.

What two African countries border only a single other country?

Lesotho and Gambia. Lesotho is surrounded entirely by South Africa. Gambia is bordered in the north, east, and south by Senegal; to its west lies the Atlantic Ocean.

What is the Ngorongoro Crater?

Located in northern Tanzania, Ngorongoro is the crater of a volcano that has been extinct for several million years. It has a diameter of 9 miles (14.5 km) and its walls rise about 2,000 feet (610 m) above its floor. The crater supports an abundance of wildlife, including wildebeests, elephants, rhinoceroses, hippopotamuses, lions, leopards, and flamingoes. In 1956 Ngorongoro was established as a conservation area, but its ecological balance is threatened by growing numbers of tourists and the large cattle herds of the nomadic Masai people.

Q Why is it difficult to say how large Lake Chad is?

A The lake's size fluctuates dramatically throughout the year. Numerous rivers and streams flow into Lake Chad, but it has no outlet. During the summer rainy season, floodwaters swell the lake to 10,000 square miles (25,900 sq km) and occasionally to twice that size. Even at its maximum size the lake is extremely shallow; its greatest depth is only 25 feet (8 m). By the end of the following spring, evaporation has shrunk the lake by 60%, to about 4,000 square miles (10,360 sq km). In recent decades, Lake Chad's cyclical fluctuations have been greatly affected by recurring droughts, which have reduced the flow of water into the lake and accelerated evaporation. Its volume has dropped by 80% since 1970.

Q What is significant about the location of Khartoum, Sudan?

A Khartoum, the capital of Sudan, is located at the point where the White Nile and Blue Nile rivers meet to form the Nile. Capitalizing on its strategic location, the city has become Sudan's commercial center and transportation hub. It is built on a curving strip of land that resembles the trunk of an elephant: the name "Khartoum" comes from the Arabic *Ras-al-hartum*, which means "end of the elephant's trunk."

Q What is Africa's newest country?

A Eritrea, which officially became independent in 1993. An Italian colony from 1890 to 1941, Eritrea was captured by the British during World War II. In 1952, the United Nations awarded Eritrea to Ethiopia under the condition that it be ruled as a self-governing territory. Ethiopia violated this agreement by annexing Eritrea in 1962, touching off a civil war which lasted more than 30 years. Eritrea formally declared its independence in May 1993, two years after defeating Ethiopia's Marxist regime.

Q What is the Sahel?

A The Sahel is a semiarid region that separates the Sahara Desert from the tropical savanna and rain forests of central Africa. It stretches halfway across the continent, from Mauritania in the west to Chad in the east, in a band averaging more than 1,000 miles (1,600 km) in width. Most of the Sahel is semiarid savanna, with low grasses in the north and tall grasses in the south. Annual precipitation varies from 4 inches to 24 inches (100 to 600 mm). The 8-month dry season makes farming difficult, and the region has experienced several severe droughts in this century.

Woman returning from well in the Sahel

Q In what country would you find Africa's northernmost point?

A Tunisia. The northernmost point is Cape Ben Sekka, which lies just north of the continent's northernmost town, Bechater. Parts of five European countries—Greece, Italy, Malta, Portugal, and Spain—lie farther south than Cape Ben Sekka. From the tip of the cape, Africa stretches southward approximately 5,000 miles (8,000 km) to its southernmost point, Cape Agulhas in South Africa.

Q How has the Sahara Desert changed in the last 5,000 years?

A Scientists believe that 5,000 years ago the climate of the Sahara was more temperate and far less arid than it is today. Much of the region was grassland. Around 3000 B.C. global climate patterns began to shift, and the region entered an arid period which continues today. The desert currently covers 3,500,000 square miles (9,100,000 sq km), an area nearly as large as the United States, and its size is increasing. In recent decades, recurring droughts and overgrazing in the Sahel region have contributed to the Sahara's southward expansion.

Q What is the traditional mode of transportation in the Sahara Desert?

A The camel, or more specifically, the one-humped dromedary, which was domesticated at least 3,000 years ago. Dromedaries are extremely well-suited to desert conditions. They have the ability to store water in their hump, and can tolerate water losses equal to one-fourth of their body weight. Their heavy-lidded eyes and closeable nostrils offer protection in sandstorms. Today, as the Saharan road system expands, truck convoys are replacing camel caravans, although trucks require frequent refueling, often overheat in the desert sun, and grind to a halt when sand clogs their engines.

Camel eating leaves

Q Which African country can boast the greatest known deposits, variety, and output of minerals in the world?

A South Africa. It has the world's largest known deposits of chromite, gold, manganese, platinum, and vanadium. The country leads the world in production of gold, chromite, vanadium, and the platinum group metals: platinum, palladium, iridium, rhodium, and ruthenium. It is also one of the leading producers of manganese, antimony, and gem and industrial diamonds.

Q Where is the Horn of Africa?

A This term refers to the horn-shaped area of eastern Africa that juts into the Indian Ocean. Somalia and Ethiopia occupy most of the horn. The cape of Gees Gwardafuy and the city of Caluula sit at the northeastern tip of the horn, marking the entrance to the Gulf of Aden, which connects the Arabian Sea and the Red Sea.

Q What is the Valley of the Kings?

A This narrow valley, across the Nile River from the city of Luxor, contains the tombs of the pharaohs who ruled Egypt during the New Kingdom period, 1550 B.C. to 1200 B.C. The tombs are carved deep into the sandstone walls of the valley; most have five to fifteen rooms. Among the pharaohs buried in the valley are Ramses II, Ramses VI, and Seti I. Upon their death, the pharaohs were mummified and then entombed with all of the material things that they might need in the afterlife, including gold, jeweled ornaments, furniture, clothing, and food. Most of the tombs were soon looted by robbers, who removed all items of value. However, in 1922 the tomb of Tutankhamen—"King Tut"—was discovered with most of its riches untouched.

Questions and Answers

Asia

Q What natural features form the physical boundary between Europe and Asia?

A Europe and Asia share the same huge landmass, which is known as Eurasia. The imaginary line dividing this landmass into two continents runs through the Ural Mountains, the Ural River, the Caspian Sea, the Caucasus mountains, the Black Sea, the Bosporus strait, the Sea of Marmara, and the Dardanelles strait.

Q How many countries lie partially within Europe and partially within Asia?

A Four: Azerbaijan, which is traversed by the Caucasus Mountains; Kazakhstan, whose far western lands lie west of the Ural River; Russia, which is split by the Ural Mountains, and Turkey, which includes a small area on the northwestern side of the Sea of Marmara.

Q Why was the Great Wall of China built?

A To defend China against invasion by the Huns and other enemies. Defensive walls were built in China as early as the 6th century B.C. In 214 B.C., under Emperor Shih Huang-ti, the existing walls were connected to form a single continuous wall with watchtowers. This wall was extended during the Han Dynasty (202 B.C. – A.D. 220) and the Sui Dynasty (A.D. 581 – 618). Seven hundred years later the wall had mostly crumbled, and in the late 1400s, under the Ming Emperors, it was completely rebuilt. The portions of the wall that remain today are those that were constructed during this most recent period.

The Great Wall winding through a hilly region in northern China

Q How has the Aral Sea changed in recent decades?

A It has shrunk by about 40% since 1960. The sea once covered nearly 25,000 square miles (64,720 sq km) and was the fourth-largest inland body of water in the world. Today it covers only about 13,000 square miles (33,600 sq km), and the former port city of Muynak lies 30 miles (48 km) inland. The sea's shrinkage can be blamed on cotton farming in the surrounding desert. Soviet-era efforts to establish a profitable cotton industry led to the creation of an extensive network of irrigation canals. These huge canals drain large amounts of water from the Syr Darya and Amu Darya, the only two rivers that empty into the sea.

Q What is the Ring of Fire?

A "Ring of Fire" designates the narrow band of active volcanoes encircling the Pacific Ocean basin. Of the approximately 1,500 volcanoes in the world that have been active within the last 10,000 years, more than two-thirds are part of the Ring. Over half of the Ring's active volcanoes are found in its Asian portion, which passes through Russia's Kamchatka Peninsula, the Kuril Islands, Japan, and the Philippines. The Ring of Fire's most recent major volcanic event was the 1991 eruption of Pinatubo on the Philippine island of Luzon, which prompted the evacuation of 250,000 people.

Q What part of Asia is called Indochina?

A "Indochina" refers to the southeastern Asian peninsula situated south of China and east of India. Countries located on the peninsula are Cambodia, Laos, Myanmar (Burma), Thailand, Vietnam, and the western portion of Malaysia. The eastern part of the Indochinese peninsula, including Cambodia, Laos, and Vietnam, was formerly known as French Indochina because of France's strong colonial presence there.

Q The Khyber Pass links which two countries?

A Afghanistan and Pakistan. Approximately 33 miles (53 km) long and reaching a maximum elevation of about 3,500 feet (1,067 m), the pass cuts through the Safed Koh mountains just south of the Kabul River, connecting the high plateau of Afghanistan with the Indus Valley. It has been used for centuries as a caravan route and as an invasion route into India. Today it is also traversed by a paved highway and, in Pakistan, by a railroad. In the 1980s several million refugees fleeing Afghanistan's civil war crossed into Pakistan via the pass.

Q What Persian Gulf country is a federation of seven Arab sheikdoms?

A United Arab Emirates, formed in 1971 through the unification of the sheikdoms of Abu Dhabi, Ajman, Dubai, Fujeirah, Sharjah, and Umm al-Qawain. Ras al-Khaimah joined the federation in 1972. Underdeveloped a few decades ago, the U.A.E. has been transformed by oil wealth into a modern and affluent country.

Q What Asian country contains, or is bordered by, six of the world's ten highest mountains?

A Nepal. Within Nepal or along its borders with China and India are found the following peaks: Mt. Everest (highest in the world), Kanchenjunga (3rd), Makalu (4th), Dhawalāgiri (5th), Annapurna (7th), and Xixabangma Feng (9th). Nanda Devi (10th) lies only 50 miles (80 km) northwest of Nepal's western border.

Q Where is the Empty Quarter?

A This hostile desert is found in the southern third of the Arabian Peninsula. Called *Ar Rub' Al-Khālī*, or "the Empty Quarter" in Arabic, it covers 250,000 square miles (647,000 sq km) and is the world's largest continuous sand body. Few people live in the Empty Quarter, and much of the region has never been explored.

Q What Asian volcanic eruption has been called the loudest natural explosion in recorded history?

A The 1883 eruption of Krakatau (Krakatoa), an island volcano between Sumatra and Java. Krakatau exploded three times on August 26 and 27, 1883, shooting tremendous amounts of gas and ash 50 miles (80 km) into the atmosphere. The explosions were so violent that they were heard nearly 3,000 miles (4,653 km) away on Rodrigues Island in the western Indian Ocean. Krakatau collapsed into itself, and when the explosions were over most of the island was submerged under 900 feet of water. Tsunamis up to 130 feet (40 m) high slammed the coasts of Sumatra and Java, washing away hundreds of villages and killing more than 36,000 people.

At their closest point, how far apart are Asia and North America?

At the narrowest point of the Bering Strait, Asia and North America are separated by only 56 miles (90 km). Russia's Big Diomede (Ratmanov) Island and the United States' Little Diomede Island, which lie in the middle of the strait, are only 2.5 miles (4 km) apart.

Where is the Fertile Crescent?

This term refers to a crescent-shaped area of fertile land in the Middle East which begins in the south with Egypt's Nile Valley, runs north along the eastern coast of the Mediterranean Sea, then turns southeast through Mesopotamia, the land between the Tigris and Euphrates rivers, and ends at the head of the Persian Gulf. The Fertile Crescent was the birthplace of some of the world's oldest civilizations, including the Sumerians, Babylonians, and Assyrians.

What country was Pakistan part of before it became independent?

India. Conflicts between Hindus and Muslims in British India led to the creation of Pakistan as a separate Muslim state in 1947. Originally, Pakistan included the two main centers of Muslim population, which lay in northwest and east India. The two areas, West Pakistan and East Pakistan, were separated by 1,000 miles (1,600 km). In 1971, East Pakistan declared its independence and changed its name to Bangladesh. The name "Pakistan" comes from the Urdu words *pakh*, meaning "pure," and *stan*, meaning "land."

What was Sri Lanka called before 1972?

Ceylon, which is the name the British had given to the island when they claimed it in 1796. The island became independent in 1948, and in 1972 was renamed Sri Lanka, which in the Sinhala language means "Resplendent Land."

The Taj Mahal

What is India's most famous tomb?

The Taj Mahal, located in the city of Agra. Often described as one of the world's most beautiful buildings, it was built by the Mogul emperor Shah Jahan to honor the memory of his wife, Mumtaz-i-Mahal. Construction began in 1631 and was completed in 1648.

What two seas are linked by the Suez Canal?

The Red Sea and the Mediterranean Sea. Before the 101-mile (163-km) canal was built in the mid-1800s, ships traveling between Europe and the Far East had to sail all the way around the southern tip of Africa. Depending on the origin and destination of the ship, the canal could shorten its trip dramatically. For example, a ship sailing from London to Bombay would have to travel almost 11,000 miles (17,700 km) around the African continent. Using the Suez Canal, the trip could be shortened to 6,300 miles (10,140 km), a distance reduction of over 40%.

Which independent Asian country has the highest population density?

The tiny republic of Singapore, with 11,874 people per square mile (4,593 per sq km). Singapore's 2,921,000 people occupy an island measuring only 26 miles east-to-west and 14 miles north-to-south. If non-independent entities are included, the Portuguese dependency of Macau has the continent's highest density, with 57,571 people per square mile (22,000 per sq km).

How long is Japan, from north to south?

The islands of Japan stretch approximately 1,900 miles (3,060 km) from Hokkaido in the north to the Sakishima Archipelago in the south. This is approximately equal to the distance between New York City and Denver.

Landscape on Hokkaido, Japan's northernmost island

What region is known as the "Roof of the World"?

Tibet, the high plateau region which lies north of the Himalayas. Covering 471,000 square miles (1,220,000 sq km), and with an average elevation of 15,000 feet (4,600 m), the Tibetan Plateau is the largest and highest plateau in the world. Much of Tibet is uninhabited; the region's fewer than two million people are concentrated in the valleys of the Brahmaputra (Yarlung) River and its tributaries.

Which Asian country leads the world in number of earthquake-related deaths recorded in this century?

China, where 48 deadly earthquakes have killed an estimated 967,420 people since 1900. During the same period Iran has lost 147,293 people in 57 earthquakes, and in Japan 32 earthquakes have killed 123,462 people.

What cities mark the endpoints of the Trans-Siberian Railway?

The longest railway line in the world, the Trans-Siberian Railway stretches 5,764 miles (9,297 km) between Moscow in the west and the Pacific Coast port city of Nakhodka (near Vladivostok) in the east. The eight-day journey between the two cities includes stops in 92 Russian cities and towns.

How many people live on the Indonesian island of Java?

Java is home to approximately 118 million people. It is the world's most populous island, although it is only the 13th-largest in area. By contrast, the island of Cuba is four-fifths the size of Java, but its population is only one-eleventh as large.

What was the name of Ho Chi Minh City, Vietnam, prior to 1975?

Saigon. When the city fell to North Vietnamese forces in 1975, it was renamed for Ho Chi Minh, founder of the Indochina Communist Party and president of North Vietnam from 1945 until his death in 1969.

Questions and Answers

What is Oceania?

The name "Oceania" refers to the scattered islands of a vast area of the Pacific Ocean, from Palau in the west to Easter Island in the east, and from the Midway Islands in the north to New Zealand in the south. The three main island groups of Oceania are Melanesia, Micronesia, and Polynesia. The continent of Australia and the islands of New Zealand are sometimes considered part of Oceania.

What is the Outback?

This nickname refers to Australia's vast, largely uninhabited interior. Over the years, the Outback's harsh beauty and its remoteness from the rest of Australia have made it popular with adventurous explorers and travelers. Through depictions in literature, art, and film, the region has become an integral part of Australia's identity. However, it is difficult to characterize the Outback, for its boundaries are undefined and its landscape varies from hot deserts to lush wilderness.

Eucalyptus tree in the Outback, Northern Territory

Why is Australia sometimes referred to as "the Land Down Under"?

This nickname originated with the British, who began colonizing Australia in the late 1700s. Because of its extreme southern location in relation to Britain, Australia was considered "Down." The "Under" part of the phrase refers to the continent's position "under" the Eurasian landmass. But while people from the Northern Hemisphere think of Australia as "Down Under," Australians do not.

How much of Australia is arid or semiarid?

More than two-thirds of the continent is considered to be arid or semiarid. The arid areas comprise several large deserts, including the Great Victoria Desert, the Gibson Desert, the Great Sandy Desert, and the Simpson Desert.

What distinction does Wellington, New Zealand have among national capitals of independent countries?

Located at 41°18' south latitude, Wellington is the world's southernmost national capital. In second place is Canberra, Australia, which lies at 35°17' south latitude.

What is unusual about how the island of Nauru was formed?

Nauru, the world's smallest republic, began as a coral atoll. Over the millennia, accumulated bird droppings filled in the central lagoon and created an 8-square-mile (21-sq-km) island whose highest point rises 210 feet (64 m) above sea level. The droppings are a rich source of phosphate, which is used in making fertilizers. Phosphate mining has long been Nauru's economic mainstay, but the resource will soon be exhausted.

What are the principal islands of New Zealand?

Two islands, North Island and South Island, account for more than 98% of New Zealand's total land area. The country also includes Stewart Island, the Chatham Islands, the Antipodes Islands, the Auckland Islands, and hundreds of tiny islets.

What is Ayers Rock?

Ayers Rock, now called by its Aboriginal name, Uluru, is a huge, red, oval-shaped rock outcropping that rises 2,831 feet (863 m) above the plains of central Australia. One of the largest monoliths in the world, Uluru is actually the summit of a massive sandstone hill, most of which is hidden underground. Aborigines consider Uluru sacred and incorporate numerous places around it into their ceremonial life.

What is the ratio of sheep to humans in Australia and New Zealand?

Because both countries are major wool, mutton, and lamb producers, Australia and New Zealand each have a high ratio of sheep to humans. In Australia, there are 132 million sheep, or seven sheep for each human in the country. In New Zealand, the ratio is even greater: the country's 50 million sheep translate into 14 sheep for each human.

How many of Oceania's countries have become independent since 1975?

Eight. Papua New Guinea became independent in 1975, the Solomon Islands and Tuvalu in 1978, Kiribati in 1979, Vanuatu in 1980, the Marshall Islands and the Federated States of Micronesia in 1986, and Palau (Belau) in 1994.

What is the Great Barrier Reef?

This vast coral reef system is the longest in the world, stretching 1,181 miles (1,900 km) along Australia's northeast coast. It is composed of reefs, shoals, and hundreds of islands. Popular with divers, the Great Barrier Reef is home to a myriad of aquatic creatures.

On what island is Robert Louis Stevenson buried?

Stevenson, author of *Dr. Jekyll and Mr. Hyde*, *Kidnapped*, and *Treasure Island*, is buried on the island of Upolu in Western Samoa. Born in Edinburgh, Scotland in 1850, Stevenson sailed to the South Pacific in 1888 and settled permanently in Samoa in 1890. He died there in 1894.

Where does Sydney rank among Australia's most populous cities?

Measured by actual city population, Sydney is not even ranked in the top hundred: only 13,501 people live within its tiny city limits. Brisbane is Australia's largest city, with 751,115 people. The Sydney metropolitan area, however, is by far the largest in Australia, with 3,538,749 people.

Harbor and skyline of Sydney

What is Australia's only island state?

Tasmania, which lies about 150 miles (240 km) south of the Australian mainland. Measuring 26,200 square miles (67,800 sq km) in area, it is the smallest of Australia's six states and accounts for less than 1% of the country's area. Originally part of New South Wales, Tasmania became a separate colony in 1825 and a state in 1901. Hobart, its capital, is home to 45% of the state's population.

World

Q Which country has the most time zones?

A Russia, with ten. The United States and Canada are tied for second place with six times zones each. Interestingly, China, the world's third largest country, has only one time zone, although the sun rises and sets almost four hours earlier at the country's eastern edge than at its western edge. Many other countries, including Nepal, Norway, and Algeria, have also adopted a single time zone to simplify daily life. *(Refer to World Time Zones map on pages 64-65.)*

Q Through how many continents does the International Dateline pass?

A Only one: Antarctica. The Dateline runs through the Pacific Ocean, between the North and South poles. Its jagged course approximately follows the 180° longitude line, although in places it veers as much as 750 miles (1,200 km) east or west of this line.

Q Which of the world's rivers flows through, or along the border of, the most countries?

A The Danube. The second-longest river in Europe (after the Volga), the Danube originates in southwestern Germany and flows through or borders eight countries: Germany, Austria, Slovakia, Hungary, Croatia, Yugoslavia, Romania, and Bulgaria. The Danube's drainage basin spreads over a total of 15 countries.

Q What is the longest mountain system in the world?

A The Andes, which stretch for almost 4,500 miles (7,200 km) along the western edge of South America from Venezuela in the north to Tierra del Fuego in the south. The second-longest system is the Rocky Mountains, the major mountain system of North America. The Rockies extend for 2,500 miles (4,000 km) from northern Canada south to northern New Mexico.

Q What are Pangaea and Panthalassa?

A Scientists believe that all of the landmasses of the world were once joined together in a single supercontinent. Given the name Pangaea, Greek for "all land," this supercontinent was surrounded by a vast universal ocean called Panthalassa, meaning "all seas." Between 225 and 190 million years ago, shifting of the Earth's crustal plates caused Pangaea to break up into northern and southern landmasses, referred to as Laurasia and Gondwanaland. As the plates continued to move, these two landmasses eventually split up into the six landmasses that exist today.

Q What is the one man-made structure that can be seen from space, with an unaided eye?

A The Great Wall of China. To astronauts orbiting hundreds of miles above the Earth, the 4,000-mile (6,500-km)-long Great Wall—the largest structure ever built by human hands—appears as nothing more than a fine line meandering across the hills and plains of northern China. It was once thought that the wall would be visible from the moon, but during a 1969 lunar mission, astronaut Alan Bean found this to be untrue.

Q Which continent has the highest population density?

A Asia, which has a density of 198 people per square mile (76 per square km). Excluding Antarctica, which is uninhabited, the lowest continental density is found in Australia, where there are only 6 people per square mile (2.4 per sq km).

Q Which continent has the most countries?

A Africa, which has 53 independent countries and eight dependencies: Ascension, British Indian Ocean Territory, Mayotte, Reunion, St. Helena, Spanish North Africa, Tristan da Cunha, and Western Sahara. Asia ranks second, with 47 independent countries, one internally self-governing country (Bhutan), and one dependency (Macau). Antarctica has no countries, and the entire continent of Australia is covered by the country of the same name.

Q What country borders the most other countries?

A The People's Republic of China is the most "neighborly" country in the world, for it shares its borders with 15 countries or dependencies: Kazakhstan, Kyrgyzstan, Tajikistan, Afghanistan, Pakistan, India, Nepal, Bhutan, Myanmar, Laos, Vietnam, Macau, North Korea, Russia, and Mongolia. Russia is in second place, bordering 14 countries: Finland, Norway, Estonia, Latvia, Belarus, Lithuania, Poland, Ukraine, Georgia, Azerbaijan, Kazakhstan, China, Mongolia, and North Korea. However, Macau will soon drop from China's list. Currently administered by the Portugal, the territory will revert to Chinese control in 1999.

Q What were the Seven Wonders of the Ancient World?

A The Colossus of Rhodes (in modern-day Greece), the Hanging Gardens of Babylon (Iraq), the Pyramids and Sphinx of Egypt, the Temple of Artemis at Ephesus (Turkey), the Statue of Zeus at Olympia (Greece), the Mausoleum at Halicarnassus (Turkey), and the Pharos of Alexandria (Egypt). Of these seven wonders, only the Pyramids and Sphinx remain standing today.

People and pyramids at Khufu, Giza Plateau, Cairo

Q Where would you be if you were at 0° latitude, 0° longitude?

A The point where 0° latitude, the Equator, intersects 0° longitude, the Prime Meridian, is located in the Atlantic Ocean off the western coast of Africa, 380 miles (610 km) south of Ghana and 670 miles (1,080 km) west of Gabon.

Q What are the official languages of the United Nations?

A There are more than 2,000 known languages in the world, but official business of the United Nations is conducted in only the following six, which are among the most widely spoken: Mandarin Chinese, English, Arabic, Spanish, Russian, and French.

The Universe and Solar System

The Milky Way Galaxy

Our star, the Sun, is one of 200 billion stars banded together in the enormous gravitational spiral nebula called the Milky Way Galaxy, which is but one of millions of known galaxies in the universe.

The Milky Way is huge; it would take light — which travels at 186,000 miles per second — 100,000 years to go from one end of the galaxy to the other. In addition to the billions of stars, Earth shares the Milky Way with eight other known planets.

Statistical Data for the Milky Way Galaxy

Diameter: 100,000 light-years

Mass: About 200 billion suns

Distance between spiral arms: 6,500 light years

Thickness of galactic disk: 1,300 light-years

Satellite galaxies: 2 (visible only in the southern sky)

Sun

The Sun's diameter — more than 865,000 miles — is 109 times greater than that of the Earth. Even so, the Sun is actually a fairly small star. Somewhere in the vastness of the universe astronomers have located a star that is 3,500 times larger than the Sun.

Diameter: 865,000 miles (1,392,000 km)
Mass: 333,000 times that of the Earth
Surface temperature: 10,300° F (5,700° C)
Central temperature: 27 million° F (15 million° C)
Composition: 70% hydrogen, 27% helium
Spin (at equator): 26 days, 21 hours

Mercury

Distance from the Sun: 35,985,000 miles (57,909,000 km), or 39% that of the Earth
Diameter: 3,031 miles (4,878 km), or 38% that of the Earth
Average surface temperature: 340° F (171° C)
Atmosphere: Extremely thin, contains helium and hydrogen
Length of day: 58 days, 15 hours, 30 minutes
Length of year: 87.97 days
Satellites: None

Venus

Distance from the Sun: 67,241,000 miles (108,209,000 km), or 72% that of the Earth
Diameter: 7,521 miles (12,104 km), or 95% that of the Earth
Surface temperature: 867° F (464° C)
Surface pressure: 90 times that of the Earth, equivalent to the pressure at a water depth of 3,000 feet (900 meters)
Atmosphere: 96% carbon dioxide
Length of day: 243 days, 14 minutes. The planet spins opposite to the rotation of the Earth.
Length of year: 224.7 days
Satellites: None

Earth

Distance from the Sun: 92,960,000 miles (149,598,000 km)
Diameter: 7,926 miles (12,756 km)
Average surface temperature: 58° F (14° C)
Surface pressure: 1 atmosphere
Atmosphere: 78% nitrogen, 21% oxygen
Length of day: 23 hours, 56 minutes and 4 seconds
Length of year: 365.25 days
Satellites: 1

The Moon

The Moon is the Earth's only natural satellite. About 2,160 miles (3,746 km) across, the Moon is an airless, waterless world just one-fourth the size of the Earth. It circles the planet once every 27 days at an average distance of about 238,000 miles (384,000 km).

Jupiter

By any measure, Jupiter is the solar system's giant. To equal Jupiter's bulk would take 318 Earths. Over 1,300 Earth-sized balls could fit within this enormous planet.

Distance from the Sun: 483,631,000 miles (778,292,000 km), or 5.2 times that of the Earth
Diameter: 88,700 miles (142,800 km), or 11.3 times that of the Earth
Temperature at cloud tops: −234° F (−148° C)

Mars

Distance from the Sun: 141,642,000 miles (227,940,000 km), about 1.5 times that of the Earth
Diameter: 4,222 miles (6,794 km), or 53% that of the Earth
Average surface temperature: −13° F (−25° C)
Surface pressure: 0.7% (1/150 th) that of the Earth
Atmosphere: 95% carbon dioxide, 2.7% nitrogen
Length of day: 24 hours, 37 minutes
Length of year: 1 year, 321.73 days
Satellites: 2

Spatial Relationships of the Sun and the Planets

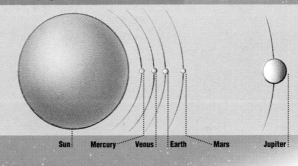

Sun   Mercury   Venus   Earth   Mars   Jupiter   Saturn

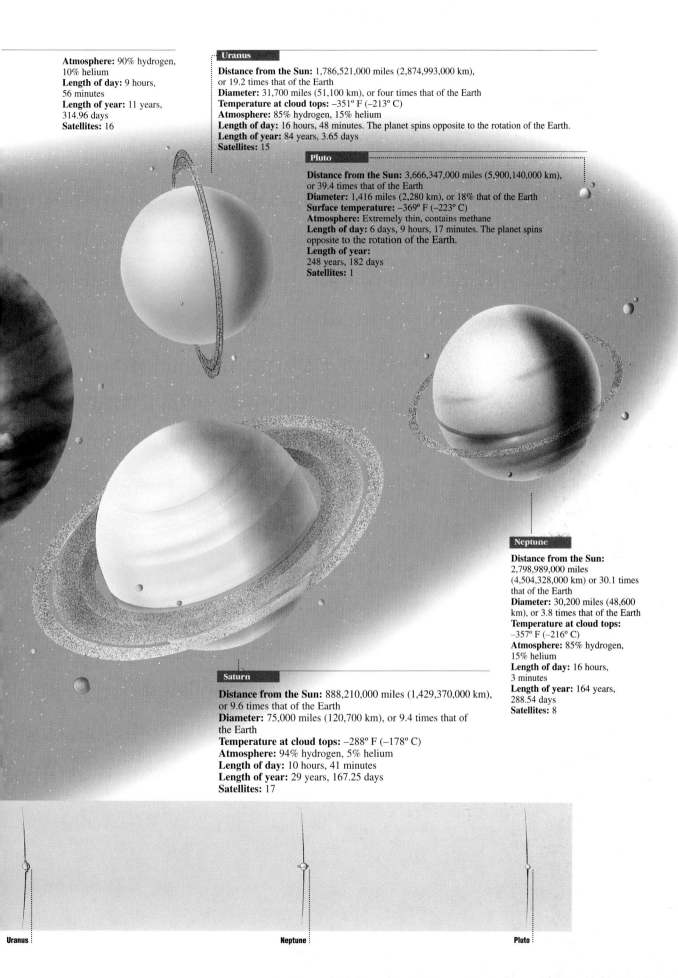

Atmosphere: 90% hydrogen, 10% helium
Length of day: 9 hours, 56 minutes
Length of year: 11 years, 314.96 days
Satellites: 16

Uranus

Distance from the Sun: 1,786,521,000 miles (2,874,993,000 km), or 19.2 times that of the Earth
Diameter: 31,700 miles (51,100 km), or four times that of the Earth
Temperature at cloud tops: –351° F (–213° C)
Atmosphere: 85% hydrogen, 15% helium
Length of day: 16 hours, 48 minutes. The planet spins opposite to the rotation of the Earth.
Length of year: 84 years, 3.65 days
Satellites: 15

Pluto

Distance from the Sun: 3,666,347,000 miles (5,900,140,000 km), or 39.4 times that of the Earth
Diameter: 1,416 miles (2,280 km), or 18% that of the Earth
Surface temperature: –369° F (–223° C)
Atmosphere: Extremely thin, contains methane
Length of day: 6 days, 9 hours, 17 minutes. The planet spins opposite to the rotation of the Earth.
Length of year: 248 years, 182 days
Satellites: 1

Neptune

Distance from the Sun: 2,798,989,000 miles (4,504,328,000 km) or 30.1 times that of the Earth
Diameter: 30,200 miles (48,600 km), or 3.8 times that of the Earth
Temperature at cloud tops: –357° F (–216° C)
Atmosphere: 85% hydrogen, 15% helium
Length of day: 16 hours, 3 minutes
Length of year: 164 years, 288.54 days
Satellites: 8

Saturn

Distance from the Sun: 888,210,000 miles (1,429,370,000 km), or 9.6 times that of the Earth
Diameter: 75,000 miles (120,700 km), or 9.4 times that of the Earth
Temperature at cloud tops: –288° F (–178° C)
Atmosphere: 94% hydrogen, 5% helium
Length of day: 10 hours, 41 minutes
Length of year: 29 years, 167.25 days
Satellites: 17

Uranus   **Neptune**   **Pluto**

The Earth

History of the Earth

Estimated age of the Earth:
At least 4.6 billion (4,600,000,000) years.

Formation of the Earth:
It is generally thought that the Earth was formed from a cloud of gas and dust (A) revolving around the early Sun. Gravitational forces pulled the cloud's particles together into an ever denser mass (B), with heavier particles sinking to the center. Heat from radioactive elements caused the materials of the embryonic Earth to melt and gradually settle into core and mantle layers. As the surface cooled, a crust formed. Volcanic activity released vast amounts of steam, carbon dioxide and other gases from the Earth's interior. The steam condensed into water to form the oceans, and the gases, prevented by gravity from escaping, formed the beginnings of the atmosphere (C).

The calm appearance of our planet today (D) belies the intense heat of its interior and the violent tectonic forces which are constantly reshaping its surface.

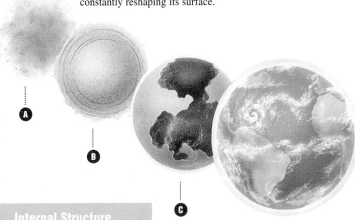

Periods in Earth's history

Earth's history is divided into different **eras**, which are subdivided into **periods**.

The most recent periods are themselves subdivided into **epochs**. The main divisions and subdivisions are shown below.

	Began	Ended	
	(million years ago)		
Precambrian Era			
Archean Period	3,800	2,500	Start of life
Proterozoic Period	2,500	590	Life in the seas
Paleozoic Era			
Cambrian Period	590	500	Sea life
Ordovician Period	505	438	First fishes
Silurian Period	438	408	First land plants
Devonian Period	408	360	Amphibians
Carboniferous Period	360	286	First reptiles
Permian Period	286	248	Spread of reptiles
Mesozoic Era			
Triassic Period	248	213	Reptiles and early mammals
Jurassic Period	213	144	Dinosaurs
Cretaceous Period	144	65	Dinosaurs, dying out at the end
Cenozoic Era			
Tertiary Period			
Paleocene	65	55	Large mammals
Eocene	55	38	Primates begin
Oligocene	38	25	Development of primates
Miocene	25	5	Modern-type animals
Pliocene	5	2	Australopithecus ape, ancestor to the human race
Quaternary Period			
Pleistocene	2	0.01	Ice ages; true humans
Holocene	0.01	Present	Modern humans

Source: *Atlas of the Universe* by Patrick Moore, Reed International Books Limited, 1994.

Internal Structure of the Earth

In its simplest form, the Earth is composed of a crust, a mantle with an upper and lower layer, and a core, which has an inner region.

Temperatures in the Earth increase with depth, as is observed in a deep mine shaft or borehole, but the prediction of temperatures within the Earth is made difficult by the fact that different rocks conduct heat at different rates: rock salt, for example, has 10 times the heat conductivity of coal. Also, estimates have to take into account the abundance of heat-generating atoms in a rock. Radioactive atoms are concentrated toward the Earth's surface, so the planet has, in effect, a thermal blanket to keep it warm. The temperature at the center of the Earth is believed to be approximately 5,400° F (3,000° C).

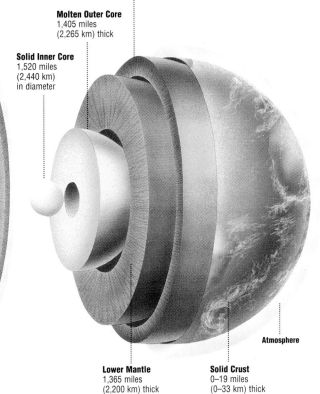

Upper Mantle
415 miles
(667 km) thick

Molten Outer Core
1,405 miles
(2,265 km) thick

Solid Inner Core
1,520 miles
(2,440 km)
in diameter

Atmosphere

Lower Mantle
1,365 miles
(2,200 km) thick

Solid Crust
0–19 miles
(0–33 km) thick

Chemical composition of the Earth:

The chemical composition of the Earth varies from crust to core. The upper crust of continents, called sial, is mainly granite, rich in aluminum and silicon. Oceanic crust, or sima, is largely basalt, made of magnesium and silicon. The mantle is composed of rocks that are rich in magnesium and iron silicates, whereas the core, it is believed, is made of iron and nickel oxides.

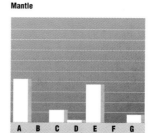

- Sial
- Sima
- Upper Mantle
- Lower Mantle
- Outer Core
- Inner Core

A. Silicon
B. Aluminum
C. Iron
D. Calcium
E. Magnesium
F. Nickel
G. Other

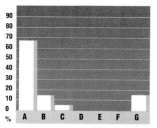

Sial (upper crust of continents)

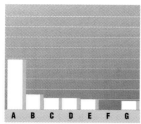

Sima (oceanic crust)

Mantle

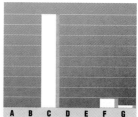

Core

Measurements of the Earth

Equatorial circumference of the Earth: 24,901.45 miles (40,066.43 km)

Polar circumference of the Earth: 24,855.33 miles (39,992.22 km)

Equatorial diameter of the Earth: 7,926.38 miles (12,753.54 km)

Polar diameter of the Earth: 7,899.80 miles (12,710.77 km)

Equatorial radius of the Earth: 3,963.19 miles (6,376.77 km)

Polar radius of the Earth: 3,949.90 miles (6,355.38 km)

Estimated weight of the Earth:

6,600,000,000,000,000,000,000 tons, or 6,600 billion billion tons (5,940 billion billion metric tons)

Total surface area of the Earth: 197,000,000 square miles (510,230,000 sq km)

Total land area of the Earth (including inland water and Antarctica): 57,900,000 square miles (150,100,000 sq km)

Total ocean area of the Earth: 139,200,000 square miles (360,528,000 sq km), or 70% of the Earth's surface area

Total area of the Earth's surface covered with water (oceans and all inland water): 147,750,000 square miles (382,672,500 sq km), or 75% of the Earth's surface area

Types of water: 97% of the Earth's water is salt water; 3% is fresh water

Life on Earth

Number of plant species on Earth: About 350,000

Number of animal species on Earth: More than one million

Estimated total human population of the Earth: 5,628,000,000

Movements of the Earth

Mean distance of the Earth from the Sun: About 93 million miles (149.6 million km)

Period in which the Earth makes one complete orbit around the Sun: 365 days, 5 hours, 48 minutes, and 46 seconds

Speed of the Earth as it orbits the Sun: 66,700 miles (107,320 km) per hour

Period in which the Earth makes one complete rotation on its axis: 23 hours, 56 minutes and 4 seconds

Equatorial speed at which the Earth rotates on its axis: More than 1,000 miles (1,600 km) per hour

The Shape of the Earth

Comparing the Earth's equatorial and polar dimensions reveals that our planet is actually not a perfect sphere but rather an oblate spheroid, flattened at the poles and bulging at the equator. This is the result of a combination of gravitational and centrifugal forces.

An even more precise term for the Earth's shape is "geoid" — the actual shape of sea level, which is lumpy, with variations away from spheroid of up to 260 feet (80 m). This lumpiness reflects major variations in density in the Earth's outer layers.

The Seasons
(Northern Hemisphere)

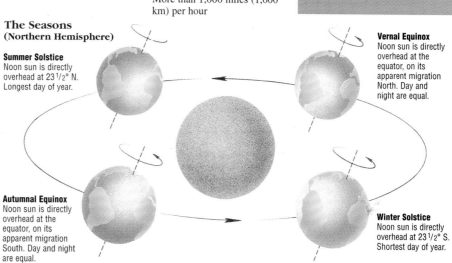

Summer Solstice
Noon sun is directly overhead at 23 1/2° N. Longest day of year.

Vernal Equinox
Noon sun is directly overhead at the equator, on its apparent migration North. Day and night are equal.

Autumnal Equinox
Noon sun is directly overhead at the equator, on its apparent migration South. Day and night are equal.

Winter Solstice
Noon sun is directly overhead at 23 1/2° S. Shortest day of year.

Continents and Islands

The word "continents" designates the largest continuous masses of land in the world.

For reasons that are mainly historical, seven continents are generally recognized: Africa, Antarctica, Asia, Australia, Europe, North America, and South America. Since Asia and Europe actually share the same land mass, they are sometimes identified as a single continent, Eurasia.

The lands of the central and south Pacific, including Australia, New Zealand, Micronesia, Melanesia, and Polynesia, are sometimes grouped together as Oceania.

The Continents

Africa

Area in square miles (sq km):
11,700,000 (30,300,000)
Estimated population (Jan. 1, 1995):
697,600,000
Population per square mile (sq km):
60 (23)
Mean elevation in feet (meters):
1,900 (580)
Highest elevation in feet (meters):
Kilimanjaro, Tanzania, 19,340 (5,895)
Lowest elevation in feet (meters):
Lac Assal, Djibouti, 515 (157) below sea level

Antarctica

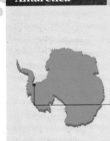

Area in square miles (sq km):
5,400,000 (14,000,000)
Estimated population (Jan. 1, 1995):
Uninhabited
Population per square mile (sq km):
0 (0)
Mean elevation in feet (meters):
6,000 (1,830)
Highest elevation in feet (meters):
Vinson Massif, 16,066 (4,897)
Lowest elevation in feet (meters):
Deep Lake, 184 (56) below sea level

Asia

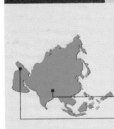

Area in square miles (sq km):
17,300,000 (44,900,000)
Estimated population (Jan. 1, 1995):
3,422,700,000
Population per square mile (sq km):
198 (76)
Mean elevation in feet (meters):
3,000 (910)
Highest elevation in feet (meters):
Mt. Everest, China (Nepal)–Tibet, 29,028 (8,848)
Lowest elevation in feet (meters):
Dead Sea, Israel–Jordan, 1,339 (408) below sea level

Australia

Area in square miles (sq km):
2,966,155 (7,682,300)
Estimated population (Jan. 1, 1995):
18,205,000
Population per square mile (sq km):
6.1 (2.4)
Mean elevation in feet (meters):
1,000 (305)
Highest elevation in feet (meters):
Mt. Kosciusko, New South Wales, 7,310 (2,228)
Lake Eyre, South Australia, 52 (16) below sea level

Europe

Area in square miles (sq km):
3,800,000 (9,900,000)
Estimated population (Jan. 1, 1995):
712,100,000
Population per square mile (sq km):
187 (72)
Mean elevation in feet (meters):
980 (300)
Highest elevation in feet (meters):
Gora El'brus, Russia, 18,510 (5,642)
Lowest elevation in feet (meters):
Caspian Sea, Asia-Europe, 92 (28) below sea level

North America

Area in square miles (sq km):
9,500,000 (24,700,000)
Estimated population (Jan. 1, 1995):
453,300,000
Population per square mile (sq km):
48 (18)
Mean elevation in feet (meters):
2,000 (610)
Highest elevation in feet (meters):
Mt. McKinley, Alaska, U.S., 20,320 (6,194)
Lowest elevation in feet (meters):
Death Valley, California, U.S., 282 (84) below sea level

Oceania *(incl. Australia)*

Area in square miles (sq km):
3,300,000 (8,500,000)
Estimated population (Jan. 1, 1995):
28,400,000
Population per square mile (sq km):
8.6 (3.3)
Mean elevation in feet (meters):
0 (0)
Highest elevation in feet (meters):
Mt. Wilhelm, Papua New Guinea, 14,793 (4,509)
Lowest elevation in feet (meters):
Lake Eyre, South Australia, 52 (16) below sea level

South America

Area in square miles (sq km):
6,900,000 (17,800,000)
Estimated population (Jan. 1, 1995):
313,900,000
Population per square mile (sq km):
45 (18)
Mean elevation in feet (meters):
1,800 (550)
Highest elevation in feet (meters):
Cerro Aconcagua, Argentina, 22,831 (6,959)
Lowest elevation in feet (meters):
Salinas Chicas, Argentina, 138 (42) below sea level

World

Area in square miles (sq km):
57,900,000 (150,100,000)
Estimated population (Jan. 1, 1995):
5,628,000,000
Population per square mile (sq km):
97 (37)
Mean elevation in feet (meters):
0 (0)
Highest elevation in feet (meters):
Mt. Everest, China–Nepal, 29,028 (8,848)
Lowest elevation in feet (meters):
Dead Sea, Israel–Jordan, 1,339 (408) below sea level

Largest Islands

Rank	Name	Area square miles	square km
1	Greenland, North America	840,000	2,175,600
2	New Guinea, Asia-Oceania	309,000	800,000
3	Borneo (Kalimantan), Asia	287,300	744,100
4	Madagascar, Africa	226,500	587,000
5	Baffin Island, Canada	195,928	507,451
6	Sumatra (Sumatera), Indonesia	182,860	473,606
7	Honshū, Japan	89,176	230,966
8	Great Britain, United Kingdom	88,795	229,978
9	Victoria Island, Canada	83,897	217,291
10	Ellesmere Island, Canada	75,767	196,236
11	Celebes (Sulawesi), Indonesia	73,057	189,216
12	South Island, New Zealand	57,708	149,463
13	Java (Jawa), Indonesia	51,038	132,187
14	North Island, New Zealand	44,332	114,821
15	Cuba, North America	42,800	110,800
16	Newfoundland, Canada	42,031	108,860
17	Luzon, Philippines	40,420	104,688
18	Iceland, Europe	39,800	103,000
19	Mindanao, Philippines	36,537	94,630
20	Ireland, Europe	32,600	84,400
21	Hokkaidō, Japan	32,245	83,515
22	Sakhalin, Russia	29,500	76,400
23	Hispaniola, North America	29,400	76,200
24	Banks Island, Canada	27,038	70,028
25	Tasmania, Australia	26,200	67,800
26	Sri Lanka, Asia	24,900	64,600
27	Devon Island, Canada	21,331	55,247
28	Berkner Island, Antarctica	20,005	51,829
29	Alexander Island, Antarctica	19,165	49,652
30	Tierra del Fuego, South America	18,600	48,200
31	Novaya Zemlya, north island, Russia	18,436	47,764
32	Kyūshū, Japan	17,129	44,363
33	Melville Island, Canada	16,274	42,149
34	Southampton Island, Canada	15,913	41,214
35	Axel Heiberg, Canada	15,498	40,151
36	Spitsbergen, Norway	15,260	39,523
37	New Britain, Papua New Guinea	14,093	36,500
38	Taiwan, Asia	13,900	36,000
39	Hainan Dao, China	13,100	34,000
40	Prince of Wales Island, Canada	12,872	33,339
41	Novaya Zemlya, south island, Russia	12,633	32,730
42	Vancouver Island, Canada	12,079	31,285
43	Sicily, Italy	9,926	25,709
44	Somerset Island, Canada	9,570	24,786
45	Sardinia, Italy	9,301	24,090
46	Bathurst Island, Canada	7,600	19,684
47	Shikoku, Japan	7,258	18,799
48	Ceram (Seram), Indonesia	7,191	18,625
49	North East Land, Norway	6,350	16,446
50	New Caledonia, Oceania	6,252	16,192
51	Prince Patrick Island, Canada	5,986	15,509
52	Timor, Indonesia	5,743	14,874
53	Sumbawa, Indonesia	5,549	14,377
54	Ostrov Oktyabr'skoy Revolyutsii, Russia	5,511	14,279
55	Flores, Indonesia	5,502	14,250
56	Samar, Philippines	5,100	13,080
57	King William Island, Canada	4,961	12,853
58	Negros, Philippines	4,907	12,710
59	Thurston Island, Antarctica	4,854	12,576
60	Palawan, Philippines	4,550	11,785

Islands, Islands, Everywhere

Four islands — Hokkaidō, Honshū, Kyūshū, and Shikoku — constitute 98% of Japan's total land area, but the country is actually comprised of more than 3,000 islands. Similarly, two islands — Great Britain and Ireland — make up 93% of the total land area of the British Isles, but the island group also includes more than 5,000 smaller islands.

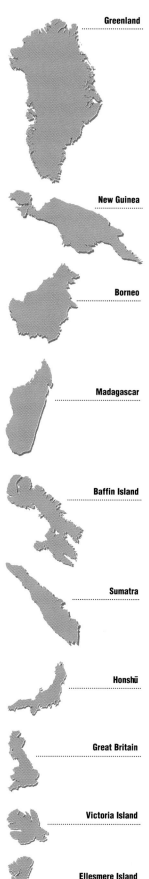

Greenland
New Guinea
Borneo
Madagascar
Baffin Island
Sumatra
Honshū
Great Britain
Victoria Island
Ellesmere Island

Major World Island Groups

Aleutian Islands (Pacific Ocean)
Alexander Archipelago (Pacific Ocean)
Azores (Atlantic Ocean)
Bahamas (Atlantic Ocean)
Balearic Islands (Mediterranean Sea)
Bismarck Archipelago (Pacific Ocean)
British Isles (Atlantic Ocean)
Cape Verde Islands (Atlantic Ocean)
Dodecanese (Mediterranean Sea)
Faeroe Islands (Atlantic Ocean)
Falkland Islands (Atlantic Ocean)
Fiji Islands (Pacific Ocean)
Galapagos Islands (Pacific Ocean)
Greater Sunda Islands (Indian/Pacific Oceans)
Hawaiian Islands (Pacific Ocean)
Ionian Islands (Mediterranean Sea)
Islas Canarias (Atlantic Ocean)
Japan (Pacific Ocean)
Kikládhes (Mediterranean Sea)
Kuril Islands (Pacific Ocean)
Lesser Sunda Islands (Indian Ocean)
Moluccas (Pacific Ocean)
Nansei Shotō (Pacific Ocean)
New Hebrides (Atlantic Ocean)
New Siberian Islands (Arctic Ocean)
Novaya Zemlya (Arctic Ocean)
Philippine Islands (Pacific Ocean)
Severnaya Zemlya (Arctic Ocean)
Solomon Islands (Pacific Ocean)
Spitsbergen (Arctic Ocean)
West Indies (Atlantic Ocean)

Contrasting Population Densities

Some islands are among the most densely populated places on Earth, while others are among the least densely populated. This fact is dramatically illustrated by the following comparison of five islands:

Manhattan, N.Y., U.S., (pop. 1,488,000) — 67,636/ sq mile (26,105/ sq km)

Singapore Island, Singapore (pop. 2,921,000) — 11,874/ sq mile (4,593/ sq km)

Long Island, N.Y., U.S. (pop. 6,863,000) — 4,984/ sq mile (1,925/ sq km)

Population per square mile (sq km)

Baffin Island, Canada (pop. 8,800) — 0.04/ sq mile (0.02/ sq km)

Greenland (pop. 57,000) — 0.07/ sq mile (0.03/ sq km)

Mountains, Volcanoes, and Earthquakes

The Tallest Mountain in the World

With its peak reaching 29,028 feet (8,848 m) above sea level, Mt. Everest ranks as the *highest* mountain in the world, but not the *tallest*. That title goes to Mauna Kea, one of the five volcanic mountains that make up the island of Hawaii. From its base on the floor of the Pacific Ocean, Mauna Kea rises 33,476 feet (10,210 m)—more than six miles—although only the top 13,796 feet (4,205 m) are above sea level.

Seafloor Atop Mt. Everest

When Sir Edmund Percival Hillary and Tenzing Norgay reached the summit of Mt. Everest in 1953, they probably did not realize they were standing on the seafloor.

The Himalayan mountain system was formed through the process of plate tectonics. Ocean once separated India and Asia, but 180 million years ago the Indo-Australian crustal plate, on which India sits, began a northward migration and eventually collided with the Eurasian plate. The seafloor between the two landmasses crumpled and was slowly thrust upward. Rock layers that once lay at the bottom of the ocean now crown the peaks of the highest mountains in the world.

Principal Mountain Systems and Ranges of the World

Alaska Range (North America)
Alps (Europe)
Altai (Asia)
Andes (South America)
Appennino (Europe)
Atlas Mountains (Africa)
Appalachian Mountains (North America)
Brooks Range (North America)
Carpathian Mountains (Europe)
Cascade Range (North America)
Caucasus (Europe/Asia)
Coast Mountains (North America)
Coast Ranges (North America)
Great Dividing Range (Australia)
Greater Khingan Range (Asia)
Himalayas (Asia)
Hindu Kush (Asia)
Karakoram Range (Asia)
Kunlun Shan (Asia)
Madre Occidental, Sierra (North America)
Madre Oriental, Sierra (North America)
Nevada, Sierra (North America)
Pamirs (Asia)
Pyrenees (Europe)
Rocky Mountains (North America)
Sayan Khrebet (Asia)
Southern Alps (New Zealand)
Tien Shan (Asia)
Urals (Europe)
Zagros Mountains (Asia)

Principal Mountains of the World
Δ = Highest mountain in range, region, country, or state named

Location	Height Feet	Meters
Africa		
Kilimanjaro, Δ Tanzania (Δ Africa)	19,340	5,895
Kirinyaga (Mount Kenya), Δ Kenya	17,058	5,199
Margherita Peak, Δ Uganda-Δ Zaire	16,763	5,109
Ras Dashen Terara, Δ Ethiopia	15,158	4,620
Meru, Mount, Tanzania	14,978	4,565
Karisimbi, Volcan, Δ Rwanda-Zaire	14,787	4,507
Elgon, Mount, Kenya-Uganda	14,178	4,321
Toubkal, Jebel, Δ Morocco (Δ Atlas Mts.)	13,665	4,165
Cameroon Mountain, Δ Cameroon	13,451	4,100
Antarctica		
Vinson Massif, Δ Antarctica	16,066	4,897
Kirkpatrick, Mount	14,856	4,528
Markham, Mount	14,049	4,282
Jackson, Mount	13,747	4,190
Sidley, Mount	13,717	4,181
Wade, Mount	13,396	4,083
Asia		
Everest, Mount, Δ China-Δ Nepal (Δ Tibet; Δ Himalayas; Δ Asia; Δ World)	29,028	8,848
K2 (Qogir Feng), China-Δ Pakistan (Δ Kashmir; Δ Karakoram Range)	28,250	8,611
Kanchenjunga, Δ India-Nepal	28,208	8,598
Makalu, China-Nepal	27,825	8,481
Dhawalāgiri, Nepal	26,810	8,172
Nanga Parbat, Pakistan	26,660	8,126
Annapurna, Nepal	26,504	8,078
Gasherbrum, China-Pakistan	26,470	8,068
Xixabangma Feng, China	26,286	8,012
Nanda Devi, India	25,645	7,817
Kamet, China-India	25,447	7,756
Namjagbarwa Feng, China	25,446	7,756
Muztag, China (Δ Kunlun Shan)	25,338	7,723
Tirich Mir, Pakistan (Δ Hindu Kush)	25,230	7,690
Gongga Shan, China	24,790	7,556
Kula Kangri, Δ Bhutan	24,784	7,554
Kommunizma, Pik, Δ Tajikistan (Δ Pamir)	24,590	7,495
Nowshak, Δ Afghanistan-Pakistan	24,557	7,485
Pobedy, Pik, China-Russia	24,406	7,439
Chomo Lhari, Bhutan-China	23,997	7,314
Muztag, China	23,891	7,282
Lenina, Pik, Δ Kyrgyzstan-Tajikistan	23,406	7,134
Api, Nepal	23,399	7,132
Kangrinboqê Feng, China	22,028	6,714
Hkakabo Razi, Δ Myanmar	19,296	5,881
Damavand, Qolleh-ye, Δ Iran	18,386	5,604
Agri Dagi (Mount Ararat), Δ Turkey	16,854	5,137
Fuladi, Kuh-e, Afghanistan	16,847	5,135
Jaya, Puncak, Δ Indonesia (Δ New Guinea)	16,503	5,030
Klyuchevskaya, Vulkan, Russia (Δ Poluostrov Kamchatka)	15,584	4,750
Trikora, Puncak, Indonesia	15,584	4,750
Belukha, Gora, Kazakhstan-Russia	14,783	4,506
Turgen, Mount, Mongolia	14,311	4,362
Kinabalu, Gunong, Δ Malaysia (Δ Borneo)	13,455	4,101
Yü Shan, Δ Taiwan	13,114	3,997
Erciyes Dağı, Turkey	12,851	3,917
Kerinci, Gunung, Indonesia (Δ Sumatra)	12,467	3,800
Fuji San, Δ Japan (Δ Honshu)	12,388	3,776
Rinjani, Gunung, Indonesia (Δ Lombok)	12,224	3,726
Semeru, Gunung, Indonesia (Δ Java)	12,060	3,676
Hadūr Shu'ayb, Jabal an-, Δ Yemen (Δ Arabian Peninsula)	12,008	3,660
Australia / Oceania		
Wilhelm, Mt., Δ Papua New Guinea	14,793	4,509
Giluwe, Mt., Papua New Guinea	14,330	4,368
Bangeta, Mt., Papua New Guinea	13,520	4,121
Victoria, Mt., Papua New Guinea (Δ Owen Stanley Range)	13,238	4,035
Cook, Mt., Δ New Zealand (Δ South Island)	12,316	3,754
Europe		
El'brus, Gora, Δ Russia (Δ Caucasus; Δ Europe)	18,510	5,642
Dykhtau, Mt., Russia	17,073	5,204
Blanc, Mont (Monte Bianco) Δ France-Δ Italy (Δ Alps)	15,771	4,807

Location	Height Feet	Meters
Dufourspitze, Italy-Δ Switzerland	15,203	4,634
Weisshorn, Switzerland	14,783	4,506
Matterhorn, Italy-Switzerland	14,692	4,478
Finsteraarhorn, Switzerland	14,022	4,274
Jungfrau, Switzerland	13,642	4,158
Écrins, Barre des, France	13,458	4,102
Viso, Monte, Italy (Δ Cottian Alps)	12,602	3,841
Grossglockner, Δ Austria	12,461	3,798
Teide, Pico de, Δ Spain (Δ Canary Is.)	12,188	3,715
North America		
McKinley, Mt., Δ Alaska (Δ United States; Δ North America)	20,320	6,194
Logan, Mt., Δ Canada (Δ Yukon; Δ St. Elias Mts.)	19,551	5,959
Orizaba, Pico de, Δ Mexico	18,406	5,610
St. Elias, Mt., Alaska-Canada	18,008	5,489
Popocatépetl, Volcán, Mexico	17,930	5,465
Foraker, Mt., Alaska	17,400	5,304
Iztaccíhuatl, Mexico	17,159	5,230
Lucania, Mt., Canada	17,147	5,226
Fairweather, Mt., Alaska-Canada (Δ British Columbia)	15,300	4,663
Whitney, Mt., Δ California	14,494	4,418
Elbert, Mt., Δ Colorado (Δ Rocky Mts.)	14,433	4,399
Massive, Mt., Colorado	14,421	4,396
Harvard, Mt., Colorado	14,420	4,395
Rainier, Mt., Δ Washington (Δ Cascade Range)	14,410	4,392
Williamson, Mt., California	14,370	4,380
La Plata Pk., Colorado	14,361	4,377
Blanca Pk., Colorado (Δ Sangre de Cristo Mts.)	14,345	4,372
Uncompahgre Pk., Colorado (Δ San Juan Mts.)	14,309	4,361
Grays Pk., Colorado (Δ Front Range)	14,270	4,349
Evans, Mt., Colorado	14,264	4,348
Longs Pk., Colorado	14,255	4,345
Wrangell, Mt., Alaska	14,163	4,317
Shasta, Mt., California	14,162	4,317
Pikes Pk., Colorado	14,110	4,301
Colima, Nevado de, Mexico	13,991	4,240
Tajumulco, Volcán, Δ Guatemala (Δ Central America)	13,845	4,220
Gannett Pk., Δ Wyoming	13,804	4,207
Mauna Kea, Δ Hawaii	13,796	4,205
Grand Teton, Wyoming	13,770	4,197
Mauna Loa, Hawaii	13,679	4,169
Kings Pk., Δ Utah	13,528	4,123
Cloud Pk., Wyoming (Δ Bighorn Mts.)	13,167	4,013
Waddington, Mt., Canada (Δ Coast Mts.)	13,163	4,012
Wheeler Pk., Δ New Mexico	13,161	4,011
Boundary Pk., Δ Nevada	13,140	4,005
Robson, Mt., Canada (Δ Canadian Rockies)	12,972	3,954
Granite Pk., Δ Montana	12,799	3,901
Borah Pk., Δ Idaho	12,662	3,859
Humphreys Pk., Δ Arizona	12,633	3,851
Chirripó, Volcán, Δ Costa Rica	12,530	3,819
Columbia, Mt., Canada (Δ Alberta)	12,294	3,747
Adams, Mt., Washington	12,276	3,742
Gunnbjørn Fjeld, Δ Greenland	12,139	3,700
South America		
Aconcagua, Cerro, Δ Argentina (Δ Andes; Δ South America)	22,831	6,959
Ojos del Salado, Nevado, Argentina-Δ Chile	22,615	6,893
Bonete, Cerro, Argentina	22,546	6,872
Huascarán, Nevado, Δ Peru	22,133	6,746
Llullaillaco, Volcán, Argentina-Chile	22,110	6,739
Yerupaja, Nevado, Peru	21,765	6,634
Tupungato, Cerro, Argentina-Chile	21,555	6,570
Sajama, Nevado, Bolivia	21,463	6,542
Illampu, Nevado, Bolivia	21,066	6,421
Illimani, Nevado, Bolivia	20,741	6,322
Chimborazo, Δ Ecuador	20,702	6,310
Antofalla, Volcán, Argentina	20,013	6,100
Cotopaxi, Ecuador	19,347	5,897
Misti, Volcán, Peru	19,101	5,822
Huila, Nevado de, Colombia (Δ Cordillera Central)	18,865	5,750
Bolívar, Pico, Δ Venezuela	16,427	5,007

Notable Volcanic Eruptions

Year	Volcano Name, Location	Comments
ca. 4895 B.C.	Crater Lake, Oregon, U.S.	Collapse forms caldera that now contains Crater Lake.
ca. 4350 B.C.	Kikai, Ryukyu Islands, Japan	Japan's largest known eruption.
ca. 1628 B.C.	Santorini (Thira), Greece	Eruption devastates late Minoan civilization.
79 A.D.	Vesuvius (Vesuvio), Italy	Roman towns of Pompeii and Herculaneum are buried.
ca. 180	Taupo, New Zealand	Area measuring 6,200 square miles (16,000 sq km) is devastated.
ca. 260	Ilopango, El Salvador	Thousands killed, with major impact on Mayan civilization.
915	Towada, Honshu, Japan	Japan's largest historic eruption.
ca. 1000	Baitoushan, China/Korea	Largest known eruption on Asian mainland.
1259	Unknown	Evidence from polar ice cores suggests that a huge eruption, possibly the largest of the millennium, occurred in this year.
1586	Kelut, Java	Explosions in crater lake; mudflows kill 10,000.
1631	Vesuvius (Vesuvio), Italy	Eruption kills 4,000.
ca. 1660	Long Island, Papua New Guinea	"The time of darkness" in tribal legends on Papua New Guinea.
1672	Merapi, Java	Pyroclastic flows and mudflows kill 3,000.
1711	Awu, Sangihe Islands, Indonesia	Pyroclastic flows kill 3,000.
1760	Makian, Halmahera, Indonesia	Eruption kills 2,000; island evacuated for seven years.
1772	Papandayan, Java	Debris avalanche causes 2,957 fatalities.
1783	Lakagigar, Iceland	Largest historic lava flows; 9,350 deaths.
1790	Kilauea, Hawaii	Hawaii's last large explosive eruption.
1792	Unzen, Kyushu, Japan	Tsunami and debris avalanche kill 14,500.
1815	Tambora, Indonesia	History's most explosive eruption; 92,000 deaths.
1822	Galunggung, Java	Pyroclastic flows and mudflows kill 4,011.
1856	Awu, Sangihe Islands, Indonesia	Pyroclastic flows kill 2,806.
1883	Krakatau, Indonesia	Caldera collapse; 36,417 people killed, most by tsunami.
1888	Ritter Island, Papua New Guinea	3,000 killed, most by tsunami created by debris avalanche.
1902	Mont Pelee, West Indies	Town of St. Pierre destroyed; 28,000 people killed.
1902	Santa Maria, Guatemala	5,000 killed as 10 villages are buried by volcanic debris.
1912	Novarupta (Katmai), Alaska	Largest 20th-century eruption.
1914	Lassen, California, U.S.	California's last historic eruption.
1919	Kelut, Java	Mudflows devastate 104 villages and kill 5,110 people.
1930	Merapi, Java	1,369 people are killed as 42 villages are totally or partially destroyed.
1943	Parícutin, Mexico	Fissure in cornfield erupts, building cinder cone 1,500 feet (460 m) high within two years. One of the few volcano births ever witnessed.
1951	Lamington, Papua New Guinea	Pyroclastic flows kill 2,942.
1963	Surtsey, Iceland	Submarine eruption builds new island.
1977	Nyiragongo, Zaire	One of the shortest major eruptions and fastest lava flows ever recorded.
1980	St. Helens, Washington, U.S.	Lateral blast; 230-square-mile (600 sq km) area devastated.
1982	El Chichón, Mexico	Pyroclastic surges kill 1,877.
1985	Ruiz, Colombia	Mudflows kill 23,080.
1991	Pinatubo, Luzon, Philippines	Major eruption in densely populated area prompts evacuation of 250,000 people; fatalities number fewer than 800. Enormous amount of gas released into stratosphere lowers global temperatures for more than a year.
1993	Juan de Fuca Ridge, off the coast of Oregon, U.S.	Deep submarine rift eruptions account for three-fourths of all lava produced; this is one of the very few such eruptions that have been well-documented.

Eruption of Mt. St. Helens in 1980

Sources: Smithsonian Institution Global Volcanism Program; Volcanoes of the World, Second Edition, by Tom Simkin and Lee Siebert, Geoscience Press and Smithsonian Institution, 1994.

Significant Earthquakes through History

Year	Estimated Magnitude	Number of Deaths	Place
365		50,000	Knossos, Crete
844		50,000	Damascus, Syria; Antioch, Turkey
856		150,000	Dāmghān, Kashan, Qumis, Iran
893		150,000	Caucasus region
894		180,000	western India
1042		50,000	Palmyra, Baalbek, Syria
1138		230,000	Aleppo, Gansana, Syria
1139	6.8	300,000	Gänca, Kiapas, Azerbaijan
1201		50,000	upper Egypt to Syria
1290	6.7	100,000	eastern China
1556		820,000	Shanxi Province, China
1662		300,000	China
1667	6.9	80,000	Caucasus region, northern Iran
1668		50,000	Shandong Province, China
1693		93,000	Sicily, Italy
1727		77,000	Tabrīz, Iran
1731		100,000	Beijing, China
1739		50,000	China
1755		62,000	Morocco, Portugal, Spain
1780	6.7	100,000	Tabrīz, Iran
1868	7.7	70,000	Ecuador, Colombia
1908	7.5	83,000	Calabria, Messina, Italy
1920	8.5	200,000	Gansu and Shanxi provinces, China
1923	8.2	142,807	Tokyo, Yokohama, Japan
1927	8.3	200,000	Gansu and Qinghai provinces, China
1932	7.6	70,000	Gansu Province, China
1970	7.8	66,794	northern Peru
1976	7.8	242,000	Tangshan, China
1990	7.7	50,000	northwestern Iran

Some Significant U.S. Earthquakes

Year	Estimated Magnitude	Number of Deaths	Place
1811–12	8.6, 8.4, 8.7	<10	New Madrid, Missouri (series)
1886	7.0	60	Charleston, South Carolina
1906	8.3	3,000	San Francisco, California
1933	6.3	115	Long Beach, California
1946	7.4	5 ‡	Alaska
1964	8.4	125	Anchorage, Alaska
1971	6.8	65	San Fernando, California
1989	7.1	62	San Francisco Bay Area, California
1994	6.8	58	Northridge, California

‡ A tsunami generated by this earthquake struck Hilo, Hawaii, killing 159 people.
Sources: Lowell S. Whiteside, National Geophysical Data Center; Catalog of Significant Earthquakes 2150 B.C.—1991 A.D. by Paula K. Dunbar, Patricia A. Lockridge, and Lowell S. Whiteside, National Geophysical Data Center, National Oceanic and Atmospheric Administration.

Oceans and Lakes

	Area		Volume of water		Mean depth		Greatest known depth		
	sq. miles	sq. km.	cubic miles	cubic km.	feet	meters	feet	meters	
Pacific Ocean	63,800,000	165,200,000	169,650,000	707,100,000	12,987	3,957	35,810	10,922	Mariana Trench
Atlantic Ocean	31,800,000	82,400,000	79,199,000	330,100,000	11,821	3,602	28,232	8,610	Puerto Rico Trench
Indian Ocean	28,900,000	74,900,000	68,282,000	284,600,000	12,261	3,736	23,812	7,258	Weber Basin
Arctic Ocean	5,400,000	14,000,000	4,007,000	16,700,000	3,712	1,131	17,897	5,453	Lat. 77° 45'N, long. 175°W
Coral Sea	1,850,000	4,791,000	2,752,000	11,470,000	7,857	2,394	30,079	9,165	
Arabian Sea	1,492,000	3,864,000	2,416,000	10,070,000	8,973	2,734	19,029	5,803	
South China Sea	1,331,000	3,447,000	943,000	3,929,000	3,741	1,140	18,241	5,563	
Caribbean Sea	1,063,000	2,753,000	1,646,000	6,860,000	8,175	2,491	25,197	7,685	Off Cayman Islands
Mediterranean Sea	967,000	2,505,000	901,000	3,754,000	4,916	1,498	16,470	5,023	Off Cape Matapan, Greece
Bering Sea	876,000	2,269,000	911,000	3,796,000	5,382	1,640	25,194	7,684	Off Buldir Island
Bengal, Bay of	839,000	2,173,000	1,357,000	5,616,000	8,484	2,585	17,251	5,261	
Okhotsk, Sea of	619,000	1,603,000	316,000	1,317,000	2,694	821	1,029	3,374	Lat. 146° 10'E, long. 46° 50'N
Norwegian Sea	597,000	1,546,000	578,000	2,408,000	5,717	1,742	13,189	4,022	
Mexico, Gulf of	596,000	1,544,000	560,000	2,332,000	8,205	2,500	14,370	4,382	Sigsbee Deep
Hudson Bay	475,000	1,230,000	22,000	92,000	328	100	850	259	Near entrance
Greenland Sea	465,000	1,204,000	417,000	1,740,000	4,739	1,444	15,899	4,849	
Japan, Sea of	413,000	1,070,000	391,000	1,630,000	5,037	1,535	12,041	3,669	
Arafura Sea	400,000	1,037,000	49,000	204,000	646	197	12,077	3,680	
East Siberian Sea	357,000	926,000	14,000	61,000	216	66	508	155	
Kara Sea	349,000	903,000	24,000	101,000	371	113	2,034	620	
East China Sea	290,000	752,000	63,000	263,000	1,145	349	7,778	2,370	
Banda Sea	268,000	695,000	511,000	2,129,000	10,056	3,064	24,418	7,440	
Baffin Bay	263,000	681,000	142,000	593,000	2,825	861	7,010	2,136	
Laptev Sea	262,000	678,000	87,000	363,000	1,772	540	9,780	2,980	
Timor Sea	237,000	615,000	60,000	250,000	1,332	406	10,863	3,310	
Andaman Sea	232,000	602,000	158,000	660,000	3,597	1,096	13,777	4,198	
Chukchi Sea	228,000	590,000	11,000	45,000	252	77	525	160	
North Sea	214,000	554,000	12,000	52,000	315	96	2,655	809	
Java Sea	185,000	480,000	5,000	22,000	147	45	292	89	
Beaufort Sea	184,000	476,000	115,000	478,000	3,295	1,004	12,245	3,731	
Red Sea	174,000	450,000	60,000	251,000	1,831	558	8,648	2,635	
Baltic Sea	173,000	448,000	5,000	20,000	157	48	1,506	459	
Celebes Sea	168,000	435,000	380,000	1,586,000	11,962	3,645	19,173	5,842	
Black Sea	166,000	431,000	133,000	555,000	3,839	1,170	7,256	2,211	
Yellow Sea	161,000	417,000	4,000	17,000	131	40	344	105	
Sulu Sea	134,000	348,000	133,000	553,000	5,221	1,591	18,300	5,576	
Molucca Sea	112,000	291,000	133,000	554,000	6,242	1,902	16,311	4,970	
Ceram Sea	72,000	187,000	54,000	227,000	3,968	1,209	17,456	5,319	
Flores Sea	47,000	121,000	53,000	222,000	6,003	1,829	16,813	5,123	
Bali Sea	46,000	119,000	12,000	49,000	1,349	411	4,253	1,296	
Savu Sea	41,000	105,000	43,000	178,000	5,582	1,701	11,060	3,370	
White Sea	35,000	91,000	1,000	4,400	161	49	1,083	330	
Azov, Sea of	15,000	40,000	100	400	29	9	46	14	
Marmara, Sea of	4,000	11,000	1,000	4,000	1,171	357	4,138	1,261	

Source: Atlas of World Water Balance, *USSR National Committee for the International Water Decade and UNESCO, 1977.*

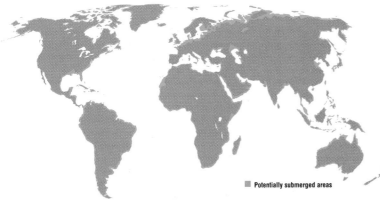

■ Potentially submerged areas

Fluctuating Sea Level

Changes in the Earth's climate have a dramatic effect on the sea level. Only 20,000 years ago, at the height of the most recent ice age, a vast amount of the Earth's water was locked up in ice sheets and glaciers, and the sea level was 330 feet (100 meters) lower than it is today. As the climate warmed slowly, the ice began to melt and the oceans began to rise.

Today there is still a tremendous amount of ice on the Earth. More than nine-tenths of it resides in the enormous ice cap which covers Antarctica. Measuring about 5.4 million square miles (14 million sq km) in surface area, the ice cap is on average one mile (1.6 km) thick but in some places is nearly three miles (4.8 km) thick. If it were to melt, the oceans would rise another 200 feet (60 m), and more than half of the world's population would have to relocate.

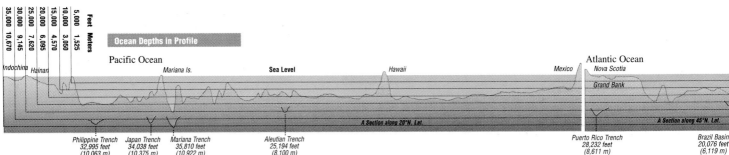

Ocean Depths in Profile

Pacific Ocean

Atlantic Ocean

Philippine Trench
32,995 feet
(10,063 m)

Japan Trench
34,038 feet
(10,375 m)

Mariana Trench
35,810 feet
(10,922 m)

Aleutian Trench
25,194 feet
(8,100 m)

Puerto Rico Trench
28,232 feet
(8,611 m)

Brazil Basin
20,076 feet
(6,119 m)

Deepest Lakes

	Lake	Greatest depth feet	meters
1	Baikal, Lake, Russia	5,315	1,621
2	Tanganyika, Lake, Africa	4,800	1,464
3	Caspian Sea, Asia-Europe	3,363	1,025
4	Nyasa, Lake (Lake Malawi), Malawi-Mozambique-Tanzania	2,317	706
5	Issyk-Kul', Lake, Kyrgyzstan	2,303	702
6	Great Slave Lake, NWT, Canada	2,015	614
7	Matana, Lake, Indonesia	1,936	590
8	Crater Lake, Oregon, U.S.	1,932	589
9	Toba, Lake (Danau Toba), Indonesia	1,736	529
10	Sarez, Lake, Tajikistan	1,657	505
11	Tahoe, Lake, California-Nevada, U.S.	1,645	502
12	Kivu, Lake, Rwanda-Zaire	1,628	496
13	Chelan, Lake, Washington, U.S.	1,605	489
14	Quesnel Lake, BC, Canada	1,560	476
15	Adams Lake, BC, Canada	1,500	457

Lakes with the Greatest Volume of Water

	Lake	Volume of water cubic mi	cubic km
1	Caspian Sea, Asia-Europe	18,900	78,200
2	Baikal, Lake, Russia	5,500	23,000
3	Tanganyika, Lake, Africa	4,500	18,900
4	Superior, Lake, Canada-U.S.	2,900	12,200
5	Nyasa, Lake (Lake Malawi), Malawi-Mozambique-Tanzania	1,900	7,725
6	Michigan, Lake, U.S.	1,200	4,910
7	Huron, Lake, Canada-U.S.	860	3,580
8	Victoria, Lake, Kenya-Tanzania-Uganda	650	2,700
9	Issyk-Kul', Lake, Kyrgyzstan	415	1,730
10	Ontario, Lake, Canada-U.S.	410	1,710
11	Great Slave Lake, Canada	260	1,070
12	Aral Sea, Kazakhstan-Uzbekistan	250	1,020
13	Great Bear Lake, Canada	240	1,010
14	Ladozhskoye, Ozero, Russia	220	908
15	Titicaca, Lago, Bolivia-Peru	170	710

Sources for volume and depth information: Atlas of World Water Balance, USSR National Committee for the International Water Decade and UNESCO, 1977; Principal Rivers and Lakes of the World, National Oceanic and Atmospheric Administration, 1982.

Principal Lakes

	Lake	Area sq mi	sq km
1	Caspian Sea, Asia-Europe	143,240	370,990
2	Superior, Lake, Canada-U.S.	31,700	82,100
3	Victoria, Lake, Kenya-Tanzania-Uganda	26,820	69,463
4	Aral Sea, Kazakhstan-Uzbekistan	24,700	64,100
5	Huron, Lake, Canada-U.S.	23,000	60,000
6	Michigan, Lake, U.S.	22,300	57,800
7	Tanganyika, Lake, Africa	12,350	31,986
8	Baikal, Lake, Russia	12,200	31,500
9	Great Bear Lake, Canada	12,095	31,326
10	Nyasa, Lake (Lake Malawi), Malawi-Mozambique-Tanzania	11,150	28,878
11	Great Slave Lake, Canada	11,030	28,568
12	Erie, Lake, Canada-U.S.	9,910	25,667
13	Winnipeg, Lake, Canada	9,416	24,387
14	Ontario, Lake, Canada-U.S.	7,540	19,529
15	Balqash koli (Lake Balkhash), Kazakhstan	7,100	18,300
16	Ladozhskoye, Ozero, Russia	6,833	17,700
17	Chad, Lake (Lac Tchad), Cameroon-Chad-Nigeria	6,300	16,300
18	Onezhskoye, Ozero, Russia	3,753	9,720
19	Eyre, Lake, Australia	3,700	9,500
20	Titicaca, Lago, Bolivia-Peru	3,200	8,300
21	Nicaragua, Lago de, Nicaragua	3,150	8,158
22	Mai-Ndombe, Lac, Zaire	3,100	8,000
23	Athabasca, Lake, Canada	3,064	7,935
24	Reindeer Lake, Canada	2,568	6,650
25	Tônlé Sap, Cambodia	2,500	6,500
26	Rudolf, Lake, Ethiopia-Kenya	2,473	6,405
27	Issyk-Kul', Ozero, Kyrgyzstan	2,425	6,280
28	Torrens, Lake, Australia	2,300	5,900
29	Albert, Lake, Uganda-Zaire	2,160	5,594
30	Vänern, Sweden	2,156	5,584
31	Nettilling Lake, Canada	2,140	5,542
32	Winnipegosis, Lake, Canada	2,075	5,374
33	Bangweulu, Lake, Zambia	1,930	4,999
34	Nipigon, Lake, Canada	1,872	4,848
35	Orumiyeh, Daryacheh-ye, Iran	1,815	4,701
36	Manitoba, Lake, Canada	1,785	4,624
37	Woods, Lake of the, Canada-U.S.	1,727	4,472
38	Kyoga, Lake, Uganda	1,710	4,429
39	Great Salt Lake, U.S.	1,680	4,351

Lake Baikal

Russia's Great Lake

On a map of the world, Lake Baikal is easy to overlook — a thin blue crescent adrift in the vastness of Siberia. But its inconspicuousness is deceptive, for Baikal is one of the greatest bodies of fresh water on Earth.

Although lakes generally have a life span of less than one million years, Baikal has existed for perhaps as long as 25 million years, which makes it the world's oldest body of fresh water. It formed in a rift that tectonic forces had begun to tear open in the Earth's crust. As the rift grew, so did Baikal. Today the lake is 395 miles (636 km) long and an average of 30 miles (48 km) wide. Only seven lakes in the world have a greater surface area.

Baikal is the world's deepest lake. Its maximum depth is 5,315 feet (1,621 m) — slightly over a mile, and roughly equal to the greatest depth of the Grand Canyon. The lake bottom lies 4,250 feet (1,295 m) below sea level and two-and-a-third miles (3.75 km) below the peaks of the surounding mountains. The crustal rift which Baikal occupies is the planet's deepest land depression, extending to a depth of more than five-and-a-half miles (9 km). The lake sits atop at least four miles (6.4 km) of sediment, the accumulation of 25 million years.

More than 300 rivers empty into Baikal, but only one, the Angara, flows out of it. Despite having only 38% of the surface area of North America's Lake Superior, Baikal contains more water than all five of the Great Lakes combined. Its volume of 5,500 cubic miles (23,000 cubic km) is greater than that of any other freshwater lake in the world and represents approximately one-fifth of all of the Earth's unfrozen fresh water.

Caspian Sea · · · · · · · · · · · · Lake Superior · · · · · · · · · · Lake Victoria · · · · · · · · Aral Sea

Lake Huron · · · · · · · · · · · · · Lake Michigan · · · · · · · · · · Lake Tanganyika

Lake Baikal · · · · · · · · · · · · · Great Bear Lake · · · · · · · · · · Lake Nyasa (Malawi)

Mediterranean Sea   Indian Ocean   Arctic Ocean   Pacific Ocean   South Pole

France   Gibraltar   Malta   Israel   Sea Level   Sumba   North Pole   65°N 65°S

A Section along 10°N. Lat.

Rivers

World's Longest Rivers

Rank	River	Length (Miles)	Length (Kilometers)	Rank	River	Length (Miles)	Length (Kilometers)
1	Nile, Africa	4,145	6,671	36	Murray, Australia	1,566	2,520
2	Amazon (Amazonas)-Ucayali, South America	4,000	6,400	37	Ganges, Asia	1,560	2,511
3	Yangtze (Chang), Asia	3,900	6,300	38	Pilcomayo, South America	1,550	2,494
4	Mississippi-Missouri, North America	3,740	6,019	39	Euphrates, Asia	1,510	2,430
5	Huang (Yellow), Asia	3,395	5,464	40	Ural, Asia	1,509	2,428
6	Ob'-Irtysh, Asia	3,362	5,410	41	Arkansas, North America	1,459	2,348
7	Río de la Plata-Paraná, South America	3,030	4,876	42	Colorado, North America (U.S.-Mexico)	1,450	2,334
8	Congo (Zaïre), Africa	2,900	4,700	43	Aldan, Asia	1,412	2,273
9	Paraná, South America	2,800	4,500	44	Syr Darya, Asia	1,370	2,205
10	Amur-Argun, Asia	2,761	4,444	45	Dnieper, Europe	1,350	2,200
11	Lena, Asia	2,700	4,400	46	Araguaia, South America	1,350	2,200
12	Mackenzie, North America	2,635	4,241	47	Cassai (Kasai), Africa	1,338	2,153
13	Mekong, Asia	2,600	4,200	48	Tarim, Asia	1,328	2,137
14	Niger, Africa	2,600	4,200	49	Kolyma, Asia	1,323	2,129
15	Yenisey, Asia	2,543	4,092	50	Orange, Africa	1,300	2,100
16	Missouri-Red Rock, North America	2,533	4,076	51	Negro, South America	1,300	2,100
17	Mississippi, North America	2,348	3,779	52	Ayeyarwady (Irrawaddy), Asia	1,300	2,100
18	Murray-Darling, Australia	2,330	3,750	53	Red, North America	1,270	2,044
19	Missouri, North America	2,315	3,726	54	Juruá, South America	1,250	2,012
20	Volga, Europe	2,194	3,531	55	Columbia, North America	1,240	2,000
21	Madeira, South America	2,013	3,240	56	Xingu, South America	1,230	1,979
22	São Francisco, South America	1,988	3,199	57	Ucayali, South America	1,220	1,963
23	Grande, Rio (Río Bravo), North America	1,885	3,034	58	Saskatchewan-Bow, North America	1,205	1,939
24	Purús, South America	1,860	2,993	59	Peace, North America	1,195	1,923
25	Indus, Asia	1,800	2,900	60	Tigris, Asia	1,180	1,899
26	Danube, Europe	1,776	2,858	61	Don, Europe	1,162	1,870
27	Brahmaputra, Asia	1,770	2,849	62	Songhua, Asia	1,140	1,835
28	Yukon, North America	1,770	2,849	63	Pechora, Europe	1,124	1,809
29	Salween (Nu), Asia	1,750	2,816	64	Kama, Europe	1,122	1,805
30	Zambezi, Africa	1,700	2,700	65	Limpopo, Africa	1,120	1,800
31	Vilyuy, Asia	1,647	2,650	66	Angara, Asia	1,105	1,779
32	Tocantins, South America	1,640	2,639	67	Snake, North America	1,038	1,670
33	Orinoco, South America	1,615	2,600	68	Uruguay, South America	1,025	1,650
34	Paraguay, South America	1,610	2,591	69	Churchill, North America	1,000	1,600
35	Amu Darya, Asia	1,578	2,540	70	Marañón, South America	995	1,592

The World's Greatest River

Although the Nile is slightly longer, the Amazon surpasses all other rivers in volume, size of drainage basin, and in nearly every other important category. If any river is to be called the greatest in the world, surely it is the Amazon.

It has been estimated that one-fifth of all of the flowing water on Earth is carried by the Amazon. From its 150-mile (240-km)-wide mouth, the river discharges 6,180,000 cubic feet (174,900 cubic m) of water per second — four-and-a-half times as much as the Congo, ten times as much as the Mississippi, and fifty-six times as much as the Nile. The Amazon's tremendous outflow turns the waters of the Atlantic from salty to brackish for more than 100 miles (160 km) offshore.

Covering more than one-third of the entire continent of South America, the Amazon's vast drainage basin measures 2,669,000 square miles (6,915,000 sq km) and is nearly twice as large as that of the second-ranked Congo. The Amazon begins its 4,000-mile (6,400-km) journey to the Atlantic from high up in the Andes, only 100 miles (160 km) from the Pacific. Along its course it receives the waters of more than 1,000 tributaries, which rise principally from the Andes, the Guiana Highlands, and the Brazilian Highlands. Seven of the tributaries are more than 1,000 miles (1,600 km) long, and one, the Madeira, is more than 2,000 miles (3,200 km) long.

The depth of the Amazon throughout most of its Brazilian segment exceeds 150 feet (45 m). Depths of more than 300 feet (90 m) have been recorded at points near the mouth. The largest ocean-going vessels can sail as far inland as Manaus, 1,000 miles (1,600 km) from the mouth. Freighters and small passenger vessels can navigate to Iquitos, 2,300 miles (3,700 km) from the mouth, even during times of low water.

Drainage basin of the Amazon River

Rivers with the Greatest Volume of Water

Rank	River Name	Flow of water per second at mouth		Rank	River Name	Flow of water per second at mouth	
		cubic feet	cubic meters			cubic feet	cubic meters
1	Amazon (Amazonas), South America	6,180,000	174,900	18	Para-Tocantins, South America (joins Amazon at mouth)	360,000	10,200
2	Congo, Africa	1,377,000	39,000	19	Salween, Asia	353,000	10,000
3	Negro, South America (tributary of Amazon)	1,236,000	35,000	20	Cassai (Kasai), Africa (trib. of Congo)	351,000	9,900
4	Orinoco, South America	890,000	25,200	21	Mackenzie, North America	343,000	9,700
5	Río de la Plata-Paraná, South America	809,000	22,900	22	Volga, Europe	271,000	7,700
6	Yangtze (Chang), Asia;	770,000	21,800	23	Ohio, North America (trib. of Mississippi)	257,000	7,300
	Madeira, South America (trib. of Amazon)	770,000	21,800	24	Yukon, North America	240,000	6,800
7	Missouri, North America (trib. of Mississippi)	763,000	21,600	25	Indus, Asia	235,000	6,600
8	Mississippi, North America*	640,300	18,100	26	Danube, Europe	227,000	6,400
9	Yenisey, Asia	636,000	18,000	27	Niger, Africa	215,000	6,100
10	Brahmaputra, Asia	575,000	16,300	28	Atchafalaya, North America	181,000	5,100
11	Lena, Asia	569,000	16,100	29	Paraguay, South America	155,000	4,400
12	Zambezi, Africa	565,000	16,000	30	Ob'-Katun, Asia	147,000	4,200
13	Mekong, Asia	500,000	14,100	31	São Francisco, South America	120,000	3,400
14	Saint Lawrence, North America	460,000	13,000	32	Tunguska, Asia	118,000	3,350
15	Ayeyarwady (Irrawaddy), Asia	447,000	12,600	33	Huang (Yellow), Asia	116,000	3,300
16	Ob'-Irtysh, Asia; Ganges, Asia	441,000	12,500	34	Nile, Africa	110,000	3,100
17	Amur, Asia	390,000	11,000				

*Approximately one-third of the Mississippi's water is diverted above Baton Rouge, Louisiana, and reaches the Gulf of Mexico via the Atchafalaya River.

Principal Rivers of the Continents

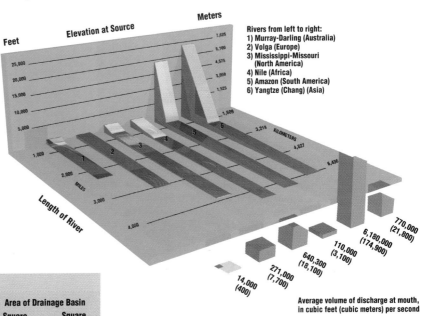

Rivers from left to right:
1) Murray-Darling (Australia)
2) Volga (Europe)
3) Mississippi-Missouri (North America)
4) Nile (Africa)
5) Amazon (South America)
6) Yangtze (Chang) (Asia)

Average volume of discharge at mouth, in cubic feet (cubic meters) per second

Rivers with the Largest Drainage Basins

Rank	River	Area of Drainage Basin	
		Square Miles	Square Kilometers
1	Amazon (Amazonas), South America	2,669,000	6,915,000
2	Congo (Zaire), Africa	1,474,500	3,820,000
3	Mississippi-Missouri, North America	1,243,000	3,220,000
4	Río de la Plata-Paraná, South America	1,197,000	3,100,000
5	Ob'-Irtysh, Asia	1,154,000	2,990,000
6	Nile, Africa	1,108,000	2,870,000
7	Yenisey-Angara, Asia	1,011,000	2,618,500
8	Lena, Asia	961,000	2,490,000
9	Niger, Africa	807,000	2,090,000
10	Amur-Argun, Asia	792,000	2,051,300
11	Yangtze (Chang), Asia	705,000	1,826,000
12	Volga, Europe	525,000	1,360,000
13	Zambezi, Africa	513,500	1,330,000
14	St. Lawrence, North America	503,000	1,302,800
15	Huang (Yellow), Asia	486,000	1,258,700

Sources for volume and drainage basin information: Atlas of World Water Balance, *USSR National Committee for the International Hydrological Decade and UNESCO, 1977;* Principal Rivers and Lakes of the World, *National Oceanic and Atmospheric Administration, 1982.*

Climate and Weather

Temperature Extremes by Continent

Africa
Highest recorded temperature
Al 'Azīzīyah, Libya, September 13, 1922:
136° F (58° C),
Lowest recorded temperature
Ifrane, Morocco, February 11, 1935:
-11° F (-24° C)

Antarctica
Highest recorded temperature
Vanda Station, January 5, 1974:
59° F (15° C)
Lowest recorded temperature
Vostok, July 21, 1983:
-129° F (-89° C)

Asia
Highest recorded temperature
Tirat Zevi, Israel, June 21, 1942:
129° F (54° C)
Lowest recorded temperature
Oymyakon and Verkhoyansk,
Russia, February 5 and 7, 1892,
and February 6, 1933: -90° F (-68° C)

Australia / Oceania
Highest recorded temperature
Cloncurry, Queensland, January 16, 1889:
128° F (53° C)
Lowest recorded temperature
Charlottes Pass, New South Wales,
June 14, 1945, and July 22, 1947: -8° F (-22° C)

Europe
Highest recorded temperature
Sevilla, Spain, August 4, 1881:
122° F (50° C)
Lowest recorded temperature
Ust' Ščugor, Russia, (date not known):
-67° F (-55° C)

North America
Highest recorded temperature
Death Valley, California, United States,
July 10, 1913: 134° F (57° C)
Lowest recorded temperature
Northice, Greenland, January 9, 1954:
-87° F (-66° C)

South America
Highest recorded temperature
Rivadavia, Argentina, December 11, 1905:
120° F (49° C)
Lowest recorded temperature
Sarmiento, Argentina, June 1, 1907:
-27° F (-33° C)

World
Highest recorded temperature
Al 'Azīzīyah, Libya, September 13, 1922:
136° F (58° C)
Lowest recorded temperature
Vostok, Antarctica, July 21, 1983:
-129° F (-89° C)

World Temperature Extremes

Highest mean annual temperature Dalol, Ethiopia, 94° F (34° C)
Lowest mean annual temperature Plateau Station, Antarctica: -70° F (-57° C)

Greatest difference between highest and lowest recorded temperatures
Verkhoyansk, Russia. The highest temperature ever recorded there is 93.5° F (34.2° C); the lowest is -89.7° F (-67.6° C)
— a difference of 183° F (102° C).

Highest temperature ever recorded at the South Pole 7.5° F (-14° C) on December 27, 1978

Most consecutive days with temperatures of 100° F (38° C) or above Marble Bar, Australia, 162 days: October 30, 1923 to April 7, 1924

Greatest rise in temperature within a 12-hour period
Granville, North Dakota, on February 21, 1918. The temperature rose 83° F (46° C), from -33° F (-36° C)
in early morning to +50° F (10° C) in late afternoon

Greatest drop in temperature within a 12-hour period
Fairfield, Montana, on December 24, 1924. The temperature dropped 84° F (46° C), from 63° F (17° C)
at noon to -21° F (-29° C) by midnight

Temperature Ranges for 14 Major Cities around the World

City	Mean Temperature		City	Mean Temperature	
	Coldest Winter Month	**Hottest Summer Month**		**Coldest Winter Month**	**Hottest Summer Month**
Bombay, India	Jan: 74.3° F (23.5° C)	May: 85.5° F (29.7° C)	Moscow, Russia	Feb: 14.5° F (-9.7° C)	Jul: 65.8° F (18.8° C)
Buenos Aires, Argentina	Aug: 51.3° F (10.7° C)	Jan: 75.0° F (23.9° C)	New York City, U.S.	Jan: 32.9° F (0.5° C)	Jul: 77.0° F (25.0° C)
Calcutta, India	Jan: 67.5° F (19.7° C)	May: 88.5° F (31.4° C)	Osaka, Japan	Jan: 40.6° F (4.8° C)	Aug: 82.2° F (27.9° C)
London, England	Feb: 39.4° F (4.1° C)	Jul: 63.9° F (17.7° C)	Rio de Janeiro, Brazil	Jul: 70.2° F (21.2° C)	Jan: 79.9° F (26.6° C)
Los Angeles, U.S.	Jan: 56.3° F (13.5° C)	Jul: 74.1° F (23.4° C)	São Paulo, Brazil	Jul: 58.8° F (14.9° C)	Jan: 71.1° F (21.7° C)
Manila, Philippines	Jan: 77.7° F (25.4° C)	May: 84.9° F (29.4° C)	Seoul, South Korea	Jan: 23.2° F (-4.9° C)	Aug: 77.7° F (25.4° C)
Mexico City, Mexico	Jan: 54.1° F (12.3° C)	May: 64.9° F (18.3° C)	Tokyo, Japan	Jan: 39.6° F (4.2° C)	Aug: 79.3° F (26.3° C)

Precipitation

Greatest local average annual rainfall
Mt. Waialeale, Kauai, Hawaii,
460 inches (1,168 cm)

Lowest local average annual rainfall
Arica, Chile, .03 inches (.08 cm)

Greatest rainfall in 12 months
Cherrapunji, India, August 1860 to August 1861:
1,042 inches (2,647 cm)

Greatest rainfall in one month
Cherrapunji, India, July 1861: 366 inches (930 cm)

Greatest rainfall in 24 hours
Cilaos, Reunion, March 15 and 16, 1952:
74 inches (188 cm)

Greatest rainfall in 12 hours
Belouve, Reunion, February 28 and 29, 1964:
53 inches (135 cm)

Most thunderstorms annually
Kampala, Uganda, averages 242 days per
year with thunderstorms

Between 1916 and 1920, Bogor, Indonesia,
averaged 322 days per year with thunderstorms

Longest dry period
Arica, Chile, October, 1903
to January, 1918 — over 14 years

Largest hailstone ever recorded
Coffeyville, Kansas, U.S., September 3, 1970:
circumference 17.5 inches (44.5 cm)
diameter 5.6 inches (14 cm),
weight 1.67 pounds (758 grams)

Heaviest hailstone ever recorded
Kazakhstan, 1959: 4.18 pounds (1.9 kilograms)

North America's greatest snowfall in one season
Rainier Paradise Ranger Station, Washington,
U.S., 1971–1972: 1,122 inches (2,850 cm)

North America's greatest snowfall in one storm
Mt. Shasta Ski Bowl, California, U.S.,
February 13 to 19, 1959: 189 inches (480 cm)

North America's greatest snowfall in 24 hours
Silver Lake, Colorado, U.S., April 14 and 15, 1921:
76 inches (1 92.5 cm)

N. America's greatest depth of snowfall on the ground
Tamarack, California, U.S., March 11, 1911:
451 inches (1,145.5 cm)

Foggiest place on the U.S. West Coast
Cape Disappointment, Washington,
averages 2,552 hours of fog per year

Foggiest place on the U.S. East Coast
Mistake Island, Maine, averages
1,580 hours of fog per year

Wind

Highest 24-hour mean surface wind speed
Mt. Washington, New Hampshire, U.S.,
April 11 and 12, 1934: 128 mph (206 kph)

Highest 5-minute mean surface wind speed
Mt. Washington, New Hampshire, U.S.,
April 12, 1934: 188 mph (303 kph)

Highest surface wind peak gust:
Mt. Washington, New Hampshire, U.S.,
April 12, 1934: 231 mph (372 kph)

Windiest U.S. Cities

Chicago is sometimes called "The Windy City."
It earned this nickname because of long-winded politicians,
not because it has the strongest gales.

The windiest cities in the U.S. are as follows:

Cities	Average wind speed	
	mph	kph
Great Falls, Montana	13.1	21.0
Oklahoma City, Oklahoma	13.0	20.9
Boston, Massachusetts	12.9	20.7
Cheyenne, Wyoming	12.8	20.6
Wichita, Kansas	12.7	20.4

Chicago ranks 16th, with a 10.4 mph (16.7 kph) average.

Deadliest Hurricanes in the U.S. since 1900

Rank	Place	Year	Number of Deaths
1	Texas (Galveston)	1900	>6,000
2	Louisiana	1893	2,000
3	Florida (Lake Okeechobee)	1928	1,836
4	South Carolina, Georgia	1893	>1,000
5	Florida (Keys)	1919	>600
6	New England	1938	600
7	Florida (Keys)	1935	408
8	Southwest Louisiana, north Texas— "Hurricane Audrey"	1957	390
	Northeast U.S.	1944	390
9	Louisiana (Grand Isle)	1909	350
10	Louisana (New Orleans)	1915	275

Tornadoes in the U.S., 1950—1993

Rank	State	Total Number of Tornadoes	Yearly Average	Total Number of Deaths
1	Texas	5,303	120	471
2	Oklahoma	2,259	51	217
3	Kansas	2,068	47	199
4	Florida	1,932	44	81
5	Nebraska	1,618	37	51
	U.S. Total	33,120	753	4,045

Deadliest Floods in the U.S. since 1900

Rank	Place	Year	Number of Deaths
1	Ohio River and tributaries	1913	467
2	Mississippi Valley	1927	313
3	Black Hills, South Dakota	1972	237
4	Texas rivers	1921	215
5	Northeastern U.S., following Hurricane Dianne	1955	187
6	Texas rivers	1913	177
7	James River basin, Virginia	1969	153
8	Big Thompson Canyon, Colorado	1976	139
9	Ohio and Lower Mississippi river basins	1937	137
10	Buffalo Creek, West Virginia	1972	125

Population

During the first two million years of our species' existence, human population grew at a very slow rate, and probably never exceeded 10 million. With the development of agriculture circa 8000 B.C., the growth rate began to rise sharply: by the year A.D. 1, the world population stood at approximately 250 million.

By 1650 the population had doubled to 550 million, and within only 200 years it doubled again, reaching almost 1.2 billion by 1850. Each subsequent doubling has taken only about half as long as the previous one: 100 years to reach 2.5 billion, and 40 years to reach 5.2 billion.

Experts have estimated that today's world population of 5.6 billion represents 5.5% of all of the people who have ever lived on Earth.*

* Population Today, *Population Reference Bureau, February 1995*

World Population

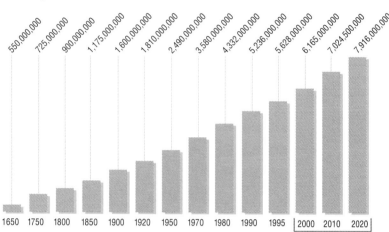

550,000,000	1650	
725,000,000	1750	
900,000,000	1800	
1,175,000,000	1850	
1,600,000,000	1900	
1,810,000,000	1920	
2,490,000,000	1950	
3,580,000,000	1970	
4,332,000,000	1980	
5,236,000,000	1990	
5,628,000,000	1995	
6,165,000,000	2000	
7,024,500,000	2010	
7,916,000,000	2020	

Projected Population

The World's Estimated Population (as of January 1, 1995): 5,628,000,000
Population Density: 97 people per square mile (37 people per square kilometer)

Historical Populations of the Continents and the World

Year	Africa	Asia	Australia	Europe	North America	Oceania, incl. Australia	South America	World
1650	*100,000,000*	335,000,000	*<1,000,000*	*100,000,000*	*5,000,000*	*2,000,000*	*8,000,000*	*550,000,000*
1750	*95,000,000*	476,000,000	*<1,000,000*	*140,000,000*	*5,000,000*	*2,000,000*	*7,000,000*	*725,000,000*
1800	*90,000,000*	593,000,000	*<1,000,000*	*190,000,000*	*13,000,000*	*2,000,000*	*12,000,000*	*900,000,000*
1850	*95,000,000*	754,000,000	*<1,000,000*	*265,000,000*	*39,000,000*	*2,000,000*	*20,000,000*	*1,175,000,000*
1900	*118,000,000*	932,000,000	4,000,000	400,000,000	106,000,000	6,000,000	38,000,000	*1,600,000,000*
1920	*140,000,000*	1,000,000,000	6,000,000	453,000,000	147,000,000	9,000,000	61,000,000	*1,810,000,000*
1950	199,000,000	1,418,000,000	8,000,000	530,000,000	219,000,000	13,000,000	111,000,000	*2,490,000,000*
1970	346,900,000	2,086,200,000	12,460,000	623,700,000	316,600,000	19,200,000	187,400,000	3,580,000,000
1980	463,800,000	2,581,000,000	14,510,000	660,000,000	365,000,000	22,700,000	239,000,000	4,332,000,000
1990	648,300,000	3,156,100,000	16,950,000	688,000,000	423,600,000	26,300,000	293,700,000	5,236,000,000

Figures for years prior to 1970 are rounded to the nearest million. Figures in italics represent rough estimates.

The 50 Most Populous Countries

Rank	Country	Population	Rank	Country	Population	Rank	Country	Population
1	China	1,196,980,000	18	United Kingdom	58,430,000	35	Algeria	27,965,000
2	India	909,150,000	19	Egypt	58,100,000	36	Morocco	26,890,000
3	United States	262,530,000	20	France	58,010,000	37	Sudan	25,840,000
4	Indonesia	193,680,000	21	Italy	57,330,000	38	Korea, North	23,265,000
5	Brazil	159,690,000	22	Ethiopia	55,070,000	39	Peru	23,095,000
6	Russia	150,500,000	23	Ukraine	52,140,000	40	Uzbekistan	22,860,000
7	Pakistan	129,630,000	24	Myanmar	44,675,000	41	Romania	22,745,000
8	Japan	125,360,000	25	Korea, South	44,655,000	42	Venezuela	21,395,000
9	Bangladesh	119,370,000	26	South Africa	44,500,000	43	Nepal	21,295,000
10	Nigeria	97,300,000	27	Zaire	43,365,000	44	Taiwan	21,150,000
11	Mexico	93,860,000	28	Spain	39,260,000	45	Iraq	20,250,000
12	Germany	81,710,000	29	Poland	38,730,000	46	Afghanistan	19,715,000
13	Vietnam	73,760,000	30	Colombia	34,870,000	47	Malaysia	19,505,000
14	Philippines	67,910,000	31	Argentina	34,083,000	48	Uganda	18,270,000
15	Iran	63,810,000	32	Kenya	28,380,000	49	Sri Lanka	18,240,000
16	Turkey	62,030,000	33	Tanzania	28,350,000	50	Australia	18,205,000
17	Thailand	59,870,000	34	Canada	28,285,000			

Most Densely Populated Countries

Rank	Country (Population)	Population per Square Mile	Population per Square Kilometer
1	Monaco (31,000)	44,286	16,316
2	Singapore (2,921,000)	11,874	4,593
3	Vatican City (1,000)	5,000	2,500
4	Malta (368,000)	3,016	1,165
5	Maldives (251,000)	2,183	842
6	Bangladesh (119,370,000)	2,147	829
7	Guernsey (64,000)	2,133	821
8	Bahrain (563,000)	2,109	815
9	Jersey (86,000)	1,911	741
10	Barbados (261,000)	1,572	607
11	Taiwan (21,150,000)	1,522	587
12	Mauritius (1,121,000)	1,423	550
13	Nauru (10,000)	1,235	476
14	Korea, South (44,655,000)	1,168	451
15	Puerto Rico (3,625,000)	1,031	398

Least Densely Populated Countries

Rank	Country (Population)	Population per Square Mile	Population per Square Kilometer
1	Greenland (57,000)	0.07	0.03
2	Mongolia (2,462,000)	4.1	1.6
3	Namibia (1,623,000)	5.1	2.0
4	Mauritania (2,228,000)	5.6	2.2
5	Australia (18,205,000)	6.1	2.4
6	Botswana (1,438,000)	6.4	2.5
7	Iceland (265,000), Suriname (426,000)	6.7	2.6
8	Canada (28,285,000)	7.3	2.8
9	Libya (5,148,000)	7.6	2.9
10	Guyana (726,000)	8.7	3.4
11	Gabon (1,035,000)	10.1	3.9
12	Chad (6,396,000)	12.9	5.0
13	Central African Republic (3,177,000)	13.0	5.1
14	Bolivia (6,790,000)	16.0	6.2
15	Kazakhstan (17,025,000)	16.3	6.3

Most Highly Urbanized Countries

Country	Urban pop. as a % of total pop.
Vatican City	100%
Singapore	100%
Monaco	100%
Belgium	96%
Kuwait	96%
San Marino	92%
Israel (excl. Occupied Areas)	92%
Venezuela	91%
Iceland	91%
Qatar	90%
Uruguay	89%
Netherlands	89%
United Kingdom	89%
Malta	87%
Argentina	86%

Least Urbanized Countries

Country	Urban pop. as a % of total pop.
Bhutan	5%
Burundi	5%
Rwanda	6%
Nepal	11%
Oman	11%
Uganda	11%
Ethiopia	12%
Cambodia (Kampuchea)	12%
Malawi	12%
Burkina Faso	15%
Eritrea	15%
Grenada	15%
Solomon Islands	15%
Bangladesh	16%
Northern Mariana Islands	16%

World's Largest Metropolitan Areas

Rank	Name	Population
1	Tokyo-Yokohama, Japan	30,300,000
2	New York City, U.S.	18,087,000
3	São Paulo, Brazil	16,925,000
4	Osaka-Kobe-Kyoto, Japan	16,900,000
5	Seoul, South Korea	15,850,000
6	Los Angeles, U.S.	14,531,000
7	Mexico City, Mexico	14,100,000
8	Moscow, Russia	13,150,000
9	Bombay, India	12,596,000
10	London, England	11,100,000
11	Rio de Janeiro, Brazil	11,050,000
12	Calcutta, India	11,022,000
13	Buenos Aires, Argentina	11,000,000
14	Paris, France	10,275,000
15	Jakarta, Indonesia	10,200,000

Fastest-Growing and Slowest-Growing Countries

A country's rate of natural increase is determined by subtracting the number of deaths from the number of births for a given period. Immigration and emigration are not included in this formulation.

The highest rate of natural increase among major countries today is Syria's 3.74%. At this rate, Syria's 1995 population of 14,100,000 will double in 19 years and triple in 30 years.

In Hungary and Ukraine deaths currently outnumber births, and the two countries share the same negative rate of natural increase, -0.026%, the lowest in the world.

When all of the countries of the world are compared, pronounced regional patterns become apparent. Of the 35 fastest-growing countries, 30 are found in either Africa or the Middle East. Of the 45 slowest-growing countries, 42 are found in Europe.

The World's Most Populous Cities

The following table lists the most populous cities of the world by continent and in descending order of population. It includes all cities with central city populations of 500,000 or greater. Cities with populations of less than 500,000 but with metropolitan area populations of 1,000,000 or greater have also been included in the table.

The city populations listed are the latest available census figures or official estimates. For a few cities, only unofficial estimates are available. The year in which the census was taken or to which the estimate refers is provided in parentheses preceding the city population. When comparing populations it is important to keep in mind that some figures are more current than others.

Figures in parentheses represent metropolitan area populations — the combined populations of the cities and their suburbs.

The sequence of information in each listing is as follows: city name, country name (metropolitan area population) (date of census or estimate) city population.

The Most Populous City in the World, through History

With more than 30 million people, Japan's Tokyo-Yokohama agglomeration ranks as the most populous metropolitan area in the world today. New York City held this title from the mid-1920's through the mid-1960's. But what city was the most populous in the world five hundred years ago? Five *thousand* years ago?

The following time line represents one expert's attempt to name the cities that have reigned as the most populous in the world since 3200 B.C. The time line begins with Memphis, the capital of ancient Egypt, which was possibly the first city in the world to attain a population of 20,000.

Listed after each city name is the name of the political entity to which the city belonged during the time that it was the most populous city in the world. The name of the modern political entity in which the city, its ruins, or its site is located, where this entity differs from the historic political entity, is listed in parentheses.

For the purpose of this time line, the word "city" is used in the general sense to denote a city, metropolitan area, or urban agglomeration.

It is important to note that reliable census figures are not available for most of the 5,200 years covered by this time line. Therefore the time line is somewhat subjective and conjectural.

Africa

Cairo (Al Qāhirah),
Egypt (9,300,000) ('86) 6,068,695
Kinshasa, Zaire ('86) 3,000,000
Alexandria (Al Iskandarīyah),
Egypt (3,350,000) ('86) 2,926,859
Casablanca (Dar-el-Beida),
Morocco (2,475,000) ('82) 2,139,204
Abidjan, Cote d'Ivoire ('88) 1,929,079
Addis Ababa, Ethiopia (1,990,000) ('90). . 1,912,500
Giza (Al Jīzah), Egypt ('86) 1,883,189
Algiers (El Djazaïr),
Algeria (2,547,983)('87) 1,507,241
Nairobi, Kenya ('90) 1,505,000
Dakar, Senegal ('88) 1,490,450
Luanda, Angola ('89) 1,459,900
Antananarivo, Madagascar ('88) 1,250,000
Lagos, Nigeria (3,800,000) ('87) 1,213,000
Ibadan, Nigeria ('87) 1,144,000
Dar es Salaam, Tanzania ('85) 1,096,000
Maputo, Mozambique ('89) 1,069,727
Lusaka, Zambia ('90) 982,362
Accra, Ghana (1,390,000) ('87) 949,113
Cape Town,
South Africa (1,900,000) ('91) 854,616
Conakry, Guinea ('86) 800,000
Kampala, Uganda ('91) 773,463
Durban, South Africa (1,740,000) ('91) . . . 715,669
Shubrā al Khaymah, Egypt ('86) 714,594
Johannesburg,
South Africa (4,000,000) ('91) 712,507
Douala, Cameroon ('87) 712,251
Brazzaville, Congo ('89) 693,712
Harare, Zimbabwe (955,000) ('83) 681,000
Bamako, Mali ('87) 658,275
Oran, Algeria ('87) 628,558
Mogadishu (Muqdisho), Somalia ('84) . . . 600,000
Bangui, Central African Republic ('89) . . . 596,800
Tunis, Tunisia (1,225,000) ('84) 596,654
Soweto, South Africa ('91) 596,632
Tripoli (Ṭarābulus),
Libya (960,000) ('88) 591,062
Ogbomosho, Nigeria ('87) 582,900
Lubumbashi, Zaire ('84) 564,830
Yaoundé, Cameroon ('87) 560,785
Kano, Nigeria ('87) 538,300
Mombasa, Kenya ('90) 537,000
Cotonou, Benin ('92) 533,212
Omdurman (Umm Durmān),
Sudan ('83) 526,192
Pretoria, South Africa (1,100,000) ('91) . . . 525,583
Rabat, Morocco (980,000) ('82) 518,616
Lomé, Togo ('87) 500,000
N'Djamena, Chad ('88) 500,000
Khartoum (Al Kharṭūm),
Sudan (1,450,000) ('83) 473,597

Asia

Seoul (Sŏul),
South Korea (15,850,000) ('90) 10,627,790
Bombay, India (12,596,243) ('91) 9,925,891
Jakarta, Indonesia (10,200,000) ('90) . . . 8,227,746
Tōkyō, Japan (30,300,000) ('90) 8,163,573
Shanghai, China (9,300,000) ('88) 7,220,000
Delhi, India (8,419,084) ('91) 7,206,704
Beijing (Peking),
China (7,320,000) ('88) 6,710,000
İstanbul, Turkey (7,550,000) ('90) 6,620,241
Tehrān, Iran (7,550,000) ('86) 6,042,584

Bangkok (Krung Thep),
Thailand (7,060,000) ('91) 5,620,591
Tianjin (Tientsin), China ('88) 4,950,000
Karāchi, Pakistan (5,300,000) ('81) 4,901,627
Calcutta, India (11,021,918) ('91) 4,399,819
Shenyang (Mukden), China ('88) 3,910,000
Madras, India (5,421,985) ('91) 3,841,396
Baghdād, Iraq ('87) 3,841,268
Pusan, South Korea (3,800,000) ('90) . . . 3,797,566
Dhaka (Dacca),
Bangladesh (6,537,308) ('91) 3,637,892
Wuhan, China ('88) 3,570,000
Yokohama, Japan ('90) 3,220,331
Guangzhou (Canton), China ('88) 3,100,000
Hyderābād, India (4,344,437) ('91) 3,043,896
Ahmadābād, India (3,312,216) ('91) 2,876,710
Ho Chi Minh City (Saigon),
Vietnam (3,300,000) ('89) 2,796,229
Harbin, China ('88) 2,710,000
Lahore, Pakistan (3,025,000) ('81) 2,707,215
T'aipei, Taiwan (6,130,000) ('92) 2,706,453
Singapore, Singapore (3,025,000) ('90) . . 2,690,100
Bangalore, India (4,130,288) ('91) 2,660,088
Ōsaka, Japan (16,900,000) ('90) 2,623,801
Ankara, Turkey (2,650,000) ('90) 2,559,471
Rangoon (Yangon),
Myanmar (2,650,000) ('83) 2,513,023
Chongqing (Chungking), China ('88) 2,502,000
Surabaya, Indonesia ('90) 2,473,272
Nanjing (Nanking), China ('88) 2,390,000
P'yŏngyang, North Korea ('81) 2,355,000
Dalian (Dairen), China ('88) 2,280,000
Taegu, South Korea ('90) 2,228,834
Xi'an (Sian), China ('88) 2,210,000
Nagoya, Japan (4,800,000) ('90) 2,154,793
Tashkent,
Uzbekistan (2,325,000) ('91) 2,113,300
Bandung, Indonesia (2,220,000) ('90) . . . 2,058,122
Chengdu (Chengtu), China ('88) 1,884,000
Kānpur, India (2,029,889) ('91) 1,874,409
Changchun, China ('88) 1,822,000
Inch'ŏn, South Korea ('90) 1,818,293
İzmir, Turkey (1,900,000) ('90) 1,757,414
Medan, Indonesia ('90) 1,730,052
Taiyuan, China ('88) 1,700,000
Sapporo, Japan (1,900,000) ('90) 1,671,742
Quezon City, Philippines ('90) 1,666,766
Nāgpur, India (1,664,006) ('91) 1,624,752
Lucknow, India (1,669,204) ('91) 1,619,115
Manila, Philippines (9,650,000) ('90) 1,598,918
Aleppo, Syria (1,640,000) ('94) 1,591,400
Pune, India (2,493,987) ('91) 1,566,651
Chittagong, Bangladesh (2,342,662) ('91) 1,566,070
Damascus (Dimashq),
Syria (2,230,000) ('94) 1,549,932
Jinan (Tsinan), China ('88) 1,546,000
New Kowloon (Xinjiulong),
Hong Kong ('86) 1,526,910
Sūrat, India (1,518,950) ('91) 1,498,817
Kōbe, Japan ('90) 1,477,410
Mashhad, Iran ('86) 1,463,508
Kyōto, Japan ('90) 1,461,103
Jaipur, India (1,518,235) ('91) 1,458,483
Novosibirsk, Russia (1,600,000) ('91) . . . 1,446,300
Kābul, Afghanistan ('88) 1,424,400
Kaohsiung, Taiwan (1,845,000) ('92) . . . 1,401,239
Anshan, China ('88) 1,330,000
Kunming, China ('88) 1,310,000
Jiddah, Saudi Arabia ('80) 1,300,000
Qingdao (Tsingtao), China ('88) 1,300,000
Lanzhou (Lanchow), China ('88) 1,297,000
Hangzhou (Hangchow), China ('88) 1,290,000

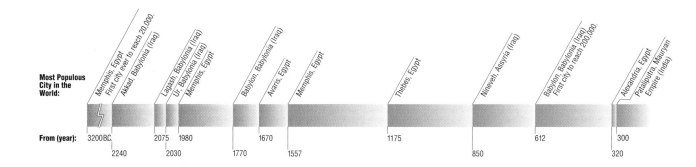

Most Populous City in the World:	Memphis, Egypt. First city ever to reach 20,000.	Akkad, Babylonia (Iraq)	Lagash, Babylonia (Iraq)	Ur, Babylonia (Iraq) Memphis, Egypt	Babylon, Babylonia (Iraq)	Avaris, Egypt	Memphis, Egypt	Thebes, Egypt	Nineveh, Assyria (Iraq)	Babylon, Babylonia (Iraq). First city to reach 200,000.	Alexandria, Egypt Pataliputra, Mauryan Empire (India)
From (year):	3200BC	2075	1980		1670	1557		1175	850	612	300
	2240		2030	1770							320

Fushun (Funan), China ('88) 1,290,000
Tbilisi, Georgia (1,460,000) ('91) 1,279,000
Victoria, Hong Kong (4,770,000) ('91) . . 1,250,993
Riyadh (Ar-Riyāḍ), Saudi Arabia ('80) . . . 1,250,000
Semarang, Indonesia ('90) 1,249,230
Fukuoka, Japan (1,750,000) ('90) 1,237,062
Changsha, China ('88) 1,230,000
Shijiazhuang, China ('88) 1,220,000
Jilin (Kirin), China ('88) 1,200,000
Yerevan, Armenia (1,315,000) ('89) 1,199,000
Qiqihar (Tsitsihar), China ('88) 1,180,000
Kawasaki, Japan ('90) 1,173,603
Omsk, Russia (1,190,000) ('91) 1,166,800
Alma-Ata (Almaty),
   Kazakhstan (1,190,000) ('91) 1,156,200
Zhengzhou (Chengchow), China ('88) . . 1,150,000
Chelyabinsk, Russia (1,325,000) ('91) . . 1,148,300
Kwangju, South Korea ('90) 1,144,695
Palembang, Indonesia ('90) 1,144,047
Baotou (Paotow), China ('88) 1,130,000
Faisalabad (Lyallpur), Pakistan ('81) . . . 1,104,209
Indore, India (1,109,056) ('91) 1,091,674
Nanchang, China ('88) 1,090,000
Hiroshima, Japan (1,575,000) ('90) 1,085,705
Baku (Bakı),
   Azerbaijan (2,020,000) ('91) 1,080,500
Tangshan, China ('88) 1,080,000
Bhopāl, India ('91) 1,062,771
Taejŏn, South Korea ('90) 1,062,084
Ürümqi, China ('88) 1,060,000
Ludhiāna, India ('91) 1,042,740
Vadodara, India (1,126,824) ('91) 1,031,346
Guiyang (Kweiyang), China ('88) 1,030,000
Kitakyūshū, Japan (1,525,000) ('90) . . . 1,026,455
Kalyān, India ('91) 1,014,557
Eṣfahān, Iran (1,175,000) ('86) 986,753
Tabrīz, Iran ('86) 971,482
Hāora, India ('91) 950,435
Ujungpandang (Makasar), Indonesia ('90) . 944,372
Madurai, India (1,085,914) ('91) 940,989

'Ammān, Jordan (1,625,000) ('89) 936,300
Vārānasi (Benares), India (1,030,863) ('91) 929,270
Krasnoyarsk, Russia ('91) 924,400
Kuala Lumpur, Malaysia (1,475,000) ('80) . 919,610
Sendai, Japan (1,175,000) ('90) 918,398
Patna, India (1,099,647) ('91) 917,243
Adana, Turkey ('90) 916,150
Fuzhou, China ('88) 910,000
Hanoi, Vietnam (1,275,000) ('89) 905,939
Āgra, India (948,063) ('91) 891,790
Wuxi (Wuhsi), China ('88) 880,000
Handan, China ('88) 870,000
Xuzhou (Süchow), China ('88) 860,000
Benxi (Penhsi), China ('88) 860,000
Shīrāz, Iran ('86) 848,289
Zibo (Zhangdian), China ('88) 840,000
Yichun, China ('88) 840,000
Bursa, Turkey ('90) 834,576

Chiba, Japan ('90) 829,455
Coimbatore, India (1,100,746) ('91) 816,321
Datong, China ('88) 810,000
Sakai, Japan ('90) 807,765
Thāna, India ('91) 803,369
Allahābād, India (844,546) ('91) 792,858
T'aichung, Taiwan ('92) 785,182
Kowloon (Jiulong), Hong Kong ('86) 774,781
Caloocan, Philippines ('90) 761,011
Luoyang (Loyang), China ('88) 760,000
Meerut, India (849,799) ('91) 753,778
Vishākhapatnam, India (1,057,118) ('91) . . 752,037
Jabalpur, India (888,916) ('91) 741,927
Suzhou (Soochow), China ('88) 740,000
Hefei, China ('88) 740,000
Nanning, China ('88) 720,000
Jinzhou (Chinchou), China ('88) 710,000
Amritsar, India ('91) 708,835
Hyderābād, Pakistan (800,000) ('81) 702,539
Vijayawāda, India (845,756) ('91) 701,827
Fuxin, China ('88) 700,000
Jixi, China ('88) 700,000
Huainan, China ('88) 700,000
Multān, Pakistan (732,070) ('81) 696,316
Malang, Indonesia ('90) 695,089
T'ainan, Taiwan ('92) 692,116
Gwalior, India (717,780) ('91) 690,765
Ulsan, South Korea ('90) 682,978
Liuzhou, China ('88) 680,000
Hohhot, China ('88) 670,000
Bucheon, South Korea ('90) 667,777
Jodhpur, India ('91) 666,279
Nāshik, India (725,341) ('91) 656,925
Mudanjiang, China ('88) 650,000
Hubli-Dhārwār, India ('91) 648,298
Vladivostok, Russia ('91) 648,000
Suwŏn, South Korea ('90) 644,968
Himṣ, Syria ('94) 644,204
Irkutsk, Russia ('91) 640,500
Daqing, China ('88) 640,000
Bishkek, Kyrgyzstan ('91) 631,300
Phnum Pénh, Cambodia ('90) 620,000
Xining (Sining), China ('88) 620,000
Farīdābad, India ('91) 617,717
Al Basrah, Iraq ('85) 616,700
Khabarovsk, Russia ('91) 613,300
Colombo, Sri Lanka (2,050,000) ('89) 612,000
Cebu, Philippines (825,000) ('90) 610,417
Qaraghandy, Kazakhstan ('91) 608,600
Barnaul, Russia (673,000) ('91) 606,800
Solāpur, India (620,846) ('91) 604,215
Gaziantep, Turkey ('90) 603,434
Novokuznetsk, Russia ('91) 601,900
Khulna, Bangladesh (966,096) ('91) 601,051
Gujrānwāla, Pakistan (658,753) ('81) 600,993
Rānchi, India (614,795) ('91) 599,306
Srīnagar, India (606,002) ('81) 594,775
Okayama, Japan ('90) 593,730
Hegang, China ('86) 588,300
Bareilly, India (617,350) ('91) 587,211
Guwāhāti, India ('91) 584,342
Dushanbe, Tajikistan ('91) 582,400
Ahvāz, Iran ('86) 579,826
Dandong, China ('86) 579,800
Kumamoto, Japan ('90) 579,306
Ulan Bator, Mongolia ('91) 575,000
Aurangābād, India (592,709) ('91) 573,272
Al-Mawṣil, Iraq ('85) 570,926
Ningbo, China ('88) 570,000
Cochin, India (1,140,605) ('91) 564,589
Bākhtarān (Kermānshāh), Iran ('86) 560,514
Shantou (Swatow), China ('88) 560,000
Rājkot, India (654,490) ('91) 559,407

Mecca (Makkah), Saudi Arabia ('80) 550,000
Qom, Iran ('86) 543,139
Sŏngnam, South Korea ('90) 540,764
T'aipeihsien, Taiwan ('91) 538,954
Kota, India ('91) 537,371
Kagoshima, Japan ('90) 536,752
Hamamatsu, Japan ('90) 534,620
Funabashi, Japan ('90) 533,270
Mandalay, Myanmar ('83) 532,949
Sagamihara, Japan ('90) 531,542
Jerusalem (Yerushalayim) (Al-Quds),
   Israel (560,000) ('91) 524,500
Trivandrum, India (826,225) ('91) 524,006
Changzhou (Changchow), China ('86) . . . 522,700
Davao, Philippines ('90) 521,525
Kemerovo, Russia ('91) 520,700
Higashiōsaka, Japan ('90) 518,319

Chŏnju, South Korea ('90) 517,104
Pimpri-Chinchwad, India ('91) 517,083
Tsuen Wan (Quanwan), Hong Kong ('86) . . 514,241
Konya, Turkey ('90) 513,346
Jalandhar, India ('91) 509,510
Beirut (Bayrūt), Lebanon (1,675,000) ('82) . 509,000
Peshāwar, Pakistan (566,248) ('81) 506,896
Tomsk, Russia ('91) 505,600
Gorakhpur, India ('91) 505,566
Chandīgarh, India (575,829) ('91) 504,094
Surakarta, Indonesia (590,000) ('90) 503,827
Zhangjiakou (Kalgan), China ('88) 500,000
Rāwalpindi, Pakistan (1,040,000) ('81) . . . 457,091
Tel Aviv-Yafo, Israel (1,735,000) ('91) . . . 339,400
Kuwait (Al-Kuwayt),
   Kuwait (1,375,000) ('85) 44,335

Australia and Oceania

Brisbane, Australia (1,334,017) ('91) 751,115
Perth, Australia (1,143,249) ('91) 80,517
Melbourne, Australia (3,022,439) ('91) 60,476
Adelaide, Australia (1,023,597) ('91) 14,843
Sydney, Australia (3,538,749) ('91) 13,501

Europe

Moscow (Moskva),
   Russia (13,150,000) ('91) 8,801,500
London, England, U.K. (11,100,000) ('81) 6,574,009
Saint Petersburg (Leningrad),
   Russia (5,525,000) ('91) 4,466,800
Berlin, Germany (4,150,000) ('91) 3,433,695
Madrid, Spain (4,650,000) ('88) 3,102,846
Rome (Roma), Italy (3,175,000) ('91) . . . 2,693,383
Kiev (Kyyiv), Ukraine (3,250,000) ('91) . . 2,635,000
Paris, France (10,275,000) ('90) 2,152,423
Bucharest (Bucureşti),
   Romania (2,300,000) ('92) 2,064,474
Budapest, Hungary (2,515,000) ('90) . . . 2,016,774
Barcelona, Spain (4,040,000) ('88) 1,714,355
Hamburg, Germany (2,385,000) ('91) . . . 1,652,363

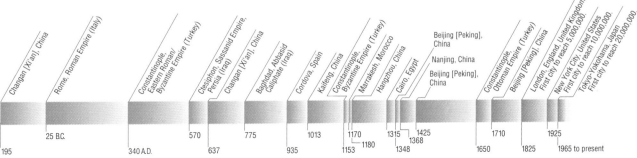

Source: Four Thousand Years of Urban Growth *by Tertius Chandler, Edwin Mellen Press, 1987.*

Warsaw (Warszawa), Poland (2,312,000) ('93) . . . 1,644,500
Minsk, Belarus (1,694,000) ('91) . . . 1,633,600
Kharkiv (Kharkov), Ukraine (2,050,000) ('91) . . . 1,622,800
Vienna (Wien), Austria (1,900,000) ('91) . 1,539,848
Nizhniy Novgorod (Gorky), Russia (2,025,000) ('91) . . . 1,445,000
Yekaterinburg, Russia (1,620,000) ('91) . 1,375,400
Milan (Milano), Italy (3,750,000) ('91) . . 1,371,008
Samara (Kuybyshev), Russia (1,505,000) ('91) . . . 1,257,300
Munich (München), Germany (1,900,000) ('91) . . . 1,229,026
Prague (Praha), Czech Republic (1,328,000) ('91) . . . 1,212,010
Dnipropetrovs'k, Ukraine (1,600,000) ('91) . . . 1,189,300
Sofia (Sofiya), Bulgaria (1,205,000) ('89) 1,136,875
Belgrade (Beograd), Yugoslavia (1,554,826) ('91) . . . 1,136,786
Donets'k, Ukraine (2,125,000) ('91) . . . 1,121,300
Perm', Russia (1,180,000) ('91) . . . 1,110,400
Kazan', Russia (1,165,000) ('91) . . . 1,107,300
Odesa, Ukraine (1,185,000) ('91) . . . 1,100,700
Ufa, Russia (1,118,000) ('91) . . . 1,097,000
Rostov-na-Donu, Russia (1,165,000) ('91) . . . 1,027,600
Naples (Napoli), Italy (2,875,000) ('91) . 1,024,601
Birmingham, England, U.K. (2,675,000) ('81) . . . 1,013,995
Volgograd (Stalingrad), Russia (1,360,000) ('91) . . . 1,007,300
Turin (Torino), Italy (1,550,000) ('91) . . . 961,916
Cologne, Germany (1,810,000) ('91) . . . 953,551
Łódź, Poland (950,000) ('93) . . . 938,400
Saratov, Russia (1,155,000) ('91) . . . 911,100
Rīga, Latvia (1,005,000) ('91) . . . 910,200
Voronezh, Russia ('91) . . . 900,000
Zaporizhzhya, Ukraine ('91) . . . 896,600
Lisbon (Lisboa), Portugal (2,250,000) ('81) 807,167
L'viv (L'vov), Ukraine ('91) . . . 802,200
Marseille, France (1,225,000) ('90) . . . 800,550
Athens (Athínai), Greece (3,096,775) ('91) . 748,110
Kraków, Poland (823,000) ('93) . . . 744,000
València, Spain (1,270,000) ('88) . . . 743,933
Kryvyy Rih, Ukraine ('91) . . . 724,000
Amsterdam, Netherlands (1,875,000) ('92) . 713,407
Zagreb, Croatia ('87) . . . 697,925
Palermo, Italy ('91) . . . 697,162
Glasgow, Scotland, U.K. (1,800,000) ('90) . 689,210
Chişinău (Kishinev), Moldova ('91) . . . 676,700
Genoa (Genova), Italy (805,000) ('91) . . . 675,639
Stockholm, Sweden (1,491,726) ('91) . . . 674,452
Sevilla, Spain (945,000) ('88) . . . 663,132
Tol'yatti, Russia ('91) . . . 654,700
Ul'yanovsk, Russia ('91) . . . 648,300
Izhevsk, Russia ('91) . . . 646,800
Frankfurt (Frankfurt am Main), Germany (1,935,000) ('91) . . . 644,865
Wrocław (Breslau), Poland ('93) . . . 640,700
Yaroslavl', Russia ('91) . . . 638,100
Krasnodar, Russia ('91) . . . 631,200
Essen, Germany (5,050,000) ('91) . . . 626,973
Dortmund, Germany ('91) . . . 599,055
Vilnius, Lithuania ('92) . . . 596,900
Rotterdam, Netherlands (1,120,000) ('92) . 589,707
Poznań, Poland (666,000) ('93) . . . 582,900
Zaragoza, Spain ('88) . . . 582,239
Stuttgart, Germany (2,005,000) ('91) . . . 579,988
Düsseldorf, Germany (1,225,000) ('91) . . . 575,794
Málaga, Spain ('88) . . . 574,456
Orenburg, Russia ('91) . . . 556,500
Bremen, Germany (790,000) ('91) . . . 551,219
Penza, Russia ('91) . . . 551,100
Tula, Russia (640,000) ('91) . . . 543,600
Liverpool, England, U.K. (1,525,000) ('81) . 538,809
Duisburg, Germany ('91) . . . 535,447
Ryazan', Russia ('91) . . . 527,200
Mariupol' (Zhdanov), Ukraine ('91) . . . 521,800
Hannover, Germany (1,000,000) ('91) . . . 513,010
Astrakhan', Russia ('91) . . . 511,900
Mykolayiv, Ukraine ('91) . . . 511,600
Leipzig, Germany (720,000) ('91) . . . 511,079
Naberezhnyye Chelny, Russia ('91) . . . 510,100
Luhans'k, Ukraine (650,000) ('91) . . . 503,900
Gomel', Belarus ('91) . . . 503,300
Dublin, Ireland (1,140,000) ('86) . . . 502,749
Helsinki (Helsingfors), Finland (1,045,000) ('93) . . . 501,514
Nürnberg, Germany (1,065,000) ('91) . . . 493,692
Antwerp, Belgium (1,140,000) ('91) . . . 467,518
Copenhagen (København), Denmark (1,670,000) ('92) . . . 464,566
Leeds, England, U.K. (1,540,000) ('81) . . . 445,242
Manchester, England, U.K. (2,775,000) ('81) . . . 437,612
Lyon, France (1,335,000) ('90) . . . 415,487
Katowice, Poland (2,770,000) ('93) . . . 359,900
Porto, Portugal (1,225,000) ('81) . . . 327,368
Mannheim, Germany (1,525,000) ('91) . . . 310,411
Newcastle upon Tyne, England, U.K. (1,300,000) ('81) . . . 199,064
Lille, France (1,050,000) ('90) . . . 172,142
Brussels (Bruxelles), Belgium (2,385,000) ('91) . . . 136,424

North America

Mexico City (Ciudad de México), Mexico (14,100,000) ('90) . . . 8,235,744
New York, N.Y., U.S. (18,087,251) ('90) . 7,322,564
Los Angeles, Ca., U.S. (14,531,529) ('90) 3,485,398
Chicago, Il., U.S. (8,065,633) ('90) . . . 2,783,726
Santo Domingo, Dominican Republic ('90) . . . 2,411,900
Havana (La Habana), Cuba (2,210,000) ('91) . . . 2,119,059
Guadalajara, Mexico (2,325,000) ('90) . . 1,650,042
Houston, Tx., U.S. (3,711,043) ('90) . . . 1,630,553
Philadelphia, Pa., U.S. (5,899,345) ('90) . 1,585,577
Nezahualcóyotl, Mexico ('90) . . . 1,255,456
Ecatepec, Mexico ('90) . . . 1,218,135
San Diego, Ca., U.S. (2,949,000) ('90) . . 1,110,549
Monterrey, Mexico (2,015,000) ('90) . . . 1,068,996
Guatemala, Guatemala (1,400,000) ('89) . 1,057,210
Detroit, Mi., U.S. (4,665,236) ('90) . . . 1,027,974
Montréal, P.Q., Canada (3,127,242) ('91) . 1,017,666
Puebla, Mexico (1,200,000) ('90) . . . 1,007,170
Dallas, Tx., U.S. (3,885,415) ('90) . . . 1,006,877
Phoenix, Az., U.S. (2,122,101) ('90) . . . 983,403
San Antonio, Tx., U.S. (1,302,099) ('90) . . 935,933
Naucalpan de Juárez, Mexico ('90) . . . 845,960
Port-au-Prince, Haiti (880,000) ('87) . . . 797,000
Ciudad Juárez, Mexico ('90) . . . 789,522
San Jose, Ca., U.S. (1,497,577) ('90) . . . 782,248
León, Mexico ('90) . . . 758,279
Baltimore, Md., U.S. (2,382,172) ('90) . . . 736,014
Indianapolis, In., U.S. (1,249,822) ('90) . . 731,327
San Francisco, Ca., U.S. (6,253,311) ('90) . 723,959
Calgary, Ab., Canada (754,033) ('91) . . . 710,677

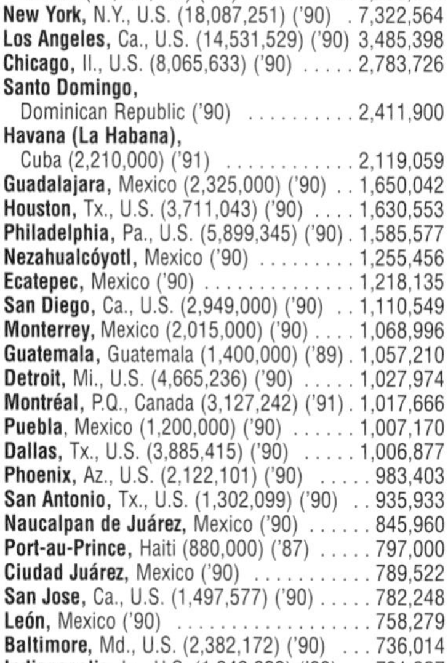

Tlalnepantla, Mexico ('90) . . . 702,270
Tijuana, Mexico ('90) . . . 698,752
Managua, Nicaragua ('85) . . . 682,000
Zapopan, Mexico ('90) . . . 668,323
Toronto, On., Canada (3,893,046) ('91) . . . 635,395
Jacksonville, Fl., U.S. (906,727) ('90) . . . 635,230
Columbus, Oh., U.S. (1,377,419) ('90) . . . 632,910
Milwaukee, Wi., U.S. (1,607,183) ('90) . . . 628,088
Winnipeg, Mb., Canada (652,354) ('91) . . . 616,790
Edmonton, Ab., Canada (839,924) ('91) . . . 616,741
Memphis, Tn., U.S. (981,747) ('90) . . . 610,337
Washington, D.C., U.S. (3,923,574) ('90) . . 606,900
Kingston, Jamaica (890,000) ('91) . . . 587,798
Tegucigalpa, Honduras ('88) . . . 576,661
Boston, Ma., U.S. (4,171,643) ('90) . . . 574,283
North York, On., Canada ('91) . . . 562,564
Guadalupe, Mexico ('90) . . . 535,332
Scarborough, On., Canada ('91) . . . 524,598
Mérida, Mexico ('90) . . . 523,422
Seattle, Wa., U.S. (2,559,164) ('90) . . . 516,259
Chihuahua, Mexico ('90) . . . 516,153
Acapulco de Juárez, Mexico ('90) . . . 515,374
El Paso, Tx., U.S. (1,211,300) ('90) . . . 515,342
Cleveland, Oh., U.S. (2,759,823) ('90) . . . 505,616
New Orleans, La., U.S. (1,238,816) ('90) . . 496,938
Vancouver, B.C., Canada (1,602,502) ('91) . 471,844
Denver, Co., U.S. (1,848,319) ('90) . . . 467,610
Fort Worth, Tx., U.S. (1,332,053) ('90) . . . 447,619
Portland, Or., U.S. (1,477,895) ('90) . . . 437,319
Kansas City, Mo., U.S. (1,566,280) ('90) . . 435,146
San Juan, Puerto Rico (1,877,000) ('90) . . 426,832
Saint Louis, Mo., U.S. (2,444,099) ('90) . . 396,685
Charlotte, N.C., U.S. (1,162,093) ('90) . . . 395,934
Atlanta, Ga., U.S. (2,833,511) ('90) . . . 394,017
Oakland, Ca., U.S. (2,082,914) ('90) . . . 372,242
Pittsburgh, Pa., U.S. (2,242,798) ('90) . . . 369,879
Sacramento, Ca., U.S. (1,481,102) ('90) . . 369,365
Minneapolis, Mn., U.S. (2,464,124) ('90) . 368,383
Cincinnati, Oh., U.S. (1,744,124) ('90) . . . 364,040
Miami, Fl., U.S. (3,192,582) ('90) . . . 358,548
Buffalo, N.Y., U.S. (1,189,288) ('90) . . . 328,123
Tampa, Fl., U.S. (2,067,959) ('90) . . . 280,015
San José, Costa Rica (1,355,000) ('88) . . . 278,600
Newark, N.J., U.S. (1,824,321) ('90) . . . 275,221
Anaheim, Ca., U.S. (2,410,556) ('90) . . . 266,406
Norfolk, Va., U.S. (1,396,107) ('90) . . . 261,229
Rochester, N.Y., U.S. (1,002,410) ('90) . . . 231,636
Riverside, Ca., U.S. (2,588,793) ('90) . . . 226,505
Orlando, Fl., U.S. (1,072,748) ('90) . . . 164,693
Providence, R.I., U.S. (1,141,510) ('90) . . . 160,728
Salt Lake City, Ut., U.S. (1,072,227) ('90) . 159,936
Fort Lauderdale, Fl., U.S. (1,255,488) ('90) 149,377
Hartford, Ct., U.S. (1,085,837) ('90) . . . 139,739

South America

São Paulo, Brazil (16,925,000) ('91) . . . 9,393,753
Rio de Janeiro, Brazil (11,050,000) ('91) . 5,473,909
Bogotá (Santa Fe de Bogotá), Colombia (4,260,000) ('85) . . . 3,982,941
Buenos Aires, Argentina (11,000,000) ('91) . . . 2,960,976
Salvador, Brazil (2,340,000) ('91) . . . 2,070,296
Caracas, Venezuela (4,000,000) ('90) . . . 1,824,654
Belo Horizonte, Brazil (3,340,000) ('91) . 1,529,566
Brasília, Brazil ('91) . . . 1,513,470
Guayaquil, Ecuador ('90) . . . 1,508,444
Medellín, Colombia (2,095,000) ('85) . . . 1,468,089
Cali, Colombia (1,400,000) ('85) . . . 1,350,565
Recife, Brazil (2,880,000) ('91) . . . 1,296,995
Montevideo, Uruguay (1,550,000) ('85) . 1,251,647
Maracaibo, Venezuela ('90) . . . 1,249,670
Porto Alegre, Brazil (2,850,000) ('91) . . . 1,247,352
Córdoba, Argentina (1,260,000) ('91) . . . 1,148,305
San Justo, Argentina ('91) . . . 1,111,811
Quito, Ecuador (1,300,000) ('90) . . . 1,100,847
Manaus, Brazil ('91) . . . 1,005,634
Goiânia, Brazil (1,130,000) ('91) . . . 912,136
Valencia, Venezuela ('90) . . . 903,621
Barranquilla, Colombia (1,140,000) ('85) . 899,781
Rosario, Argentina (1,190,000) ('91) . . . 894,645
Curitiba, Brazil (1,815,000) ('91) . . . 841,882
Belém, Brazil (1,355,000) ('91) . . . 765,476
Campinas, Brazil (1,290,000) ('91) . . . 759,032
Fortaleza, Brazil (2,040,000) ('91) . . . 743,335
La Paz, Bolivia (1,120,000) ('92) . . . 713,378
Santa Cruz de la Sierra, Bolivia ('92) . . . 697,278
General Sarmiento (San Miguel), Argentina ('91) . . . 646,891
Morón, Argentina ('91) . . . 641,541
Barquisimeto, Venezuela ('90) . . . 625,450
Lomas de Zamora, Argentina ('91) . . . 572,769
Osasco, Brazil ('91) . . . 566,949
Nova Iguaçu, Brazil ('91) . . . 562,062
Teresina, Brazil (665,000) ('91) . . . 556,073
Maceió, Brazil ('91) . . . 554,727
São Bernardo do Campo, Brazil ('91) . . . 550,030
Guarulhos, Brazil ('91) . . . 546,417
Cartagena, Colombia ('85) . . . 531,426
La Plata, Argentina ('91) . . . 520,449
Mar del Plata, Argentina ('91) . . . 519,707
Santo André, Brazil ('91) . . . 518,272
Campo Grande, Brazil ('91) . . . 516,403
Quilmes, Argentina ('91) . . . 509,445
Asunción, Paraguay (700,000) ('92) . . . 502,426
Santos, Brazil (1,165,000) ('91) . . . 415,554
Lima, Perú (4,608,010) ('81) . . . 371,122
Santiago, Chile (4,100,000) ('82) . . . 232,667

Countries and Flags

This 12-page section presents basic information about each of the world's countries, along with an illustration of each country's flag. A total of 199 countries are listed: the world's 191 fully independent countries, and 8 internally independent countries which are under the protection of other countries in matters of defense and foreign affairs. Colonies and other dependent political entities are not listed.

The categories of information provided for each country are as follows.

Flag: In many countries two or more versions of the national flag exist. For example, there is often a "civil" version which the average person flies, and a "state" version which is flown only at government buildings and government functions. A common difference between the two is the inclusion of a coat of arms on the state version. The flag versions shown here are the ones that each country has chosen to fly at the United Nations.

Country name: The short form of the English translation of the official country name.

Official name: The long form of the English translation of the official country name.

Population: The population figures listed are 1995 estimates based on U.S. census bureau figures and other available information.

Area: Figures provided represent total land area and all inland water. They are based on official data or U.N. data.

Population density: The number of people per square mile and square kilometer, calculated by dividing the country's population figure by its area figure.

Capital: The city that serves as the official seat of government. Population figures follow the capital name. These figures are based upon the latest official data.

AFGHANISTAN
Official Name: Islamic State of
 Afghanistan
Population: 19,715,000
Area: 251,826 sq mi (652,225 sq km)
Density: 78/sq mi (30/sq km)
Capital: Kābul, 1,424,400

ALGERIA
Official Name: Democratic and
 Popular Republic of Algeria
Population: 27,965,000
Area: 919,595 sq mi (2,381,741 sq km)
Density: 30/sq mi (12/sq km)
Capital: Algiers (El Djazaïr),1,507,241

ANGUILLA
Official Name: Anguilla
Population: 7,100
Area: 35 sq mi (91 sq km)
Density: 203/sq mi (78/sq km)
Capital: The Valley, 1,042

ALBANIA
Official Name: Republic of Albania
Population: 3,394,000
Area: 11,100 sq mi (28,748 sq km)
Density: 306/sq mi (118/sq km)
Capital: Tiranë, 238,100

ANDORRA
Official Name: Principality of Andorra
Population: 59,000
Area: 175 sq mi (453 sq km)
Density: 337/sq mi (130/sq km)
Capital: Andorra, 20,437

ANTIGUA AND BARBUDA
Official Name: Antigua and Barbuda
Population: 67,000
Area: 171 sq mi (442 sq km)
Density: 392/sq mi (152/sq km)
Capital: St. John's, 24,359

ANGOLA
Official Name: Republic of Angola
Population: 10,690,000
Area: 481,354 sq mi (1,246,700 sq km)
Density: 22/sq mi (8.6/sq km)
Capital: Luanda, 1,459,900

Countries
and Flags
continued

BAHAMAS
Official Name: Commonwealth of the
  Bahamas
Population: 275,000
Area: 5,382 sq mi (13,939 sq km)
Pop. Density: 51/sq mi (20/sq km)
Capital: Nassau, 141,000

BELIZE
Official Name: Belize
Population: 212,000
Area: 8,866 sq mi (22,963 sq km)
Pop. Density: 24/sq mi (9.2/sq km)
Capital: Belmopan, 5,256

ARGENTINA
Official Name: Argentine Republic
Population: 34,083,000
Area: 1,073,519 sq mi (2,780,400 sq km)
Pop. Density: 32/sq mi (12/sq km)
Capital: Buenos Aires (de facto), 2,960,976,
  and Viedma (future), 40,452

BAHRAIN
Official Name: State of Bahrain
Population: 563,000
Area: 267 sq mi (691 sq km)
Pop. Density: 2,109/sq mi (815/sq km)
Capital: Al Manāmah, 82,700

BENIN
Official Name: Republic of Benin
Population: 5,433,000
Area: 43,475 sq mi (112,600 sq km)
Pop. Density: 125/sq mi (48/sq km)
Capital: Porto-Novo (designated), 164,000,
  and Cotonou (de facto), 533,212

ARMENIA
Official Name: Republic of Armenia
Population: 3,794,000
Area: 11,506 sq mi (29,800 sq km)
Pop. Density: 330/sq mi (127/sq km)
Capital: Yerevan, 1,199,000

BANGLADESH
Official Name: People's Republic of
  Bangladesh
Population: 119,370,000
Area: 55,598 sq mi (143,998 sq km)
Pop. Density: 2,147/sq mi (829/sq km)
Capital: Dhaka (Dacca), 3,637,892

BHUTAN
Official Name: Kingdom of Bhutan
Population: 1,758,000
Area: 17,954 sq mi (46,500 sq km)
Pop. Density: 98/sq mi (38/sq km)
Capital: Thimphu, 12,000

AUSTRALIA
Official Name: Commonwealth of Australia
Population: 18,205,000
Area: 2,966,155 sq mi (7,682,300 sq km)
Pop. Density: 6.1/sq mi (2.4/sq km)
Capital: Canberra, 276,162

BARBADOS
Official Name: Barbados
Population: 261,000
Area: 166 sq mi (430 sq km)
Pop. Density: 1,572/sq mi (607/sq km)
Capital: Bridgetown, 5,928

BOLIVIA
Official Name: Republic of Bolivia
Population: 6,790,000
Area: 424,165 sq mi (1,098,581 sq km)
Pop. Density: 16/sq mi (6.2/sq km)
Capital: La Paz (seat of government),
  713,378, and Sucre (legal capital), 131,769

AUSTRIA
Official Name: Republic of Austria
Population: 7,932,000
Area: 32,377 sq mi (83,856 sq km)
Pop. Density: 245/sq mi (95/sq km)
Capital: Vienna (Wien), 1,539,848

BELARUS
Official Name: Republic of Belarus
Population: 10,425,000
Area: 80,155 sq mi (207,600 sq km)
Pop. Density: 130/sq mi (50/sq km)
Capital: Minsk, 1,633,600

BOSNIA AND HERZEGOVINA
Official Name: Republic of Bosnia and
  Herzegovina
Population: 4,481,000
Area: 19,741 sq mi (51,129 sq km)
Pop. Density: 227/sq mi (88/sq km)
Capital: Sarajevo, 341,200

AZERBAIJAN
Official Name: Azerbaijani Republic
Population: 7,491,000
Area: 33,436 sq mi (86,600 sq km)
Pop. Density: 224/sq mi (87/sq km)
Capital: Baku (Bakı), 1,080,500

BELGIUM
Official Name: Kingdom of Belgium
Population: 10,075,000
Area: 11,783 sq mi (30,518 sq km)
Pop. Density: 855/sq mi (330/sq km)
Capital: Brussels (Bruxelles), 136,424

BOTSWANA
Official Name: Republic of Botswana
Population: 1,438,000
Area: 224,711 sq mi (582,000 sq km)
Pop. Density: 6.4/sq mi (2.5/sq km)
Capital: Gaborone, 133,468

BRAZIL
Official Name: Federative Republic of Brazil
Population: 159,690,000
Area: 3,286,500 sq mi (8,511,996 sq km)
Pop. Density: 49/sq mi (19/sq km)
Capital: Brasília, 1,513,470

CAMEROON
Official Name: Republic of Cameroon
Population: 13,330,000
Area: 183,568 sq mi (475,440 sq km)
Pop. Density: 73/sq mi (28/sq km)
Capital: Yaoundé, 560,785

CHINA
Official Name: People's Republic of China
Population: 1,196,980,000
Area: 3,689,631 sq mi (9,556,100 sq km)
Pop. Density: 324/sq mi (125/sq km)
Capital: Beijing (Peking), 6,710,000

BRUNEI
Official Name: Negara Brunei Darussalam
Population: 289,000
Area: 2,226 sq mi (5,765 sq km)
Pop. Density: 130/sq mi (50/sq km)
Capital: Bandar Seri Begawan, 22,777

CANADA
Official Name: Canada
Population: 28,285,000
Area: 3,849,674 sq mi (9,970,610 sq km)
Pop. Density: 7.3/sq mi (2.8/sq km)
Capital: Ottawa, 313,987

COLOMBIA
Official Name: Republic of Colombia
Population: 34,870,000
Area: 440,831 sq mi (1,141,748 sq km)
Pop. Density: 79/sq mi (31/sq km)
Capital: Santa Fe de Bogotá (Bogotá),
3,982,941

BULGARIA
Official Name: Republic of Bulgaria
Population: 8,787,000
Area: 42,855 sq mi (110,994 sq km)
Pop. Density: 205/sq mi (79/sq km)
Capital: Sofia (Sofiya), 1,136,875

CAPE VERDE
Official Name: Republic of Cape Verde
Population: 429,000
Area: 1,557 sq mi (4,033 sq km)
Pop. Density: 276/sq mi (106/sq km)
Capital: Praia, 61,644

COMOROS
Official Name: Federal Islamic Republic of
the Comoros
Population: 540,000
Area: 863 sq mi (2,235 sq km)
Pop. Density: 626/sq mi (242/sq km)
Capital: Moroni, 23,432

BURKINA FASO
Official Name: Burkina Faso
Population: 10,275,000
Area: 105,792 sq mi (274,000 sq km)
Pop. Density: 97/sq mi (38/sq km)
Capital: Ouagadougou, 441,514

CENTRAL AFRICAN REPUBLIC
Official Name: Central African Republic
Population: 3,177,000
Area: 240,535 sq mi (622,984 sq km)
Pop. Density: 13/sq mi (5.1/sq km)
Capital: Bangui, 596,800

CONGO
Official Name: Republic of the Congo
Population: 2,474,000
Area: 132,047 sq mi (342,000 sq km)
Pop. Density: 19/sq mi (7.2/sq km)
Capital: Brazzaville, 693,712

BURUNDI
Official Name: Republic of Burundi
Population: 6,192,000
Area: 10,745 sq mi (27,830 sq km)
Pop. Density: 576/sq mi (222/sq km)
Capital: Bujumbura, 226,628

CHAD
Official Name: Republic of Chad
Population: 6,396,000
Area: 495,755 sq mi (1,284,000 sq km)
Pop. Density: 13/sq mi (5/sq km)
Capital: N'Djamena, 500,000

COOK ISLANDS
Official Name: Cook Islands
Population: 19,000
Area: 91 sq mi (236 sq km)
Pop. Density: 209/sq mi (81/sq km)
Capital: Avarua, 10,886

CAMBODIA
Official Name: Kingdom of Cambodia
Population: 9,713,000
Area: 69,898 sq mi (181,035 sq km)
Pop. Density: 139/sq mi (54/sq km)
Capital: Phnum Pénh (Phnom Penh), 620,000

CHILE
Official Name: Republic of Chile
Population: 14,050,000
Area: 292,135 sq mi (756,626 sq km)
Pop. Density: 48/sq mi (19/sq km)
Capital: Santiago, 232,667

COSTA RICA
Official Name: Republic of Costa Rica
Population: 3,379,000
Area: 19,730 sq mi (51,100 sq km)
Pop. Density: 171/sq mi (66/sq km)
Capital: San José, 278,600

Countries and Flags
continued

CZECH REPUBLIC
Official Name: Czech Republic
Population: 10,430,000
Area: 30,450 sq mi (78,864 sq km)
Pop. Density: 343/sq mi (132/sq km)
Capital: Prague (Praha), 1,212,010

EGYPT
Official Name: Arab Republic of Egypt
Population: 58,100,000
Area: 386,662 sq mi (1,001,449 sq km)
Pop. Density: 150/sq mi (58/sq km)
Capital: Cairo (Al Qāhirah), 6,068,695

COTE D'IVOIRE
Official Name: Republic of Cote d'Ivoire
Population: 14,540,000
Area: 124,518 sq mi (322,500 sq km)
Pop. Density: 117/sq mi (45/sq km)
Capital: Abidjan (de facto), 1,929,079, and
Yamoussoukro (future), 106,786

DENMARK
Official Name: Kingdom of Denmark
Population: 5,207,000
Area: 16,639 sq mi (43,094 sq km)
Pop. Density: 313 sq mi (121/sq km)
Capital: Copenhagen (København), 464,566

EL SALVADOR
Official Name: Republic of El Salvador
Population: 5,280,000
Area: 8,124 sq mi (21,041 sq km)
Pop. Density: 650/sq mi (251/sq km)
Capital: San Salvador, 462,652

CROATIA
Official Name: Republic of Croatia
Population: 4,801,000
Area: 21,829 sq mi (56,538 sq km)
Pop. Density: 220/sq mi (85/sq km)
Capital: Zagreb, 697,925

DJIBOUTI
Official Name: Republic of Djibouti
Population: 557,000
Area: 8,958 sq mi (23,200 sq km)
Pop. Density: 62/sq mi (24/sq km)
Capital: Djibouti, 329,337

EQUATORIAL GUINEA
Official Name: Republic of Equatorial Guinea
Population: 394,000
Area: 10,831 sq mi (28,051 sq km)
Pop. Density: 36/sq mi (14/sq km)
Capital: Malabo, 31,630

CUBA
Official Name: Republic of Cuba
Population: 11,560,000
Area: 42,804 sq mi (110,861 sq km)
Pop. Density: 270/sq mi (104/sq km)
Capital: Havana (La Habana), 2,119,059

DOMINICA
Official Name: Commonwealth of Dominica
Population: 89,000
Area: 305 sq mi (790 sq km)
Pop. Density: 292/sq mi (113/sq km)
Capital: Roseau, 9,348

ERITREA
Official Name: State of Eritrea
Population: 3,458,000
Area: 36,170 sq mi (93,679 sq km)
Pop. Density: 96/sq mi (37/sq km)
Capital: Asmera, 358,100

CYPRUS
Official Name: Republic of Cyprus
Population: 551,000
Area: 2,276 sq mi (5,896 sq km)
Pop. Density: 242/sq mi (93/sq km)
Capital: Nicosia (Levkosía), 48,221

DOMINICAN REPUBLIC
Official Name: Dominican Republic
Population: 7,896,000
Area: 18,704 sq mi (48,442 sq km)
Pop. Density: 422/sq mi (163/sq km)
Capital: Santo Domingo, 2,411,900

ESTONIA
Official Name: Republic of Estonia
Population: 1,515,000
Area: 17,413 sq mi (45,100 sq km)
Pop. Density: 87/sq mi (34/sq km)
Capital: Tallinn, 481,500

CYPRUS, NORTH
Official Name: Turkish Republic of
Northern Cyprus
Population: 182,000
Area: 1,295 sq mi (3,355 sq km)
Pop. Density: 141/sq mi (54/sq km)
Capital: Nicosia (Lefkoşa), 37,400

ECUADOR
Official Name: Republic of Ecuador
Population: 11,015,000
Area: 105,037 sq mi (272,045 sq km)
Pop. Density: 105/sq mi (40/sq km)
Capital: Quito, 1,100,847

ETHIOPIA
Official Name: Ethiopia
Population: 55,070,000
Area: 446,953 sq mi (1,157,603 sq km)
Pop. Density: 123/sq mi (48/sq km)
Capital: Addis Ababa (Adis Abeba), 1,912,500

FIJI
Official Name: Republic of Fiji
Population: 775,000
Area: 7,056 sq mi (18,274 sq km)
Pop. Density: 110/sq mi (42/sq km)
Capital: Suva, 69,665

GERMANY
Official Name: Federal Republic of Germany
Population: 81,710,000
Area: 137,822 sq mi (356,955 sq km)
Pop. Density: 593/sq mi (229/sq km)
Capital: Berlin (designated), 3,433,695, and
Bonn (de facto), 292,234

GUINEA
Official Name: Republic of Guinea
Population: 6,469,000
Area: 94,926 sq mi (245,857 sq km)
Pop. Density: 68/sq mi (26/sq km)
Capital: Conakry, 800,000

FINLAND
Official Name: Republic of Finland
Population: 5,098,000
Area: 130,559 sq mi (338,145 sq km)
Pop. Density: 39/sq mi (15/sq km)
Capital: Helsinki (Helsingfors), 501,514

GHANA
Official Name: Republic of Ghana
Population: 17,210,000
Area: 92,098 sq mi (238,533 sq km)
Pop. Density: 187/sq mi (72/sq km)
Capital: Accra, 949,113

GUINEA-BISSAU
Official Name: Republic of Guinea-Bissau
Population: 1,111,000
Area: 13,948 sq mi (36,125 sq km)
Pop. Density: 80/sq mi (31/sq km)
Capital: Bissau, 125,000

FRANCE
Official Name: French Republic
Population: 58,010,000
Area: 211,208 sq mi (547,026 sq km)
Pop. Density: 275/sq mi (106/sq km)
Capital: Paris, 2,152,423

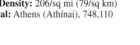

GREECE
Official Name: Hellenic Republic
Population: 10,475,000
Area: 50,949 sq mi (131,957 sq km)
Pop. Density: 206/sq mi (79/sq km)
Capital: Athens (Athínai), 748,110

GUYANA
Official Name: Co-operative Republic of
Guyana
Population: 726,000
Area: 83,000 sq mi (214,969 sq km)
Pop. Density: 8.7/sq mi (3.4/sq km)
Capital: Georgetown, 78,500

GABON
Official Name: Gabonese Republic
Population: 1,035,000
Area: 103,347 sq mi (267,667 sq km)
Pop. Density: 10/sq mi (3.9/sq km)
Capital: Libreville, 235,700

GREENLAND
Official Name: Greenland
Population: 57,000
Area: 840,004 sq mi (2,175,600 sq km)
Pop. Density: 0.1/sq mi (0.03/sq km)
Capital: Godthåb (Nuuk), 12,217

HAITI
Official Name: Republic of Haiti
Population: 7,069,000
Area: 10,714 sq mi (27,750 sq km)
Pop. Density: 660/sq mi (255/sq km)
Capital: Port-au-Prince, 797,000

GAMBIA
Official Name: Republic of the Gambia
Population: 1,082,000
Area: 4,127 sq mi (10,689 sq km)
Pop. Density: 262/sq mi (101/sq km)
Capital: Banjul, 44,188

GRENADA
Official Name: Grenada
Population: 92,000
Area: 133 sq mi (344 sq km)
Pop. Density: 692/sq mi (267/sq km)
Capital: St. George's, 4,439

HONDURAS
Official Name: Republic of Honduras
Population: 5,822,000
Area: 43,277 sq mi (112,088 sq km)
Pop. Density: 135/sq mi (52/sq km)
Capital: Tegucigalpa, 576,661

GEORGIA
Official Name: Republic of Georgia
Population: 5,704,000
Area: 26,911 sq mi (69,700 sq km)
Pop. Density: 212/sq mi (82/sq km)
Capital: Tbilisi, 1,279,000

GUATEMALA
Official Name: Republic of Guatemala
Population: 10,420,000
Area: 42,042 sq mi (108,889 sq km)
Pop. Density: 248/sq mi (96/sq km)
Capital: Guatemala, 1,057,210

HUNGARY
Official Name: Republic of Hungary
Population: 10,270,000
Area: 35,919 sq mi (93,030 sq km)
Pop. Density: 286/sq mi (110/sq km)
Capital: Budapest, 2,016,774

Countries and Flags
continued

IRELAND
Official Name: Ireland
Population: 3,546,000
Area: 27,137 sq mi (70,285 sq km)
Pop. Density: 131/sq mi (50/sq km)
Capital: Dublin (Baile Átha Cliath), 502,749

KAZAKHSTAN
Official Name: Republic of Kazakhstan
Population: 17,025,000
Area: 1,049,156 sq mi (2,717,300 sq km)
Pop. Density: 16/sq mi (6.3/sq km)
Capital: Alma-Ata (Almaty), 1,156,200, and Akmola (future), 286,000

ICELAND
Official Name: Republic of Iceland
Population: 265,000
Area: 39,769 sq mi (103,000 sq km)
Pop. Density: 6.7/sq mi (2.6/sq km)
Capital: Reykjavik, 100,850

ISRAEL
Official Name: State of Israel
Population: 5,059,000
Area: 8,019 sq mi (20,770 sq km)
Pop. Density: 631/sq mi (244/sq km)
Capital: Jerusalem (Yerushalayim), 524,500

KENYA
Official Name: Republic of Kenya
Population: 28,380,000
Area: 224,961 sq mi (582,646 sq km)
Pop. Density: 126/sq mi (49/sq km)
Capital: Nairobi, 1,505,000

INDIA
Official Name: Republic of India
Population: 909,150,000
Area: 1,237,062 sq mi (3,203,975 sq km)
Pop. Density: 735/sq mi (284/sq km)
Capital: New Delhi, 301,297

ITALY
Official Name: Italian Republic
Population: 57,330,000
Area: 116,324 sq mi (301,277 sq km)
Pop. Density: 493/sq mi (190/sq km)
Capital: Rome (Roma), 2,693,383

KIRIBATI
Official Name: Republic of Kiribati
Population: 79,000
Area: 313 sq mi (811 sq km)
Pop. Density: 252/sq mi (97/sq km)
Capital: Bairiki, 2,226

INDONESIA
Official Name: Republic of Indonesia
Population: 193,680,000
Area: 752,410 sq mi (1,948,732 sq km)
Pop. Density: 257/sq mi (99/sq km)
Capital: Jakarta, 8,227,746

JAMAICA
Official Name: Jamaica
Population: 2,568,000
Area: 4,244 sq mi (10,991 sq km)
Pop. Density: 605/sq mi (234/sq km)
Capital: Kingston, 587,798

KOREA, NORTH
Official Name: Democratic People's Republic of Korea
Population: 23,265,000
Area: 46,540 sq mi (120,538 sq km)
Pop. Density: 500/sq mi (193/sq km)
Capital: P'yŏngyang, 2,355,000

IRAN
Official Name: Islamic Republic of Iran
Population: 63,810,000
Area: 632,457 sq mi (1,638,057 sq km)
Pop. Density: 101/sq mi (39/sq km)
Capital: Tehrān, 6,042,584

JAPAN
Official Name: Japan
Population: 125,360,000
Area: 145,870 sq mi (377,801 sq km)
Pop. Density: 859/sq mi (332/sq km)
Capital: Tōkyō, 8,163,573

KOREA, SOUTH
Official Name: Republic of Korea
Population: 44,655,000
Area: 38,230 sq mi (99,016 sq km)
Pop. Density: 1,168/sq mi (451/sq km)
Capital: Seoul (Sŏul), 10,627,790

IRAQ
Official Name: Republic of Iraq
Population: 20,250,000
Area: 169,235 sq mi (438,317 sq km)
Pop. Density: 120/sq mi (46/sq km)
Capital: Baghdād, 3,841,268

JORDAN
Official Name: Hashemite Kingdom of Jordan
Population: 4,028,000
Area: 35,135 sq mi (91,000 sq km)
Pop. Density: 115/sq mi (44/sq km)
Capital: 'Ammān, 936,300

KUWAIT
Official Name: State of Kuwait
Population: 1,866,000
Area: 6,880 sq mi (17,818 sq km)
Pop. Density: 271/sq mi (105/sq km)
Capital: Kuwait (Al Kuwayt), 44,335

KYRGYZSTAN
Official Name: Kyrgyz Republic
Population: 4,541,000
Area: 76,641 sq mi (198,500 sq km)
Pop. Density: 59/sq mi (23/sq km)
Capital: Bishkek, 631,300

LIBYA
Official Name: Socialist People's Libyan
Arab Jamahiriya
Population: 5,148,000
Area: 679,362 sq mi (1,759,540 sq km)
Pop. Density: 7.6/sq mi (2.9/sq km)
Capital: Tripoli (Ṭarābulus), 591,062

MALAWI
Official Name: Republic of Malawi
Population: 8,984,000
Area: 45,747 sq mi (118,484 sq km)
Pop. Density: 196/sq mi (76/sq km)
Capital: Lilongwe, 223,318

LAOS
Official Name: Lao People's Democratic
Republic
Population: 4,768,000
Area: 91,429 sq mi (236,800 sq km)
Pop. Density: 52/sq mi (20/sq km)
Capital: Viangchan (Vientiane), 377,409

LIECHTENSTEIN
Official Name: Principality of Liechtenstein
Population: 30,000
Area: 62 sq mi (160 sq km)
Pop. Density: 484/sq mi (188/sq km)
Capital: Vaduz, 4,887

MALAYSIA
Official Name: Malaysia
Population: 19,505,000
Area: 127,320 sq mi (329,758 sq km)
Pop. Density: 153/sq mi (59/sq km)
Capital: Kuala Lumpur, 919,610

LATVIA
Official Name: Republic of Latvia
Population: 2,532,000
Area: 24,595 sq mi (63,700 sq km)
Pop. Density: 103/sq mi (40/sq km)
Capital: Rīga, 910,200

LITHUANIA
Official Name: Republic of Lithuania
Population: 3,757,000
Area: 25,212 sq mi (65,300 sq km)
Pop. Density: 149/sq mi (58/sq km)
Capital: Vilnius, 596,900

MALDIVES
Official Name: Republic of Maldives
Population: 251,000
Area: 115 sq mi (298 sq km)
Pop. Density: 2,183/sq mi (842/sq km)
Capital: Male', 55,130

LEBANON
Official Name: Republic of Lebanon
Population: 3,660,000
Area: 4,015 sq mi (10,400 sq km)
Pop. Density: 912/sq mi (352/sq km)
Capital: Beirut (Bayrūt), 509,000

LUXEMBOURG
Official Name: Grand Duchy of Luxembourg
Population: 396,000
Area: 998 sq mi (2,586 sq km)
Pop. Density: 397/sq mi (153/sq km)
Capital: Luxembourg, 75,377

MALI
Official Name: Republic of Mali
Population: 9,585,000
Area: 482,077 sq mi (1,248,574 sq km)
Pop. Density: 20/sq mi (7.7/sq km)
Capital: Bamako, 658,275

LESOTHO
Official Name: Kingdom of Lesotho
Population: 1,967,000
Area: 11,720 sq mi (30,355 sq km)
Pop. Density: 168/sq mi (65/sq km)
Capital: Maseru, 109,382

MACEDONIA
Official Name: Republic of Macedonia
Population: 2,102,000
Area: 9,928 sq mi (25,713 sq km)
Pop. Density: 212/sq mi (82/sq km)
Capital: Skopje, 444,900

MALTA
Official Name: Republic of Malta
Population: 368,000
Area: 122 sq mi (316 sq km)
Pop. Density: 3,016/sq mi (1,165/sq km)
Capital: Valletta, 9,199

LIBERIA
Official Name: Republic of Liberia
Population: 2,771,000
Area: 38,250 sq mi (99,067 sq km)
Pop. Density: 72/sq mi (28/sq km)
Capital: Monrovia, 465,000

MADAGASCAR
Official Name: Republic of Madagascar
Population: 13,645,000
Area: 226,658 sq mi (587,041 sq km)
Pop. Density: 60/sq mi (23/sq km)
Capital: Antananarivo, 1,250,000

MARSHALL ISLANDS
Official Name: Republic of the Marshall
Islands
Population: 55,000
Area: 70 sq mi (181 sq km)
Pop. Density: 786/sq mi (304/sq km)
Capital: Majuro (island)

Countries
and Flags
continued

MONACO
Official Name: Principality of Monaco
Population: 31,000
Area: 0.7 sq mi (1.9 sq km)
Pop. Density: 44,286/sq mi (16,316/sq km)
Capital: Monaco, 31,000

NAURU
Official Name: Republic of Nauru
Population: 10,000
Area: 8.1 sq mi (21 sq km)
Pop. Density: 1,235/sq mi (476/sq km)
Capital: Yaren District

MAURITANIA
Official Name: Islamic Republic of
 Mauritania
Population: 2,228,000
Area: 395,956 sq mi (1,025,520 sq km)
Pop. Density: 5.6/sq mi (2.2/sq km)
Capital: Nouakchott, 285,000

MONGOLIA
Official Name: Mongolia
Population: 2,462,000
Area: 604,829 sq mi (1,566,500 sq km)
Pop. Density: 4.1/sq mi (1.6/sq km)
Capital: Ulan Bator (Ulaanbaatar), 575,000

NEPAL
Official Name: Kingdom of Nepal
Population: 21,295,000
Area: 56,827 sq mi (147,181 sq km)
Pop. Density: 375/sq mi (145/sq km)
Capital: Kathmandu, 421,258

MAURITIUS
Official Name: Republic of Mauritius
Population: 1,121,000
Area: 788 sq mi (2,040 sq km)
Pop. Density: 1,423/sq mi (550/sq km)
Capital: Port Louis, 141,870

MOROCCO
Official Name: Kingdom of Morocco
Population: 26,890,000
Area: 172,414 sq mi (446,550 sq km)
Pop. Density: 156/sq mi (60/sq km)
Capital: Rabat, 518,616

NETHERLANDS
Official Name: Kingdom of the Netherlands
Population: 15,425,000
Area: 16,164 sq mi (41,864 sq km)
Pop. Density: 954/sq mi (368/sq km)
Capital: Amsterdam (designated), 713,407,
 and The Hague ('s-Gravenhage) (seat of
 government), 445,287

MEXICO
Official Name: United Mexican States
Population: 93,860,000
Area: 759,534 sq mi (1,967,183 sq km)
Pop. Density: 124/sq mi (48/sq km)
Capital: Mexico City (Ciudad de México),
 8,235,744

MOZAMBIQUE
Official Name: Republic of Mozambique
Population: 17,860,000
Area: 308,642 sq mi (799,380 sq km)
Pop. Density: 58/sq mi (22/sq km)
Capital: Maputo, 1,069,727

NEW ZEALAND
Official Name: New Zealand
Population: 3,558,000
Area: 104,454 sq mi (270,534 sq km)
Pop. Density: 34/sq mi (13/sq km)
Capital: Wellington, 150,301

MICRONESIA, FEDERATED STATES OF
Official Name: Federated States of
 Micronesia
Population: 122,000
Area: 271 sq mi (702 sq km)
Pop. Density: 450/sq mi (174/sq km)
Capital: Kolonia (de facto), 6,169, and
 Paliker (future)

MYANMAR
Official Name: Union of Myanmar
Population: 44,675,000
Area: 261,228 sq mi (676,577 sq km)
Pop. Density: 171/sq mi (66/sq km)
Capital: Rangoon (Yangon), 2,513,023

NICARAGUA
Official Name: Republic of Nicaragua
Population: 4,438,000
Area: 50,054 sq mi (129,640 sq km)
Pop. Density: 89/sq mi (34/sq km)
Capital: Managua, 682,000

MOLDOVA
Official Name: Republic of Moldova
Population: 4,377,000
Area: 13,012 sq mi (33,700 sq km)
Pop. Density: 336/sq mi (130/sq km)
Capital: Chişinău (Kishinev), 676,700

NAMIBIA
Official Name: Republic of Namibia
Population: 1,623,000
Area: 318,253 sq mi (824,272 sq km)
Pop. Density: 5.1/sq mi (2.0/sq km)
Capital: Windhoek, 114,500

NIGER
Official Name: Republic of Niger
Population: 9,125,000
Area: 489,191 sq mi (1,267,000 sq km)
Pop. Density: 19/sq mi (7.2/sq km)
Capital: Niamey, 392,165

NIGERIA
Official Name: Federal Republic of Nigeria
Population: 97,300,000
Area: 356,669 sq mi (923,768 sq km)
Pop. Density: 273/sq mi (105/sq km)
Capital: Lagos (de facto),1,213,000, and
Abuja (designated), 250,000

PALAU
Official Name: Republic of Palau
Population: 17,000
Area: 196 sq mi (508 sq km)
Pop. Density: 87/sq mi (33/sq km)
Capital: Koror (de facto), 9,018, and
Melekeok (future)

POLAND
Official Name: Republic of Poland
Population: 38,730,000
Area: 121,196 sq mi (313,895 sq km)
Pop. Density: 320/sq mi (123/sq km)
Capital: Warsaw (Warszawa), 1,644,500

NIUE
Official Name: Niue
Population: 1,900
Area: 100 sq mi (259 sq km)
Pop. Density: 19/sq mi (7.3/sq km)
Capital: Alofi, 706

PANAMA
Official Name: Republic of Panama
Population: 2,654,000
Area: 29,157 sq mi (75,517 sq km)
Pop. Density: 91/sq mi (35/sq km)
Capital: Panamá, 411,549

PORTUGAL
Official Name: Portuguese Republic
Population: 9,907,000
Area: 35,516 sq mi (91,985 sq km)
Pop. Density: 279/sq mi (108/sq km)
Capital: Lisbon (Lisboa), 807,167

NORTHERN MARIANA ISLANDS
Official Name: Commonwealth of the
Northern Mariana Islands
Population: 51,000
Area: 184 sq mi (477 sq km)
Pop. Density: 277/sq mi (107/sq km)
Capital: Saipan (island)

PAPUA NEW GUINEA
Official Name: Independent State of Papua
New Guinea
Population: 4,057,000
Area: 178,704 sq mi (462,840 sq km)
Pop. Density: 23/sq mi (8.8/sq km)
Capital: Port Moresby, 193,242

PUERTO RICO
Official Name: Commonwealth of Puerto Rico
Population: 3,625,000
Area: 3,515 sq mi (9,104 sq km)
Pop. Density: 1,031/sq mi (398/sq km)
Capital: San Juan, 426,832

NORWAY
Official Name: Kingdom of Norway
Population: 4,339,000
Area: 149,412 sq mi (386,975 sq km)
Pop. Density: 29/sq mi (11/sq km)
Capital: Oslo, 470,204

PARAGUAY
Official Name: Republic of Paraguay
Population: 4,400,000
Area: 157,048 sq mi (406,752 sq km)
Pop. Density: 28/sq mi (11/sq km)
Capital: Asunción, 502,426

QATAR
Official Name: State of Qatar
Population: 519,000
Area: 4,412 sq mi (11,427 sq km)
Pop. Density: 118/sq mi (45/sq km)
Capital: Ad Dawḥah (Doha), 217,294

OMAN
Official Name: Sultanate of Oman
Population: 2,089,000
Area: 82,030 sq mi (212,457 sq km)
Pop. Density: 25/sq mi (9.8/sq km)
Capital: Muscat (Masqat), 30,000

PERU
Official Name: Republic of Peru
Population: 23,095,000
Area: 496,225 sq mi (1,285,216 sq km)
Pop. Density: 47/sq mi (18/sq km)
Capital: Lima, 371,122

ROMANIA
Official Name: Romania
Population: 22,745,000
Area: 91,699 sq mi (237,500 sq km)
Pop. Density: 248/sq mi (96/sq km)
Capital: Bucharest (Bucureşti), 2,064,474

PAKISTAN
Official Name: Islamic Republic of Pakistan
Population: 129,630,000
Area: 339,732 sq mi (879,902 sq km)
Pop. Density: 382/sq mi (147/sq km)
Capital: Islāmābād, 204,364

PHILIPPINES
Official Name: Republic of the Philippines
Population: 67,910,000
Area: 115,831 sq mi (300,000 sq km)
Pop. Density: 586/sq mi (226/sq km)
Capital: Manila, 1,598,918

RUSSIA
Official Name: Russian Federation
Population: 150,500,000
Area: 6,592,849 sq mi (17,075,400 sq km)
Pop. Density: 23/sq mi (8.8/sq km)
Capital: Moscow (Moskva), 8,801,500

Countries and Flags
continued

SAO TOME AND PRINCIPE
Official Name: Democratic Republic of Sao Tome and Principe
Population: 127,000
Area: 372 sq mi (964 sq km)
Pop. Density: 341/sq mi (132/sq km)
Capital: São Tomé, 5,245

SLOVAKIA
Official Name: Slovak Republic
Population: 5,353,000
Area: 18,933 sq mi (49,035 sq km)
Pop. Density: 283/sq mi (109/sq km)
Capital: Bratislava, 441,453

RWANDA
Official Name: Republic of Rwanda
Population: 7,343,000
Area: 10,169 sq mi (26,338 sq km)
Pop. Density: 722/sq mi (279/sq km)
Capital: Kigali, 232,733

SAUDI ARABIA
Official Name: Kingdom of Saudi Arabia
Population: 18,190,000
Area: 830,000 sq mi (2,149,690 sq km)
Pop. Density: 22/sq mi (8.5/sq km)
Capital: Riyadh (Ar Riyād), 1,250,000

SLOVENIA
Official Name: Republic of Slovenia
Population: 1,993,000
Area: 7,820 sq mi (20,253 sq km)
Pop. Density: 255/sq mi (98/sq km)
Capital: Ljubljana, 233,200

ST. KITTS AND NEVIS
Official Name: Federation of St. Kitts and Nevis
Population: 42,000
Area: 104 sq mi (269 sq km)
Pop. Density: 404/sq mi (156/sq km)
Capital: Basseterre, 14,725

SENEGAL
Official Name: Republic of Senegal
Population: 8,862,000
Area: 75,951 sq mi (196,712 sq km)
Pop. Density: 117/sq mi (45/sq km)
Capital: Dakar, 1,490,450

SOLOMON ISLANDS
Official Name: Solomon Islands
Population: 393,000
Area: 10,954 sq mi (28,370 sq km)
Pop. Density: 36/sq mi (14/sq km)
Capital: Honiara, 30,413

ST. LUCIA
Official Name: St. Lucia
Population: 138,000
Area: 238 sq mi (616 sq km)
Pop. Density: 580/sq mi (224/sq km)
Capital: Castries, 11,147

SEYCHELLES
Official Name: Republic of Seychelles
Population: 75,000
Area: 175 sq mi (453 sq km)
Pop. Density: 429/sq mi (166/sq km)
Capital: Victoria, 23,000

SOMALIA
Official Name: Somalia
Population: 7,187,000
Area: 246,201 sq mi (637,657 sq km)
Pop. Density: 29/sq mi (11/sq km)
Capital: Mogadishu (Muqdisho), 600,000

ST. VINCENT AND THE GRENADINES
Official Name: St. Vincent and the Grenadines
Population: 110,000
Area: 150 sq mi (388 sq km)
Pop. Density: 733/sq mi (284/sq km)
Capital: Kingstown, 15,466

SIERRA LEONE
Official Name: Republic of Sierra Leone
Population: 4,690,000
Area: 27,925 sq mi (72,325 sq km)
Pop. Density: 168/sq mi (65/sq km)
Capital: Freetown, 469,776

SOUTH AFRICA
Official Name: Republic of South Africa
Population: 44,500,000
Area: 471,010 sq mi (1,219,909 sq km)
Pop. Density: 94/sq mi (36/sq km)
Capital: Pretoria (administrative), 525,583, Cape Town (legislative), 854,616, and Bloemfontein (judicial), 126,867

SAN MARINO
Official Name: Republic of San Marino
Population: 24,000
Area: 24 sq mi (61 sq km)
Pop. Density: 1,000/sq mi (393/sq km)
Capital: San Marino, 2,794

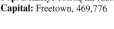

SINGAPORE
Official Name: Republic of Singapore
Population: 2,921,000
Area: 246 sq mi (636 sq km)
Pop. Density: 11,874/sq mi (4,593/sq km)
Capital: Singapore, 2,921,000

SPAIN
Official Name: Kingdom of Spain
Population: 39,260,000
Area: 194,885 sq mi (504,750 sq km)
Pop. Density: 201/sq mi (78/sq km)
Capital: Madrid, 3,102,846

SRI LANKA
Official Name: Democratic Socialist Republic
of Sri Lanka
Population: 18,240,000
Area: 24,962 sq mi (64,652 sq km)
Pop. Density: 731/sq mi (282/sq km)
Capital: Colombo (designated), 612,000, and
Sri Jayawardenepura (seat of government),
108,000

SYRIA
Official Name: Syrian Arab Republic
Population: 14,100,000
Area: 71,498 sq mi (185,180 sq km)
Pop. Density: 197/sq mi (76/sq km)
Capital: Damascus (Dimashq), 1,549,932

TONGA
Official Name: Kingdom of Tonga
Population: 110,000
Area: 288 sq mi (747 sq km)
Pop. Density: 382/sq mi (147/sq km)
Capital: Nuku'alofa, 21,265

SUDAN
Official Name: Republic of the Sudan
Population: 25,840,000
Area: 967,500 sq mi (2,505,813 sq km)
Pop. Density: 27/sq mi (10/sq km)
Capital: Khartoum (Al Kharṭum), 473,597

TAIWAN
Official Name: Republic of China
Population: 21,150,000
Area: 13,900 sq mi (36,002 sq km)
Pop. Density: 1,522/sq mi (587/sq km)
Capital: T'aipei, 2,706,453

TRINIDAD AND TOBAGO
Official Name: Republic of Trinidad and
Tobago
Population: 1,281,000
Area: 1,980 sq mi (5,128 sq km)
Pop. Density: 647/sq mi (250/sq km)
Capital: Port of Spain, 50,878

SURINAME
Official Name: Republic of Suriname
Population: 426,000
Area: 63,251 sq mi (163,820 sq km)
Pop. Density: 6.7/sq mi (2.6/sq km)
Capital: Paramaribo, 241,000

TAJIKISTAN
Official Name: Republic of Tajikistan
Population: 6,073,000
Area: 55,251 sq mi (143,100 sq km)
Pop. Density: 110/sq mi (42/sq km)
Capital: Dushanbe, 582,400

TUNISIA
Official Name: Republic of Tunisia
Population: 8,806,000
Area: 63,170 sq mi (163,610 sq km)
Pop. Density: 139/sq mi (54/sq km)
Capital: Tunis, 596,654

SWAZILAND
Official Name: Kingdom of Swaziland
Population: 889,000
Area: 6,704 sq mi (17,364 sq km)
Pop. Density: 133/sq mi (51/sq km)
Capital: Mbabane (administrative), 38,290,
and Lobamba (legislative)

TANZANIA
Official Name: United Republic of Tanzania
Population: 28,350,000
Area: 341,217 sq mi (883,749 sq km)
Pop. Density: 83/sq mi (32/sq km)
Capital: Dar es Salaam (de facto), 1,096,000,
and Dodoma (legislative), 85,000

TURKEY
Official Name: Republic of Turkey
Population: 62,030,000
Area: 300,948 sq mi (779,452 sq km)
Pop. Density: 206/sq mi (80/sq km)
Capital: Ankara, 2,559,471

SWEDEN
Official Name: Kingdom of Sweden
Population: 8,981,000
Area: 173,732 sq mi (449,964 sq km)
Pop. Density: 52/sq mi (20/sq km)
Capital: Stockholm, 674,452

THAILAND
Official Name: Kingdom of Thailand
Population: 59,870,000
Area: 198,115 sq mi (513,115 sq km)
Pop. Density: 302/sq mi (117/sq km)
Capital: Bangkok (Krung Thep), 5,620,591

TURKMENISTAN
Official Name: Turkmenistan
Population: 4,035,000
Area: 188,456 sq mi (488,100 sq km)
Pop. Density: 21/sq mi (8.3/sq km)
Capital: Ashkhabad, 412,200

SWITZERLAND
Official Name: Swiss Confederation
Population: 7,244,000
Area: 15,943 sq mi (41,293 sq km)
Pop. Density: 454/sq mi (175/sq km)
Capital: Bern (Berne), 136,338

TOGO
Official Name: Republic of Togo
Population: 4,332,000
Area: 21,925 sq mi (56,785 sq km)
Pop. Density: 198/sq mi (76/sq km)
Capital: Lomé, 500,000

TUVALU
Official Name: Tuvalu
Population: 10,000
Area: 10 sq mi (26 sq km)
Pop. Density: 1,000/sq mi (385/sq km)
Capital: Funafuti, 2,191

Countries and Flags
continued

URUGUAY
Official Name: Oriental Republic of Uruguay
Population: 3,317,000
Area: 68,500 sq mi (177,414 sq km)
Pop. Density: 48/sq mi (19/sq km)
Capital: Montevideo, 1,251,647

WESTERN SAMOA
Official Name: Independent State of Western Samoa
Population: 172,000
Area: 1,093 sq mi (2,831 sq km)
Pop. Density: 157/sq mi (61/sq km)
Capital: Apia, 34,126

UGANDA
Official Name: Republic of Uganda
Population: 18,270,000
Area: 93,104 sq mi (241,139 sq km)
Pop. Density: 196/sq mi (76/sq km)
Capital: Kampala, 773,463

UZBEKISTAN
Official Name: Republic of Uzbekistan
Population: 22,860,000
Area: 172,742 sq mi (447,400 sq km)
Pop. Density: 132/sq mi (51/sq km)
Capital: Tashkent, 2,113,300

YEMEN
Official Name: Republic of Yemen
Population: 12,910,000
Area: 203,850 sq mi (527,968 sq km)
Pop. Density: 63/sq mi (24/sq km)
Capital: San'ā', 427,150

UKRAINE
Official Name: Ukraine
Population: 52,140,000
Area: 233,090 sq mi (603,700 sq km)
Pop. Density: 224/sq mi (86/sq km)
Capital: Kiev (Kyyiv), 2,635,000

VANUATU
Official Name: Republic of Vanuatu
Population: 161,000
Area: 4,707 sq mi (12,190 sq km)
Pop. Density: 34/sq mi (13/sq km)
Capital: Port Vila, 18,905

YUGOSLAVIA
Official Name: Socialist Federal Republic of Yugoslavia
Population: 10,765,000
Area: 39,449 sq mi (102,173 sq km)
Pop. Density: 273/sq mi (105/sq km)
Capital: Belgrade (Beograd), 1,136,786

UNITED ARAB EMIRATES
Official Name: United Arab Emirates
Population: 2,855,000
Area: 32,278 sq mi (83,600 sq km)
Pop. Density: 88/sq mi (34/sq km)
Capital: Abū Ẓaby (Abu Dhabi), 242,975

VATICAN CITY
Official Name: State of the Vatican City
Population: 1,000
Area: 0.2 sq mi (0.4 sq km)
Pop. Density: 5,000/sq mi (2,500/sq km)
Capital: Vatican City, 1,000

ZAIRE
Official Name: Republic of Zaire
Population: 43,365,000
Area: 905,355 sq mi (2,344,858 sq km)
Pop. Density: 48/sq mi (18/sq km)
Capital: Kinshasa, 3,000,000

UNITED KINGDOM
Official Name: United Kingdom of Great Britain and Northern Ireland
Population: 58,430,000
Area: 94,249 sq mi (244,101 sq km)
Pop. Density: 620/sq mi (239/sq km)
Capital: London, 6,574,009

VENEZUELA
Official Name: Republic of Venezuela
Population: 21,395,000
Area: 352,145 sq mi (912,050 sq km)
Pop. Density: 61/sq mi (23/sq km)
Capital: Caracas, 1,822,465

ZAMBIA
Official Name: Republic of the Zambia
Population: 8,809,000
Area: 290,587 sq mi (752,618 sq km)
Pop. Density: 30/sq mi (12/sq km)
Capital: Lusaka, 982,362

UNITED STATES
Official Name: United States of America
Population: 262,530,000
Area: 3,787,425 sq mi (9,809,431 sq km)
Pop. Density: 69/sq mi (27/sq km)
Capital: Washington, D.C., 606,900

VIETNAM
Official Name: Socialist Republic of Vietnam
Population: 73,760,000
Area: 127,428 sq mi (330,036 sq km)
Pop. Density: 579/sq mi (223/sq km)
Capital: Hanoi, 905,939

ZIMBABWE
Official Name: Republic of Zimbabwe
Population: 11,075,000
Area: 150,872 sq mi (390,757 sq km)
Pop. Density: 73/sq mi (28/sq km)
Capital: Harare (Salisbury), 681,000

Legend

Continental and regional coverage of the world's land areas is provided by the following section of physical-political reference maps. The section falls into a continental arrangement: North America, South America, Europe, Africa, Asia, and Oceania. Introducing each regional reference map section are several basic thematic maps.

To aid the reader in understanding the relative sizes of continents and of some of the countries and regions, uniform scales for comparable areas were used as far as possible. Most of the world is covered by a series of regional maps at scales of 1:16,000,000 and 1:12,000,000. Maps at 1:10,000,000 provide even greater detail for parts of Europe. The United States and parts of South America are mapped at 1:4,000,000.

Many of the symbols used are self-explanatory. A complete legend below provides a key to the symbols on the reference maps in the atlas.

The color tints on the maps depict the varying elevations and depths of land areas and bodies of water. The Relief legend that accompanies each map shows the specific elevation or depth that each color tint represents.

The surface configuration is represented by hill-shading, which gives the three-dimensional impression of landforms. This terrain representation is superimposed on the layer tints to convey a realistic and readily visualized impression of the surface. The combination of altitudinal tints and hill-shading best shows elevation, relief, steepness of slope, and ruggedness of terrain.

If the world used one alphabet and language, no particular difficulty would arise in understanding place-names. However, some of the people of the world, the Chinese and the Japanese, for example, use non-alphabetic languages. Their symbols are transliterated into the Roman alphabet. In this atlas, a "local-name" policy generally was used for naming cities, towns, and all local topographic and water features. However, for a few major cities the Anglicized name was preferred and the local name given in parentheses: for instance, Moscow (Moskva), Vienna (Wien), Bangkok (Krung Thep). In countries where more than one official language is used, a name appears in the dominant local language. The generic parts of local names for topographic and water features are self-explanatory in many cases because of the associated map symbols or type styles. A complete list of foreign generic names is given in the Glossary.

Physical-Political Reference Map Legend

Cultural Features

Political Boundaries

International
(Demarcated, Undemarcated, and Administrative) (over water)

Disputed de facto

Claim Boundary

Indefinite or Undefined

Secondary, State, Provincial, etc. (over water)

Parks, Indian Reservations

City Limits ▪ Urbanized Areas

▫ Neighborhoods, Sections of City

Populated Places

⊙ 1,000,000 and over

◎ 250,000 to 1,000,000

⊙ 100,000 to 250,000

• 25,000 to 100,000

◦ 0 to 25,000

TŌKYŌ National Capitals

Boise Secondary Capitals

Note: On maps at 1:20,000,000 and smaller the town symbols do not follow the specific population classification shown above. On all maps, type size indicates the relative importance of the city.

Transportation

Railroads

Railroads
On 1:1,000,000 scale maps

Railroad Ferries

Roads

Major
On 1:1,000,000 scale maps
Other

Major
On 1:4,000,000 scale maps
Other

On other scale maps

Caravan Routes

✈ Airports

Other Cultural Features

Dams

Pipelines

▲ Points of Interest

∴ Ruins

Land Features

△ Peaks, Spot Heights

= Passes

Sand

Contours

Water Features

Lakes and Reservoirs

Fresh Water

Fresh Water: Intermittent

Salt Water

Salt Water: Intermittent

Other Water Features

Salt Basins, Flats

Swamps

Ice Caps and Glaciers

Rivers

Intermittent Rivers

Aqueducts and Canals

Ship Channels

Falls

Rapids

Springs

△ Water Depths

Fishing Banks

Sand Bars

Reefs

Note: Country populations used throughout the atlas are 1995 estimates based on U.S. Census Bureau figures and other available information. City populations reflect the latest available official data.

ARCTIC OCEAN

ZEML'A FRANCA-IOSIFA
NOVAJA ZEML'A
Barents Sea
Karskoje More
More Laptevych
NOVOSIBIRSKIJE OSTROVA

• Noril'sk
Arctic Circle
• Anadyr'

R U S S I A
• Jenisej
Lena
• Jakutsk

SWEDEN
FINLAND
Helsinki
• Archangel'sk
Ob'
60°
Bering Sea
ALEUTIAN IS. (U.S.)

SANKT-PETERBURG
MOSKVA
• Jekaterinburg
Sea of Okhotsk
OSTROV SACHALIN
• Petropavlovsk-Kamcatskij

EST.
LAT.
LITH.
BELA.
• Niznij Novgorod
URAL'SKIJE GORY

E U R O P E
POLAND
UKRAINE
KYIV
Volga
• Karaganda
K A Z A K H S T A N
Aral Sea
A S I A
• Novosibirsk

Ozero Bajkal
MONGOLIA
Harbin

SLVK.
HUNG.
MOLD.
ROM.
Caspian Sea
UZBEK.
KYRG.
ALTAI
GOBI

ITALY
BOS.
BUL.
Black Sea
Gora El'brus 5633
GEOR.
ARM.
AZER.
Taskent
TAJIK.
TURKMENISTAN
C H I N A
BEIJING PEKING
Sea of Japan
KOREA
SEOUL
JAPAN
OSAKA
TOKYO

GREECE
TURKEY
Istanbul
SYRIA
IRAN
AFGHANISTAN
HIMALAYA
Xi'an
Yellow Sea
Japan

MALTA
Sea
ISRAEL
JORDAN
IRAQ
KUWAIT
Tehrān
Chongqing
Wuhan
SHANGHAI

LIBYA
AL-QĀHIRAH
CAIRO
EGYPT
SAUDI ARABIA
QATAR
UNITED ARAB EMIRATES
OMAN
PAKISTAN
Karāchi
DELHI
NEPAL
Mount Everest 8848
BHU.
BNGL.
CALCUTTA
Guangzhou
HONG KONG (U.K.)
TAIWAN
PACIFIC OCEAN
WAKE ISLAND (U.S.)

Red Sea
Tropic of Cancer
I N D I A
MYANMAR BURMA
South
China
Sea
Philippine Sea
MANILA
GUAM (U.S.)

CHAD
SUDAN
Al-Khartūm
ERITREA
YEMEN
Aden
BOMBAY
Arabian Sea
Madras
Bay of Bengal
THAILAND
VIETNAM
Krung Thep
Bangkok
CAMB.
PHILIPPINES
MICRONESIA

CEN. AFR. REP.
ETHIOPIA
DJIBOUTI
SOMALIA
SRI LANKA
Colombo
BRUNEI
MALAYSIA
Singapore

UGANDA
KENYA
Nairobi
MALDIVES
Equator
SUMATRA
BORNEO
SULAWESI
INDONESIA
PAPUA NEW GUINEA
SOLOMON ISLANDS
KIRIBATI
TUVALU

Muqdisho
Lake Victoria
Kilimanjaro 5895
SEYCHELLES
JAKARTA
NEW GUINEA
MELANESIA

CONGO
ZAIRE
Kinshasa
RWANDA
BURUNDI
TANZANIA
CHAGOS ARCHIPELAGO (B.I.O.T.)
JAWA
TIMOR
Port Moresby
SOLOMON ISLANDS
VANUATU

Luanda
ANGOLA
ZAMBIA
I N D I A N
CHRISTMAS ISLAND (Austl.)
NEW CALEDONIA (Fr.)
FIJI

NAMIBIA
ZIMBABWE
MOZAMBIQUE
MADAGASCAR
Mozambique Channel
O C E A N
MAURITIUS
REUNION (Fr.)
Cairns
Coral Sea

BOTSWANA
Johannesburg
SWAZILAND
Tropic of Capricorn
A U S T R A L I A
Brisbane

LESOTHO
SOUTH AFRICA
Durban
Perth
Sydney

Cape Town
CAPE OF GOOD HOPE
Mount Kosciusko 2230
Melbourne
Tasman Sea
NEW ZEALAND

TASMANIA
Wellington

ÎLES KERGUELEN (F.S.A.T.)

Antarctic Circle

ENDERBY LAND
WILKES LAND

A N T A R C T I C A

Copyright © by Rand McNally & Co.
Map prepared by Rand McNally & Co.
C-510000-264

Kilometers
0   1000   2000   3000 Km.
Miles
0   1000   2000   3000 Mi.

Robinson Projection

WORLD TERRAIN

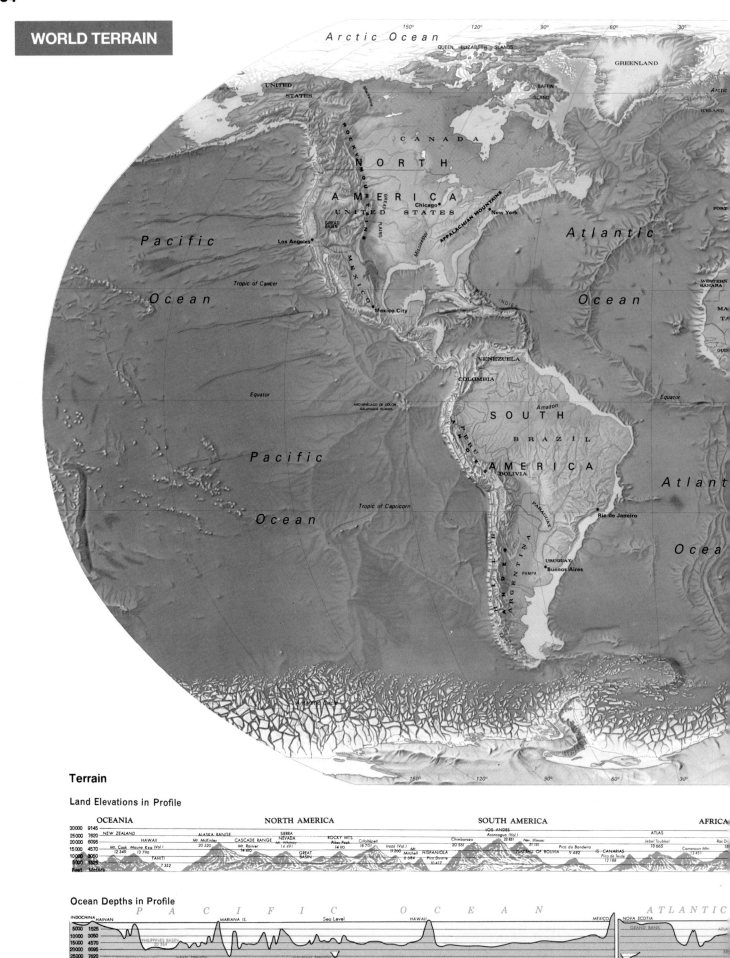

Terrain

Land Elevations in Profile

Ocean Depths in Profile

Arctic Ocean

30° 60° 90° 120° 150°

Arctic Circle

NORWAY
SWEDEN
FINLAND
RUSSIA
Ob'
Moscow
Volga
Berlin
POLAND
BELARUS
GERMANY
EUROPE
UKRAINE
ris
ITALY
Rome
Black Sea
Mediterranean Sea
TURKEY
KAZAKHSTAN
A S I A
MONGOLIA
GOBI
TURKMENISTAN
SYRIA
ISRAEL
Tehran
Qolleh-ye
IRAQ
IRAN
CHINA
Beijing
JAPAN
Tokyo
Cairo
EGYPT
SAUDI
ARABIA
PAKISTAN
HIMALAYA
Ganges
INDIA
BNGL
Calcutta
Shanghai
Pacific
Ocean
LIBYA
NIGER
CHAD
SUDAN
Red Sea
Nile
AFRICA
NIGERIA
CENTRAL
AFRICAN
REPUBLIC
ETHIOPIA
SOMALIA
Tropic of Cancer
Bombay
THAILAND
VIETNAM
CAMB
PHILIPPINES
GABON
CONGO
ZAIRE
RIFT
TANZANIA
Lake
Victoria
VALLEY
MALAYSIA
Congo
Equator
Jakarta
INDONESIA
PAPUA
NEW GUINEA
Equator
ANGOLA
ZAMBIA
ZIMBABWE
MADAGASCAR
MOZAMBIQUE
Indian
NAMIBIA
KALAHARI
DESERT
BOTSWANA
GREAT
SANDY
DESERT
JAVA
Tropic of Capricorn
Ocean
SOUTH
AFRICA
Cape Town
GREAT
VICTORIA
DESERT
AUSTRALIA
GREAT DIVIDING RANGE
Sydney
NEW
ZEALAND
Antarctic Circle
ARCTICA
A-510000-792-1

30° 60° 90° 120° 150°

Scale

| 0 | 1000 | 2000 Mi. |
| 0 | 1000 | 2000 Km. |

©1990 Rand McNally & Co.

EUROPE
ASIA
OCEANIA

ALPS
PYRENEES
Mt. Blanc
15 771
Pico de Aneto
11 168
KJÖLEN
Glittertinden
8110
Etna (Vol.)
10 902
CAUCASUS
Gora Elbrus
18 510
ELBURZ
Damāvand
18 386
Dj. esh-Shaikh
(Hermon)
9 232
PAMIRS
K2
28 250
Everest
29 028
Kanchenjunga
28 208
Gongga Shan
24 790
SUMATRA
BORNEO
NEW GUINEA
7620 25000
9145 30000
Fuji-San
(Vol.)
12 388
Klyuchevskaya
15 584
Kinabalu
13 455
Mt. Apo
9692
Puncak Jaya 4570 15000
Semeru
12 060
6095 20000
MADAGASCAR
omokotro
9436
Hekla (Vol.)
4 892
Narodnaya
6 217
IRAN
Pāmāmāgala
86 141M.A.
PLATEAU OF TIBET
HIMALAYA
GOBI DESERT
JAVA
PHILIPPINES
AUSTRALIA
Semeru
12 060
G. Kerinci
12 467
Mt. Kosciuszko 1525 5000
3050 10000
Meters Feet

FRANCE
GIBRALTAR
MALTA
ISRAEL
MEDITERRANEAN SEA
INDIAN OCEAN
Sea Level
SOEMBA
ARCTIC OCEAN
NORTH POLE
PACIFIC OCEAN
SOUTH POLE
LITTLE AMERICA
n feet
A Section along 10°S. Lat
1525 5000
3050 10000
4570 15000
6095 20000
7620 25000
9145 30000
10670 35000
Meters Feet

World Climate

World Climate Zones

Tropical

	Tropical rain forest
	Tropical savanna

Dry

	Steppe
	Desert

Temperate - Mild and rainy winter

	Mediterranean
	Humid subtropical
	Marine West Coast

Temperate - Cold and snowy winter

	Humid continental, warm summer
	Humid continental, cool summer
	Subarctic

Polar

	Tundra
	Ice cap
	Highlands

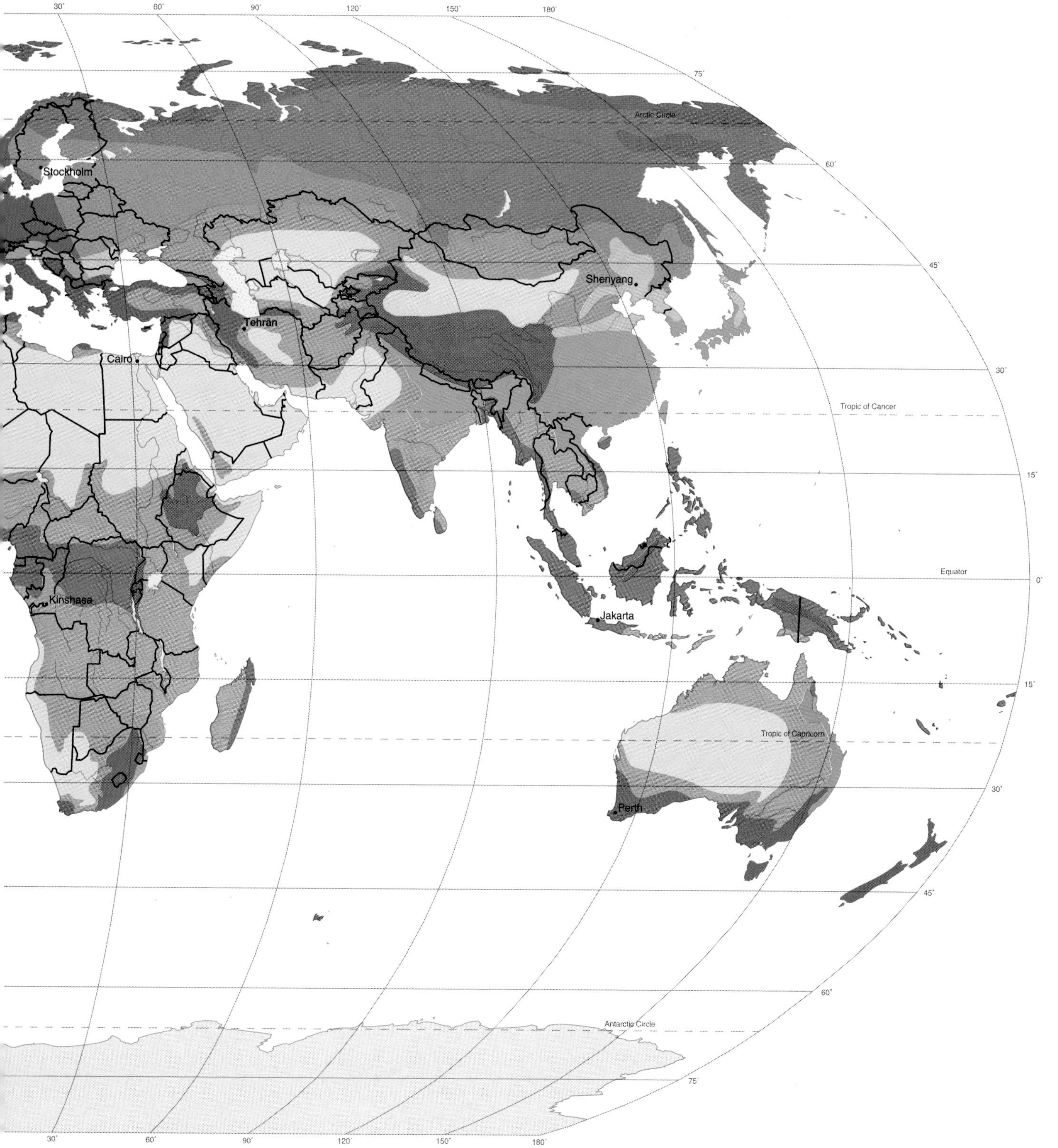

30° 60° 90° 120° 150° 180° 75°

Arctic Circle

60°

Stockholm

45°

Shenyang

Tehrān

30°

Cairo

Tropic of Cancer

15°

Kinshasa

Equator 0°

Jakarta

15°

Tropic of Capricorn

Perth

30°

45°

60°

Antarctic Circle

75°

30° 60° 90° 120° 150° 180°

Tinted areas show temperature in degrees Fahrenheit. Vertical bars show precipitation in inches.

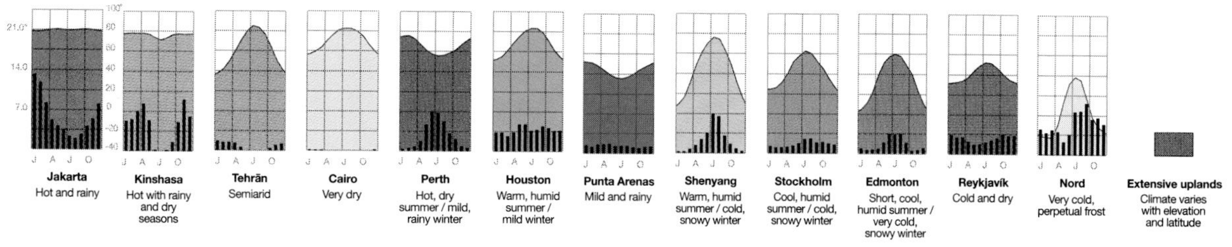

Jakarta Hot and rainy	
Kinshasa Hot with rainy and dry seasons	
Tehrān Semiarid	
Cairo Very dry	
Perth Hot, dry summer / mild, rainy winter	
Houston Warm, humid summer / mild winter	
Punta Arenas Mild and rainy	
Shenyang Warm, humid summer / cold, snowy winter	
Stockholm Cool, humid summer / cold, snowy winter	
Edmonton Short, cool, humid summer / very cold, snowy winter	
Reykjavik Cold and dry	
Nord Very cold, perpetual frost	
Extensive uplands Climate varies with elevation and latitude	

World Vegetation

© Rand McNally & Co.
M-510000-8N-EL1-•-5-•-7

Arctic Circle
Tropic of Cancer
Equator
Tropic of Capricorn
Antarctic Circle

ROCKY MOUNTAINS
Great Plains
APPALACHIAN MTS.
New York
Mexico City
Amazon Basin
ANDES MOUNTAINS
Rio de Janeiro
Buenos Aires
Patagonia

Vegetation Regions

Tropical and sub-tropical forests

Savanna

Desert

Mediterranean

Temperate grassland

S i b e r i a

URALS

Moscow

Arctic Circle

ALPS

Balkan
Peninsula

Beijing

Tōkyō

Cairo

ra

Arabian
Peninsula

Tropic of Cancer

HIMALAYAS

Equator

Congo
Basin

MADAGASCAR

Great Sandy
Desert

Tropic of Capricorn

Johannesburg

Sydney

Melbourne

Antarctic Circle

Temperate forest

Taiga (northern
forests)

Tundra (lichen
and moss)

Mountain

Polar and high
mountain

World Population

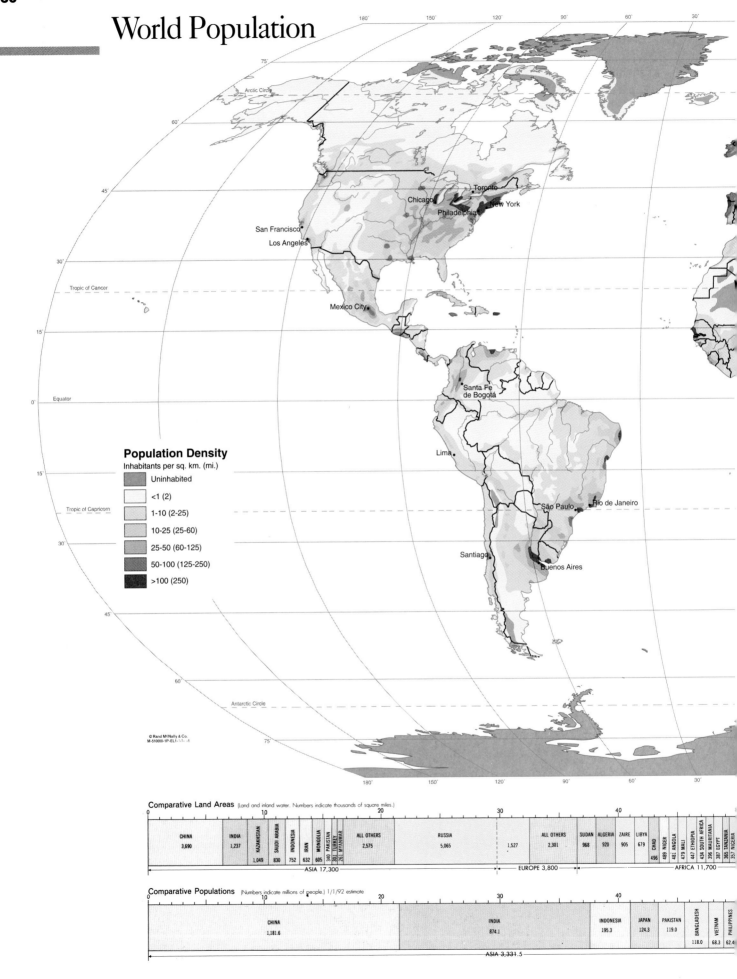

Population Density
Inhabitants per sq. km. (mi.)

	Uninhabited
	<1 (2)
	1-10 (2-25)
	10-25 (25-60)
	25-50 (60-125)
	50-100 (125-250)
	>100 (250)

Arctic Circle
Tropic of Cancer
Equator
Tropic of Capricorn
Antarctic Circle

Toronto
Chicago
New York
Philadelphia
San Francisco
Los Angeles
Mexico City
Santa Fe de Bogotá
Lima
São Paulo
Rio de Janeiro
Santiago
Buenos Aires

© Rand McNally & Co.
M-510000-1P-EL1-1-1-1--1

Comparative Land Areas (Land and inland water. Numbers indicate thousands of square miles.)

CHINA 3,690	INDIA 1,237	KAZAKHSTAN 1,049	SAUDI ARABIA 830	INDONESIA 752	IRAN 632	MONGOLIA 605	PAKISTAN 340	TURKEY 301	MYANMAR 261	ALL OTHERS 2,575	RUSSIA 5,065	1,527	ALL OTHERS 2,301	SUDAN 968	ALGERIA 920	ZAIRE 905	LIBYA 679	CHAD 496	NIGER 489	ANGOLA 481	MALI 479	ETHIOPIA 447	SOUTH AFRICA 434	MAURITANIA 396	EGYPT 387	TANZANIA 365	NIGERIA 357

ASIA 17,300
EUROPE 3,800
AFRICA 11,700

Comparative Populations (Numbers indicate millions of people.) 1/1/92 estimate

CHINA 1,181.6	INDIA 874.1	INDONESIA 195.3	JAPAN 124.3	PAKISTAN 119.0	BANGLADESH 118.0	VIETNAM 68.3	PHILIPPINES 62.4

ASIA 3,331.5

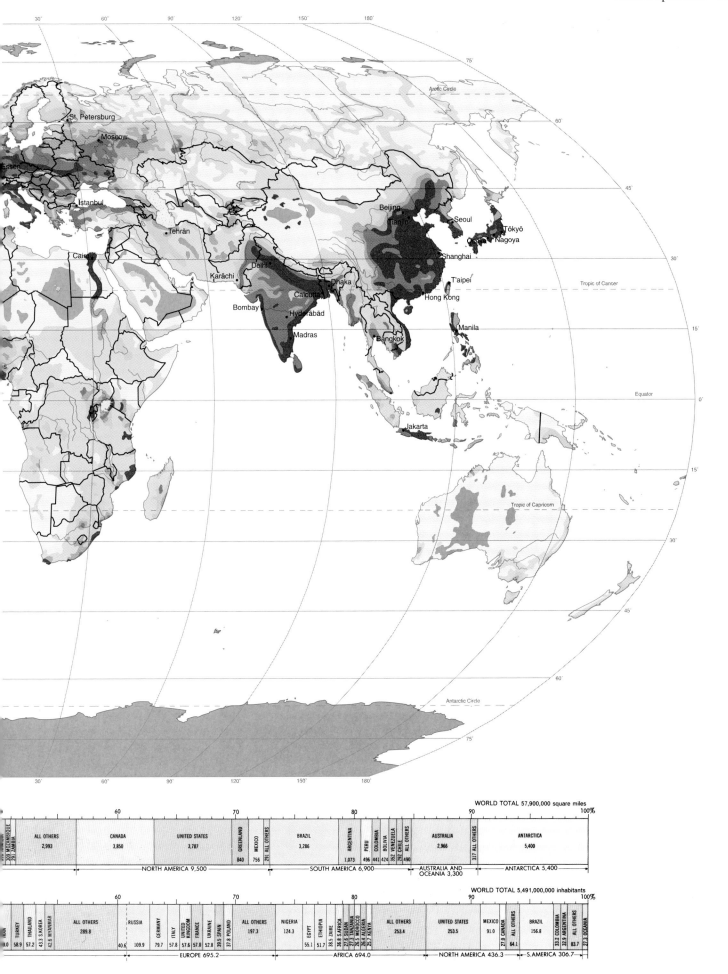

WORLD TOTAL 57,900,000 square miles

	60		70			80					90		100%

| MOZAMBIQUE 303 | ZAMBIA 291 | ALL OTHERS 2,993 | CANADA 3,850 | UNITED STATES 3,787 | GREENLAND 840 | MEXICO 756 | ALL OTHERS 291 | BRAZIL 3,286 | ARGENTINA 1,073 | PERU 496 | BOLIVIA 424 | VENEZUELA 352 | CHILE 292 | ALL OTHERS 490 | AUSTRALIA 2,966 | ALL OTHERS 317 | ANTARCTICA 5,400 |

NORTH AMERICA 9,500 — SOUTH AMERICA 6,900 — AUSTRALIA AND OCEANIA 3,300 — ANTARCTICA 5,400

WORLD TOTAL 5,491,000,000 inhabitants

	60		70			80					90		100%

| PAKISTAN 0.0 | TURKEY 58.9 | THAILAND 57.2 | S.KOREA 43.3 | MYANMAR 42.6 | ALL OTHERS 289.8 | RUSSIA 40.6 | GERMANY 109.9 | ITALY 79.7 | UNITED KINGDOM 57.8 | FRANCE 57.6 | UKRAINE 57.0 | SPAIN 52.8 | POLAND 39.5 | 37.8 | ALL OTHERS 197.3 | NIGERIA 124.3 | EGYPT 55.1 | ETHIOPIA 51.7 | ZAIRE 38.5 | S.AFRICA 36.8 | SUDAN 27.6 | TANZANIA 26.5 | MOROCCO 26.4 | ALGERIA 25.7 | KENYA 25.7 | ALL OTHERS 253.4 | UNITED STATES 253.5 | MEXICO 91.0 | CANADA 27.0 | ALL OTHERS 64.1 | BRAZIL 156.8 | COLOMBIA 33.2 | ARGENTINA 32.9 | ALL OTHERS 83.7 | OCEANIA 27.3 |

EUROPE 695.2 — AFRICA 694.0 — NORTH AMERICA 436.3 — S.AMERICA 306.7

World Environments

Environments

Urban

Cropland

Cropland, woodland

Cropland, grazing land

Grassland, grazing land

© Rand McNally & Co.
M-510000-8L-EL1-1- - -1

Forest, woodland	Swamp, marsh	Tundra	Shrub, sparse grass, wasteland	Barren land

Time Zones

▨	Standard time zone of even-numbered hours from Greenwich time
▨	Standard time zone of odd-numbered hours from Greenwich time
▨	Time varies from the standard time zone by half an hour
▨	Time varies from the standard time zone by other than half an hour

h m	hours, minutes

GREENWICH MERIDIAN

Scale (approx.) 1:125,000,000 1 inch equals 1,975 miles
Mercator Projection
True scale only on the Equator
Encyclopaedia Britannica, Inc. 039

U.S. Naval Oceanographic Office
A-510000-1T74   -11-11-19

The standard time zone system, fixed by international agreement and by law in each country, is based on a theoretical division of the globe into 24 zones of 15° longitude each. The mid-meridian of each zone fixes the hour for the entire zone. The zero time zone extends 7½° east and 7½° west of the Greenwich meridian, 0° longitude. Since the earth rotates toward the east, time zones to the west of Greenwich are earlier, to the east, later.

Plus and minus hours at the top of the map are added to or subtracted from local time to find Greenwich time. Local standard time can be determined for any area in the world by adding one hour for each time zone counted in an easterly direction from one's own, or by subtracting one hour for each zone counted in a westerly direction. To separate one day from the next, the 180th meridian has been designated as the international date line. On both sides of the line the time of day is the same, but west of the line it is one day later than it is to the east. Countries that adhere to the international zone system adopt the zone applicable to their location. Some countries, however, establish time zones based on political boundaries, or adopt the time zone of a neighboring unit. For all or part of the year some countries also advance their time by one hour, thereby utilizing more daylight hours each day.

North America

North America is the world's third-largest continent, covering an area of 9.5 million square miles (24.7 million sq km). It lies primarily between the Arctic Circle and the Tropic of Cancer, and comes within 500 miles (800 km) of both the North Pole and the Equator. The continent's western flank is dominated by the spectacular Rocky Mountains. Covering vast stretches of the central United States and Canada are the fertile Great Plains, a large part of which is drained by the Mississippi River and its tributaries.

In the north, Hudson Bay is frozen for much of the year. Mexico, located in the continent's southern third, is mostly mountainous and dry, but farther south, the climate is wet. Many of the small Central American countries have volcanoes along the Pacific Coast.

North America at a glance

Land area: 9,500,000 square miles (24,700,000 sq km)

Estimated population (January 1, 1995): 453,300,000

Population density: 48/square mile (18/sq km)

Mean elevation: 2,000 feet (610 m)

Highest point: Mt. McKinley, Alaska, U.S. 20,230 feet (6,194 m)

Lowest point: Death Valley, California, U.S., 282 feet (86 m) below sea level

Longest river: Mississippi-Missouri, 3,740 mi (6,019 km)

Number of countries (incl. dependencies): 38

Largest independent country: Canada, 3,849,674 square miles (9,970,610 sq km)

Smallest independent country: St. Kitts and Nevis, 101 square miles (261 sq km)

Most populous independent country: United States, 262,530,000

Least populous independent country: St. Kitts and Nevis, 44,000

Largest city: Mexico City, pop. 8,235,744 (1990)

Coldest place: Northice, Greenland -87°F (-66° C)

Highest point: Mt. McKinley, Alaska 20,230 ft (6,194 m)

Wettest place: Henderson Lake, British Columbia 256 inches (650 cm)/year

Lowest point: Death Valley, California 282 ft (86 m) below sea level

Hottest place: Death Valley, California 134°F (57°C)

Driest place: Bataques, Mexico 1.2 inches (3 cm)/year

Landforms

- Mountains
- Widely spaced mountains
- High tablelands
- Hills and low tablelands
- Plains
- Depresssions, basins
- High tablelands and ice caps
- Mountains and ice caps

© Rand McNally & Co.
M-520000-7C-EL1- - - -

Lake Louise in the Canadian Rockies

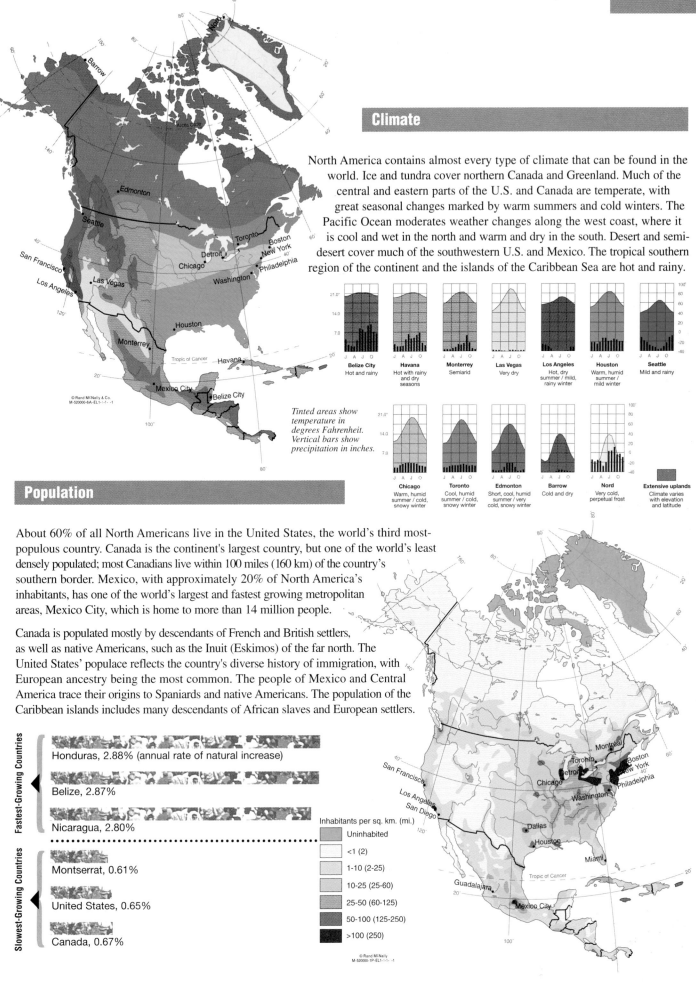

Climate

North America contains almost every type of climate that can be found in the world. Ice and tundra cover northern Canada and Greenland. Much of the central and eastern parts of the U.S. and Canada are temperate, with great seasonal changes marked by warm summers and cold winters. The Pacific Ocean moderates weather changes along the west coast, where it is cool and wet in the north and warm and dry in the south. Desert and semi-desert cover much of the southwestern U.S. and Mexico. The tropical southern region of the continent and the islands of the Caribbean Sea are hot and rainy.

Tinted areas show temperature in degrees Fahrenheit. Vertical bars show precipitation in inches.

Belize City — Hot and rainy

Havana — Hot with rainy and dry seasons

Monterrey — Semiarid

Las Vegas — Very dry

Los Angeles — Hot, dry summer / mild, rainy winter

Houston — Warm, humid summer / mild winter

Seattle — Mild and rainy

Chicago — Warm, humid summer / cold, snowy winter

Toronto — Cool, humid summer / cold, snowy winter

Edmonton — Short, cool, humid summer / very cold, snowy winter

Barrow — Cold and dry

Nord — Very cold, perpetual frost

Extensive uplands — Climate varies with elevation and latitude

© Rand McNally & Co.
M-520000-6A-EL1-1-1- -1

Population

About 60% of all North Americans live in the United States, the world's third most-populous country. Canada is the continent's largest country, but one of the world's least densely populated; most Canadians live within 100 miles (160 km) of the country's southern border. Mexico, with approximately 20% of North America's inhabitants, has one of the world's largest and fastest growing metropolitan areas, Mexico City, which is home to more than 14 million people.

Canada is populated mostly by descendants of French and British settlers, as well as native Americans, such as the Inuit (Eskimos) of the far north. The United States' populace reflects the country's diverse history of immigration, with European ancestry being the most common. The people of Mexico and Central America trace their origins to Spaniards and native Americans. The population of the Caribbean islands includes many descendants of African slaves and European settlers.

Fastest-Growing Countries

Honduras, 2.88% (annual rate of natural increase)

Belize, 2.87%

Nicaragua, 2.80%

Slowest-Growing Countries

Montserrat, 0.61%

United States, 0.65%

Canada, 0.67%

Inhabitants per sq. km. (mi.)

Uninhabited
<1 (2)
1-10 (2-25)
10-25 (25-60)
25-50 (60-125)
50-100 (125-250)
>100 (250)

© Rand McNally
M-520000-1P-EL1-1-1- -1

Environments and Land Use

Although only 12% of the continent is suitable for agriculture, North America is the world's leading food producer. Unlike other parts of the world, famine is virtually unknown. Large quantities of food, such as grains from the central U.S. and Canada, are exported worldwide. Sixteen percent of the continent is used for grazing, and the livestock raised on these lands are also an important source of food at home and abroad.

Forests cover one-third of the land, and the timber and paper industries are important to the U.S. and Canada. The continent has an extremely long coastline, and many countries send great fishing fleets to sea. This is especially true of Canada, whose eastern-most provinces are fittingly known as the "Maritime Provinces." However, sharp declines in catches due to over-fishing have put the industry in economic turmoil.

Blue waters, sunny skies, and idyllic beaches draw millions of tourists to the Caribbean each year. While tourism provides income for island countries that have few other assets, the economic gap between the visitors and the people who serve them remains dramatic.

One of the greatest challenges facing North America in the coming decades is a familiar one: coping with a growing population and dwindling resources. Pollution and the environment are divisive issues. Although the United States has begun to clean up its air and water, economic pressures will continue to be an argument for a relaxation of policies. Meanwhile, in Mexico, environmental issues have been pushed aside by concerns about the economy and the exploding population.

Urban

Cropland

Cropland and woodland

Cropland and grazing land

Grassland, grazing land

Forest, woodland

Swamp, marsh

Tundra

Shrub, sparse grass, wasteland

Barren land

© Rand McNally & Co.
M-520000-8L-EL1-!-!- -!

0	200	400	600	800	1000 Miles
0	300	600	900	1200	1500 Kilometers

Field of corn in the midwestern United States

Urbanization in North America

Seen from the air, large portions of North America still bear the checkerboard imprint left by the people who settled the continent: a vast array of small farms that could be worked by one man and a horse. As industrialization swept through the United States in the second half of the 19th century, many farmers left their farms. Great numbers moved to fast-growing cities such as Chicago and St. Louis. Many small towns saw their populations dwindle.

In the cities, change was continuous. The former farm families were joined by waves of European immigrants. Over the next 100 years, urban populations con- tinued to grow, and cities that had once been separate became part of vast urban megalopolises. An example can be seen in the eastern United States, where a band of urban centers stretches almost continuously from Boston south through New York City to Washington D.C. (see map at right).

After World War II, as the U. S. middle class expanded, large numbers of fami- lies moved out of the city centers into suburban communities of mass-pro- duced, affordable homes. Many of those who remained were economically disad- vantaged. A shrinking tax base meant that cities could not support their infra- structures, and conditions in the inner cities worsened. In the suburbs the opposite was true: vast sums were spent building new roads, houses, and shopping centers.

The same process that transformed the U.S. is now occurring in Mexico. In 1945, 25% of the population was considered urban, but today the figure surpasses 70% (see graph above). Not content to lead lives as subsistence farmers, scores of Mexicans arrive in the cities each day in search of jobs that will enable them to provide a better life for their families.

Sadly, these dreams are often elusive. Most of the people end up in low-paying jobs, with their meager wages going to pay for the food that they once grew themselves. City officials are hard-pressed to provide clean water to their ever-growing populations, let alone electricity, trans- portation and education.

As elsewhere in the world, coping with the pressures of growing popu- lations is one of the greatest challenges facing North Americans today.

Rising Urban Population
Urban population as a percentage of total population, 1900-2000 (estimated)

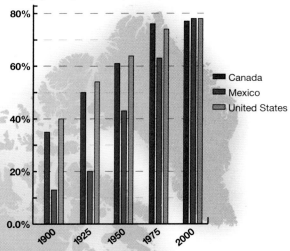

- Canada
- Mexico
- United States

(The definition of "urban" varies from country to country. In Canada, all towns with more than 1,000 people are considered urban, while in the U.S. and Mexico only towns with more than 2,500 people are defined as urban.)

Urban Centers

50,000-99,999 people

100,000-500,000 people

Over 500,000 people

© Rand McNally
M-520000-9E-EL1-¹-¹- -1

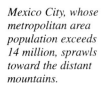

Mexico City, whose metropolitan area population exceeds 14 million, sprawls toward the distant mountains.

Scale 1:40 000 000; one inch to 630 miles. Lambert's Azimuthal Equal Area Projection
Elevations and depressions are given in feet

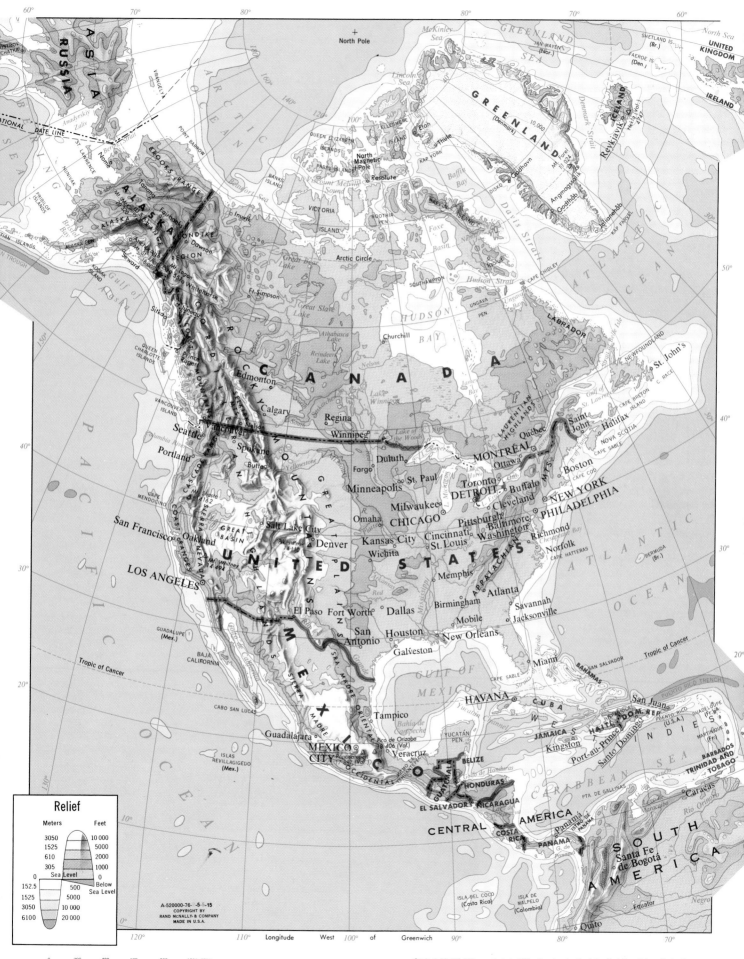

Relief

Meters	Feet
3050	10 000
1525	5000
610	2000
305	1000
0 Sea Level	0
	Below
152.5	Sea Level
	500
1525	5000
3050	10 000
6100	20 000

A-520000-76- -5-5-15
COPYRIGHT BY
RAND McNALLY & COMPANY
MADE IN U.S.A.

Scale 1:40 000 000; one inch to 630 miles. Lambert's Azimuthal Equal Area Projection
Elevations and depressions are given in feet

Scale 1: 12 000 000; one inch to 190 miles. Conic Projection
Elevations and depressions are given in feet

Longitude West of Greenwich

Scale 1:12 000 000; one inch to 190 miles. Polyconic Proje

Elevations and depressions are given in feet

Cities
and
Towns

0 to 50,000

50,000 to 500,000

500,000 to 1,000,000

1,000,000 and over

40,000 SQ MI
AREA

0   100   200

Miles

Scale 1:12 000 000; one inch to 190 miles. Polyconic Proje

Elevations and depressions are given in feet

Meters		Feet
3050		10 000
1525		5000
610		2000
305		1000
152.5		500
0	Sea Level	0
		Below
152.5		500 Sea Level
1525		5 000
3050		10 000
6100		20 000

Relief

Cities
and
Towns

0 to 50,000   500,000 to 1,000,000

50,000 to 500,000   1,000,000 and over

50 75 100   200   300   400   500 Miles

100   200   400   600   800 Kilometers

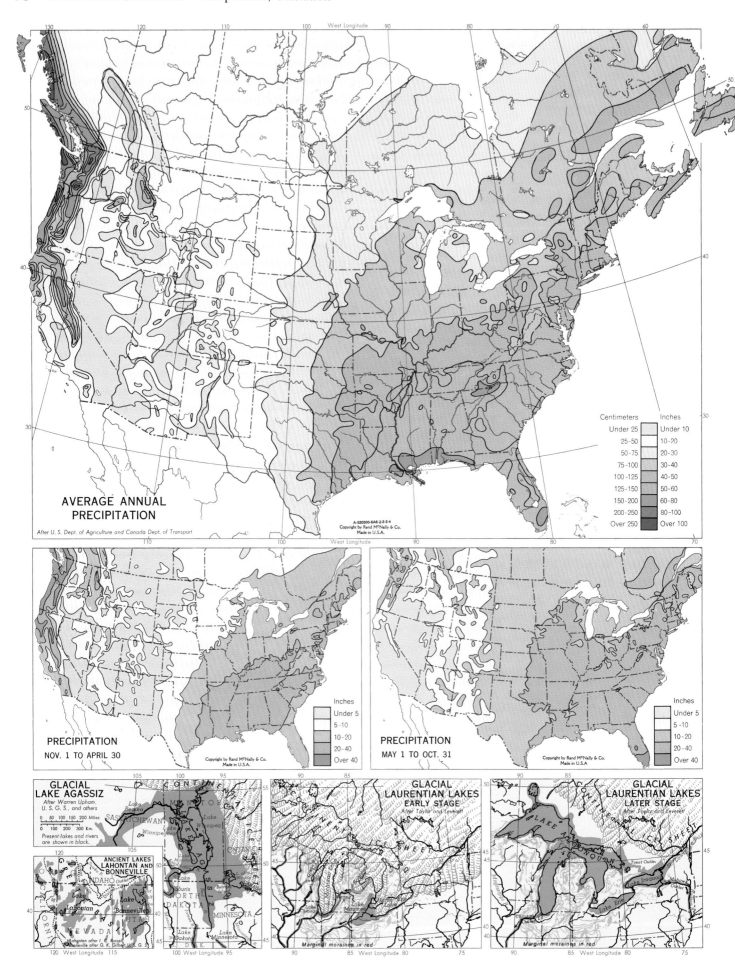

AVERAGE ANNUAL
PRECIPITATION

After U.S. Dept. of Agriculture and Canada Dept. of Transport

A-580500-6A6-2-2-2-4
Copyright by Rand McNally & Co.
Made in U.S.A.

Centimeters	Inches
Under 25	Under 10
25–50	10–20
50–75	20–30
75–100	30–40
100–125	40–50
125–150	50–60
150–200	60–80
200–250	80–100
Over 250	Over 100

PRECIPITATION

NOV. 1 TO APRIL 30

Copyright by Rand McNally & Co.
Made in U.S.A.

Inches
Under 5
5–10
10–20
20–40
Over 40

PRECIPITATION

MAY 1 TO OCT. 31

Copyright by Rand McNally & Co.
Made in U.S.A.

Inches
Under 5
5–10
10–20
20–40
Over 40

GLACIAL
LAKE AGASSIZ
*After Warren Upham,
U. S. G. S., and others*

0 50 100 150 200 Miles
0 100 200 300 Km.

*Present lakes and rivers
are shown in black.*

ANCIENT LAKES
LAHONTAN AND
BONNEVILLE

*Lahontan after I. C. Russell
Bonneville after G. K. Gilbert, U. S. G. S.*

GLACIAL
LAURENTIAN LAKES
EARLY STAGE
After Taylor and Leverett

Marginal moraines in red

GLACIAL
LAURENTIAN LAKES
LATER STAGE
After Taylor and Leverett

Marginal moraines in red

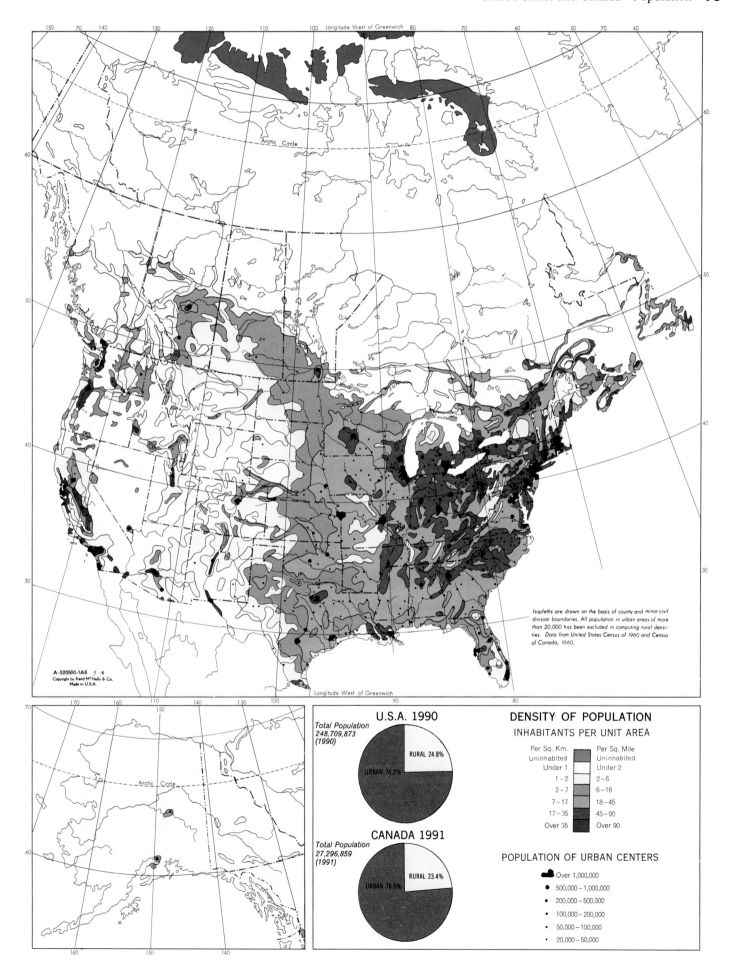

Longitude West of Greenwich

Arctic Circle

60

50

40

30

60

50

40

30

Isopleths are drawn on the basis of county and minor civil division boundaries. All population in urban areas of more than 20,000 has been excluded in computing rural densities. Data from United States Census of 1960 and Census of Canada, 1960.

A-520500-1A6 -5 -6
Copyright by Rand McNally & Co.
Made in U.S.A.

Longitude West of Greenwich

Arctic Circle

U.S.A. 1990

Total Population
248,709,873
(1990)

RURAL 24.8%

URBAN 75.2%

CANADA 1991

Total Population
27,296,859
(1991)

RURAL 23.4%

URBAN 76.6%

DENSITY OF POPULATION
INHABITANTS PER UNIT AREA

Per Sq. Km.	Per Sq. Mile
Uninhabited	Uninhabited
Under 1	Under 2
1–2	2–6
2–7	6–18
7–17	18–45
17–35	45–90
Over 35	Over 90

POPULATION OF URBAN CENTERS

Over 1,000,000

500,000 – 1,000,000

200,000 – 500,000

100,000 – 200,000

50,000 – 100,000

20,000 – 50,000

Scale 1: 32 000 000; One inch to 500 miles.   LAMBERT CONFORMAL CONIC PROJECTION

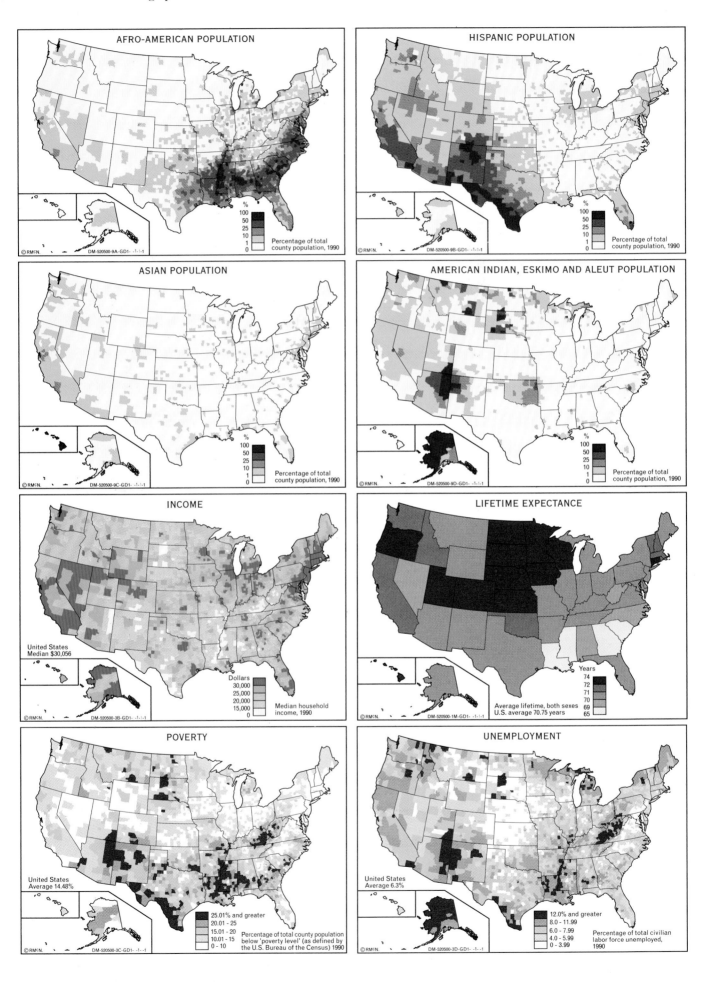

AFRO-AMERICAN POPULATION

%
100
50
25
10
1
0

Percentage of total
county population, 1990

HISPANIC POPULATION

%
100
50
25
10
1
0

Percentage of total
county population, 1990

ASIAN POPULATION

%
100
50
25
10
1
0

Percentage of total
county population, 1990

AMERICAN INDIAN, ESKIMO AND ALEUT POPULATION

%
100
50
25
10
1
0

Percentage of total
county population, 1990

INCOME

United States
Median $30,056

Dollars
30,000
25,000
20,000
15,000
0

Median household
income, 1990

LIFETIME EXPECTANCE

Years
74
72
71
70
69
65

Average lifetime, both sexes
U.S. average 70.75 years

POVERTY

United States
Average 14.48%

25.01% and greater
20.01 - 25
15.01 - 20
10.01 - 15
0 - 10

Percentage of total county population
below 'poverty level' (as defined by
the U.S. Bureau of the Census) 1990

UNEMPLOYMENT

United States
Average 6.3%

12.0% and greater
8.0 - 11.99
6.0 - 7.99
4.0 - 5.99
0 - 3.99

Percentage of total civilian
labor force unemployed,
1990

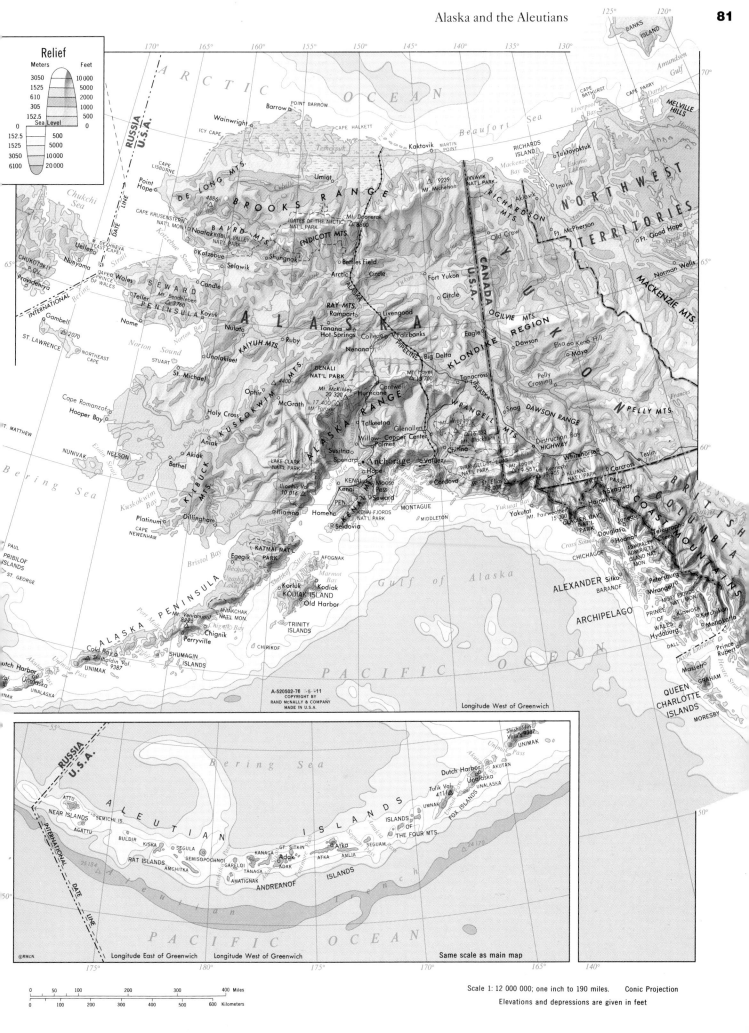

Relief

Meters	Feet
3050	10 000
1525	5000
610	2000
305	1000
152.5	500
0	0

Sea Level

152.5	500
1525	5000
3050	10 000
6100	20 000

ARCTIC OCEAN

Beaufort Sea

RUSSIA
U.S.A.

Chukchi Sea

Point Barrow
Barrow
Wainwright
ICY CAPE
CAPE HALKETT
Kaktovik
MARTIN POINT

CAPE LISBURNE
Point Hope
Umiat
Mt. Michelson △9239

RICHARDS ISLAND
Tuktoyaktuk
Inuvik

NORTHWEST TERRITORIES

DE LONG MTS.
△4886
BROOKS RANGE
BAIRD MTS.
ENDICOTT MTS.
Mt. Doonerak △7610
Mt. Chamberlin △9020

RICHARDSON MTS.
Aklavik
Old Crow
Ft. McPherson
Ft. Good Hope
Great Bear Lake

MELVILLE HILLS

CAPE KRUSENSTERN NAT'L MON.
Noatak
KOBUK VALLEY NAT'L PARK
GATES OF THE ARCTIC NAT'L PARK
Shungnak
Bettles Field

YUKON REGION
OGILVIE MTS.
Dawson
Elsa oo Keno Hill
Mayo

MACKENZIE MTS.
Norman Wells

Kotzebue
Selawik
Candle
Arctic
Circle
Circle
Fort Yukon
Eagle

M. DEZHNEVA
CAPE PRINCE OF WALES
Cape Wales
Teller
SEWARD PENINSULA
Mt. Bendeleben △3760
Nome
Koyuk
Nulato
Ruby
Tanana
Rampart
RAY MTS.
Livengood
College Fairbanks
Nenana
Big Delta

KLONDIKE
Tanacross Tok
Shag
DAWSON RANGE
PELLY MTS.
Destruction Bay HIGHWAY
Whitehorse
Teslin

ALASKA

Uelleno
Chukotski P.O.V.
Providenya
Gambell
ST. LAWRENCE △2070
NORTHEAST CAPE

St. Michael
Unalakleet
Ophir
McGrath
KAIYUH MTS.
KUSKOKWIM MTS. △4400

DENALI NAT'L PARK
Mt. McKinley 20 320
Mt. Foraker 17 400
Hurricane
Cantwell

Mt. Hayes △13 700

WRANGELL MTS.

ST. MATTHEW
Cape Romanzof
Hooper Bay
Holy Cross
ALASKA RANGE
Talkeetna
Willow Palmer
Glenallen
Copper Center
Chitina
Mt. Wrangell △14 163
Mt. Blackburn
WRANGELL-ST. ELIAS NAT'L PARK
Mt. Logan 19 550
KLUANE NAT'L PARK
Carcross
Skagway

BRITISH COLUMBIA

COAST MOUNTAINS

NUNIVAK
NELSON
Aniak
Akiak
Bethel
KILBUCK MTS.
LAKE CLARK NAT'L PARK
Iliamna Vol. 10 016
Susitna
Spenard
Anchorage
Hope
KENAI
Moose Pass
Valdez
Cordova
Mt. St. Elias 18 008

Bering Sea

PAUL
PRIBILOF ISLANDS
ST. GEORGE

Platinum
CAPE NEWENHAM
Dillingham
Iliamna
Homer
Seldovia
KENAI FJORDS NAT'L PARK
MONTAGUE
MIDDLETON
Yakutat
Mt. Fairweather 15 300
GLACIER BAY NAT'L PARK
Haines
Juneau
Douglas
Hoonah

Kenai
PEN.
Seward

Gulf of Alaska

ALEXANDER
Sitka
BARANOF
CHICHAGOF
ADMIRALTY ISLAND NAT'L MON.
Petersburg
Wrangell
MISTY FJORDS NAT'L MON.

Bristol Bay
KATMAI NAT'L PARK
Egegik
Becharof Lake
Ugashik Lakes
ANIAKCHAK NAT'L MON.
Chignik
Perryville
SHUMAGIN ISLANDS
Cold Bay
Shishaldin Vol. 9387
UNIMAK

Korluk
Kodiak
KODIAK ISLAND
Old Harbor
AFOGNAK
Marmot Bay
TRINITY ISLANDS
CHIRIKOF

ARCHIPELAGO
PRINCE OF WALES
Hydaburg
DALL

QUEEN CHARLOTTE ISLANDS
MORESBY

ALASKA PENINSULA
Mt. Veniaminof △8225
Dutch Harbor
Unalaska

A-520502-76 -5 -11
COPYRIGHT BY
RAND McNALLY & COMPANY
MADE IN U.S.A.

Longitude West of Greenwich

PACIFIC OCEAN

RUSSIA
U.S.A.

Bering Sea

ALEUTIAN ISLANDS

ATTU
NEAR ISLANDS
AGATTU
SEMICHI IS.
BULDIR
KISKA
SEGULA
RAT ISLANDS
AMCHITKA
SEMISOPOCHNOI
GARELOI
TANAGA
AMATIGNAK
KANAGA
GT. SITKIN
Adak
ADAK
ANDREANOF ISLANDS
ATKA
Atka
AMLIA
SEGUAM
ISLANDS OF THE FOUR MTS.
UMNAK
Tulik Vol. 4111
Shishaldin Vol. △9387
UNIMAK
Dutch Harbor
AKUTAN
Unalaska
FOX ISLANDS
UNALASKA

PACIFIC OCEAN

INTERNATIONAL DATE LINE

Longitude East of Greenwich
Longitude West of Greenwich
Same scale as main map

0 50 100 200 300 400 Miles
0 100 200 300 400 500 600 Kilometers

124° 122° 120° 118° 116°

BRITISH COLUMBIA

CANADA
U.S.A.

VANCOUVER ISLAND

Strait of Georgia

Nanaimo
Ladysmith
Duncan
Esquimalt
Victoria
CAPE FLATTERY
MAKAH IND. RES.
Cape Flattery
Strait of Juan de Fuca
Port Angeles
Port Townsend

N. Vancouver
Vancouver
New Westminster
Steveston
Blaine
Lynden
Chilliwack

Bellingham
SAN JUAN ISLANDS
Anacortes
Sedro Woolley
Concrete
Newhalem
Mt. Baker 10,778
Ross Lake

Grand Forks
Rossland
Trail
Oroville
Northport
Porthill
Troy
Libby

CABINET MTS.

Mount Vernon
Arlington
TULALIP IND. RES.
Everett
Snohomish
Monroe
Kirkland
Bellevue

Glacier Peak 10,541
Lake Chelan
Okanogan
COLVILLE IND. RES.
Republic
Colville
KALISPEL IND. RES.
Chewelah
Newport
Sandpoint
Priest Lake
Lake Pend Oreille
Bonners Ferry

OLYMPIC MTS.
OLYMPIC NATIONAL PARK
Mt. Olympus 7965
QUINAULT IND. RES.
Moclips

SEATTLE
Tacoma
Lakewood Center
Auburn
Puyallup
Carbonado
Enumclaw

Cascade Tunnel
Leavenworth
Cashmere
Wenatchee
ROCK ISLAND DAM
Chelan
Waterville
Mansfield
WELLS DAM
GRAND COULEE DAM

Davenport
Spokane
Deer Park
SPOKANE IND. RES.
Medical Lake
Cheney
Spirit Lake
Opportunity
Coeur d'Alene
Kellogg
Wallace
Mullan
Thompson Falls
COEUR D'ALENE IND. RES.
St. Maries

PACIFIC OCEAN

Grays Harbor
Hoquiam
Aberdeen
Montesano
Cosmopolis
Elma
Olympia

Shelton

WASHINGTON

Ellensburg
Roslyn
Cle Elum
Yakima
Ephrata
Moses Lake
Ritzville
Odessa
Crab Cr.
Colfax
Pullman
Moscow
Palouse
Elk River
Tekoa

Willapa Bay
Raymond
South Bend
Centralia
Chehalis
Castle Rock
Warrenton
Astoria
Longview
Kelso
Rainier
Kalama
Ilwaco

Columbia R.

Mt. Rainier 14,410
MOUNT RAINIER NATIONAL PARK

Mt. St. Helens 8307
Mt. Adams 12,276
YAKIMA INDIAN RESERVATION
Toppenish
Sunnyside
Prosser
Kennewick
Richland
Pasco
Wallula

PRIEST RAPIDS DAM
LOWER MONUMENTAL DAM
LITTLE GOOSE DAM
LOWER GRANITE DAM
Pomeroy
ICE HARBOR DAM
Waitsburg
Dayton
Walla Walla
Clarkston
Lewiston
NEZ PERCE IND. RES.
Winchester
Nez Perce
Asotin

Seaside
Saint Helens
Scappoose

Vancouver
Camas
Gresham
Portland
Oregon City
W. Linn
Milwaukie
Lake Oswego
Hillsboro
Forest Grove
Beaverton
McMinnville
Newberg
Sheridan
Dallas
Independence
Salem
Silverton
Woodburn

Goldendale
JOHN DAY DAM
BONNEVILLE DAM
The Dalles
THE DALLES DAM
Wasco
Hood River
Mt. Hood 11,239

McNARY DAM
Milton-Freewater
Pendleton
UMATILLA IND. RES.
Elgin
Heppner
Condon

Wallowa
Enterprise
BLUE MOUNTAINS
La Grande
Union
WALLOWA MTS.
HELLS CANYON
New Meadows
Baker

CLEARWATER MOUNTAINS
Grangeville

Newport
Toledo
Corvallis
Albany
Lebanon

WARM SPRINGS IND. RES.
Mt. Jefferson 10,497
Detroit
Green Peter Lake

OREGON

John Day
Prineville
Bend
PRINEVILLE RES.
Burns
Vale
Ontario
Payette
Weiser
Emmett
Caldwell
Nampa
Boise

IDAHO

SALMON R.

Reedsport
Cottage Grove
Diamond Peak 8744
Crescent Lake
Waldo Lake
Lookout Pt. Lake
Cougar Res.
Crane Prairie Res.
Wickiup Res.
Eugene
Springfield

GREAT SANDY DESERT
HARNEY BASIN
Harney Lake
Malheur Lake
Lake Owyhee
BEULAH RES.
WARM SPRS. RES.
C.J. STRIKE RES.
Mountain Home
Glenns Ferry

Coos Bay
North Bend
Coos Bay
Coquille
Bandon
Myrtle Point
CAPE BLANCO
Roseburg

CRATER LAKE NATIONAL PARK
Mt. Scott 8926
Crater Lake
Lake Abert
Lake Summit
Sycan

OWYHEE MTS.
Paradise Valley
Midas
Tuscarora

Grants Pass
Medford
Ashland
Mt. McLoughlin 9495
OREGON CAVES NAT'L MON.
Klamath Falls

Lakeview
Paisley
WARNER MTS.
STEENS MTN.
FORT McDERMITT IND. RES.
DUCK VALLEY IND. RES.

Crescent City
Happy Camp
Yreka
KLAMATH MTS.
Lower Klamath Lake
LAVA BEDS NAT'L MON.
Clear Lake Res.
Goose Lake
Upper Lake
Lower Lake
Alturas
SUMMIT LAKE IND. RES.
PINE FOREST RA.
BLACK ROCK DESERT
SANTA ROSA RA.
INDEPENDENCE MTS.

HOOPA VALLEY IND. RES.
Weed
Mt. Shasta 14,162
Mt. Shasta
Dunsmuir
Eagle Peak 9892

CALIFORNIA
NEVADA

Arcata
Fieldbrook
Eureka
Humboldt Bay
Fortuna
Ferndale
Scotia
CAPE MENDOCINO
Weaverville

Redding
Anderson
LASSEN VOLCANIC NAT'L PARK
Lassen Peak (Vol.) 10,457
Eagle Lake

SMOKE CREEK DESERT
Winnemucca
Battle Mountain
Rye Patch Res.
Elko

A-520597-76
COPYRIGHT BY
RAND McNALLY & CO.
MADE IN U.S.A.

Scale 1: 4,000,000; one inch to 64 miles. Conic Projection
Elevations and depressions are given in feet

Longitude West of Greenwich

48° 46° 44° 42°

ALBERTA — CANADA — U.S.A. — SASKATCHEWAN

MONTANA

WYOMING

UTAH — COLO. — N. DAK.

Great Falls · Havre · Chinook · Harlem · Malta · Glasgow · Wolf Point · Poplar · Sidney · Williston · Grenora · Plentywood · Scobey · Opheim

Browning · Shelby · Cut Bank · Sunburst · Conrad · Valier · Choteau · Fort Benton · Winifred · Hogeland · Morgan

FORT PECK IND. RES. · Fort Peck Lake · Ft. Peck

BLACKFEET IND. RES. · ROCKY BOYS IND. RES. · FT. BELKNAP IND. RES.

Lewistown · Winnett · Roundup · Harlowton · White Sulphur Spgs. · Neihart · Belt · Townsend · Helena · East Helena · Deer Lodge

LITTLE BELT MTS. · BIG BELT MTS. · CRAZY MTS. · SWAN RANGE

Missoula · Lolo · Stevensville · Hamilton · Philipsburg · Anaconda · Butte · Walkerville · Three Forks · Bozeman · Livingston · Big Timber · Columbus · Laurel · Billings · Hardin · Huntley · Crow Agency · Lame Deer · Colstrip · Forsyth · Miles City · Terry · Glendive · Baker · Marmarth · Beach

CROW IND. RES. · NORTHERN CHEYENNE IND. RES. · CUSTER BATTLEFIELD NAT'L MON.

Red Lodge · Granite Peak 12 799 · Bear Creek · Electric Peak 10 992 · Gardiner · Mt. Washburn 10 243 · Mammoth Hot Springs

ABSAROKA RANGE · BIGHORN MOUNTAINS

YELLOWSTONE NATIONAL PARK · 7733 ft above sea level · Yellowstone Lake · Shoshone Lake · Hebgen Lake

BIG HOLE NAT'L BATTLEFIELD · PIONEER MTS. · Homer Youngs Peak 10 621 · Dillon · Twin Bridges · Ennis Lake

BEAVERHEAD MTS. · LEMHI RANGE · LOST RIVER RA. · Borah Pk. 12 662 · Mackay · Arco · Hyndman Peak 12 009

Salmon · Stevensville · NATIONAL BISON RANGE · Ronan · Flathead · Blackfoot

Sheridan · Buffalo · Gillette · Moorcroft · Sundance · DEVILS TOWER NAT'L MON.

Cloud Peak 13 167 · Basin · Greybull · Powell · Lovell · Cody · Worland · Ten Sleep · Gebo · Thermopolis · Kaycee · Midwest · Powder River

GRAND TETON NAT'L PARK · Grand Teton 13 770 · Jackson · WIND RIVER RANGE · Garnett Peak 13 804 · Fremont Peak 13 745 · Gannett Peak

WIND RIVER IND. RES. · Shoshoni · Riverton · Lander · Hudson

St. Anthony · Ashton · Rexburg · Rigby · Idaho Falls · Shelley · Blackfoot · Pocatello · American Falls · Rupert · Burley

CRATERS OF THE MOON NAT'L MON. · SNAKE RIVER PLAIN

American Falls Res. · FORT HALL IND. RES. · Blackfoot Reservoir

Soda Springs · Lava Hot Spgs. · Meade Peak 9957 · Afton · Montpelier

WIND RIVER RANGE · GREAT DIVIDE BASIN

Casper · Douglas · Orin · Glenrock · Powder River · Sweetwater · Pathfinder Res. · Alcova Res. · Seminoe Res. · Medicine Bow · Hanna · Rawlins · Wheatland

Kemmerer · Granger · Green River · Rock Springs · Superior · Fontenelle Res. · Flaming Gorge Res.

Malad City · Preston · Richmond · Smithfield · Logan · Providence · Wellsville · Brigham · Huntsville · Ogden · Morgan · Farmington · Bountiful · Murray · Salt Lake City · Midvale · Park City · Heber City · Midway

GREAT SALT LAKE DESERT · Great Salt Lake · Lucin · Wendover · Oakley · Tooele

BEAR RIVER RANGE · WASATCH RANGE · UINTA MTS. · Kings Peak 13 528 · Mt. Emmons 13 440

DINOSAUR NAT'L MON. · UINTAH AND OURAY IND. RES. · Vernal · Craig · Steamboat Spgs. · Oak Creek

PARK RANGE

Missouri R. · Milk R. · Marias R. · Teton R. · Sun R. · Musselshell · Bighorn Lake · Yellowstone · Powder R. · Green R. · Snake R. · Bear L.

Relief

Meters		Feet
3050		10000
1525		5000
610		2000
305		1000
152.5		500
0	Sea Level	0
1525		500

0 20 40 60 80 100 120 Miles
0 20 40 60 80 100 120 140 160 180 200 Kilometers

84

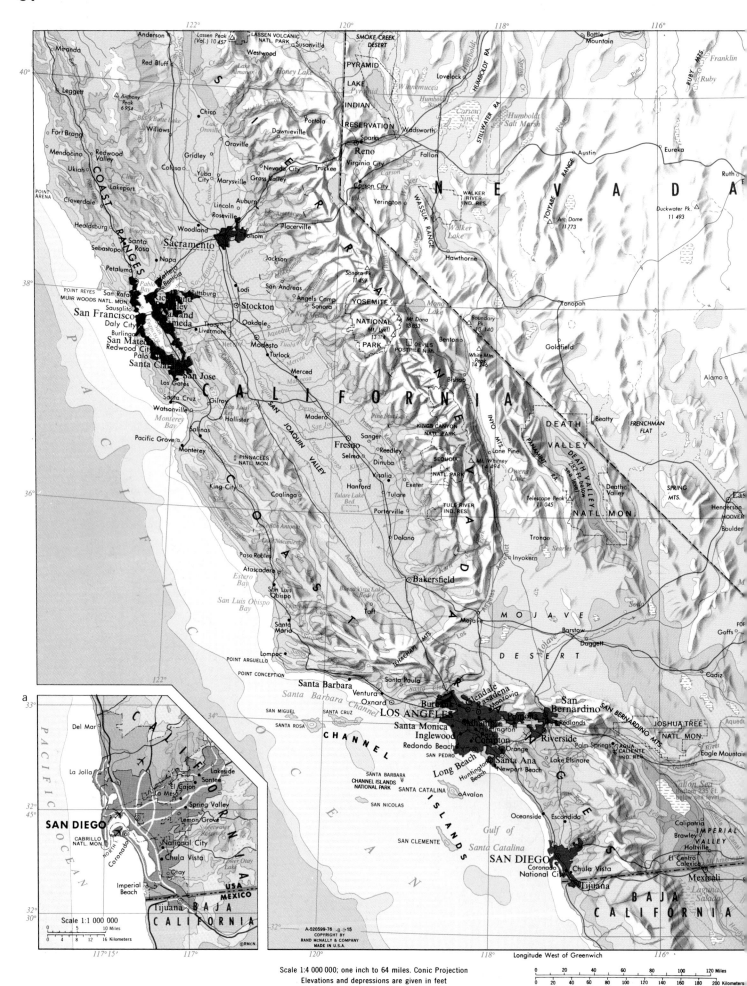

Scale 1:4 000 000; one inch to 64 miles. Conic Projection
Elevations and depressions are given in feet

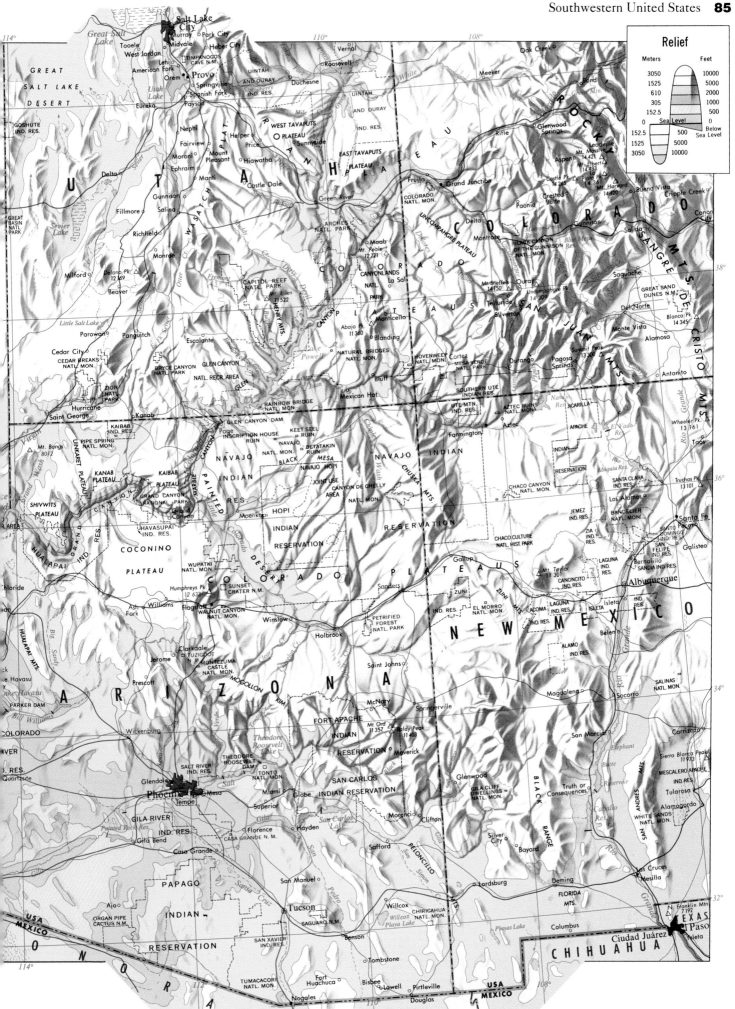

Relief

Meters	Feet
3050	10000
1525	5000
610	2000
152.5	500
0	Sea Level
152.5	500 Below
1525	5000 Sea Level
3050	10000

Relief

Meters		Feet
3050		10 000
1525		5000
610		2000
305		1000
152.5		500
0	Sea Level	0

Cities and Towns

0 to 50,000 ○
50,000 to 500,000 ⊙
500,000 to 1,000,000 ◉
1,000,000 and over

A-511006-76-   -7₁-11
COPYRIGHT BY
RAND McNALLY & COMPANY
MADE IN U.S.A.

Longitude West of Greenwich

Scale 1:4 000 000; one inch to 64 miles. Conic Projectio
Elevations and depressions are given in feet.

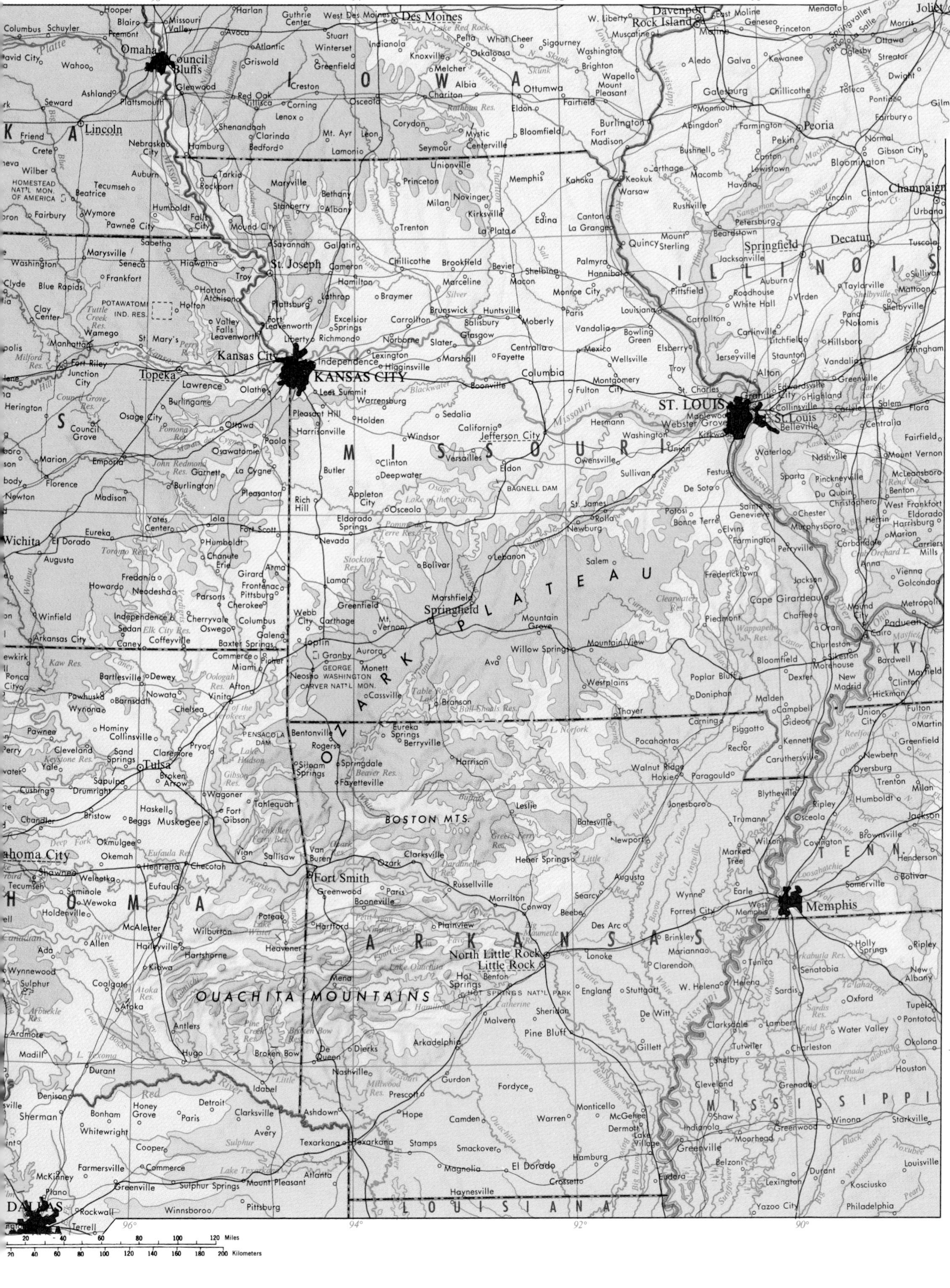

AURORA
CHICAGO
Joliet

96° 94° 92° 90° 88°

IOWA
ILLINOIS
MISSOURI
KANSAS
NEBRASKA
OKLAHOMA
ARKANSAS
LOUISIANA
MISSISSIPPI
TENN.
KY.

Omaha
Council Bluffs
Lincoln
Des Moines
West Des Moines
Davenport
Rock Island

St. Joseph
Kansas City
KANSAS CITY
Topeka
Lawrence

Springfield
Decatur

ST. LOUIS
St. Louis
Belleville

Jefferson City
Columbia

Wichita

Tulsa
Springfield
OZARK PLATEAU

Branson
Cape Girardeau
Cairo
Paducah

BOSTON MTS.

Fort Smith
OUACHITA MOUNTAINS

Memphis

North Little Rock
Little Rock
Hot Springs
HOT SPRINGS NAT'L PARK

oma City
DALLAS

Texarkana

Red River

20 40 60 80 100 120 Miles
20 40 60 80 100 120 140 160 180 200 Kilometers

40°
38°
36°
34°

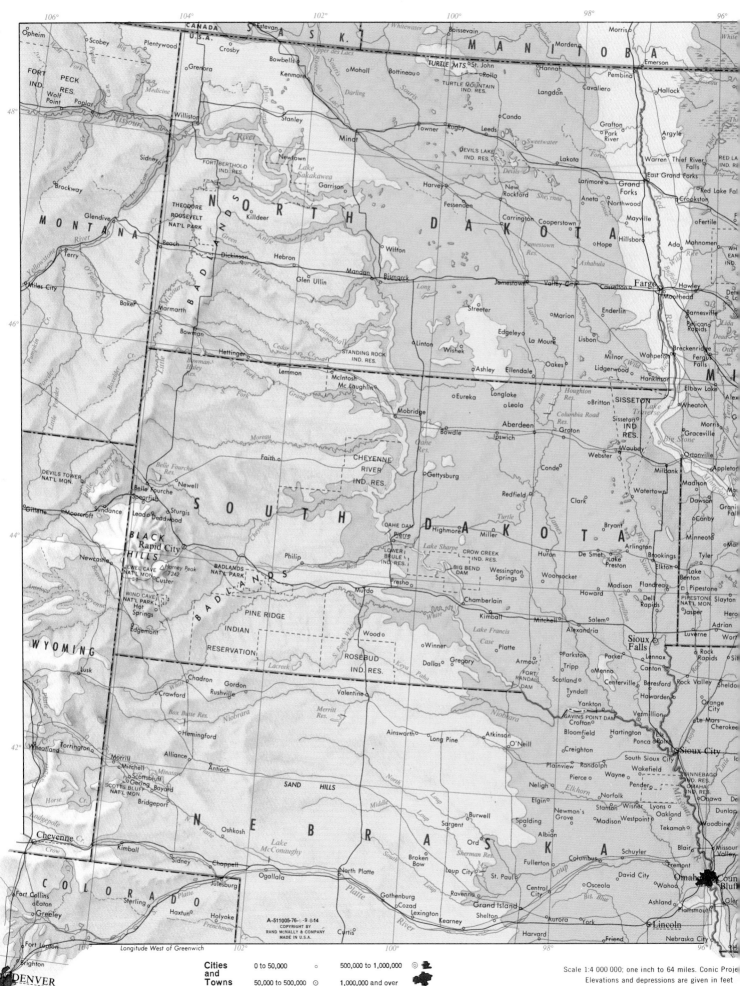

Cities
and
Towns

0 to 50,000 ○
50,000 to 500,000 ⊙
500,000 to 1,000,000 ◎
1,000,000 and over

A-511005-76- -9-8-14
COPYRIGHT BY
RAND McNALLY & COMPANY
MADE IN U.S.A.

Longitude West of Greenwich

Scale 1:4 000 000; one inch to 64 miles. Conic Projection
Elevations and depressions are given in feet

ONTARIO

Lake of the Woods

Rainy Lake

Fort Frances
International Falls

Thunder Bay

CANADA
U.S.A.

LAKE SUPERIOR
Surface elev. 600 Feet above Sea Level
Maximum depth 1333 Feet

ISLE ROYALE NAT'L PARK

Copper Harbor

GRAND PORTAGE NAT'L
GRAND PORTAGE IND. RES.

Sault Ste. Marie

MICHIPICOTEN NATIONAL PARK

Michipicoten Harbour

QUETICO PROVINCIAL PARK

VOYAGEURS PARK

NETT LAKE IND. RES.

GREATER LEECH LAKE IND. RES.

VERMILION RANGE

MISQUAH HILLS

Lower Red Lake

Cass Lake

Deer River
Grand Rapids
Coleraine
Nashwauk
Keewatin
Hibbing
Chisholm Buhl
Virginia Biwabik
Eveleth Gilbert Aurora

MESABI RANGE

Hill City

Silver Bay

Two Harbors

APOSTLE ISLANDS
SAND
OUTER
STOCKTON
MADELINE

RED CLIFF IND. RES.
Bayfield
BAD RIVER IND. RES.

Ontonagon

Calumet
Laurium Lake Linden
Hancock Houghton

Newberry

BAY MILLS IND. RES.

Trout Lake

GARDEN
HOG St. Ignace
Mackinaw City
BEAVER I. IND. RES.
Cheboygan

Duluth
Superior
Proctor
Cloquet
Carlton
FOND DU LAC IND. RES.

Washburn
Ashland

GOGEBIC RANGE

Bessemer Wakefield
Hurley Ironwood

MENOMINEE RANGE

Champion
L'Anse
BARAGA
L'ANSE VIEUX DESERT IND. RES.
Negaunee
Ishpeming
Marquette
Munising

M I C H I G A N

Aitkin
Crosby
Brainerd
MILLE LAC IND. RES.

Mille Lacs

Staples
Pelican
Long Prairie
Little Falls

Sandstone
Hayward
LAC COURT OREILLE IND. RES.

LAC DU FLAMBEAU IND. RES.

Iron River
Stambaugh Crystal Falls
Iron Mountain
Norway
Niagara

Gladstone
Escanaba

Manistique

Harbor Springs
Charlevoix
Petoskey

Milaca
Princeton
Cambridge

ST. CROIX IND. RES.
Cumberland
Spooner
Park Falls

Phillips
Rhinelander
Crandon
Wausaukee

Menominee
Marinette
Peshtigo
Oconto Falls Oconto

E. Jordan
Boyne City

Elk Rapids
Mancelona

Traverse City

Frankfort

MANITOU ISLANDS

L. Charlevoix
Grand Traverse Bay

St. Cloud
Sauk Rapids
Elk River
Anoka
Stillwater

Rush City
Pine City

Barron
Rice Lake
Chetek
Ladysmith
Rib Lake
Tomahawk
Antigo

DOOR PEN.

Jennings
Cadillac

Reed City

Big Rapids

MINNEAPOLIS
St. Louis Park St. Paul
Chaska South St. Paul
Shakopee Hastings
Glencoe
New Prague

Hudson
River Falls
Menomonie
Eau Claire
New Richmond
Bloomer
Chippewa Falls
Cornell
Stanley Owen
Stratford
Medford
Merrill
Marshfield
Schofield
Wausau

Shawano
STOCKBRIDGE MUNSEE IND. RES.

Clintonville
New London
De Pere
Green Bay

Kewaunee
Two Rivers
Manitowoc

Algoma

Sturgeon Bay

Manistee

Ludington

Hart Shelby

WISCONSIN

Neillsville
Wisconsin Rapids
Nekoosa
Stevens Point

Waupaca
Appleton
Menasha Neenah
Kaukauna

Lake Winnebago

Sheboygan
Sheboygan Falls

Whitehall

Muskegon Heights
Muskegon
Grand Haven
Grand Rapids
Greenville
Belding

Fremont
Newago

Holland

Allegan
Otsego

Northfield
Faribault
Kenyon
Zumbrota
Red Wing
Lake City
Wabasha
Alma
Durand
Augusta

New Ulm
St. Peter
Waterville
Waseca
Owatonna
Blooming Prairie
Winona
Galesville
Arcadia
Black River Falls
Sparta
Tomah
Adams
Wautoma
Omro
Oshkosh
Berlin
Ripon
Fond du Lac
Chilton
Kiel
Plymouth

Port Washington
Cedarburg

LAKE MICHIGAN
Surface elevation 579 Feet above Sea Level
Maximum depth 870 Feet

Rochester
Plainview
Chatfield
St. Charles
Preston
Caledonia
Westby
Viroqua

New Lisbon
Mauston
Wisconsin Dells
Montello
Princeton

Portage
Beaver Dam
Horicon
West Bend

Mequon
Whitefish Bay
Shorewood

MILWAUKEE
West Allis
Wauwatosa
Cudahy South Milwaukee

Racine
Kenosha

Waukegan
Zion
North Chicago
Lake Forest
Highland Park
Winnetka
Wilmette
Evanston

South Haven

Benton Harbor
St. Joseph

Dowagiac
Three Rivers
Niles
Sturgis

Kalamazoo

Hastings

Albert Lea
Austin
Northwood

Cresco
Decorah
Lansing
Waukon
Calmar
New Hampton
West Union
Fayette

EFFIGY MOUNDS NAT'L MON.
Prairie du Chien
McGregor
Guttenberg
Lancaster
Platteville
Darlington
Monroe

Madison
Jefferson
Fort Atkinson
Stoughton
Edgerton
Whitewater
Milton Elkhorn
Evansville
Janesville Delavan
Beloit
Lake Geneva
Walworth

Woodstock
Libertyville
Fort Sheridan

Forest City
Osage
Clear Lake
Mason City Charles City

Dodgeville
Mineral Point
Boscobel
Richland Center
Sauk City
Baraboo
Reedsburg
Columbus
Watertown
Oconomowoc

Hartford

Dubuque
Galena
Freeport
Rockford
Belvidere

Harvard

I O W A

Waterloo
Cedar Falls
Manchester
Dyersville
Monticello
Bellevue
Savanna
Oregon
Mt. Carroll
Dixon
Sterling
Rock Falls

Sycamore
De Kalb
Geneva Batavia
St. Charles
Aurora

Elgin
Joliet

CHICAGO
E. Chicago
Hammond
Gary

Michigan City
La Porte
Valparaiso

Hampton
Belmond
Clarion
Eagle Grove
Iowa Falls
Eldora
Marshalltown
Toledo
Tama

Cedar Rapids
Marion
Anamosa
Maquoketa

Clinton
De Witt
Tipton
Morrison

Crown Point
Lowell
N. Judson

Webster City
Grundy Center
Reinbeck
La Porte City
Vinton
Belle Plaine
Marengo

Davenport
Rock Island Moline
Muscatine
Geneseo

Rochelle
Princeton
La Salle
Mendota
Peru
Ottawa
Morris

DES MOINES
West Des Moines
Colfax
Newton
Grinnell

Iowa City
West Liberty

Aledo
Kewanee
Galva

Marseilles
Streator
Pontiac
Dwight

Lowell
Kankakee
Watseka

Rensselaer
Kentland
Monticello
Fowler

Indianola
Winterset
Greenfield
Knoxville
Oskaloosa
Sigourney
Washington
Brighton
Wapello

What Cheer

Springvalley
Oglesby

Chillicothe Minonk
Fairbury Gilman

IND.

Creston
Osceola
Chariton
Albia
Melcher
Red Rock
Fairfield
Mt. Pleasant

Galesburg
Monmouth
Abingdon
Farmington

Peoria

ILLINOIS

Mt. Ayr
Leon
Lamoni
Corydon
Centerville
Mystic
Seymour
Bloomfield
Eldon
Ottumwa
Burlington
Fort Madison

Relief

Meters		Feet
1525		5000
610		2000
305		1000
152.5		500
0	Sea Level	0
152.5		500

0 20 40 60 80 100 120 Miles
0 20 40 60 80 100 120 140 160 180 200 Kilometers

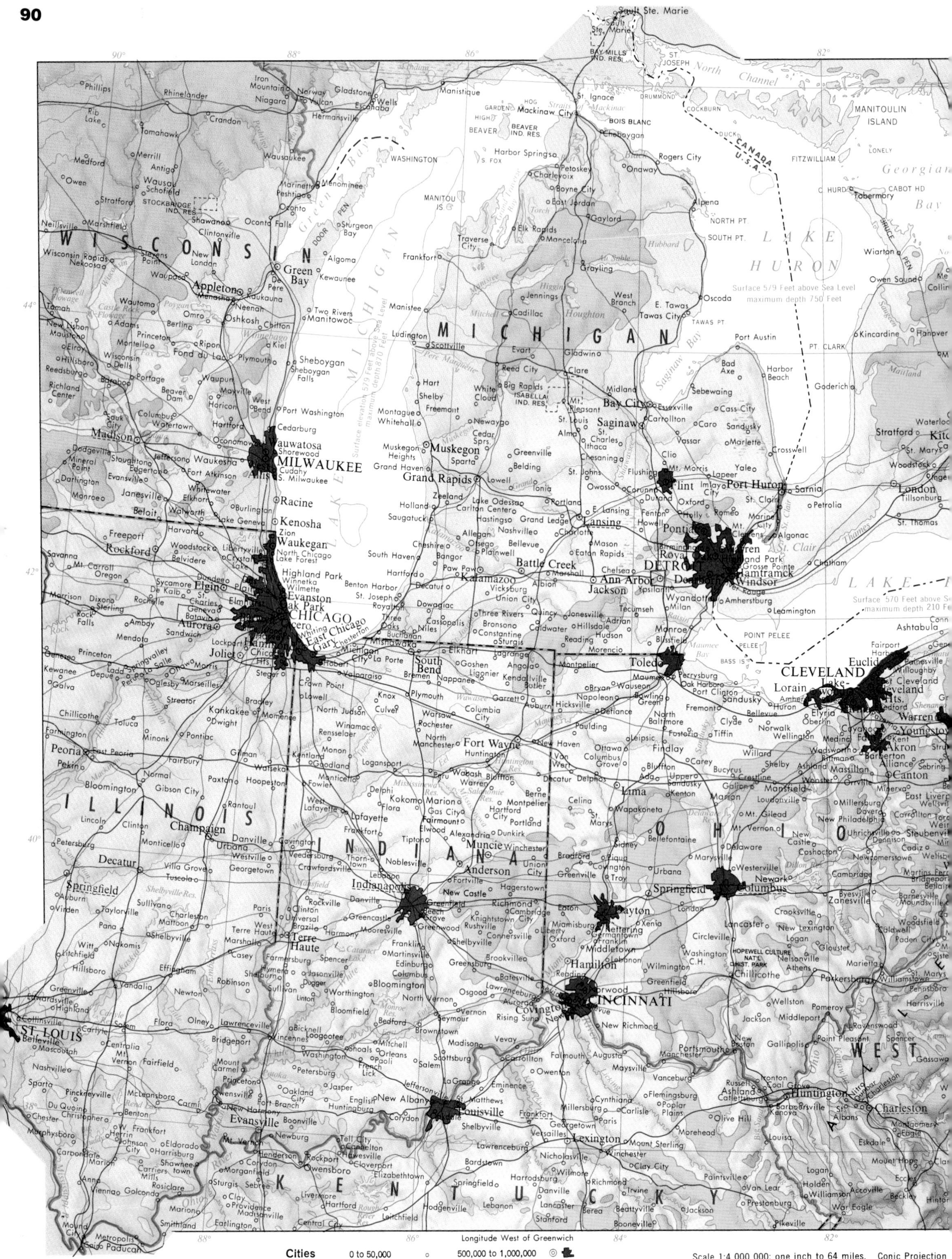

WISCONSIN
MICHIGAN
ILLINOIS
INDIANA
OHIO
KENTUCKY
WEST

LAKE HURON
Surface 5/9 Feet above Sea Level
maximum depth 750 Feet

LAKE ERIE
Surface 570 Feet above Sea Level
maximum depth 210 Feet

MANITOULIN ISLAND
Georgian Bay

MILWAUKEE
CHICAGO
DETROIT
CLEVELAND
CINCINNATI
INDIANAPOLIS
Columbus
ST. LOUIS
Louisville

Green Bay
Madison
Grand Rapids
Lansing
Toledo
Fort Wayne
Dayton
Springfield
Peoria
Rockford
Flint
Port Huron
Saginaw
Bay City
Kalamazoo
Ann Arbor
Windsor
Akron
Canton
Youngstown
Warren
Lorain
Elyria
Euclid

Longitude West of Greenwich

Cities and Towns

| | 0 to 50,000 | ○ | 500,000 to 1,000,000 | ◎ |
| | 50,000 to 500,000 | ⊙ | 1,000,000 and over | ✦ |

Scale 1:4 000 000; one inch to 64 miles. Conic Projection
Elevations and depressions are given in feet

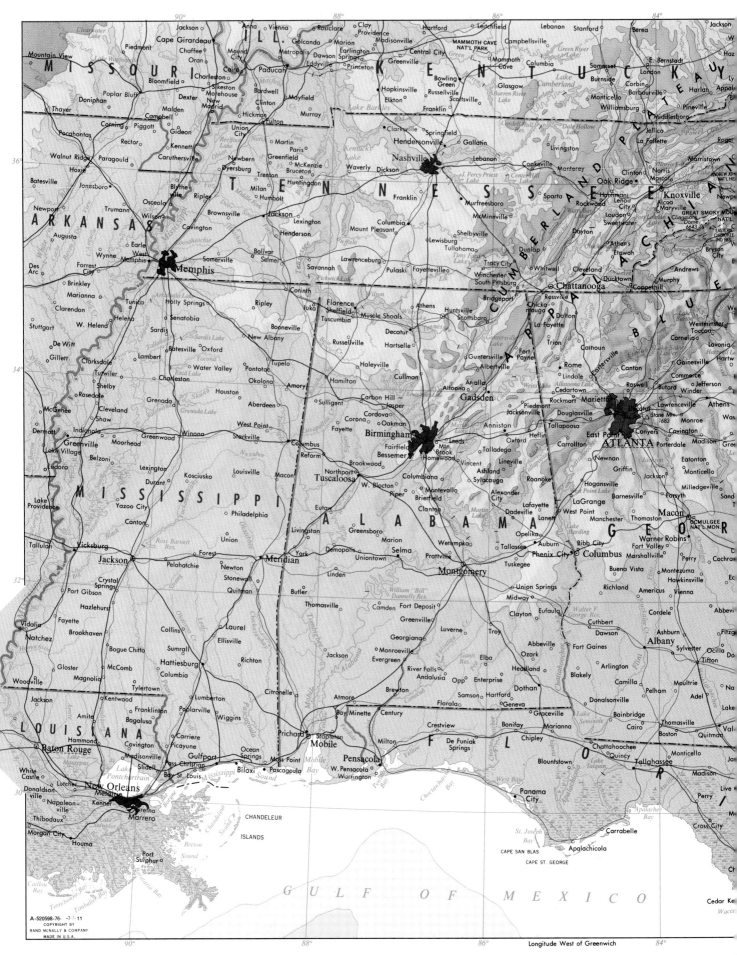

Scale 1:4 000 000; one inch to 64 miles. Conic Project
Elevations and depressions are given in feet

Relief

Meters	Feet
1525	5000
610	2000
305	1000
152.5	500
0	Sea Level	0
152.5	500
1525	5000

82° 80° 76° 74°

W.VA
Welch
Gary
Bluefield
Princeton
Pulaski
Radford
Christiansburg
Roanoke
Salem Vinton
Bedford
Lynchburg
Chester
Richmond
Williamsburg
Hopewell
Petersburg
Farmville
Crewe
Yorktown
Newport News
Hampton
Dendron
Suffolk
Norfolk
Portsmouth
Virginia Beach
CAPE HENRY
Cape Charles
CAPE CHARLES
Chesapeake Bay

V I R G I N I A

Saltville
Marion
Abingdon
Bristol
Elizabethton
North Wilkesboro
Lenoir
Grandfather Mtn.
5964

Wytheville
Fries Galax
Mount Airy
Mayodan
Madison
Eden
Reidsville
Danville
South Boston
Chase City
Lawrenceville
Franklin
Emporia
Victoria
Blackstone
South Hill
John H. Kerr Res.
Roanoke Rapids
Weldon
Ahoskie
Hertford
Edenton
Elizabeth City
Kitty Hawk
Manteo
Albemarle Sound
Currituck Sound
Great Dismal Swamp

N O R T H   C A R O L I N A

Elkin
Yadkin
Winston-Salem
Greensboro Burlington
High Point
Graham
Chapel Hill
Durham
Oxford
Henderson
Scotland Neck
Windsor
New Holland
Pamlico Sound
CAPE HATTERAS

Booker Washington Nat'l Mon.
Cooleemee
Lexington
Thomasville
Statesville
Mooresville
Siler City
Asheboro
Raleigh
Wake Forest
Clayton
Selma
Wilson
Greenville
Washington
Ayden
Belhaven

Morganton
Hickory
Newton
Lincolnton
Salisbury
Kannapolis
Concord
Albemarle
Troy
Carthage
Sanford
Smithfield
Goldsboro
Kinston
New Bern
Atlantic
Morehead City
Beaufort
CAPE LOOKOUT

Marion
Rutherfordton
Forest City
Shelby
Cherryville
Bessemer City
Gastonia
Kings Mtn.
Clover
York
Rock Hill
Charlotte
Fort Mill
Monroe
Wadesboro
Rockingham
Hamlet
Dunn
Erwin
Southern Pines
Mount Olive
Warsaw
Clinton
Fayetteville
Raeford
Laurinburg
McColl
Lumberton
Burgaw
Wilmington
Southport
CAPE FEAR

Greenville
Greer
Woodruff
Enoree
Union
Lockhart
Whitmire
Newberry
Chester
Great Falls
Winnsboro
Lancaster
Cheraw
Bennettsville
Dillon
Mullins
Marion
Chadbourn
Whiteville

S O U T H   C A R O L I N A

Clinton
Laurens
Williamston
Greenwood
Saluda
McCormick
Edgefield
Aiken
Langley
Granitville
Augusta
Barnwell
Bamberg
Allendale
Fairfax

Columbia
West Columbia
Batesburg
Orangeburg
Blackville
Denmark
Branchville
St. George
Summerville
North Charleston
Charleston
Mount Pleasant
FORT SUMTER NAT'L MON.

Sumter
St. Matthew
Manning
Kingstree
Lake City
Florence
Darlington
Hartsville
Bishopville
Camden
Timmonsville
Conway
Myrtle Beach
Georgetown
Andrews
Winyah Bay
Lake Marion
Lake Moultrie

Wateree Lake
Lake Greenwood
Lake Murray

Waynesboro
Louisville
Wadley
Millen
Sylvania
Statesboro
Metter
Lyons
Claxton
Glennville
Savannah
FORT PULASKI NAT'L MON.
Beaufort
Meggett
Edisto Island
S E A   I S L A N D S

Jesup
Ludowici
Brunswick
FORT FREDERICA NAT'L MON.
Folkston
St. Marys
Fernandina Beach
Jacksonville Beach
Jacksonville

Waycross
Okefenokee Swamp
Green Cove Springs
Starke
CASTILLO DE SAN MARCOS NAT'L MON.
St. Augustine
Palatka
FORT MATANZAS NAT'L MON.
Crescent City
Ormond Beach
Daytona Beach
New Smyrna Beach
De Land

Ocala
Dunnellon
Leesburg
Eustis
Lake George
Lake Ocklawaha
Orange Lake
Newnans Lake

A T L A N T I C   O C E A N

82° 80° 78°

20 40 60 80 100 120 Miles
20 40 60 80 100 120 140 160 180 200 Kilometers

a

Same scale as main map

Jacksonville
Jacksonville Beach
Starke
Green Cove Springs
CASTILLO DE SAN MARCOS NAT'L MON.
St. Augustine
FORT MATANZAS NAT'L MON.
Gainesville
Newnans Lake
Crescent Springs
Crescent Beach
Ormond Beach
Daytona Beach
New Smyrna Beach

A T L A N T I C

F L O R I D A

Cedar Keys
Ocala
Lake George
De Land
Sanford
Titusville
Winter Park
Orlando
CAPE CANAVERAL
Cocoa
Cocoa Beach

O C E A N

Waccasassa Bay
Inverness
Brooksville
Leesburg
Eustis
Mount Dora
Apopka
Winter Garden
Dade City
Kissimmee
St. Cloud
Haines City
Winter Haven
Melbourne

Tarpon Springs
Dunedin
Clearwater
St. Petersburg
Tampa
Plant City
Lakeland
Bartow
Fort Meade
Lake Wales
Avon Park
Sebring
Vero Beach
Fort Pierce
Okeechobee
Stuart

Bradenton
Palmetto
Wauchula
Sarasota
Arcadia
BRIGHTON INDIAN RES.
Lake Okeechobee
Riviera Beach
W Palm Beach
Palm Beach
Pahokee
Belle Glade
Lake Worth
Delray Beach

Punta Gorda
Fort Myers
SANIBEL I.
Pine I. Sound
Naples
BIG CYPRESS IND. RES.
Clewiston
Chosen
Pompano Beach
Fort Lauderdale
Hollywood

G U L F

O F

M E X I C O

Everglades City
CAPE ROMANO
TEN THOUSAND IS.
MICCOSUKEE IND. RES.
THE EVERGLADES
Tamiami Trail
Hialeah
MIAMI
Coral Gables
Miami Beach
Homestead

EVERGLADES NATIONAL PARK
CAPE SABLE
Whitewater Bay
Flamingo
Florida Bay
Biscayne Bay
KEY LARGO

FORT JEFFERSON N.M.
DRY TORTUGAS
MARQUESAS KEYS
Key West
Marathon
F L O R I D A   K E Y S

82° 80°

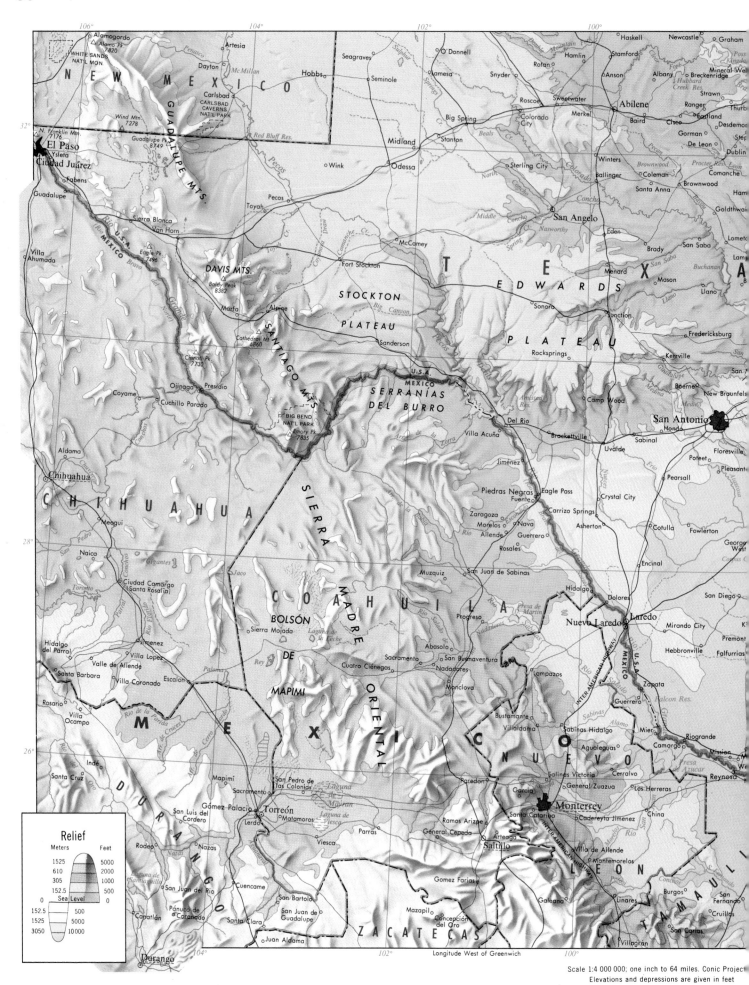

94

Scale 1:4 000 000; one inch to 64 miles. Conic Projection
Elevations and depressions are given in feet

Relief

Meters	Feet
1525	5000
610	2000
305	1000
152.5	500
0	Sea Level	0
152.5	500
1525	5000
3050	10000

Longitude West of Greenwich

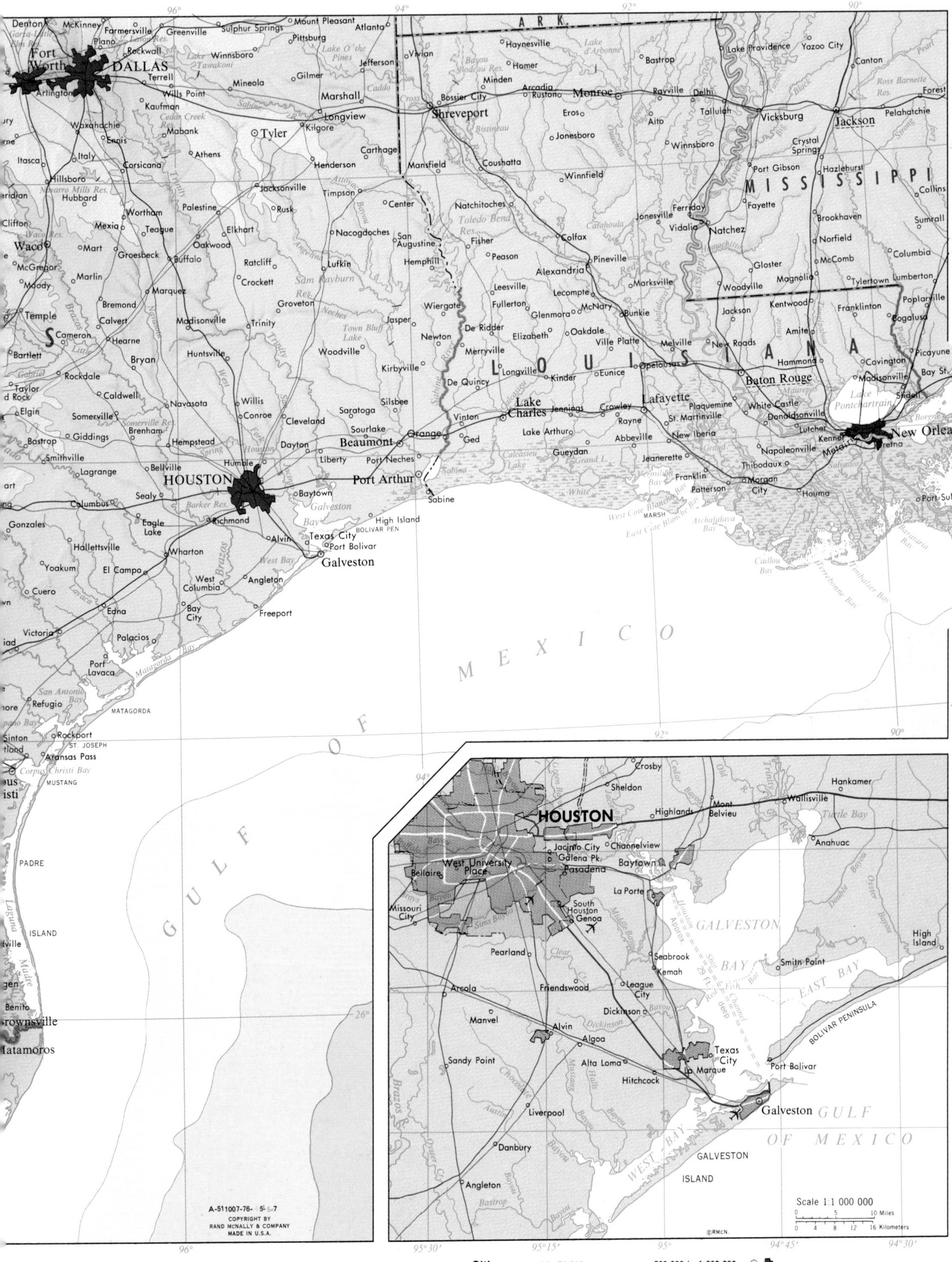

ARK.

MISSISSIPPI

LOUISIANA

GULF OF MEXICO

Fort Worth · **DALLAS** · Tyler · Shreveport · Monroe · Vicksburg · **Jackson**

Waco · Temple · Longview · Natchitoches · Alexandria · Baton Rouge · New Orleans

HOUSTON · Beaumont · Port Arthur · Lake Charles · Lafayette · Lake Pontchartrain

Galveston · Corpus Christi · Brownsville · Matamoros

Laguna Madre · PADRE ISLAND

a

HOUSTON · Crosby · Sheldon · Hankamer · Wallisville · Anahuac

West University Place · Bellaire · Missouri City · Jacinto City · Galena Pk. · Pasadena · Channelview · Baytown · Mont Belvieu

South Houston · Genoa · La Porte · GALVESTON BAY · EAST BAY · High Island

Pearland · Seabrook · Kemah · Smith Point

Arcola · Friendswood · League City · Dickinson · BOLIVAR PENINSULA

Manvel · Alvin · Algoa · La Marque · Texas City · Port Bolivar

Sandy Point · Alta Loma · Hitchcock · Galveston · GULF OF MEXICO

Liverpool · GALVESTON ISLAND

Danbury · Angleton · Bastrop

Scale 1:1 000 000

0   5   10 Miles

0 4   8   12 16 Kilometers

A-511007-76- 5-5-7

COPYRIGHT BY
RAND McNALLY & COMPANY
MADE IN U.S.A.

©RMCN.

20   40   60   80   100   120 Miles
0 20 40 60 80 100 120 140 160 180 200 Kilometers

Cities and Towns

0 to 50,000 ○	500,000 to 1,000,000 ◉
50,000 to 500,000 ⊙	1,000,000 and over

a

PANAMA

Scale 1:1 000 000

Caribbean Sea

Bahía de Panamá

©RMCN.

A-530000-76-9 6-25
COPYRIGHT BY
RAND McNALLY & COMPANY
MADE IN U.S.A.

Scale 1:16 000 000; one inch to 250 miles. Polyconic Proje
Elevations and depressions are given in feet

b

ATLANTIC OCEAN

Arecibo   San Juan
Aguadilla   Bayamón   CABEZAS DE   ST. THOMAS   TORTOLA
                          SAN JUAN   (U.S.A.)   (Br.)
PTA. HIGUERO   Utuado   Fajardo   Charlotte   ST. JOHN
Mayagüez   (U.S.A.)   Caguas   Culebra   Amalie   (U.S.A.)
PUERTO RICO
        Caamó   Cayey   Humacao   Vieques
CABO ROJO   Ponce   Salinas   Guayama   VIEQUES   Christiansted
        CARIBBEAN   SEA   SAINT CROIX
                        (U.S.A.)

Scale 1:4 000 000
0 10 20 30   40 Miles
0 10 20 30 40 50 60 Kilometers
©RMCN.

c

LITTLE   64°30′
HANS LOLLICK
OUTER BRASS   HANS LOLLICK
INNER BRASS   PICARA PT   GRASS
STORMY PT   THATCH CAY   CAY
        ST△THOMAS
        Crown Mt. (U.S.A.)   Charlotte Amalie   18°
        1558   (St. Thomas)   20′
WATER   FLAMINGO PT   St.   Nadir
        FLAMINGO PT   Thomas
©RMCN.   Harbor   Scale 1:500 000

W.VIRGINIA   Richmond   80°   75°   70°   65°   65°
Roanoke
NORTH CAROLINA   Norfolk   Chesapeake Bay   35°
Raleigh   CAPE HATTERAS
Charlotte   Pamlico
SOUTH   Wilmington
CAROLINA   Columbia   CAPE FEAR
GIA   Charleston
        Savannah
        ATLANTIC   BERMUDA
Jacksonville   (Br.)
St. Augustine
FLORIDA   Ocala   CAPE CANAVERAL   NORTH AMERICAN
mpa
Bay
        OCEAN   BASIN
W. Palm
Beach   GRAND
BAHAMA
MIAMI   GREAT ABACO
CAPE SABLE   ELEUTHERA
Key West   NASSAU   CAT   20°
FLORIDA KEYS   SAN SALVADOR (WATLING)
Straits of   ANDROS   LONG
ANA   Guanabacoa
VANA   Matanzas   S
el Río   Cárdenas   ACKLINS
        Santa Clara   PUERTO RICO TRENCH
Cienfuegos   Sancti Spíritus   GT. INAGUA
    Ciego   Nuevitas   CAICOS
ISLA   de Ávila   Camagüey   TURKS (Br.)
DE LA   Holguín   PUNTA
VENTUD   Manzanillo   MAISI   ▽ 28 374
GRAND CAYMAN   Santiago   Cap-Haïtien   Puerto Plata
(Br.)   de Cuba   Gonaïves   Santiago de los   SAMANA   Mayagüez   San Juan   VIRGIN IS.   ANGUILLA
        ÎLE DE LA   Caballeros   Sánchez   ENGAÑO   Ponce   ST. THOMAS   ANTIGUA
WEST   C. CRUZ   GONAVE   HAITI   DOMINICAN   Charlotte Amalie   BARBUDA
        Pico Duarte   REPUBLIC   PUERTO RICO   (Br.)   AND
Montego Bay   Mt.   Port-au-Prince   3 417   Santo Domingo   (U.S.A.)   SAINT CROIX   BARBUDA
    Denham   HISPANIOLA   (U.S.A.)   ST. KITTS AND NEVIS
Spanish Town   3236 Port Antonio   MONTSERRAT   Pointe-à-Pitre
JAMAICA   Kingston   ANTILLES   (Br.)   V. Soufrière   GUADELOUPE
                        4813   (Fr.)
            LESSER   Basse-Terre   DOMINICA
                    WINDWARD IS.   MARTINIQUE (Fr.)
                        Fort-de-France
                ANTILLES   ST. LUCIA
                    ST. VINCENT   BARBADOS
                    AND THE
                    GRENADINES   Bridgetown
PUNTA DE GALLINAS   GRENADA   Kingstown
Bluefields   PENÍNSULA   SAN ROMAN   ARUBA   CURAÇAO BONAIRE
    DE GUAJIRA   (Neth.)   (Neth.)(Neth.)   Willemstad   LESSER   TOBAGO
Santa Marta   Golfo de   Willemstad   ISLA DE   TRINIDAD AND TOBAGO
AMERICA   Barranquilla   Ciénaga   Venezuela   Coro   LA TORTUGA   Carúpano   Port of Spain
    Cartagena   Soledad   Maracaibo   San Felipe   Puerto   ISLA LA   ISLA DE   TRINIDAD
        San   Cabimas   Cabello   MARGARITA   Cumaná
Colón   Limón   Lorica   Sincelejo   Mompós   La Guaira   Puerto   Maturín
PANAMA   Portobelo   Magangué   Barquisimeto   CARACAS   la Cruz
    Golfo del   Montería   Valera   Maracay   El Tigre
David   Darién   Guanare   Calabozo   Morawhanna
    Golfo de   Puerto de   San Fernando   Ciudad Guayana
    Panamá   Cúcuta   San Cristóbal   Nutrias   de Apure   Ciudad Bolívar
Santiago   Pamplona   VENEZUELA   Río   Cerro Bolívar
    Barrancabermeja   Bucaramanga   Cerro Icutu   GUYANA
Medellín   7800△
Tunja   COLOMBIA
Manizales   San Fernando   SERRA PACARAIMA
Pereira   SANTA FE DE   de Atabapo
Armenia   BOGOTA   BRAZIL
Ibagué   Girardot   Villavicencio
Buenaventura   Cali   Palmira   Guaviare

Longitude West of Greenwich   80°   75°   70°   65°   60°

Relief
Meters   Feet
3050   10 000
1525   5000
610   2000
305   1000
152.5   500
0   Sea Level   0
152.5   500
1525   5000
3050   10 000
6100   20 000

50 100   200   300   500 Miles
100   200   400   600   800 Kilometers

Cities   0 to 50,000   500,000 to 1,000,000
and
Towns   50,000 to 500,000   1,000,000 and over

South America

Floodplain of the Amazon River, Brazil

With an area of 6.9 million square miles (17.8 million sq km), triangular-shaped South America is fourth among the continents in size. The Andes, which pass through seven of the continent's 13 mainland countries, are the longest mountain chain in the world. The mighty Amazon River carries a greater volume of water than any other river: 46 million gallons per second flow into the Atlantic Ocean. The Amazon basin contains an estimated one-fifth of the world's fresh water and is home to the world's largest rain forest with its countless plant and animal species. Angel Falls, in a remote Venezuelan forest, is the world's highest waterfall, dropping 3,212 feet (979 m), or almost the height of three Empire State Buildings.

One of South America's other great wonders is manmade. High in the Peruvian Andes lie the ruins of the sacred city of Machu Picchu, built centuries ago by the Incas. The city has an exquisite design and was built with remarkable skill. The Inca population, like most of South America's other native peoples, declined rapidly after the arrival of Europeans in the early 16th century.

South America at a glance

Land area: 6,900,000 square miles (17,800,000 sq km)

Estimated population (January 1, 1995): 313,900,000

Population density: 45/square mile (18/sq km)

Mean elevation: 1,800 feet (550 m)

Highest point: Aconcagua, Argentina, 22,831 feet (6,959 m)

Lowest point: Salinas Chicas, Argentina, 138 feet (42 m) below sea level

Longest river: Amazon-Ucayali, 4,000 mi (6,400 km)

Number of countries (incl. dependencies): 15

Largest independent country: Brazil, 3,286,500 square miles (8,511,996 sq km)

Smallest independent country: Suriname, 63,251 square miles (163,820 sq km)

Most populous independent country: Brazil, 159,690,000

Least populous independent country: Suriname, 426,000

Largest city: São Paulo, pop. 9,393,753 (1991)

The Andes, at the western edge of Argentina's Patagonia region.

Wettest place:
Quibdó, Colombia
354 inches (899 cm)/year

Driest place:
Arica, Chile
.03 inches (.08 cm)/year

Hottest place:
Rivadavia, Argentina
120°F (49°C)

Highest point:
Cerro Aconcagua, Argentina
22,831 ft (6,959 m)

Coldest place:
Sarmiento, Argentina
-27°F (-33°C)

Lowest point:
Salinas Chicas, Argentina
138 ft (42 m) below sea level

Orinoco
Llanos
Guiana Highlands
Equator
Amazon
Amazon Basin
Madeira
São Francisco
Pacific Ocean
ANDES MOUNTAINS
Lago Titicaca
Mato Grosso
Brazilian Highlands
Atlantic Ocean
Gran Chaco
Paraguay
Paraná
Tropic of Capricorn
Pampas
Patagonia
FALKLAND ISLANDS
TIERRA DEL FUEGO

Landforms

- Mountains
- Widely spaced mountains
- High tablelands
- Hills and low tablelands
- Plains
- Depressions, basins
- High tablelands and ice caps
- Mountains and ice caps

© Rand McNally & Co.
M-540000-7C-EL1-

© Rand McNally & Co.
M-540000-6A-EL1-1-1- -1

Climate

South America's most predominant climate zones are the vast tropical rain forests and tropical savannas which cover most of the northern half of the continent. In the rain forests, rain falls throughout the year, averaging 60 to 80 inches (152 to 203 cm) annually. Daytime temperatures usually exceed 80° F (27° C). The tropical savanna regions experience the same high temperatures but less rainfall, with a dry season in winter. A temperate climate, with milder temperatures and moderate rainfall, prevails throughout much of southern South America, east of the Andes. Arid to semiarid conditions are found in the far south and at Brazil's eastern tip.

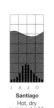
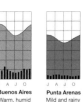

Tinted areas show temperature in degrees Fahrenheit. Vertical bars show precipitation in inches.

Manaus — Hot and rainy
Recife — Hot with rainy and dry seasons
Caracas — Semiarid
Lima — Very dry
Santiago — Hot, dry summer / mild, rainy winter
Buenos Aires — Warm, humid summer / mild winter
Punta Arenas — Mild and rainy
Extensive uplands — Climate varies with elevation and latitude

Population

South America is the fourth most-densely populated continent, with 45 people per square mile (18 per sq km). Despite this relatively low figure, the continent is intensely urban because the Andes and the Amazon rain forest render most of it either inaccessible or unsuitable for farming. More than 90% of South America's 314 million people live within 150 miles (240 km) of the coast. São Paulo, Brazil, with a metropolitan population of almost 17 million, is the world's third-largest metropolitan area. Most South Americans are *mestizo*—of mixed European and Indian descent. Spanish is the predominant language, followed by Portuguese. More than 90% of the people are Roman Catholics.

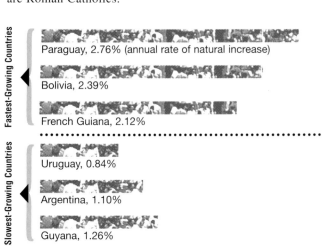

Fastest-Growing Countries

Paraguay, 2.76% (annual rate of natural increase)

Bolivia, 2.39%

French Guiana, 2.12%

Slowest-Growing Countries

Uruguay, 0.84%

Argentina, 1.10%

Guyana, 1.26%

Inhabitants per sq. km. (mi.)

Uninhabited
<1 (2)
1-10 (2-25)
10-25 (25-60)
25-50 (60-125)
50-100 (125-250)
>100 (250)

© Rand McNally & Co.
M-540000-1P-EL1-1-1- -1

Environments and Land Use

Land suitable for farming is very limited in South America, covering only about 6% of the continent. Small, family-run subsistence farms are common, and typical crops are maize, wheat, and potatoes. Despite the scarcity of arable land, commercial agriculture for export is a major part of the economies of several countries. Ecuador is the world's leading exporter of bananas, while Brazil and Colombia grow almost 40% of the world's coffee beans. Brazil is also a major exporter of sugar. Chile has developed a large trade in produce—such as tomatoes and grapes—that is exported to North America during its winter months (South America's summer months). Production of coca, the basis for illicit drugs, has become a part of the rural economies of Colombia, Bolivia and Peru.

Cattle ranching is centered on the vast, grassy Pampas region, which extends through northern Argentina, Uruguay, and southern Brazil. Sheep, raised both for meat and wool, are important throughout the Andes and southern Argentina. About 25% of the continent is suitable for grazing.

As South America's population grows, pressure builds to clear more land for farming. Much expansion has taken place in the Amazon basin at the cost of millions of acres of rain forest, which are cleared of trees and drained. Balancing the demands of the population with the need to preserve the rain forest is one of the continent's most pressing issues.

Urban
Cropland
Cropland and woodland
Cropland and grazing land
Grassland, grazing land
Forest, woodland
Swamp, marsh
Tundra
Shrub, sparse grass, wasteland
Barren land

© Rand McNally & Co.
M-540000-8L-EL1-1-1--1

| 0 | 200 | 400 | 600 | 800 | 1000 Miles |
| 0 | 300 | 600 | 900 | 1200 | 1500 Kilometers |

Coffee plantation in the Brazilian highlands

Destruction of the Rain Forest

The Amazonian rain forest contains an abundance and diversity of life that is matched by few places in the world. In fact, it has been estimated that the plant and animal species of Amazonia account for nearly one-half of those found on Earth. New plants and animals are constantly being discovered, and scientists have found in Amazonian plants a treasure trove of new substances, some of which are now being used to produce life-saving medicines. It is thought that cures for many more diseases could be found in the plants yet to be studied.

In recent decades, nearly 10% of the rain forest's original 1.58 million square miles (4.09 million sq km) has been cleared (see map below) for farming, cattle ranching, mining, and commercial logging. The most effective way to clear the land is the "slash-and-burn" method, which has been practiced by indigenous peoples on an insignificant scale for centuries. Today, widespread usage of this method is destroying vast areas of the rain forest, and smoke from the fires is polluting the atmosphere and possibly contributing to global warming. The destruction also imperils the Indians living within the forest; their numbers have shrunk by more than half in this century alone.

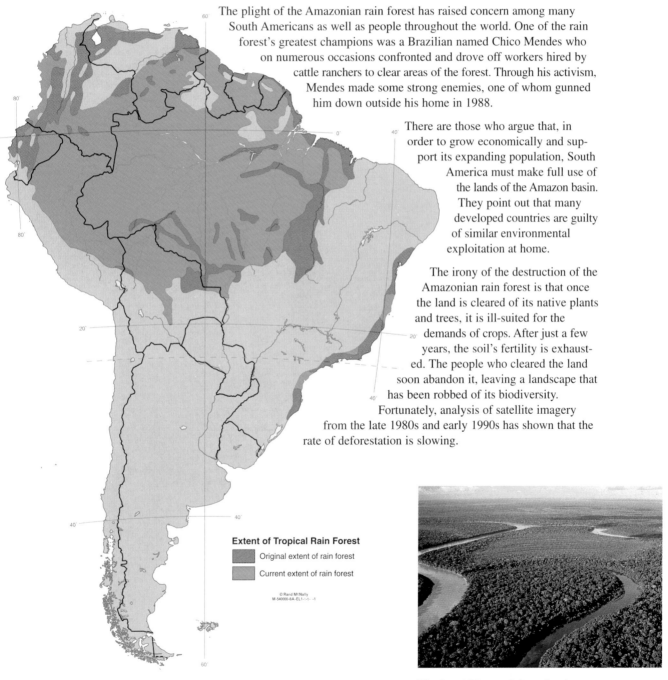

The plight of the Amazonian rain forest has raised concern among many South Americans as well as people throughout the world. One of the rain forest's greatest champions was a Brazilian named Chico Mendes who on numerous occasions confronted and drove off workers hired by cattle ranchers to clear areas of the forest. Through his activism, Mendes made some strong enemies, one of whom gunned him down outside his home in 1988.

There are those who argue that, in order to grow economically and support its expanding population, South America must make full use of the lands of the Amazon basin. They point out that many developed countries are guilty of similar environmental exploitation at home.

The irony of the destruction of the Amazonian rain forest is that once the land is cleared of its native plants and trees, it is ill-suited for the demands of crops. After just a few years, the soil's fertility is exhausted. The people who cleared the land soon abandon it, leaving a landscape that has been robbed of its biodiversity. Fortunately, analysis of satellite imagery from the late 1980s and early 1990s has shown that the rate of deforestation is slowing.

Extent of Tropical Rain Forest

Original extent of rain forest

Current extent of rain forest

© Rand McNally
M-540000-8A-EL1-·-·-· -1

The Juruá River, at left, and a clearwater slough wind through the dense Amazon rain forest near Eirunepé, Brazil.

HAVANA

CENTRAL

AMERICA

Bahía de Campeche

PEN. DE YUCATÁN

Yucatan Channel

Gulf of Honduras

Lago de Nicaragua

ISLA DEL COCO (Costa Rica)

JAMAICA

HISPANIOLA

PUERTO RICO TRENCH

San Juan

PUERTO RICO (U.S.A.)

Windward Passage

CARIBBEAN SEA

INDIES

WEST

Bahía de Campeche

NORTH AMERICAN BASIN

Tropic of Cancer

GUADELOUPE (Fr.)

MARTINIQUE (Fr.)

BARBADOS

TRINIDAD AND TOBAGO

Port of Spain

PUNTA DE GALLINAS

Golfo de Venezuela

Barranquilla

Cartagena

Golfo del Darién

Panama

Golfo de Panamá

ISLA DE MALPELO (Colombia)

Medellín

Maracaibo

Valencia

La Guaira

CARACAS

Mérida

Nevado del Tolima 17 110

SANTA FE DE BOGOTÁ

COLOMBIA

Ciudad Bolívar

Orinoco

VENEZUELA

Cerro Icutú △ 7800

Guaviare

Boa Vista do Rio Branco

Georgetown

Paramaribo

GUYANA

SURINAME

FR. GUIANA

Cayenne

GUIANA HIGHLANDS

Quito

Cotopaxi 19 347

ECUADOR

Guayaquil

Chimborazo 20 702

Golfo de Guayaquil

ARCHIPIÉLAGO DE COLÓN (GALÁPAGOS ISLANDS) (Ec.)

Iquitos

Leticia

Río Negro

Japurá

Manaus (Manáos)

Río Amazonas

Equator

ILHA DE MARAJÓ

Belém (Pará)

São Luís (Maranhão)

ROCEDOS SÃO PEDRO E SÃO PAULO (Brazil)

Rio Solimões (Amazonas)

Putumayo

Chiclayo

Trujillo

Nevs. Huascarán 22 131

Callao

LIMA

Cusco

PERU

Juruá

Purús

Rio Madeira

Pôrto Velho

Río Branco

Xingú

Tapajós

Tocantins

Rio

Fortaleza (Ceará)

Teresina

Natal

João Pessoa (Paraíba)

RECIFE (Pernambuco)

Maceió

Salvador (Bahia)

ARQUIPÉLAGO FERNANDO DE NORONHA (Brazil)

CABO DE SÃO ROQUE

Salto Paulo Afonso

Araguaia

B R A Z I L

CHAPADA DE MATO GROSSO

Cuiabá

Brasília

Diamantina

Belo Horizonte

SERRA DO PIAUÍ

SERRA DO ESPINHAÇO

Volcán Misti 19 101

Arequipa

Mollendo

La Paz

Nev. Illimani 20 741

BOLIVIA

Sucre

Potosí

Lago de Poopó

Pilcomayo

Paraguai

Paraná

Pico da Bandeira 9492

Vitória

CABO FRIO

BRAZILIAN HIGHLANDS

SÃO PAULO

Santos

RIO DE JANEIRO

Iquique

ATACAMA

DESIERTO DE ATACAMA

Antofagasta

Tropic of Capricorn

ISLA DE SAN FÉLIX (Chile)

ISLA DE SAN AMBROSIO (Chile)

ATACAMA TRENCH

Cerro Azul 19 647

Copiapó

Coquimbo

Salta

Tucumán

Bermejo

GRAN CHACO

Corrientes

PARAGUAY

Asunción

Paraná

Iguassú Falls

Florianópolis

Valparaíso

SANTIAGO

ISLAS DE JUAN FERNÁNDEZ (Chile)

Concepción

Valdivia

Aconcagua 22 835

Mendoza

Córdoba

Rosario

Santa Fe

A R G E N T I N A

BUENOS AIRES

La Plata

PAMPAS

Colorado

Salto

URUGUAY

Rio de la Plata

MONTEVIDEO

Pôrto Alegre

Rio Grande

ATLANTIC OCEAN

Bahía Blanca

Viedma

Chubut

Golfo San Matias

Puerto Montt

ISLA DE CHILOÉ

ARCHIPIÉLAGO DE LOS CHONOS

CHILE

ANDES

Monte Valentín 13 314

Comodoro Rivadavia

Golfo San Jorge

WELLINGTON

HANOVER

DESOLACIÓN

Mt. Sarmiento 8100

Punta Arenas

Río Gallegos

Estrecho de Magallanes

TIERRA DEL FUEGO

ISLA DE LOS ESTADOS

CABO DE HORNOS (CAPE HORN)

FALKLAND IS. (ISLAS MALVINAS) (Br.)

Stanley

SOUTH GEORGIA (Br.)

Drake Passage

SOUTH SHETLAND ISLANDS (Br.)

SOUTH ORKNEY IS. (Br.)

JOINVILLE

JAMES ROSS

PENINSULA

Antarctic Circle

SOUTH SANDWICH ISLANDS (Br.)

SOUTH SANDWICH TRENCH

PACIFIC OCEAN

ATLANTIC OCEAN

Longitude West of Greenwich

40,000 SQ MI AREA

0   300   600

Miles

A-540000-26

COPYRIGHT BY RAND MCNALLY & COMPANY MADE IN U.S.A.

0   200   400   600   800   1000 Miles

0   400   800   1200 1600 Kilometers

Scale 1:40 000 000, one inch to 630 miles. Lambert's Azimuthal, Equal Area Projection

Elevations and depressions are given in feet

HAVANA

CUBA

Bahía de Campeche

PEN. DE YUCATÁN

Gulf of Honduras

JAMAICA

CENTRAL AMERICA

Lago de Nicaragua

ISLA DEL COCO (Costa Rica)

ISLA DE MALPELO (Colombia)

ARCHIPIÉLAGO DE COLÓN (GALAPAGOS ISLANDS) (Ec.)

WEST INDIES

HISPANIOLA

San Juan

PUERTO RICO TRENCH

PUERTO RICO (U.S.A.)

GUADELOUPE (Fr.)

MARTINIQUE (Fr.)

BARBADOS

NORTH AMERICAN BASIN

CARIBBEAN SEA

PUNTA DE GALLINAS

Barranquilla
Cartagena

Panamá IST. DE PAN.

Golfo de Panamá

Maracaibo
Valencia

Mérida

Medellín

Nevado del Tolima 17 110

SANTA FE DE BOGOTA

COLOMBIA

Quito
Cotopaxi 19 347

ECUADOR

Guayaquil Chimborazo 20 702

Golfo de Guayaquil

La Guaira

CARACAS

Ciudad Bolívar
Cerro Cutú 7 890

VENEZUELA

TRINIDAD AND TOBAGO
Port of Spain

Georgetown

GUYANA
Paramaribo

SURINAME FR. GUIANA

Cayenne

Boa Vista do Rio Branco

GUIANA HIGHLANDS

Rio Branco

Rio Negro

Equator

ROCEDOS SÃO PEDRO E SÃO PAULO (Brazil)

Iquitos

Leticia

PERU

Chiclayo
Trujillo

Nevs Huascarán 22 133

LIMA
Callao

Cusco

Arequipa
Mollendo

Volcán Misti 19 101

La Paz
Nev. Illimani 20 741

BOLIVIA
Sucre
Potosí

Iquique

Antofagasta

Copiapó
Cerro Azufre 19 647 Vol.

Coquimbo

Valparaíso
SANTIAGO

Concepción

Valdivia

Puerto Montt

ISLA DE CHILOE

ARCHIPIÉLAGO DE LOS CHONOS

WELLINGTON

HANOVER
DESOLACIÓN

Punta Arenas

Mt. Sarmiento 8100

Manaus (Manáos)

Rio Negro

Rio Amazonas

Pôrto Velho

Rio Branco

BRAZIL

CHAPADA DE MATO GROSSO

Cuiabá

Diamantina

BRAZILIAN HIGHLANDS

Brasília

Belo Horizonte

Pico da Bandeira 9 482

Vitória

CABO FRIO

RIO DE JANEIRO

Santos

SÃO PAULO

Iguaçú Falls

Asunción

PARAGUAY

GRAN CHACO

Salta

Tucumán

Corrientes

Córdoba
Aconcagua 22 881

Mendoza

Rosario

Santa Fe

Salto

URUGUAY

Rio Grande

Pôrto Alegre

Florianópolis

BUENOS AIRES
La Plata

Rio de la Plata

MONTEVIDEO

PAMPAS

Bahía Blanca

Viedma

Golfo San Matías

ARGENTINA

ANDES

CHILE MTS.

Comodoro Rivadavia
Golfo San Jorge

Monte Valentín 13 314

Río Gallegos

FALKLAND IS. (ISLAS MALVINAS) (Br.)

Stanley

Estrecho de Magallanes

TIERRA DEL FUEGO

ISLA DE LOS ESTADOS

CABO DE HORNOS (CAPE HORN)

Drake Passage

SOUTH SHETLAND ISLANDS (Br.)

JOINVILLE

ANTARCTIC PENINSULA

JAMES ROSS

Antarctic Circle

SOUTH ORKNEY IS. (Br.)

SOUTH SANDWICH ISLANDS (Br.)

SOUTH GEORGIA (Br.)

Belém (Pará)

São Luís (Maranhão)

Fortaleza (Ceará)

Teresina

Natal
João Pessoa (Paraíba)

RECIFE (Pernambuco)

Maceió

Salvador (Bahia)

CABO DE SÃO ROQUE

ARQUIPÉLAGO DE FERNANDO DE NORONHA (Brazil)

ATLANTIC OCEAN

PACIFIC OCEAN

ISLAS DE JUAN FERNÁNDEZ (Chile)

ISLA DE SAN FÉLIX ISLA DE SAN AMBROSIO (Chile)

Tropic of Cancer

Tropic of Capricorn

Longitude West of Greenwich

Rio Amazonas

Relief

Meters		Feet
3050		10 000
1525		5000
610		2000
305		1000
	Sea Level	0
152.5		500
1525		5000
3050		10 000
6100		20 000

0 200 400 600 800 1000 Miles

0 400 800 1200 1600 Kilometers

Scale 1:40 000 000; one inch to 630 miles. Lambert's Azimuthal, Equal Area Projection
Elevations and depressions are given in feet

A-540000-76 3-5-14
COPYRIGHT BY
RAND McNALLY & COMPANY
MADE IN U.S.A.

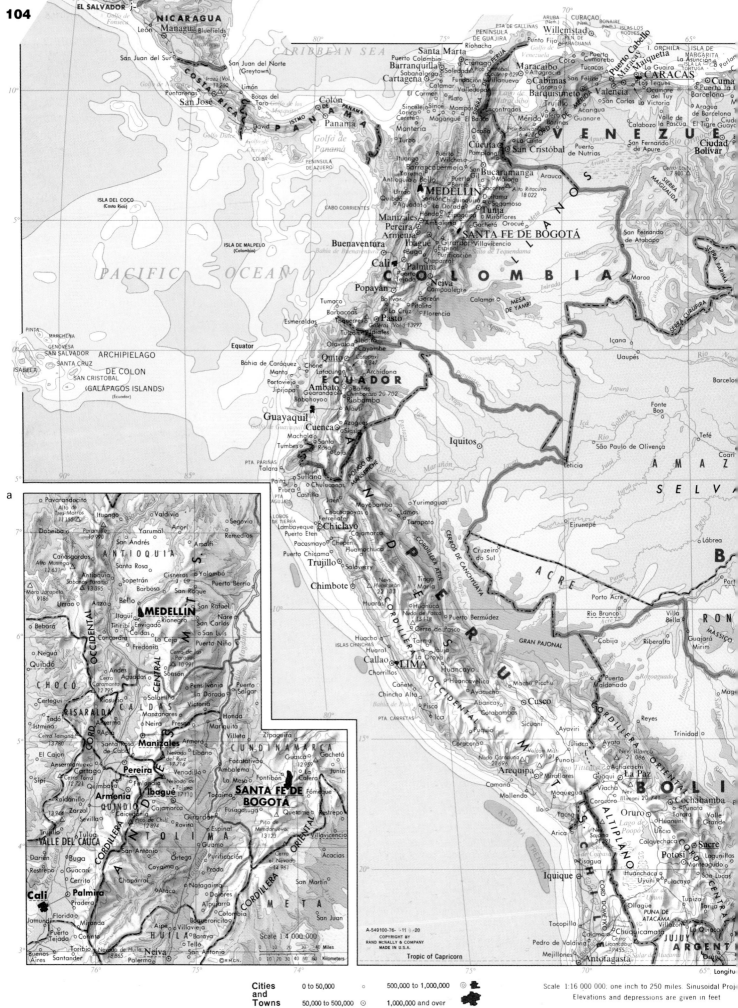

a

Cities
and
Towns

0 to 50,000 ○
50,000 to 500,000 ⊙

500,000 to 1,000,000 ◎
1,000,000 and over

Scale 1:16 000 000, one inch to 250 miles. Sinusoidal Proj
Elevations and depressions are given in feet

A-549100-76- -11 9 -20
COPYRIGHT BY
RAND McNALLY & COMPANY
MADE IN U.S.A.

Tropic of Capricorn

b

CARIBBEAN SEA

ISLA DE MARGARITA
Tocuyo de la Costa
Chichiriviche
Cayo Sombrero
Tucacas
FALCÓN
Boca del Pozo △ 2003
PUNTA ARENAS
Punta de Piedras
NUEVA ESPARTA
ISLA CUBAGUA

Puerto Cabello
Maiquetía
La Guaira
La Sabana
Carayaca
CABO CODERA
Higuerote
Río Chico
ISLA LA TORTUGA

Manicuare
Cumaná
PUNTA DE ARAYA

Morón
Montalbán Guacara
San Joaquín
Pico Codazzi 2988 △
FEDERAL
Petare
Naiguatá
CARACAS
Los Teques
Santa Lucía
San Antonio

Maracay
La Victoria
Santa Teresa
MIRANDA
Caucagua
Las Vegas
SUCRE
△ 8000
Guanta
Bergantín △

Miranda
CARABOBO
Valencia
Cagua
Ocumare del Tuy
San Francisco de Macaira
Boca de Uchire
El Guapo
Sabana de Uchire
Soublette
Puerto La Cruz
El Hatillo
Barcelona

Tinaquillo
Villa de Cura
San Sebastián
Casimira
Altagracia de Orituco
Clarines
San Miguel
El Pilar
Puerto Píritu
Santa Inés

COJEDES
San Juan de los Morros
Camatagua
San Pablo
Onoto
Santa Rosa

Scale 1:4 000 000
GUÁRICO
Dos Caminos
Libertad de Orituco
Aragua de Barcelona
Anaco
ANZOÁTEGUI

Barbacoas

of Spain
TRINIDAD AND TOBAGO
TRINIDAD

Boca Grande
Morawhanna

Georgetown
Bartica
New Amsterdam
Rosignol
Wismar
Skeldon
Rockstone
Nieuw Nickerie
Paranam

GUYANA
MERÚME MTS.
WILHELMINA GEBERGTE

Paramaribo
Moengo
St. Laurent
Sinnamary
ILE DU DIABLE (DEVIL'S I.)
CABO ORANGE
Cayenne

SURINAME
FRENCH GUIANA

Saint-Georges

ACARAÍ MTS.
TUMUC-HUMAC MTS.

Amapá

AMAPÁ

Macapá
ILHA CAVIANA
Mazagão

ATLANTIC OCEAN

Equator
0°

Manaus (Manáos)
Faro
Óbidos
Alenquer
Gurupá
ILHA DE MARAJÓ
Breves
Belém (Pará)
Abaetetuba
Marapanim
Bragança
Cururupu
São Luís (Maranhão)
Alcântara

Parintins
Itacoatiara
Santarém
Cametá
ILHA TUPINAMBARANAS
Altamira
Tucuruí

Maués
Itaituba
Brasília Legal (Fordlândia)

Borba

Tutóia
Parnaíba
Camocim
Acaraú
ARQUIPÉLAGO FERNANDO DE NORONHA (Brazil)

Rosário
Viana
Itapecuru-Mirim
Brejo
Sobral
Ipu
Baturité
Maranguape
FORTALEZA (Ceará)

Mançao
Barras
Campo Maior
Pedro II
Quixadá
Russas
Areia Branca
Macau
CABO DE SÃO ROQUE
FERNANDO DE NORONHA

PARÁ

Pedreiras
Caxias
Crateús
Mossoró
Natal
Nova Cruz

São João do Araguaia
Araguatins
MARANHÃO
Teresina
Grajaú
Barra do Corda
Senador Pompeu
CEARÁ
Iguatu
Icó
RIO GRANDE DO NORTE
Currais Novos
Campina Grande
João Pessoa (Paraíba)

Tocantinópolis
Mirador
Amarante
Picos
Crato
Juàzeiro do Norte
Patos
Flores
Sertânia
Caruaru
Nazaré da Mata
Olinda
RECIFE (Pernambuco)

B R A Z I L
Carolina
Riachão
Floriano
Oeiras
Paulistana
Granito
PERNAMBUCO
Cabrobó
Garanhuns
Palmeira dos Índios
Pôrto de Pedras

Balsas
Santa Filomena
São Raimundo Nonato
Petrolina
Juàzeiro
Propriá
ALAGOAS
Maceió

Miracema do Tocantins
PIAUÍ
Parnaguá
SERRA DO PIAUÍ
Barra
Jeremoabo
Senhor do Bonfim
Itabaiana
SERGIPE
Feneda
Aracaju

Porto Nacional
Palmas
Morro do Chapéu
Jacobina
São Cristóvão
Estância

TOCANTINS
Natividade
BAHIA
Serrinha
Inhambupe

Barreiras
Feira de Santana
Alagoinhas
Catu
Santo Amaro

Correntina
Lençóis
Nazaré
SALVADOR (Bahia)
Aratuípe

CHAPADA DE MATO GROSSO
Carinhanha
Mucugê
Jequié
Valença

Diamantino
Caetité
Vitória da Conquista
Condeúba
Ilhéus
Itabuna

MATO GROSSO
Rosário Oeste
Cuiabá
SA. DA TAQUARA
GOIÁS
Pilar de Goiás
Goiás
Cavalcante
Januária
Rio Pardo de Minas
Pedra Azul
Canavieiras
Belmonte

Mato Grosso
Barão de Melgaço
Formosa
Brasília
São Francisco
Grão Mogol
Araçuaí
Porto Seguro

Cáceres
Anápolis
Luziânia
Montes Claros
Minas Novas
Teófilo Otoni
Caravelas
ARQUIPÉLAGO DOS ABROLHOS

Goiânia
Silvânia
Paracatu
Pirapora
Diamantina
Peçanha
São Mateus

Bela Vista de Goiás
Ipameri
Corinto
Gov. Valadares
Aracruz

Rio Verde
Morrinhos
Catalão
Araguari
Patos de Minas
Curvelo
Sta. Bárbara
Vitória
Espírito Santo

Ituiutaba
Uberlândia
Araxá
Pará de Minas
BELO HORIZONTE
Ponte Nova
Guarapari

MATO GROSSO DO SUL
Coxim
Paranaíba
Uberaba
Formiga
Divinópolis
Lafaiete
Cachoeiro de Itapemirim

Campo Grande
Itapira
Franca
Passos
Barbacena
Itaperuna

Aquidauana
Três Lagoas
São José do Rio Prêto
MINAS GERAIS
Barbacena
Juiz de Fora
Campos

Bella Vista
Presidente Epitácio
Ribeirão Prêto
Pouso Alegre
Nova Friburgo
CABO FRIO

Pedro Juan Caballero
Araçatuba
Araraquara
Caxambu
Petrópolis
RIO DE JANEIRO

PARAGUAY
Marília
São Carlos
Piracicaba
Campinas
Niterói
RIO DE JANEIRO

Londrina
Bauru
SÃO PAULO
Jundiaí
Nova Iguaçu

Concepción
Jacarèzinho
Sorocaba
Taubaté
Mogi das Cruzes
Tropic of Capricorn

PARANÁ
SÃO PAULO
São Vicente
Santos

Porto Mendes
Tibagi
Itararé
Curitiba
Ponta Grossa
Guarapuava

Relief

Meters	Feet
3050	10 000
1525	5000
610	2000
305	1000
152.5	500
Sea Level	0
152.5	500
1525	5000
3050	10 000
6100	20 000

0 50 100 200 300 400 500 Miles
0 100 200 300 400 600 800 Kilometers

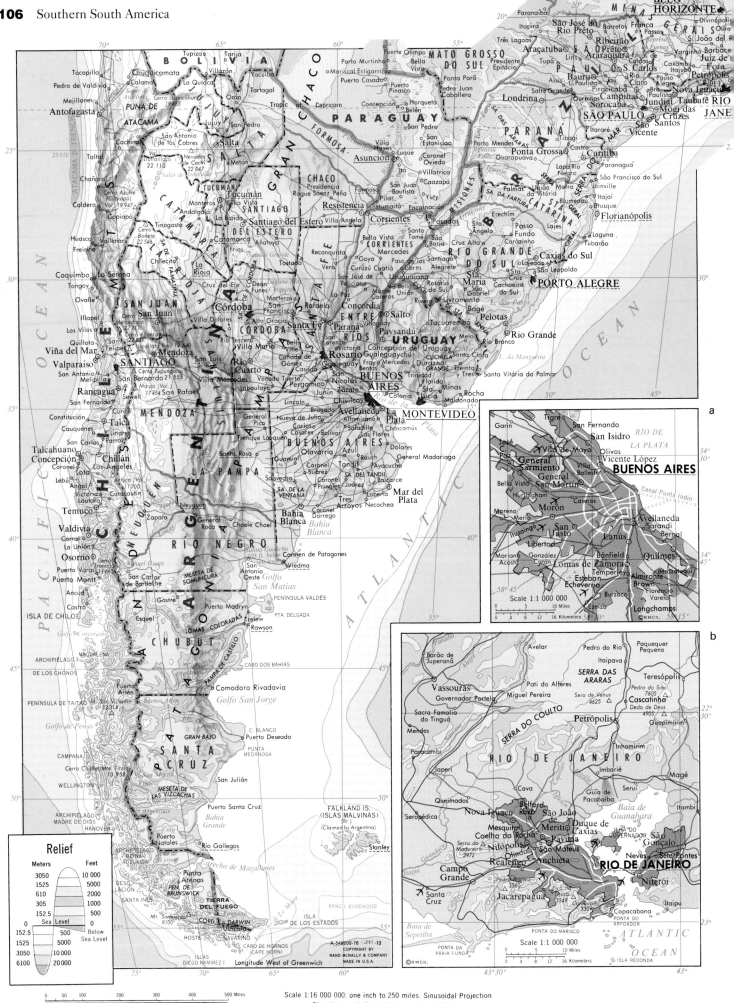

Relief

Meters	Feet
3050	10 000
1525	5000
610	2000
305	1000
152.5	500
0	Sea Level
Sea Level	0
152.5	Below
1525	Sea Level
3050	500
6100	5000
	10 000
	20 000

BUENOS AIRES

Scale 1:1 000 000

0   4   8   12   16 Kilometers

RIO DE JANEIRO

Scale 1:1 000 000

0   5   10 Miles

0   4   8   12   16 Kilometers

©RMCN.

A-549200-76 -111 -13
COPYRIGHT BY
RAND McNALLY & COMPANY
MADE IN U.S.A.

Longitude West of Greenwich

0   50   100   200   300   400   500 Miles

0   100   200   400   600   800 Kilometers

Scale 1:16 000 000, one inch to 250 miles. Sinusoidal Projection
Elevations and depressions are given in feet

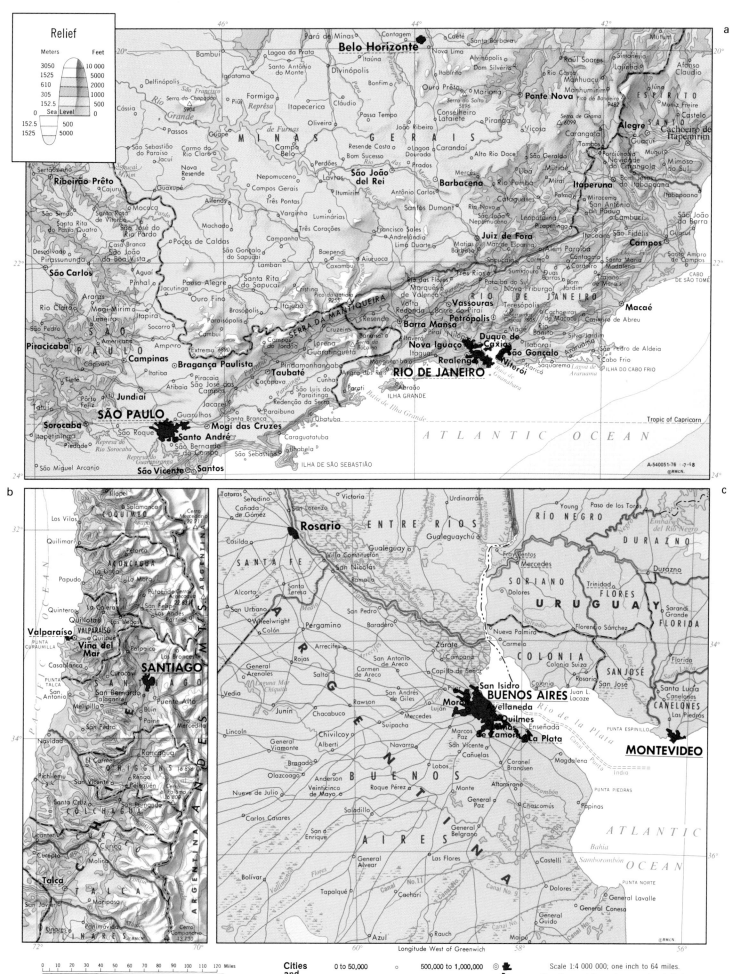

Europe

Europe is smaller than every other continent except Australia. In a sense, Europe is not really a continent at all, since it is part of the same vast landmass as Asia. Geographers sometimes refer to this landmass as a single continent, Eurasia. Europe occupies only about 18% of the land area of Eurasia.

Europe can be described as an enormous peninsula, stretching from the Ural Mountains, Ural River, and Caspian Sea in the east, to the Atlantic Ocean in the west; and from the Arctic Ocean in the north to the Mediterranean Sea, Black Sea, and Caucasus mountains in the south. The British Isles, Iceland, Corsica, Crete, and thousands of smaller islands that lie off the European mainland are usually considered as part of the continent.

A sweep of mountain ranges, including the Pyrenees, Alps and Carpathians, divides the colder, wetter north from the sun-drenched south.

Europe at a glance

Land area: 3,800,000 square miles (9,900,000 sq km)

Estimated population (January 1, 1995): 712,100,000

Population density: 187/square mile (72/sq km)

Mean elevation: 980 feet (300 m)

Highest point: Gora El' brus, Russia, 18,510 feet (5,642 m)

Lowest point: Caspian Sea, Asia-Europe, 92 feet (28 m) below sea level

Longest river: Volga, 2,194 mi (3,531 km)

Number of countries (incl. dependencies): 49

Largest independent country: Russia (Europe/Asia), 6,592,849 square miles (17,075,400 sq km)

Smallest independent country: Vatican City, 0.2 square miles (0.4 sq km)

Most populous independent country: Russia (Europe/Asia), 150,500,000

Least populous independent country: Vatican City, 1,000

Largest city: Moscow, pop. 8,801,500 (1991)

Coldest place:
Ust'- Shchugor, Russia
-67°F (-55°C)

Driest place:
Astrakhan', Russia
6.4 inches (16 cm)

Lowest point:
Caspian Sea, Asia-Eu
92 ft (28 m) below se

Highest point:
Gora El'brus, Russia
18,510 ft (5,642 m)

Wettest place:
Crkvice, Bosnia & Herzegovina
183 inches (465 cm)/year

Hottest place:
Sevilla, Spain
122°F (50°C)

Landforms

- Mountains
- Widely spaced mountains
- High tablelands
- Hills and low tablelands
- Plains
- Depresssions, basins
- High tablelands and ice caps
- Mountains and ice caps

The Alps tower above a village in the Virgen Tal valley of western Austria.

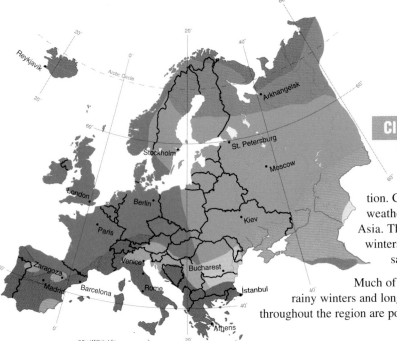

Climate

Warm, moist air masses flowing in from the Atlantic Ocean give much of Europe a mild climate and abundant precipitation. Cities like London, Paris and Rome all enjoy warmer weather than cities at similar latitudes in North America and Asia. The moderate winds don't reach eastern Europe, where the winters are long and cold and the summers short and cool. The same is true in the northern regions of Scandinavia.

Much of the south enjoys a Mediterranean climate, marked by short, rainy winters and long, dry summers. Indeed, the many beaches and islands found throughout the region are popular with vacationers year-round.

Tinted areas show temperature in degrees Fahrenheit. Vertical bars show precipitation in inches.

| Zaragoza | Athens | Venice | Paris | Bucharest | Stockholm | Arkhangelsk | Reykjavik | Extensive uplands |
| Semiarid | Hot, dry summer / mild, rainy winter | Warm, humid summer / mild winter | Mild and rainy | Warm, humid summer / cold, snowy winter | Cool, humid summer / cold, snowy winter | Short, cool, humid summer / very cold, snowy winter | Cold and dry | Climate varies with elevation and latitude |

© Rand McNally & Co.
M-550000-6A-EL1-¹-¹-¹- -1

Population

With a population of 712 million, Europe is home to 13% of the world's people. Only one continent, Asia, has a larger population. Europe's population density—187 people per square mile (72 per sq km) is also second only to Asia. However, the continent's density varies dramatically from country to country. The Netherlands, for instance, has a density of 954 people per square mile (368 per sq km), making it one of the most densely populated countries in the world. In contrast, Norway has only 29 people per square mile (11 per sq km).

A vast array of ethnic groups and cultures can be found in Europe's relatively small area. Throughout the centuries, this diversity has enriched European culture while also leading to many hostilities. Of the 60 languages spoken, the majority are derived from Latin, Germanic or Slavic roots. Most Europeans are Christian, either Protestant or Roman Catholic.

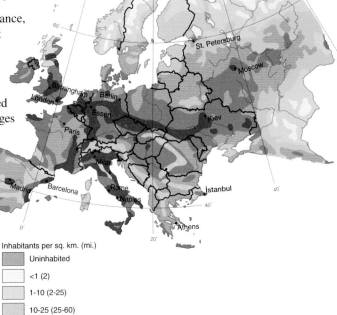

Inhabitants per sq. km. (mi.)

- Uninhabited
- <1 (2)
- 1-10 (2-25)
- 10-25 (25-60)
- 25-50 (60-125)
- 50-100 (125-250)
- >100 (250)

© Rand McNally & Co.
M-550000-1P-EL1-¹-¹-¹- -1

Fastest-Growing Countries

Albania, 1.71% (annual rate of natural increase)

Faeroe Islands, 1.04%

Iceland, 0.97%

Slowest-Growing Countries

Monaco, -0.15%

Ukraine, -0.03%

Hungary, -0.03%

Environments and Land Use

Given the high population density of Europe, it is not surprising that evidence of human development can be seen in every part of the continent, with the exception of the northern reaches of Scandinavia. In Western Europe, small farms are surrounded by towns, cities and industrial areas. Only in the east, in areas such as the vast rolling steppes of the Ukraine, can large farms and unbroken natural vistas be found.

Harvesting grapes from vineyards in Burgundy, France

The heavily industrialized countries of Western Europe boast rich economies and high standards of living. Switzerland has a per capita Gross Domestic Product (GDP) approaching U.S. $22,000, the highest in the world. The figures are generally much lower in Eastern Europe. One of the continent's poorest countries is the tiny former Communist state of Albania, which has a per capita GDP of only U.S. $998.

Pollution is an unfortunate by-product of the continent's industry. One example is the scenic Rhine River: in the 1980s, large stretches were found to be so polluted that they were devoid of life. These findings sparked a 20-year program to clean up the river. In general, the countries of Eastern Europe suffer from the worst pollution, as economic development has in the past taken precedence over environmental policies.

The vast forests of Scandinavia support a large paper and wood-products economy. Where forests survive in countries farther to the south, they are often used for recreation. Along the Mediterranean, the warm and dry lands support olive and fruit orchards. In many of these areas, agriculture is being supplemented and even replaced by tourism.

Over-fishing has depleted the seas and ocean around Europe. The fleets of countries such as Spain and Great Britain must sail far into the North Atlantic to find the ever-dwindling stocks of fish.

- Urban
- Cropland
- Cropland and woodland
- Cropland and grazing land
- Grassland, grazing land
- Forest, woodland
- Swamp, marsh
- Tundra
- Shrub, sparse grass, wasteland
- Barren land

0 100 200 300 400 Miles
0 200 400 600 Kilometers

© Rand McNally & Co.
M-550000-8L-EL1-1-1. .1

Political Changes Since 1989

Much of Europe lay in economic and physical ruin after World War II ended in 1945. Germany's cities and industrial centers had been ravaged by aerial bombardment and assaults by the Allied armies. Many other countries, such as Russia, Poland, Belgium, and the Netherlands suffered gravely from Nazi invasions and occupation.

After 1945, tensions among the victorious Allies grew, specifically between the Western powers—the United States, Great Britain and France—and the Soviet Union. It became clear that the two sides had vastly different visions for post-war Europe. In 1946, former British prime minister Winston Churchill observed that an "Iron Curtain" had gone down across Europe. It was to stay in place for almost 45 years.

Germany and the city of Berlin were divided between the Western Allies and the Soviet Union. West Germany quickly joined the other countries of Western Europe in building a stable, affluent democratic society. East Germany became part of a bloc of Eastern European countries dominated by the Soviet Union. These included Poland, Czechoslovakia, Hungary, Romania, Albania, and Bulgaria (see map at right). The economies in these countries were tightly controlled and personal freedoms were severely limited by the Communist governments in power.

The two blocs faced each other in a tense, generally non-military standoff called "The Cold War," which lasted for four decades. However, in 1985 winds of reform began sweeping through Eastern Europe. In 1989, Hungary relaxed its borders with Austria, setting off a flow of refugees from the east who had been forbidden to travel to the West. Thus began a dizzying period of change: the next two years saw the collapse of the Soviet Union, the reunification of Germany, independence for the former Soviet republics, and freedom from Soviet influence for the former bloc countries.

Although much of the old east seems intent on adopting Western ideals of democracy and freedom, the process is not without problems. Switching from communism to market economies has meant hardship for millions. It has also led to ethnic tensions that resulted in the peaceful break-up of Czechoslovakia and the violent civil wars in the former Yugoslavia.

Still, most countries in the east seem intent on one day becoming a part of the European Union, the political and economic organization that currently has 15 member countries.

East Germany and West Germany reunited in 1990.

In 1991, the Soviet Union broke up into 15 independent states: Russia, Estonia, Latvia, Lithuania, Belarus, Ukraine, Moldova, Georgia, Armenia, Azerbaijan, Kazakhstan, Turkmenistan, Kyrgyzstan, Uzbekistan, and Tajikistan.

In 1991-92 the former Yugoslavia broke up when Slovenia, Croatia, Macedonia, and Bosnia and Herzegovina declared their independence, leaving Serbia and Montenegro as the remaining Yugoslav Republcs.

In 1993, Czechoslovakia split into two separate countries: the Czech Republic and Slovakia.

Political Change Since 1989

Former Soviet Union
Former Czechoslovakia
Former Yugoslavia
Former East and West Germany
Former Soviet-bloc countries

© Rand McNally & Co.
M-550000-2P-EL1-...-1

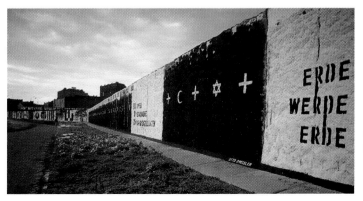

Berlin Wall memorial

40,000 SQ MI
AREA

0   100   200
Miles

ARCTIC OCEAN

ICELAND
Reykjavík
Reykjanes
Eskifjörður
Súðarkrókur
FONTUR

Arctic Circle

ATLANTIC OCEAN

Tórshavn
FÆRØE IS.
(Den.)

NORWAY
SWEDEN
FINLAND
LAPLAND
Hammerfest
Vardø
LOFOTEN IS.
Narvik
Luleå
Tornio
Oulu
Trondheim
(Nidaros)
Sundsvall
Umeå
Vaasa
Bergen
Oslo
Gävle
Turku
Helsinki
Stavanger
Karlstad
Uppsala
Hango
ST. PETERSB.
(Leningrad)
Kristiansand
Norrköping
STOCKHOLM
Tallinn
ESTONIA
Tartu
Göteborg
GOTLAND
Visby
Riga
LATVIA
Ålborg
Jelgava
Daugavpils
DENMARK
ÖLAND
Liepāja
LITHUANIA
COPENHAGEN
(København)
Malmö
Klaipėda
Kaliningrad
RUSSIA
Kaunas
Gdańsk
Vilnius
BELA
Minsk
HAMBURG
Lübeck
Szczecin
Toruń
Białystok
Grodno
Kiel
Bremen
BERLIN
POLAND
Baranovichi Bo
Hannover
Magdeburg
Poznań
Pinsk
NETHERLANDS
AMSTERDAM
Brest
The Hague
's Gravenhage
ROTTERDAM
GERMANY
Leipzig
WARSAW
Łódź
ANTWERP
ESSEN
Dresden
Wrocław
Lublin
BELGIUM
COLOGNE
Bonn
PRAGUE
KATOWICE
L'viv
BRUSSELS
FRANKFURT A.M.
Kraków
Przemyśl
LILLE
Lux.
Mainz
CZECH
Brno
Berdyc
Calais
Nürnberg
REP.
Ostrava
CZECHOSLOVAKIA
Drohobych Vinn
Le Havre
Rouen
Reims
STUTTGART
SLOVAKIA
Ivano-Fra
Cherbourg
PARIS
Strasbourg
MUNICH
Bratislava
Chernivtsi
Orléans
VIENNA
Miskolc
Debrecen
St. Nazaire
Dijon
Lausanne
(Wien)
FRANCE
Clermont-
Ferrand
Geneva
Zürich
AUSTRIA
BUDAPEST
Oradea
Cluj-
Napoca
Nantes
Bern
Graz
HUNGARY
La Rochelle
SWITZERLAND
Maribor
Szeged
ROMANIA
Tours
LYON
Ljubljana
Subotica
Bordeaux
MILAN
SLO.
Zagreb
Novi
Sad
Bayonne
TURIN
Trieste
CROATIA
CARPATI MERIDIONALI
La
Spezia
Venice
BOSNIA AND
HERZEGOVINA
Belgrade
BUCHAREST
Toulouse
Nîmes
Genoa
Bologna
Nice
SAN
Zadar
YUGOSLAVIA
MARSEILLE
MONACO
Livorno
Ancona
Split
Sofia
BULGAR
Toulon
CORSICA
(Fr.)
Florence
Sarajevo
(Sofiya)
STARA PLAN
Ajaccio
ROME
(Roma)
Niš
Plovdiv
SARDINIA
(It.)
NAPLES
(Napoli)
Vesuvio
Bari
Skopje
MACEDONIA
RHODOPE MTS.
Dubrovnik
Cetinje
Brindisi
Tiranë
Bitola
Shkodër
Durrës
Thessaloníki
Cagliari
Palermo
Messina
TYRRHENIAN
SEA
GREECE
ATHENS
(Athínai)
MEDITERRANEAN
Mt. Etna
10 902
Catania
IONIAN
SEA
Kórinthos
Kalámai
KÉRKIRA
Strait of
Otranto
C. PASSERO
SICILY
(It.)
MALTA
CRETE
Khaniá

SHETLAND IS.
(Br.)
Lerwick
NORTH
SEA

ORKNEY IS.
(Br.)

HEBRIDES

Moray
Firth
SCOTLAND
GRAMPIAN MTS.
GLASGOW
Aberdeen
Dundee
UNITED
Edinburgh
BRITISH
Firth of Forth
NORTHERN IRELAND
CHEVIOT HILLS
Belfast
Carlisle
ISLES
NEWCASTLE
IRELAND
KINGDOM
Galway
LIVERPOOL
LEEDS
Dublin
(Baile Átha Cliath)
Kingston upon Hull
CAPE CLEAR
Cork
Cobh
MANCHESTER
St. George's Chan.
BIRMINGHAM
Leicester
IRISH SEA
ISLES OF SCILLY
LANDS END
Southampton
LONDON
Portsmouth
Dover
St. of Dover
ENGLISH CHANNEL
CHANNEL IS.
(Br.)
Brest
Rennes

Bay of Biscay

SPAIN
PORTUGAL
La Coruña
C. DE FINISTERRE
El Ferrol
Vigo
Gijón
Oviedo
Santander
S. Sebastián
Bilbao
PYRENEES
ANDORRA
CORD. CANTÁBRICA
Porto
(Oporto)
Picos de Europa
Coimbra
Salamanca
Valladolid
SIERRA DE
GUADARRAMA
Zaragoza
LISBON
(Lisboa)
MADRID
Tortosa
Tarragona
BARCELONA
Valencia
SIERRA MORENA
C. DE SÃO
VICENTE
Sevilla
Murcia
Cartagena
Almería
BALEARES
MENORCA
ISLAS
(Sp.)
MALLORCA
IBIZA
C. DE LA
NAO
Palma
Cádiz
Strait of Gibraltar
Málaga
Gibraltar (Br.)
I. DEL
ALBORÁN
(Sp.)
SIERRA NEVADA
Tanger
Ceuta (Sp.)
Tétouan
Oran
Algiers
(El Djazair)
Rabat
Casablanca
MOROCCO
Fès
ALGERIA
ATLAS MOUNTAINS
Constantine
Bizerte
Tunis
TUNISIA
C. BON
C. SPARTIVENTO

Longitude West of Greenwich   0°   Longitude East of Greenwich

Scale 1: 16 000 000; one inch to 250 miles. Conic Projection
Elevations and depressions are given in feet

0   50   100   200   300   400   500 Miles
0   100   200   400   600   800 Kilometers

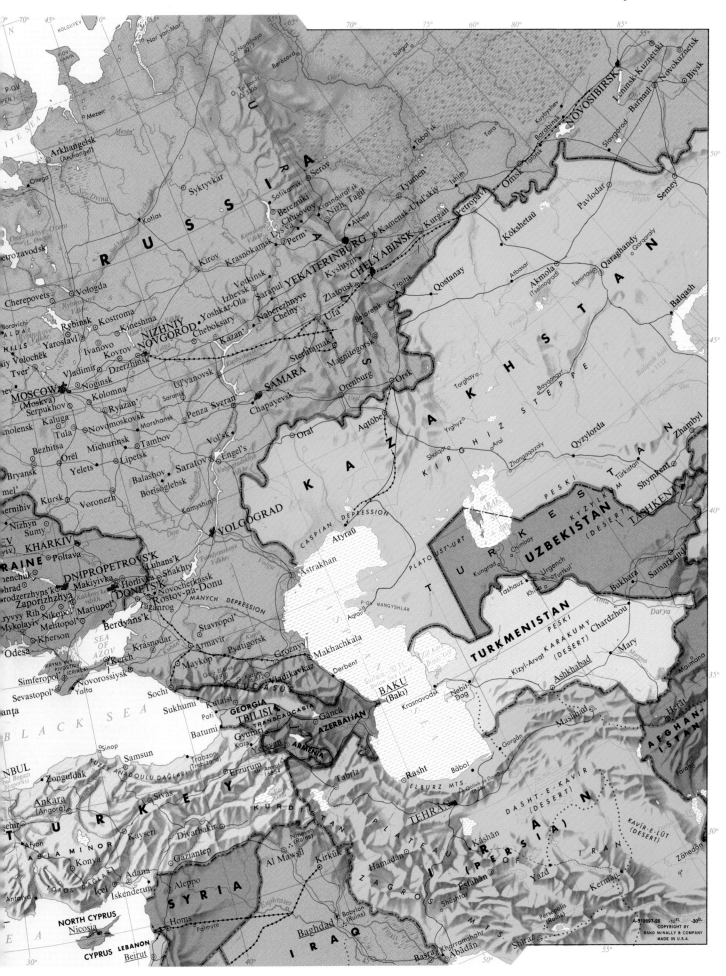

A-519697-26 · IGL · 30 EL
COPYRIGHT BY
RAND MCNALLY & COMPANY
MADE IN U.S.A.

Relief

Meters		Feet
3050		10 000
1525		5000
610		2000
305		1000
152.5		500
0	Sea Level	0
152.5		Below Sea Level
		500
1525		5000
3050		10 000

Scale 1: 16 000 000; one inch to 250 miles. Conic Projection

Elevations and depressions are given in feet

Longitude West of Greenwich   Longitude East of Greenwich

0	50	100	200	300	400	500 Miles
0	100	200	400	600	800 Kilometers	

RUSSIA
Murmansk
Polyarnyl

F I N L A N D

Helsinki
Tampere
Turku
Oulu

ESTONIA
Tallinn
Pärnu

LATVIA
Riga
Liepāja

LITHUANIA
Šiauliai
Kaunas

Klaipeda
Kaliningrad
RUSSIA
Białystok
BELA

GULF OF BOTHNIA

S W E D E N

N O R W A Y

Luleå
Boden
Skellefteå
Umeå
Örnsköldsvik
Sundsvall
Härnösand
Hudiksvall
Söderhamn
Gävle

Kiruna
Gällivare

STOCKHOLM
Uppsala
Västerås
Örebro
Norrköping
Linköping
Jönköping
Kalmar
Karlskrona
Kristianstad
GOTLAND
Visby
ÖLAND

Falun
Borlänge
Borås
Göteborg
Helsingborg
Halmstad
Malmö

Oslo
Drammen
Larvik
Uddevalla
Trollhättan
Kristiansand
Grimstad
Risör

Trondheim

Bergen
Haugesund
Stavanger
Egersund

Nesna
Bodö
Narvik

VESTERALEN
LOFOTEN
ANDOYA
SENJA

Hammerfest
Alta

DENMARK
COPENHAGEN
(København)
Odense
Ålborg
Århus
Esbjerg
Flensburg

Kattegat
Skagerrak

A R C T I C   O C E A N

N O R W E G I A N   S E A

Arctic Circle

JAN MAYEN
(Nor.)

FAEROE IS.
(Den.)
Tórshavn

SHETLAND IS.
(Br.)
Lerwick
MAINLAND

ORKNEY IS.
(Br.)
Kirkwall
Wick

KINNAIRDS HEAD
Aberdeen
Dundee

S C O T L A N D
GLASGOW
EDINBURGH
Greenock
Paisley

Inverness
Stornoway

HEBRIDES
ISLE OF SKYE
TIREE
ISLAY

NORTHERN
IRELAND
Belfast
Londonderry

BRITISH
ISLES
UNITED
KINGDOM

Newcastle-upon-Tyne
South Shields
Sunderland
Hartlepool
Middlesbrough
Tynemouth
Carlisle

Berwick-upon-Tweed

DOGGER
BANK

N O R T H   S E A

I R E L A N D

ICELAND
Reykjavík
Seydisfjördur
Eskifjördur
Vopnafjördur

GRIMSEY

N O R T H   A T L A N T I C

Relief

Feet		Meters
10 000		3050
5000		1525
2000		610
1000		305
500		152.5
0	Sea Level	Sea Level
Below Sea Level		
500		152.5
5000		1525
10000		3050

Scale 1: 10 000 000; one inch to 160 miles. Conic Proje
Elevations and depressions are given in feet

ENGLAND
LONDON
BIRMINGHAM
NETHERLANDS
AMSTERDAM
The Hague
Rotterdam
BELGIUM
BRUSSELS
ANTWERP
GERMANY
COLOGNE
ESSEN
FRANKFURT
STUTTGART
MUNICH
PRAGUE
CZECH REP.
VIENNA
BUDAPEST
HUNGARY
CROATIA
POLAND
FRANCE
PARIS
Lyon
Marseille
Toulon
Bordeaux
Toulouse
Nantes
SPAIN
MADRID
BARCELONA
Valencia
Sevilla
Málaga
Zaragoza
Bilbao
LISBON
Porto
ROME
NAPLES
Vatican City
Palermo
Messina
Bari
Brindisi
Taranto
Venice
MONACO
CORSICA (Fr.)
SARDINIA
BALEARES (Sp.)
MALLORCA
MENORCA
IBIZA
Algiers
Tunis
TUNISIA
Tangier
MOROCCO
ENGLISH CHANNEL
BAY OF BISCAY
LIGURIAN SEA
TYRRHENIAN SEA
MEDITERRANEAN SEA
ADRIATIC SEA
IONIAN SEA
Longitude West of Greenwich
Longitude East of Greenwich
50 100 150 200 250 300 Miles
100 200 300 400 500 Kilometers
A-559400-76-13-1-22
COPYRIGHT BY RAND McNALLY & COMPANY MADE IN U.S.A.

Cities
and
Towns

0 to 50,000
50,000 to 500,000
500,000 to 1,000,000
1,000,000 and over

Relief

Meters	Feet
3050	10000
1525	5000
610	2000
305	1000
152.5	500
0	Sea Level
	Below Sea Level

Sea Level
152.5 | 500
1525 | 5000
3050 | 10000

0   50   100   150   200   250   300 Miles

0   100   200   300   400   500 Kilometers

Obskaya Guba

KARA SEA

YAMAL

NENETS

WESTERN SIBERIAN LOWLAND

U R A L

KHREBET PAY-KHOY

PECHORA BASIN

T I M A N

R I D G E

NOVAYA ZEMLYA

KOLGUYEV

P-OV KANIN

MALOZEMEL'SKAYA TUNDRA

BOL'SHEZEMEL'SKAYA TUNDRA

BARENTS SEA

ARCTIC OCEAN

KOL'SKIY P-OV (KOLA PEN.)

SOLOVETSKIYE OSTROVA

Arkhangel'sk (Arkhangel)

R U S S I A

YEKATERINBURG

BASHKORTOSTAN

TATARSTAN

UDMURTIA

MARI EL

CHUVASHIA

Kazan'

NIZHNIY NOVGOROD

MOSCOW (Moskva)

ST. PETERSBURG (Sankt-Peterburg) (Leningrad)

Kronshtadt

KARELIA

LAPLAND

NORWAY

SWEDEN

FINLAND

ESTONIA

LATVIA

LITHUANIA

RUSSIA

Helsinki

Tallinn

Riga

Vilnius

Murmansk

Petrozavodsk

Vologda

Yaroslavl'

Kostroma

Rybinsk

Tver'

Novgorod

Pskov

Smolensk

Gulf of Finland

BALTIC SEA

GULF OF BOTHNIA

Perm'

Kirov

Arkhangel'sk

Syktyvkar

Ukhta

Pechora

Vorkuta

Salekhard

Arctic Circle

VALDAI HILLS

C E N T R

Scale 1:10 000 000; one inch to 160 miles. Conic Projection
Elevations and depressions are given in feet.

ATLANTIC OCEAN

BAY OF BISCAY

FRANCE

SPAIN

PORTUGAL

LISBON

MADRID

BARCELONA

Valencia

SWITZERLAND

GERMANY

FRANKFURT

MANNHEIM

STUTTGART

MUNICH

TURIN

MILAN

Venice

ROME
(Roma)

NAPLES
(Napoli)

CORSICA
(Fr.)

SARDINIA
(It.)

LIGURIAN SEA

TYRRHENIAN SEA

MEDITERRANEAN

SICILY

MALTA

MOROCCO

ATLAS MOUNTAINS

ALGERIA

TUNISIA

GRAND ERG OCCIDENTAL

GRAND ERG ORIENTAL

SAHARAN ATLAS

TARABULUS
(TRIPOLITANIA)

Tripoli (Ṭarābulus)

Relief

Meters	Feet
3050	10000
1525	5000
610	2000
305	1000
152.5	500
0 Sea Level	0
	Below
152.5	500 Sea Level
1525	5000
3050	10000

A-558300-76 18 12-33
COPYRIGHT BY
RAND McNALLY & COMPANY
MADE IN U.S.A.

Longitude West of Greenwich   Longitude East of Greenwich

Scale 1:10 000 000; one inch to 160 miles. Bonne's Projection
Elevations and depressions are given in feet

The Turkish Republic of Northern Cyprus
unilaterally declared its independence
on Nov. 15, 1983.

Areas occupied by Israel since 1967.

50	100	150	200	250	300 Miles
100	200	300	400	500 Kilometers	

Africa

Africa, the second-largest continent, comprises about one-fifth of the world's land area. From the Equator, Africa extends roughly the same distance to the north as it does to the south.

The Drakensberg Mountains mark the southern end of the African plateau.

A high plateau covers much of the continent. The edges of the plateau are marked by steep slopes, called escarpments, where the land angles sharply downward onto narrow coastal plains or into the sea. Many of the continent's great rivers plunge over these escarpments in falls or rapids, and therefore cannot be used as transportation routes from the coast into the continent's interior.

Among Africa's most significant mountain systems are the Atlas range in the far north and the Drakensberg range in the far south. A long string of mountain ranges and highlands running north-south through eastern Africa marks the course of the Great Rift Valley.

Africa at a glance

Land area: 11,700,000 square miles (30,300,000 sq km)

Estimated population (January 1, 1995): 697,600,000

Population density: 60/ square mile (23/sq km)

Mean elevation: 1,900 feet (580 m)

Highest point: Kilimanjaro, Tanzania, 19,340 feet (5,895 m)

Lowest point: Lac Assal, Djibouti, 515 feet (157 m) below sea level

Longest river: Nile, 4,145 mi (6,671 km)

Number of countries (incl. dependencies): 61

Largest independent country: Sudan, 967,500 square miles (2,505,813 sq km)

Smallest independent country: Seychelles, 175 square miles (453 sq km)

Most populous independent country: Nigeria, 97,300,000

Least populous independent country: Seychelles, 75,000

Largest city: Cairo, pop. 6,068,695 (1990)

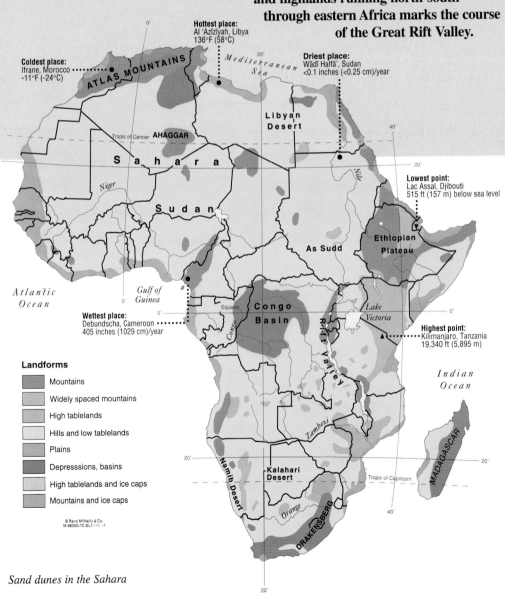

Coldest place:
Ifrane, Morocco
-11°F (-24°C)

Hottest place:
Al 'Azīzīyah, Libya
136°F (58°C)

Driest place:
Wādī Halfā', Sudan
<0.1 inches (<0.25 cm)/year

ATLAS MOUNTAINS

Mediterranean Sea

Libyan Desert

Tropic of Cancer AHAGGAR

S a h a r a

Niger

S u d a n

Nile

Lowest point:
Lac Assal, Djibouti
515 ft (157 m) below sea level

As Sudd

Ethiopian Plateau

Atlantic Ocean

Gulf of Guinea

Equator

Congo Basin

Congo

Rift Valley

Lake Victoria

Highest point:
Kilimanjaro, Tanzania
19,340 ft (5,895 m)

Wettest place:
Debundscha, Cameroon
405 inches (1029 cm)/year

Indian Ocean

Zambezi

Namib Desert

Kalahari Desert

Tropic of Capricorn

MADAGASCAR

Orange

DRAKENSBERG

Landforms

- Mountains
- Widely spaced mountains
- High tablelands
- Hills and low tablelands
- Plains
- Depresssions, basins
- High tablelands and ice caps
- Mountains and ice caps

© Rand McNally & Co.
M-580000-7C-EL1-1-1- -1

Sand dunes in the Sahara

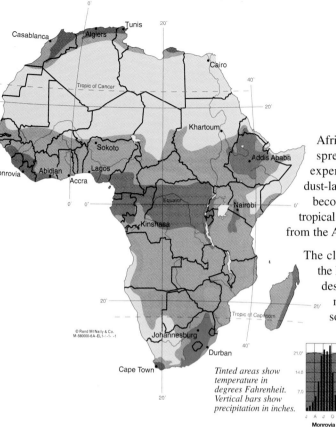

Climate

Africa's most prominent climatic region is the vast Sahara desert which spreads over much of the northern half of the continent. The Sahara experiences scorching daytime temperatures, minimal rainfall, and hot, dry, dust-laden winds that blow nearly continuously. South of the Sahara, the climate becomes increasingly humid, moving through zones of semiarid steppe and tropical savanna to the tropical rain forest that stretches across equatorial Africa from the Atlantic Ocean to the Rift Valley.

The climate patterns of northern Africa are repeated in reverse south of the Equator. The rain forest gives way to zones of decreasing humidity, and desert regions cover western South Africa and Namibia. Africa's mildest, most temperate climates are found along its Mediterranean coast, at its southwestern tip, and in eastern South Africa.

Tinted areas show temperature in degrees Fahrenheit. Vertical bars show precipitation in inches.

Monrovia	Kinshasa	Sokoto	Cairo	Tunis	Durban	Johannesburg	Extensive uplands
Hot and rainy	Hot with rainy and dry seasons	Semiarid	Very dry	Hot, dry summer / mild, rainy winter	Warm, humid summer / mild winter	Mild and rainy	Climate varies with elevation and latitude

Population

Approximately one-eighth of the world's people live in Africa. The population is almost evenly divided between the sub-Saharan countries and those bordering the Mediterranean. Large tracts of the Sahara are uninhabited. Despite recurring famines and warfare, the population is rapidly increasing. Twenty-two African countries have annual growth rates at or above 3%, which means that the number of inhabitants in each can double within 25 years.

The largest concentrations of people are generally found in regions in which one or more of the following conditions exist: moderate temperatures, ample water supply, and arable land. These regions include Egypt's fertile Nile Valley, the northern coast of the Gulf of Guinea, the highlands of East Africa, and the coastal regions of Morocco, Algeria, and Tunisia, north of the Atlas Mountains.

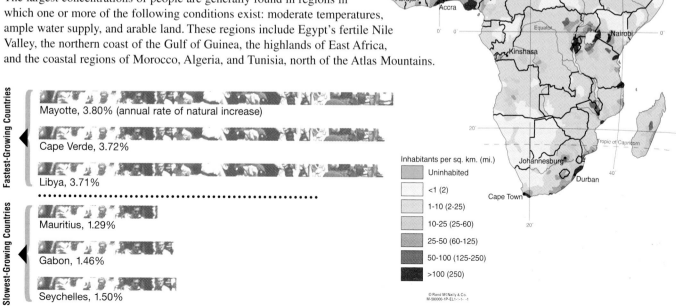

Fastest-Growing Countries

Mayotte, 3.80% (annual rate of natural increase)

Cape Verde, 3.72%

Libya, 3.71%

Slowest-Growing Countries

Mauritius, 1.29%

Gabon, 1.46%

Seychelles, 1.50%

Inhabitants per sq. km. (mi.)

	Uninhabited
	<1 (2)
	1-10 (2-25)
	10-25 (25-60)
	25-50 (60-125)
	50-100 (125-250)
	>100 (250)

© Rand McNally & Co.
M-580000-1P-EL1--!-1-.-1

Environments and Land Use

Deserts account for one-third of Africa's land area, and they claim new land every year. Drought, over-farming and over-grazing can quickly turn marginal land, such as that of the Sahel region, into barren wasteland. The huge Sahara desert has itself only existed a short time, in geological terms: cave paintings and other archeological evidence indicate that green pastureland covered the area just a few thousand years ago.

Shepherd with goats in the Sahel

Most Africans are subsistence farmers, growing sorghum, corn, millet, sweet potatoes, and other starchy foods. Commercial farms, most of which date from the colonial period, can be found throughout central and southern Africa, producing cash crops such as coffee, bananas, tobacco and cacao. One-quarter of the continent's land is suitable for grazing, but disease and drought have made raising animals difficult. Although three out of four Africans work in agriculture, Africa is the only continent that is not self-sufficient for food.

The great rain forests that cover much of equatorial Africa produce mahogany, ebony, and other valuable hardwoods. However, only limited areas of the forests are suitable for logging, and the lack of developed road networks makes it difficult and costly to transport the wood.

Vast mineral reserves are spread throughout the continent. Most are unexploited, but notable exceptions include the diamond mines of South Africa and Namibia, the copper mines of Zambia and Zaire, and the oil fields of Nigeria, Libya, and Algeria.

The great concentrations of wildlife for which Africa is famous can still be found in places such as Tanzania's Serengeti Plain and Botswana's Kalahari Desert. In many other parts of the continent, however, wildlife is quickly disappearing as humans encroach on habitat and poachers decimate entire species.

Urban

Cropland

Cropland and woodland

Cropland and grazing land

Grassland, grazing land

Forest, woodland

Swamp, marsh

Tundra

Shrub, sparse grass, wasteland

Barren land

© Rand McNally & Co.
M-580000-8L-EL1-·-·-·-·1

| 0 | 200 | 400 | 600 | 800 | 1000 Miles |
| 0 | 300 | 600 | 900 | 1200 | 1500 Kilometers |

Field of sorghum in Zimbabwe

Africa: from Colonial Rule to Independence

The origins of Europe's colonization of Africa can be traced back to the 1500s, when a lucrative slave trade developed to supply European settlers in the New World with laborers. Africa became the primary source for slaves: between the mid-1500s and the mid-1800s, 11 million Africans were captured and sold into slavery.

When the slave trade was banned across Europe in the early 1800s, commercial trade with Africa continued. In the second half of the century, competition for Africa's minerals and other raw materials intensified, and between 1880 and 1914, France, Britain, Italy, Portugal, Belgium, Spain, and Germany annexed large areas of Africa. Colonial rule was often characterized by racial prejudice and segregation.

In the late 19th and early 20th centuries, Egypt, Ethiopia, and South Africa began to break free from colonial influence. For most or Africa, however, colonial rule persisted through the mid-1900s, although it faced growing bitterness and nationalist sentiment. As the colonial powers struggled through two world wars, and as their international dominance declined, it became increasingly difficult for them to maintain their empires.

In 1951, Libya gained its independence, following a UN resolution that ended British and French control. Sudan peacefully won independence from Britain and Egypt in 1956. A year later, Britain granted independence to the Gold Coast, which became the new country of Ghana. Guinea separated from France in 1958, followed by all of the other French colonies in 1960. Anti-colonial movements gathered strength across Africa, and by the end of the 1970s, a total of 43 countries had become independent.

The end of colonial rule, however, has not brought peace and prosperity. Many of the newly freed countries were ill-prepared for independence. Their economies were oriented to fit the needs of the now-departed colonists, few transportation networks existed, and dictators and rival despots fought for power in civil wars.

People of the Samburu tribe

Further, most Africans identify themselves primarily with the tribe to which they belong. The political delineations established by the European powers have little meaning and often conflict with traditional tribal boundaries. In some cases, enemy tribes found themselves pushed together in a single country; in others, single tribes were divided among several countries. These conditions have already brought much warfare and hardship. Still, Africa is a land of promise and opportunity. The rich diversity of its people and abundance of its resources should inevitably enable the continent to realize its potential.

Africa in 1950
- Independent
- British
- French
- Portuguese
- Spanish
- Belgian
- Italian
- Other

© Rand McNally & Co.
M-480045-2S-EL1-·-·- -1

Africa Today
- Independent
- Other

1960 Date of independence

© Rand McNally & Co.
M-580000-2S-EL1-·-·- -1

Ethno-linguistic Groups

Semitic-Hamitic	Bantu	Indo-European
Mande	Central Bantoid	Kanuri
Guinean	Eastern Bantoid	Songhai
Hausa	Western Bantoid	Khoisan

Nilotic	Central/Eastern Sudanese, Bantu
Malay-Polynesian	Indo-European, Semitic-Hamitic
Kanuri, Semitic-Hamitic	Central/Eastern Sudanese, Semitic-Hamitic
Hausa, Western Bantoid	Central/Eastern Sudanese

© Rand McNally & Co.
M-580000-1D-EL1-·-·- -1

Scale 1:40 000 000; one inch to 630 miles. Lambert's Azimuthal, Equal Area Projection
Elevations and depressions are given in feet.

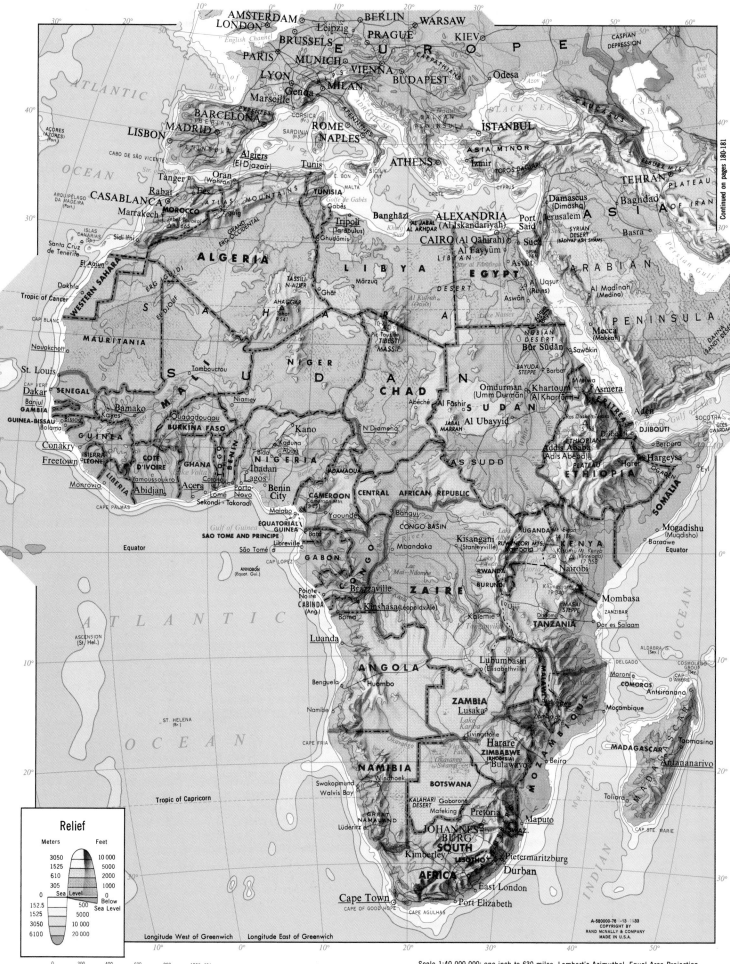

Continued on pages 180-181

Relief

Meters		Feet
3050		10 000
1525		5000
610		2000
305		1000
0	Sea Level	0
		Below
152.5		500 Sea Level
1525		5000
3050		10 000
6100		20 000

Longitude West of Greenwich   Longitude East of Greenwich

0	200	400	600	800	1000 Miles
0	400	800	1200	1600 Kilometers	

A-580000-76 -13 1933
COPYRIGHT BY
RAND McNALLY & COMPANY
MADE IN U.S.A.

Scale 1:40 000 000; one inch to 630 miles. Lambert's Azimuthal, Equal Area Projection
Elevations and depressions are given in feet.

a

ÁÇORES (AZORES)
(Port.)

GRACIOSA
TERCEIRA
SÃO JORGE
FAIAL
PICO
SÃO MIGUEL
Ponta Delgada
STA. MARIA

®RMCN.

Same scale as main map

ARQUIPÉLAGO
ILHA DE PORTO SANTO
Funchal
DA MADEIRA
ILHA DA MADEIRA
(Port.)

ISLAS CANARIAS
(Sp.)
LANZAROTE
LA PALMA
TENERIFE
Sta. Cruz
de Tenerife
San Sebastián
GOMERA
HIERRO
GRAN CANARIA
Las Palmas de
Gran Canaria
FUERTEVENTURA
CAP DRÂA

CABO BOJADOR

The Western Sahara is
occupied by Morocco

Dakhla

Tropic of Cancer

Nouadhibou
CAP BLANC
CAP D'ARGUIN

Nouamrhar
CAP TIMIRIS

Nouakchott

Saint-Louis
CAP
VERT
Rufisque
Thiès
Dakar
Kaolack
Banjul
(Bathurst)
GAMBIA
Ziguinchor
GUINEA-
BISSAU
Bissau
Bolama
Buba
ARQUIPÉLAGO
DOS BIJAGÓS
Boké
Boffa
Kindia
Forécariah
Conakry
Makeni
Freetown
SIERRA LEONE
Moyamba
Bonthe

b

SANTA ANTÃO
SÃO VICENTE
SAL
SÃO NICOLAU
BOA VISTA
CAPE VERDE
SÃO TIAGO
MAIO
FOGO
Praia

®RMCN.

Same scale as main map

SPAIN
Cádiz
Str. of Gibraltar
Gibraltar (U.K.)
Ceuta (Sp.)
Tanger
(Tangier)
Tetouan
Melilla
(Sp.)
Larache
Ouezzane
Salé
Rabat
CASABLANCA
El Jadida
Azemmour
Settat
Safi
(Asfi)
Kasba-Tadla
Marrakech
Essaouira
Jebel Toubkal
13665
Demnat
Agadir
Taroudant
Sidi Ifni
Tiznit
ANTI ATLAS
El Aaiún

WESTERN SAHARA

Algiers
(El Djazair)
Delles
Bejaïa
(Bougie)
Skikda
Annaba
Bône
Tizi-Ouzou
Cherchell
El Boulaïda
Blida
Constantine
Mestghanem
Oran
Ghilizane
M'Sila
Batna
Tébessa
Sidi bel Abbès
Saïda
El Djelfa
Beskra
Tilimsen
Laghouat
El Oued
Touggourt
Figuig
Ghardaïa
Wargla
Hassi Messaoud
Béchar
Igli
Béni Abbès
GRAND ERG OCCIDENTAL
Timimoun
GRAND ERG ORIENTAL
Adrar
El Menia
PLATEAU
DU TADEMAÏT
Bordj Omar Idriss
PLATEAU
DU TINGHERT
In Salah
Illizi
ALGERIA
TIDIKELT
TASSILI-N-AJJER

ERG CHECH
ERG IGUIDI
Tindouf
Chenachane
El MREYYÉ
EL HANK
EL DJOUF
Taoudenni
Ouallene
Djanet
Ahaggar
In Amel
Tamenghest
SAHARA
TANEZROUFT
Atar
Chinguetti
OUARANE
Mabrouk
ADRAR DES IFÓGHAS
Iferouâne
Monts Tamgak
6300
AÏR
Monts Bagzane
6906
Agadez
TUAREG

MAURITANIA

Akjoujt
Araouane
Kidal
Tidjikdja
VALLÉE DU TILEMSI
Boutilimit
Aleg
Kiffa
Oualâta
Néma
Tombouctou
(Timbuktu)
Bamba
Gao
Goundam
Bourem
MALI
NIGER
Rosso
Dagana
Kaédi
Mbout
Sélibaby
Nioro du Sahel
Niafounke
Tahoua
Madaoua
Tessaoua
Zinder
Louga
Matam
Linguère
Nara
Goumbou
Sokolo
Tillabéry
Maradi
Katsina
Nguru
Diourbel
Bakel
SENEGAL
Kayes
Bafoulabé
Mopti
Bandiagara
Niamey
Dosso
Kaura Namoda
Gusau
Kano
Say
Sokoto
Hadejia
Tambacounda
Kita
Koulikoro
Djenné
Ouahigouya
Dori
Birnin Kebbi
Zaria
Kaduna
Ségou
San
BURKINA FASO
Ouagadougou
Fada
N'gourma
Malanville
Kandi
Kontagora
Bauchi
Gombe
Bamako
Satadougou
Siguiri
SUDAN
Koutiala
Dédougou
Koudougou
Tenkodogo
Kano
Illo
Zungeru
Minna
Jos
FOUTA DJALLON
Labé
Timbo
Kankan
Bougouni
Sikasso
Bobo-
Dioulasso
Gambaga
Sansanné-Mango
Nafitingou
Gaya
Abuja
Keffi
NIGERIA
Kindia
Mamou
Kouroussa
GUINEA
Faranah
Odienné
Korhogo
Gaoua
Bole
Tamale
Yendi
Sokode
Parakou
Jebba
Baro
Ibi
Kissidougou
Kabala
Beyla
Kong
Boura
Bouna
Dabakala
Bondoukou
Kintampo
Savalou
Atakpamé
Save
Iseyin
Oyo
Ilorin
Ogbomosho
Oshogbo
Lokoja
Makurdi
Katsina Ala
Pendembu
Kolahun
Séguéla
Bouaké
KONG
GHANA
TOGO
Abomey
Ibadan
Iwo
Ife
Ilesha
Idah
Benin
City
Enugu
Onitsha
Kumasi
Koforidua
COTE D'IVOIRE
(IVORY COAST)
Yamoussoukro
Bouaflé
Palimé
Porto-Novo
Abeokuta
Ijebu Ode
Sapele
Warri
Aba
Port
Harcourt
Calabar
Mamfe
Monrovia
Buchanan
LIBERIA
River Cess
Mont Nimba
5748
Greenville
Harper
Tabou
CAPE PALMAS
Grand
Lahou
Grand
Bassam
Assini
Tarkwa
Accra
Ada
Sekondi-Takoradi
Cape Coast
Saltpond
THREE
POINTS
Lagos
Cotonou
Lomé
Keta
Forcados
Brass
Bonny
Cameroon Mtn.
13451
Malabo
BIOKO
Douala
Kribi
EQUATORIAL
GUINEA
Bata
RIO
MUNI
SÃO TOMÉ AND PRINCIPE
ILHA DO PRINCIPE
ILHA DE SÃO TOMÉ
São Tomé
Libreville

ATLANTIC OCEAN

GULF OF GUINEA

BIGHT OF BENIN

ATLANTIC
OCEAN

A-589100-76-17-...-33
COPYRIGHT BY
RAND McNALLY & COMPANY
MADE IN U.S.A.
®RMCN.

Longitude West of Greenwich
Longitude East of Greenwich

Scale 1:16 000 000; one inch to 250 miles; Sinusoidal Projection
Elevations and depressions are given in feet

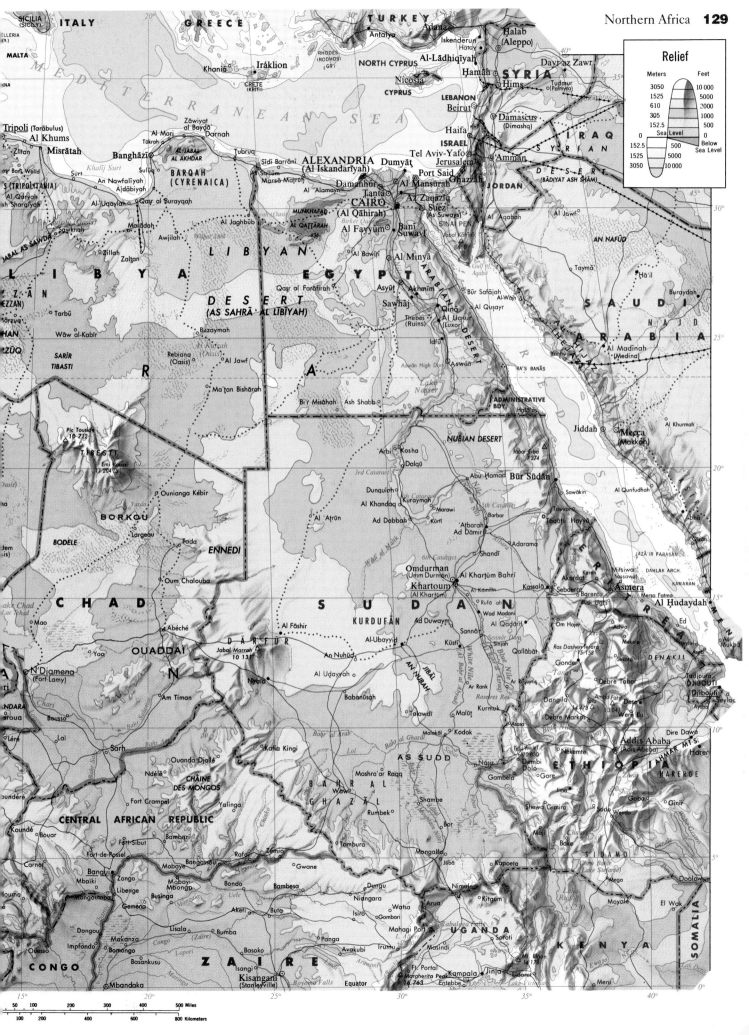

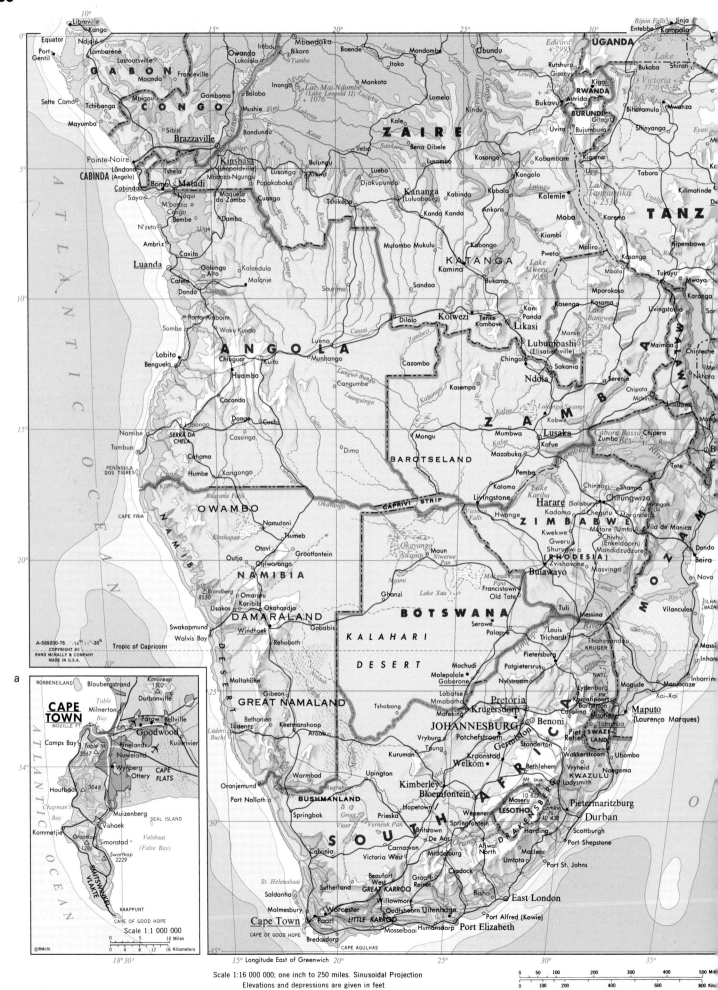

Scale 1:16 000 000; one inch to 250 miles. Sinusoidal Projection
Elevations and depressions are given in feet

b

SOMALIA / ETHIOPIA inset (top right)

YEMEN
Al Mukhá
Madinat ash Sha'b
Aden ('Adan)
SOCOTRA (Yemen)
Hadibu
ABD AL-KURI
GEES GWARDAFUY
Red Sea
ERITREA
Aseb
Bab el Mandeb
Gulf of Aden
Obock
Tadjoura
DJIBOUTI
Seylac
Aysha
Berbera
Karin
Laas Qoray
Boosaaso
Caluula
MAYD I.
Hurdiyo
RAS HAFUN
Dire Dawa
Harer
Jijiga
Hargeysa
Boorama
Burco
Shimbiris
7 897
Borraan
Bender Beyla
AHMAR MTS.
NOGAL VALLEY
Laas Caanood
Degeh Bur
Buuhoodle
Eyl
ETHIOPIA
Gaalkacyo
AUDO RANGE
Keldra
OGADEN
Ceel Buur
Hobyo
S O M A L I
KENYA
Doolow
Xuddur
Buulo Berde
Luuq
Baydhabo (Baidoa)
Cadale
El Wak
Sarahley
Afgooye
Baadheere (Barderal)
Mogadishu (Muqdisho)
Marka (Merca)
Baraawe
Shabeelle
Juba
Lach Dera

Scale 1:16 000 000;
one inch to 250 miles.
A-580051-7C

EUROPE
ASIA
AFRICA
Location of area shown on the map

c

Main map (Southern Africa / South Africa)

INDIAN OCEAN

SOMALIA
Kismaayo
Buur Gaabo
Equator

Mr. Kenya (Kirinyaga) 17,058
Hall
robi
Witu
Lamu
Malindi
Takaungu
Mombasa
Vanga
PEMBA ISLAND
Tanga
Pangani
ZANZIBAR
Zanzibar
Bagamoyo
Morogoro
Dar es Salaam
Kisaki
MAFIA
Utete
Kilwa Kivinje
Lindi
Mikindani
CABO DELGADO
Masasi
Mocímboa da Praia
Ibo
NJAZIDJA
Moroni
COMOROS
MWALI
NZWANI
ÎLES GLORIEUSES (Fr.)
Antsiranana
CAP D'AMBRE
Pemba
Lúrio
Memba
Nacala
Moçambique
Angoche
ILHA ANGOCHE
Mahajanga
CAP SAINT-ANDRÉ
Besalampy
ALDABRA IS. (Sey.)
COSMOLEDO GROUP (Sey.)
Dzaoudzi
MAYOTTE (Fr.)
NOSY BE
Iharana
Maromokotro 9436
Mataantsetra
Mandritsara
Helodrano Antongila
NOSY BORAHA
Antananarivo
Ambatondrazaka
Alaotra
Fenoarivo Atsinanana
Maintirano
ÎLE JUAN DE NOVA (Fr.)
NOSY BARREN
Moramanga
Toamasina
Tsiafajavona 8671
Vatomandry
Antsirabe
Mahanoro
Morondava
Fianarantsoa
Ambositra
Mananjary
BASSAS DA INDIA (Fr.)
Manakara
Ivohibe
EUROPA (Fr.)
Morombe
Betroka
MADAGASCAR
Mahaly
Trafonomby 4411
Faradofay
Toliara
CAP STE. MARIE
Tsaratanana

LESOTHO
Clocolan
Pitseng
Teyateyaneng
Mokhotlong
Estcourt
Kranskop
Eshowe
Greytown
Mapumulo
Cathkin Pk. 10438
Mooirivier
Mt. Gilboa 5803
New Hanover
Dalton
Wartburg
Stanger
Machache 9464
Thabana Ntlenyana 11425
Impendle
Ntshoni 5851
Howick
Pietermaritzburg
Roma
10159
Underberg
Bulwer
Richmond
Camperdown
Verulam
Pinetown
Durban
Isipingo
Donnybrook
Creighton
Mid Illovo
Umkomaas
8326
Qacha's Nek
Swartberg 7619
Franklin
EASTERN CAPE
Ixopo
Umzinkulu
Scottburgh
Park Rynie
The Twins 8820
Matatiele
Cedarville
Mt. Currie 7297
Kokstad
Harding
Sezela
Mohale's Hoek
Zastron
Mount Fletcher
1426
Kokstad
Umzimkulu
Umtentweni
Port Shepstone
Quthing
9684
Mount Frere
Mount Ayliff
Bizana
Uvongo Beach
Margate
Ben Macdhui 9846
Rhodes
Witberg 7855
Lady Grey
Herschel
Tabankulu
Port Edward
Barkly East
Maclear
Qumbu
Flagstaff
Jamestown
Rossouw
8430
Elliot
Ugie
Tsolo
Libode
Lusikisiki
Molteno
Dordrecht
Indwe
Cala
Umtata
Ngqeleni
Port St. Johns
STORMBERG
Sterkstroom
Lady Frere
Engcobo
Mqanduli
RAME HEAD
Waverly
Queenstown
Tylden
Cofimvaba
Tsomo
Idutywa
Elliotdale
Tarkastad
Cradock
Whittlesea
Cathcart
Ngamakwe
Willowvale
BANKBERG 6606
WINTERBERG 7778
Seymour
Stutterheim
Frankfort
Xama
Kei Mouth
Butterworth
Kentani
Pearston
Adelaide
Keiskammahoek
Bisho
Berlin
Morgan's Bay
Somerset East
Bedford
Fort Alice
Fort Beaufort
King William's Town
Breidbach
Gonubie
East London
SUURBERGE
Alicedale
Riebeek-Oos
Grahamstown
Peddie
Kidd's Beach
Kirkwood
Addo
Salem
Bothurst
Hamburg
Uitenhage
Alexandria
Port Alfred (Kowie)
SAINT CROIX ISLAND
BIRD ISLAND
Port Elizabeth
KAAP RECIFE

SOUTH AFRICA

DRAKENSBERG

Orange

INDIAN OCEAN

Scale 1:4 000 000
0 10 20 30   40 Miles
0 10 20 30 40 50 60 Kilometers

Relief

Meters		Feet
3050		10 000
1525		5000
610		2000
305		1000
152.5		500
0	Sea Level	0
152.5		500
1525		5000
3050		10 000

Longitude East of Greenwich

Asia

Covering nearly one-third of the Earth's land surface, Asia is by far the largest of the seven continents. It is a land of extremes and dramatic physical contrasts, containing nearly every type of landform, and many of them on a vast scale. It boasts the world's lowest point (the Dead Sea), its highest point (Mt. Everest), its highest and largest plateau (the Plateau of Tibet), and its largest inland body of water (the Caspian Sea).

Wide belts of mountain systems cover much of Asia. The Himalayas, which form a great 1,500-mile (2,400-km) arc south of Tibet, are the highest mountains in the world: more than 90 Himalayan peaks rise above 24,000 feet (7,320 m).

The beginnings of civilization can be traced to three distinct areas of Asia: Mesopotamia, around 4000 BC; the Indus River valley, around 3000 BC; and China, around 2000 BC. Eight of the world's major religions—Buddhism, Christianity, Confucianism, Hinduism, Islam, Judaism, Shinto, and Taoism—originated in Asia.

Asia at a glance

Land area:
17,300,000 square miles
(44,900,000 sq km)

Estimated population
(January 1, 1995): 3,422,700,000

Population density:
198/square mile (76/sq km)

Mean elevation: 3,000 feet
(910 m)

Highest point: Mt. Everest,
China (Tibet)-Nepal, 29,028
feet (8,848 m)

Lowest point: Dead Sea,
Israel-Jordan, 1,339 feet
(408 m) below sea level

Longest river: Yangtze
(Chang), 3,900 mi (6,300 km)

Number of countries
(incl. dependencies): 49

Largest independent country:
Russia (Europe/Asia),
6,592,849 square miles
(17,075,400 sq km)

Smallest independent country:
Maldives, 115 square miles
(298 sq km)

**Most populous independent
country:** China, 1,196,980,000

**Least populous independent
country:** Maldives, 251,000

Largest city: Seoul, South
Korea, pop. 10,627,790 (1990)

Annapurna, one of the highest mountains in the Himalayas

Coldest place:
Verkhoyansk, Russia
-90°F (-68°C)

Lowest point:
Dead Sea, Israel-Jordan
1,339 ft (408 m) below sea level

Hottest place:
Tirat Zvi, Israel
129°F (54°C)

Wettest place:
Cherrapunji, India
450 inches (1143 cm)/year

Driest place:
Aden, Yemen
1.8 inches (4.6 cm)/year

Highest point:
Mt. Everest, China (Tibet)-Nepal
29,028 ft (8,848 m)

URALS · Ob' · Yenisey · Siberia · Sea of Okhotsk · Poluostrov Kamchatka · Western Siberian Lowland · Kirghiz Steppe · ALTAI MTS. · Gobi Desert · Sea of Japan · HONSHU · CAUCASUS · ZAGROS MTS. · Plateau of Iran · PAMIRS · TIEN SHAN · KUNLUN SHAN · Huang · East China Sea · Pacific Ocean · Arabian Peninsula · HIMALAYAS · Plateau of Tibet · Indus · Yangtze · Arabian Sea · Ganges · Deccan · Bay of Bengal · LUZON · South China Sea · Malay Pen. · SUMATRA · BORNEO · NEW GUINEA · Equator

Landforms

- Mountains
- Widely spaced mountains
- High tablelands
- Hills and low tablelands
- Plains
- Depresssions, basins
- High tablelands and ice caps
- Mountains and ice caps

© Rand McNally & Co.
M-550000-7C-EL1-·-·- -1

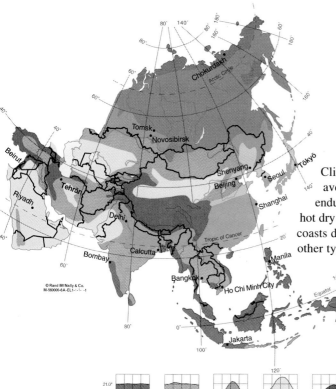

Climate

Climates vary greatly across Asia. In much of Siberia, temperatures average below -5°F (-20°C) in January, while the Persian Gulf region endures summer temperatures as high as 122°F (50°C). Monsoons interrupt hot dry spells with much-needed rain along the southeast and Indian Ocean coasts during the summer months. Between these extremes, almost every other type of climate on Earth can be found in Asia.

This climatic diversity can be explained by the continent's great expanse, from the Arctic to the tropics, and its great range in elevations.

Tinted areas show temperature in degrees Fahrenheit. Vertical bars show precipitation in inches.

    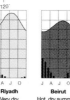 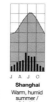

Jakarta	Ho Chi Minh City	Tehran	Riyadh	Beirut	Shanghai	Shenyang	Novosibirsk	Tomsk	Chokurdakh	Extensive uplands
Hot and rainy	Hot with rainy and dry seasons	Semiarid	Very dry	Hot, dry summer / mild, rainy winter	Warm, humid summer / mild winter	Warm, humid summer / cold, snowy winter	Cool, humid summer / cold, snowy winter	Short, cool, humid summer / very cold, snowy winter	Cold and dry	Climate varies with elevation and latitude

Population

With 3.4 billion people, Asia is nearly five times as populous as any other continent and is home to six out of every ten people in the world. If its current 2% annual growth rate continues, Asia's population will double by the year 2030. The continent contains the two most populous countries in the world, China and India, as well as the most populous metropolitan area, Tōkyō-Yokohama, Japan.

Great concentrations of people are found in India, eastern China, Japan, Vietnam, and on the Indonesian island of Java. In contrast, vast stretches of northern Siberia, Mongolia, western China, and the Arabian Peninsula are only sparsely populated. Numerous desert regions, including Arabia's Rub' al Khālī and China's Takla Makān, are uninhabited.

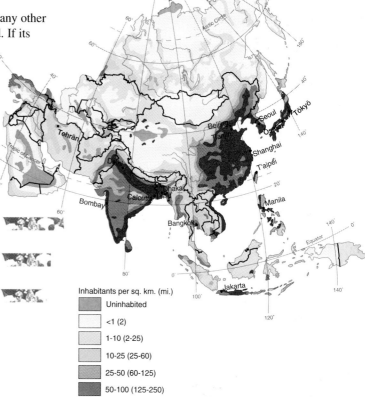

Inhabitants per sq. km. (mi.)

	Uninhabited
	<1 (2)
	1-10 (2-25)
	10-25 (25-60)
	25-50 (60-125)
	50-100 (125-250)
	>100 (250)

© Rand McNally & Co.
M-560000-1P-EL1-‑1-‑ -1

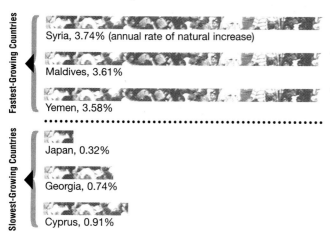

Fastest-Growing Countries

Syria, 3.74% (annual rate of natural increase)

Maldives, 3.61%

Yemen, 3.58%

Slowest-Growing Countries

Japan, 0.32%

Georgia, 0.74%

Cyprus, 0.91%

Environments and Land Use

Despite rapid industrialization in Japan, Korea, and Singapore, feeding the enormous and fast-growing population remains Asia's primary economic focus. In China, India, and Indonesia, two-thirds of the work force is engaged in farming. Where arable land exists, it is generally cultivated intensively. Rice is the most commonly grown crop: the continent produces more than 90% of the world's total. Other important crops include wheat, sorghum, millet, maize, and barley.

Asia's major agricultural regions are found in the fertile alluvial valleys, floodplains, and deltas of some of its greatest rivers, such as the Ganges and Brahmaputra in northern India, the Indus in Pakistan, the Huang (Yellow) and Yangtze in eastern China, the Irawaddy in Myanmar (Burma), the Mekong in Cambodia and Vietnam, and the Tigris and Euphrates in Iraq.

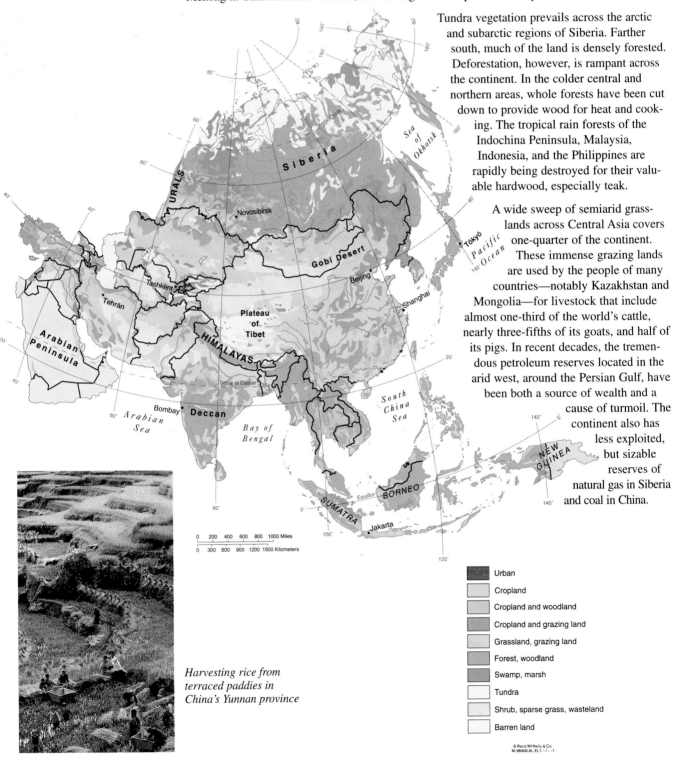

Tundra vegetation prevails across the arctic and subarctic regions of Siberia. Farther south, much of the land is densely forested. Deforestation, however, is rampant across the continent. In the colder central and northern areas, whole forests have been cut down to provide wood for heat and cooking. The tropical rain forests of the Indochina Peninsula, Malaysia, Indonesia, and the Philippines are rapidly being destroyed for their valuable hardwood, especially teak.

A wide sweep of semiarid grasslands across Central Asia covers one-quarter of the continent. These immense grazing lands are used by the people of many countries—notably Kazakhstan and Mongolia—for livestock that include almost one-third of the world's cattle, nearly three-fifths of its goats, and half of its pigs. In recent decades, the tremendous petroleum reserves located in the arid west, around the Persian Gulf, have been both a source of wealth and a cause of turmoil. The continent also has less exploited, but sizable reserves of natural gas in Siberia and coal in China.

0 200 400 600 800 1000 Miles
0 300 600 900 1200 1500 Kilometers

Harvesting rice from terraced paddies in China's Yunnan province

Urban

Cropland

Cropland and woodland

Cropland and grazing land

Grassland, grazing land

Forest, woodland

Swamp, marsh

Tundra

Shrub, sparse grass, wasteland

Barren land

The Asian Tigers

Many people have predicted that the 21st century will be "the Asian Century"—a time when the countries of that continent will come of age internationally and will assert their economic, political, and cultural influence around the world. Indeed, Asia's power has been growing steadily since the end of World War II. Japan now boasts one of the world's most powerful economies, with an annual trade surplus of more than $100 billion.

Right behind Japan in economic development are a host of countries known collectively as "the Asian Tigers." Four of these "Tigers"—Hong Kong, Singapore, South Korea and Thailand—are challenging Japanese preeminence in manufacturing and finance. Each of the four has both a government providing strong support for economic growth and a population ready to exploit the opportunity. With an annual Gross Domestic Product (GDP) growth rate of over 10%, Singapore stands out from the others. It boasts a standard of living comparable to that of the U.S. or Western Europe.

Busy shopping district in Seoul, South Korea

In the next tier of economic development are Malaysia, Thailand, and Indonesia, which have been transformed in less than a generation by rapid economic growth. Primarily rural and agricultural 20 years ago, these countries now have vibrant urban areas that attract millions from the rural areas in search of greater opportunities. As a result of this influx of people, cities like Kuala Lumpur, Bangkok, and Jakarta have enormous problems with slums, traffic, and pollution.

China, as always, is a special case. Areas such as Guangdong Province, where the Communist government has loosened economic controls, boast "Asian Tiger" rates of growth, but other regions remain quite poor.

Asia's economic dominance in the next century is by no means assured. Presently, the new wealth is limited to the "Tigers," all of which lie along the continent's eastern and southeastern edges. Many other parts of the vast continent, including Russia and the Indian subcontinent, have no comparable rates of growth and are impoverished. Also, political upheaval could derail the economies of several countries, especially Taiwan, where the shadow of China is long, and Hong Kong.

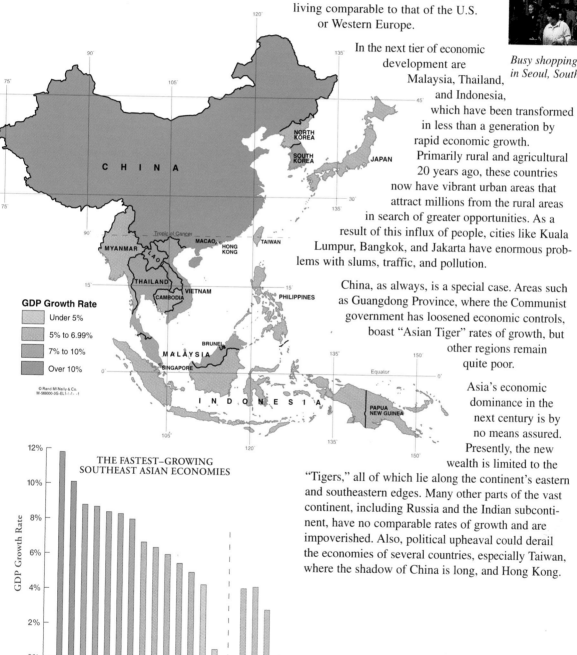

GDP Growth Rate
- Under 5%
- 5% to 6.99%
- 7% to 10%
- Over 10%

© Rand McNally & Co.
M-569300-3G-EL1-'-!- -1

THE FASTEST–GROWING SOUTHEAST ASIAN ECONOMIES

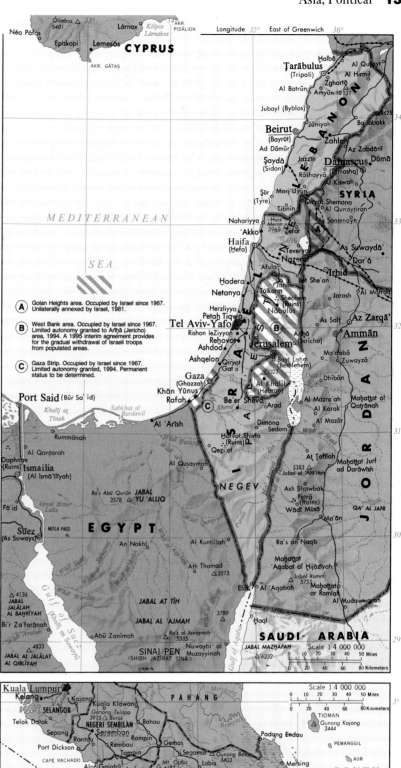

Relief

Meters		Feet
3050		10 000
1525		5000
610		2000
305		1000
0	Sea Level	0
152.5		500 Below
1525		5000 Sea Level
3050		10 000
6100		20 000

A-519695-76   -1916-38
COPYRIGHT BY
RAND MCNALLY & COMPANY
MADE IN U.S.A.

Scale 1:40 000 000; one inch to 630 miles. Lambert's Azimuthal, Equal Area Projection
Elevations and depressions are given in feet

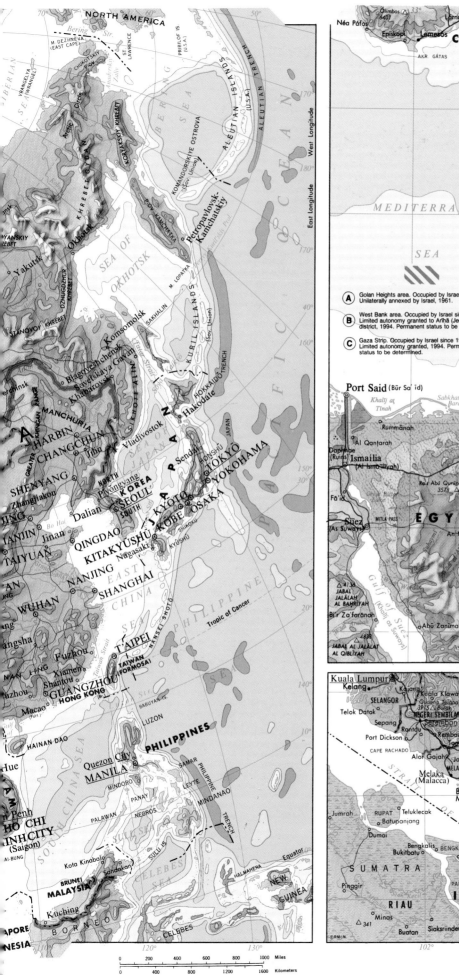

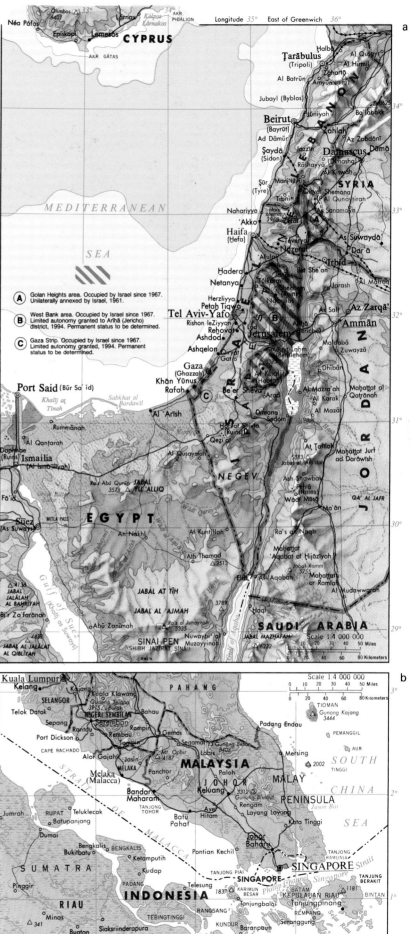

FINLAND

BARENTS SEA

KARELIA

NOVAYA ZEMLYA

KARSKOYE MORE
(Kara Sea)

ST. PETERSBURG
(Sankt-Peterburg) (Leningrad)

MOSCOW
(Moskva)

NIZHNIY NOVGOROD

NENETS

KOMI

P-OV YAMAL

P-OV GYDANSKIY

Salekhard

Dikson

Karaul

Dudinka

Noril'sk

GORY PUTOR

MORDVINIA
MARI EL

TATARSTAN

YAMAL

WESTERN

NENETS

R

U

U

SAMARA

BASHKOR

UDMURTIA

YEKATERINBURG

Nizhny Tagil

Khanty-Mansiysk

Turukhansk

Surgut

SIBERIAN

Chelyabinsk
Kopeysk
Troitsk

Tyumen'

Yeniseysk

Baykit

KAZAKHSTAN

KIRGIZ

STEPPE

LOWLAND

Tomsk

NOVOSIBIRSK

Kansk

Krasnoyarsk

Tayshet

KUZNETSK BASIN

Anzhero-Sudzhensk
Kemerovo

Barnaul

Biysk

Nizhneudinsk

Tulun

KHAKASIA

Abakan

SAYAN KHREBET

GORNO-ALTAY

Oskemen

Semey
(Semipalatinsk)

TUVA
TANNU-OLA

Kyzyl

USBEKISTAN

TASHKENT

Balqash

SARYESIK
ATYRAU
(DESERT)

M O Y Y N Q U M

MONGOLIA

HANGAYN
(HANGAY) MTS.

KYRGYZSTAN

Bishkek

Alma-Ata
(Almaty)

XINJIANG
UYGUR
(SINKIANG)

CHINA

AFGHANISTAN

PAMIR

Cities
and
Towns

0 to 50,000   o

50,000 to 500,000   ⊙

500,000 to 1,000,000   ◎

1,000,000 and over

Scale 1:16 000 000; one inch to 250 miles   Conic Project

Elevations and depressions are given in feet.

85° Longitude East of Greenwich 90°

Relief

Meters	Feet
3050	10 000
1525	5000
610	2000
305	1000
152.5	500
0	Sea Level	0
152.5	500
1525	5000
3050	10 000

BLACK SEA

İstanbul Boğazı
(Bosporus)
İstanbul
(Troy (Ruins))
Mitilini
İzmir
Bergama
Kütahya
Eskişehir
Aydın
Muğla
RHODOS

Zonguldak
Kastamonu
Çankırı
Sinop
Samsun
Merzifon
Çorum
Yozgat
Kırıkkale
T U R K E Y
Ankara
Afyon
Kütahya

Sivas
Kayseri
Kahramanmaraş
Konya
TOROS DAĞLARI
Antalya
Içel
Tarsus
Adana
İskenderun
Hatay

Giresun
Trabzon
Gümüşhane
Erzincan
Erzurum 16,854
Tavşan
Elazığ
Diyarbakır
Şanlıurfa
Siverek
Mardin
Cizre

CAUCASUS
Vladikavkaz
Kutaisi
Poti
Batumi
GEORGIA
Tbilisi
Gyumri
Kars
ARMENIA
Yerevan
AZERBAIJAN
AZER.
Khvoy
Van
Tabriz
Ardabil

RUSSIA
Grozny
Fort Shevchenko
Makhachkala
Derbent

MEDITERRANEAN SEA

NORTH CYPRUS
CYPRUS
Nicosia
Ladhiqiyah
(Latakia)
Aleppo
Tarabulus
(Tripoli)
Hims
Hamah
Beirut
Saydā (Sidon)
LEBANON
Haifa
ISRAEL
Tel Aviv-Yafo
Jerusalem
Gaza
Rashid
Damietta
ALEXANDRIA
(Al Iskandarīyah)
Port Said
(As Suways)
Suez
CAIRO
(Al Qāhirah)
Areas occupied by Israel since 1967

SYRIA
Dimashq
Damascus
As Suwayda
Al Mawsil
Rawanduz
Ninevah
As Sulaymaniyah
Irbil
Kirkūk
Zanjan
Dayr az Zawr
Palmyra (Ruins)
Abū Kamāl
Tikrit
Ar Ramadi

Orūmīyeh
Mianeh
Bandar-e Anzali
Rasht
Qazvin
ELBURZ MTS.
Bābol
Damāvand
TEHRAN
Qom
Hamadan
Sanandaj
Kangavar
Bakhtaran
Arāk
Borūjerd

Bandar-e Torkeman
Gorgan
Emāmshahr
DASHT-E KAVIR
DESERT
Daryācheh-ye Namak

KURDISTAN

JORDAN
Ammān
Amman
Ma'ān
Al 'Aqabah
Al Jawf
Sakākah
SINAI
PEN
Elat
GULF OF SUEZ
Jabal Katherina 8,398

Karbalā
An Najaf
Babylon (Ruins)
BAGHDAD
I R A Q
SYRIAN DESERT
At Turayf
Badanah
An Nāsirīyah
Ar Rafhā
Al Basrah
Az Zubayr

Dezful
Shūshtar
Masjed Soleymān
Ahvāz
Khorramshahr
Abādān
Bandar-e Khomeyni
Kāzerūn
Borāzjān

Esfahān
Qomsheh
Shiraz
Persepolis (Ruins)
Daryācheh-ye Bakhtegān

EGYPT
Bur Safājah
Al Qusayr
RED SEA

SAUDI
N A J D
ARABIA
AN NAFUD
Tayma
JABAL SHAMMAR
Hā'il
Al Qaysūmah
KUWAIT
Kuwait
(Al Kuwayt)
AL HASA
AD DAHNĀ
Al Jubayl
Al Qatif
Az Zahrān
(Dhahran)
Ad Dammām
BAHRAIN
Al Manāmah
PERSIAN GULF
RA'S AT TANNŪRAH

Bandar-e Būshehr
Jahrom
Lār
Furūr 10,760
Bandar-e Lengeh
Qeshm
QESHM
Bandar-e Abbās
Bandar Beheshti
Jāsk
Str. of Hormuz
GULF OF OMAN

Burayidah
Unayzah
Sudair
Ash Shaqrā
Riyadh
(Ar Riyād)
Ad Dilam
AL AFLAJ
NAFŪD AD DAHY
Mubarraz
Al Khurmah
Al Lidām
At Tā'if
Al Madinah
(Medina)
Yanbu
Khaybar
Jiddah
Mecca
(Makkah)
Wādī ar Rimah
JABAL RADWAH
Tropic of Cancer
Al Hufūf
JABAL TUWAYQ

QATAR
Ad Dawhah
Abū Zaby
UNITED ARAB EMIRATES
Ajman
Dubayy
Al Buraymi
JABAL AL AKHDAR
Al Khābūrah
Matrah
Muscat
Jabal ash Sham 9,957
Şūr
RA'S AL HADD

Sawākin
Būr Sūdān
Tawkar
SUDAN
Kassala
Sebderat
Keren
Akordat
Barentu
Adi Ugri
ERITREA
Asmera
Mitsiwa
(Massawa)
DAHLAK ARCH.
Mersa Fatma
ETHIOPIA
DENAKIL

Al Qunfudhah
Abha
Qizan
JAZA'IR FARASAN
Abū 'Arish
Sa'dah
NAJRAN
Najran
Hādūr Shu'ayb 12,008
KAMARĀN
Al Luhayyah
San'ā
Jabal Remā 10,720
Al Hudaydah
Al Mukhā
(Mocha)
Ta'izz
Madinat ash Sha'b
Bāb al Mandab
Aden ('Adan)
YEMEN
Ed
Beylul
'Aseb
Tadjoura
Doāa
DJIBOUTI
Djibouti
Ayshah
Seylac
Berbera
SOMALIA

ARABIA
AR RUB' AL KHĀLĪ
OMAN
RA'S AL MADRAKAH
KHŪRYĀN MŪRYĀN
(Oman)
Mirbāt
RA'S FARTAK
HADRAMAWT
Shibām
Tarim
Say'ūn
Al Hawtah
Ash Shihr
Al Mukallā
Saybūt
GULF OF ADEN
SUQUTRA (SOCOTRA)
(Yemen)
Hadibū
Caluula
GEES GWARDAFUY
Lass Qoray

PLATEAU OF IRAN
DASHT-E LŪT
(DESERT)
Yazd
Bāfq
Nā'īn
Rafsanjān
Kermān
Zāhedān
Rīgān
Bam
Khāsh
Bampūr
Zābol
CHĀH

KAZ
UZBEKISTA
Kungrad
Chimbay
Nukus
PESKI KYZ
TURKESTAN
Khiva
Turtkul
Bukhara

CASPIAN SEA
Surface 92 feet below Sea Level
Zal.
Kara-Bogaz-Gol
Krasnovodsk
Nebit-Dag
Chikishlyar

TURKMENISTAN
PESKI KARAKUMY
(DESERT)
Ashkhabad
Chardzhou
Bojnurd
KOPPEH DAGH
Mery
Kushka
Neyshābūr
Mashhad
Binalud 11,708
Dāmghān
Ferdows
Bājestān
Qāyen
Herāt
AFGH
Biriand
Farāh

A-569400-76 -21 -37
COPYRIGHT BY
RAND-McNALLY & COMPANY
MADE IN U.S.A.

Relief

Meters	Feet
3050	10 000
1525	5000
610	2000
305	1000
152.5	500
0 Sea Level	Sea Level 0
152.5	500
1525	5000
3050	10 000 Below Sea Level

ADMINISTR.
BDY.

Scale 1:16 000 000; one inch to 250 miles. Polyconic Projection
Elevations and depressions are given in feet
Longitude East of Greenw

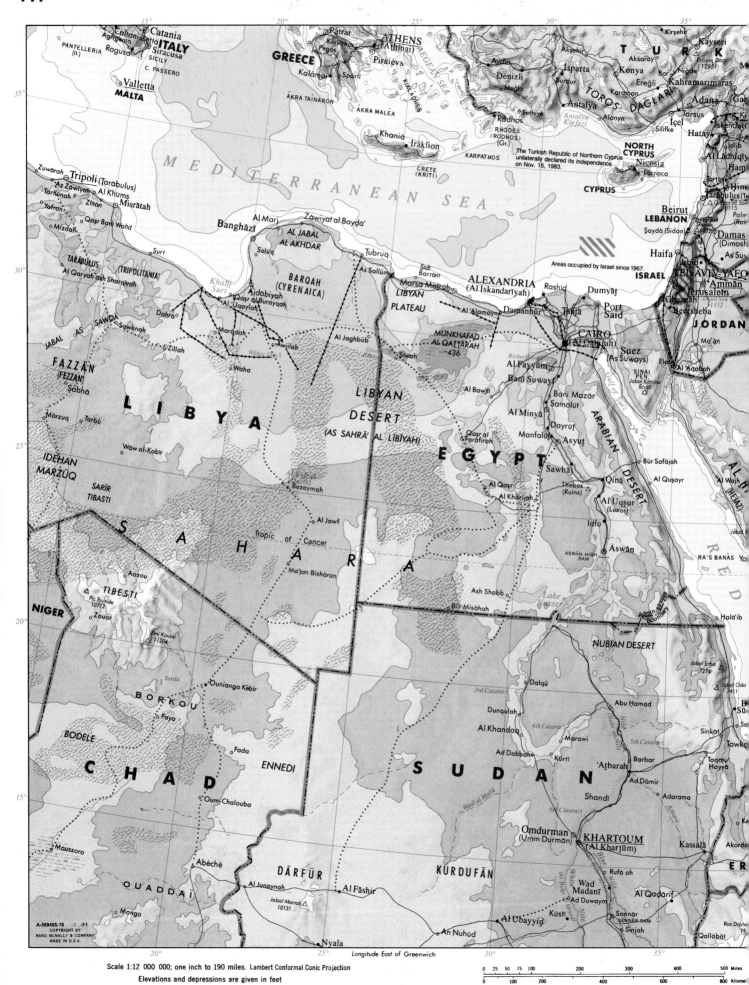

144

MEDITERRANEAN SEA

The Turkish Republic of Northern Cyprus
unilaterally declared its independence
on Nov. 15, 1983.

Areas occupied by Israel since 1967.

LIBYA

EGYPT

LIBYAN DESERT
(AS SAHRĀʾ AL LIBĪYAH)

S A H A R A

SUDAN

CHAD

Tropic of Cancer

Scale 1:12 000 000; one inch to 190 miles. Lambert Conformal Conic Projection

Elevations and depressions are given in feet

A-569495-76   -7 -11
COPYRIGHT BY
RAND McNALLY & COMPANY
MADE IN U.S.A.

Longitude East of Greenwich

0 25 50 75 100   200   300   400   500 Miles

0   100   200   400   600   800 Kilome

Yerevan
Erzurum
AZERBAIJAN
(Baki)
Nebit-Dag
Kazandzik
TURKMENISTAN
Celeken
Damghan
Mt. Ararat 16854
AZER.
Naxçivan
Xankandi (Stepanakert)
Salyan
CASPIAN SEA
Kizyl-Arvat
Bacharden
Ashkabad
KOPPEH DAGH
Quchan
Mary
Iolotan
Andkhvoy
Mus
Van
Tatvano
Bilis
Khvoy
Marand
Ahar
Astara
Surface 92 Feet Below Sea Level
Bandar-e Torkeman
Gorgan
Bojnurd
Binalud 11208
Neyshabur
Sabzevar
Sorakhs
Sandykaci
Meymaneh
Tehta-Bazar
Diyarbakir
Siirt
Orümiyah
Tabriz
Ardabil
Bandar-e Anzali
Rasht
Lahijan
Chalus
Babol
Emamshahr
Mashhad
Torbat-e Heydariyeh
Torbat-e Jam
Ghurian
Herat
KURD
Mahabad
Maragheh
Mianeh
Zanjan
Qazvin
ELBURZ MTS.
Rey
Qolleh-ye Damavand 18386
Kashmar
Ferdows
Qayen
Shindand
Al Mawsil
Irbil
As Sulaymaniyah
Sanandaj
Hamadan
TEHRAN
Qom
DASHT-E KAVIR DESERT
Bajestan
Birjand
Farah
AFGHANISTAN
Kirkuk
Khanaqin
Bakhtaran
Arak
Kashan
IRAN
Nehbandan
Tikrit
Samarra
Ba'qubah
Khorramabad
Na'in
Yazd
PLATEAU OF IRAN
DASHT-E LUT (DESERT)
Zaranj
BAGHDAD
Babylon (Ruins)
Dezful
Esfahan
Qomsheh
Chahar Borjak
Karbala'
Shushtar
Masjed Soleyman
Surmaq
Namakzar-e Shahdad
An Najaf
Al Hayy
Al 'Amarah
Haft Gel
Kalar 14100
Behbehan
Rafsanjan
Kerman
Zahedan
IRAQ
An Nasiriyah
Ahvaz
Persepolis (Ruins)
Ladiz
PAKISTAN
Khorramshahr
Bandar-e Khomeyni
Gachsaran
Shiraz
Furgun 10760
Bampur
Al Basrah
Abadan
Kazerun
Jahrom
Bandar-e 'Abbas
Gwadar
KUWAIT
Kuwait (Al Kuwayt)
Bandar-e Bushehr
Lar
Bandar-e Lengeh
Jask
Bandar Beheshti
N NAFUD
Rafha
Al 'Qaysumah
PERSIAN GULF
RA'S AT TANNURAH
BAHRAIN
Bandar-e Lengeh
OMAN
Ha'il
Al Qatif
Al Manamah
QATAR
Ash Shariqah
JABAL SHAMMAR
Burraydah
Ad Dammam
Az Zahran (Dhahran)
Dukhan
Ad Dawhah
Dubay
Al Khaburah
Muscat
SAUDI
Unayzah
Ash Shaqra
Al Hufuf
Abu Zaby
UNITED ARAB EMIRATES
AL JABAL AL AKHDAR
Sur
NAJD
Al Madinah (Medina)
Riyadh (Ar Riyad)
As Sulaymaniyah
Jabal ash Sham 9957
RA'S AL HADD
ARABIA
NAFUD AD DAHY
Al Mubarraz
Al 'Ubaylah
OMAN
Al Masirah
Mahd adh Dhahab
Mecca (Makkah)
Al Ta'if
Al Lidam
AR RUB' AL KHALI
RA'S AL MADRAKAH
Al Lith
Qal'at Bishah
Al Jawarah
ASIR
Abha
NAJRAN
KHURYAN MURYAN
Al Qunfudhah
Mirbat
JAZA'IR FARASAN
Sa'dah
RAMLAT AS SAB'ATAYN
Al Ghaydah
RA'S FARTAK
Qizan
Shibam
Say'un
HADRAMAWT
ARABIAN SEA
DAHLAK ARCH.
KAMARAN
Al Luhayyah
San'a
Sayhut
Ash Shihr
Al Hudaydah
YEMEN
Ibb
Al Mukalla
Al Hawrah
Ta'izz
Al Makha (Mocha)
Al Hawrah
Mekele
Ramlu 6988
DENAKIL
Aden ('Adan)
Madinat ash Sha'b
Hadibu
SUQUTRA (SOCOTRA) (Yemen)
DJIBOUTI
Obock
Tadjoura
Qandala
GEES GWARDAFUY
Djibouti
Caluula
SOMALIA
Seylac
GULF OF ADEN

Relief

Meters	Feet
3050	10 000
1525	5000
610	2000
305	1000
152.5	500
0 Sea Level	0 Sea Level
152.5	500 Below Sea Level
1525	5000
3050	10 000
6100	20 000

Scale 1:16 000 000; one inch to 250 miles. Polyconic Projection
Elevations and depressions are given in feet

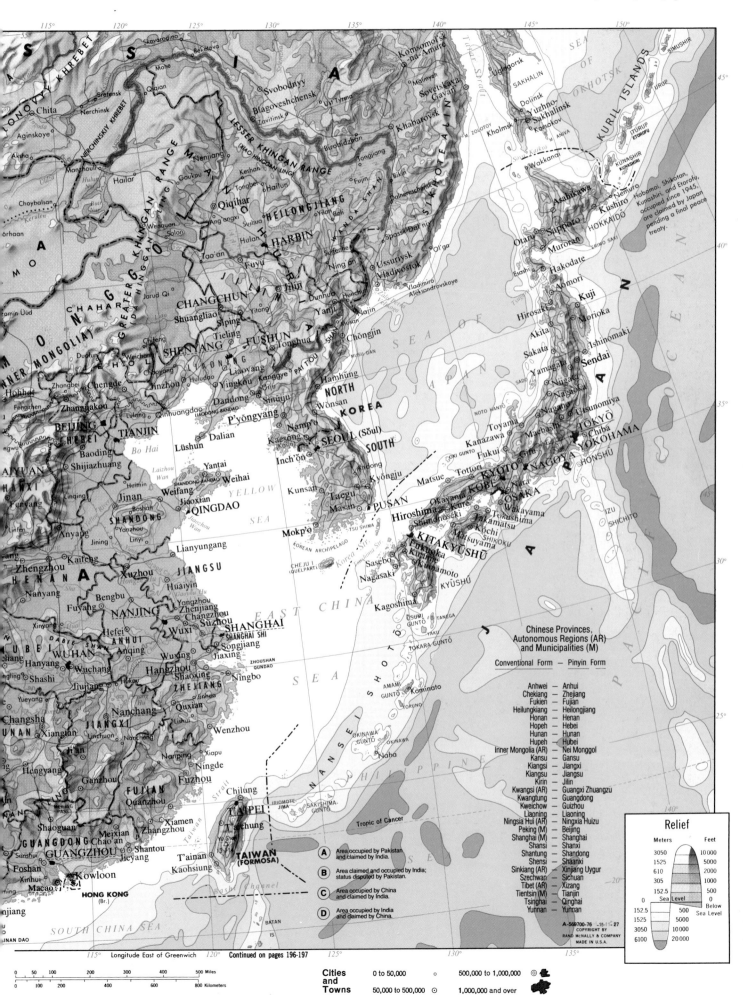

Hobomai, Shikotan, Kunashiri, and Etorofu, occupied since 1945, are claimed by Japan pending a final peace treaty.

Chinese Provinces, Autonomous Regions (AR) and Municipalities (M)

Conventional Form — Pinyin Form

Conventional	Pinyin
Anhwei	Anhui
Chekiang	Zhejiang
Fukien	Fujian
Heilungkiang	Heilongjiang
Honan	Henan
Hopeh	Hebei
Hunan	Hunan
Hupeh	Hubei
Inner Mongolia (AR)	Nei Monggol
Kansu	Gansu
Kiangsi	Jiangxi
Kiangsu	Jiangsu
Kirin	Jilin
Kwangsi (AR)	Guangxi Zhuangzu
Kwangtung	Guangdong
Kweichow	Guizhou
Liaoning	Liaoning
Ningsia Hui (AR)	Ningxia Huizu
Peking (M)	Beijing
Shanghai (M)	Shanghai
Shansi	Shanxi
Shantung	Shandong
Shensi	Shaanxi
Sinkiang (AR)	Xinjiang Uygur
Szechwan	Sichuan
Tibet (AR)	Xizang
Tientsin (M)	Tianjin
Tsinghai	Qinghai
Yunnan	Yunnan

Ⓐ Area occupied by Pakistan and claimed by India.

Ⓑ Area claimed and occupied by India; status disputed by Pakistan.

Ⓒ Area occupied by China and claimed by India.

Ⓓ Area occupied by India and claimed by China.

A-569700-76 -15-11-27

COPYRIGHT BY
RAND McNALLY & COMPANY
MADE IN U.S.A.

Relief

Meters	Feet
3050	10 000
1525	5000
610	2000
305	1000
152.5	500
0	Sea Level
Sea Level	Below
152.5	500
1525	5000
3050	10 000
6100	20 000

Continued on pages 196-197

Longitude East of Greenwich

0 50 100 200 300 400 500 Miles
0 100 200 400 600 800 Kilometers

Cities and Towns

0 to 50,000 ○ 500,000 to 1,000,000 ◉

50,000 to 500,000 ⊙ 1,000,000 and over

Scale 1:16 000 000; one inch to 250 miles. Polyconic Projection
Elevations and depressions are given in feet

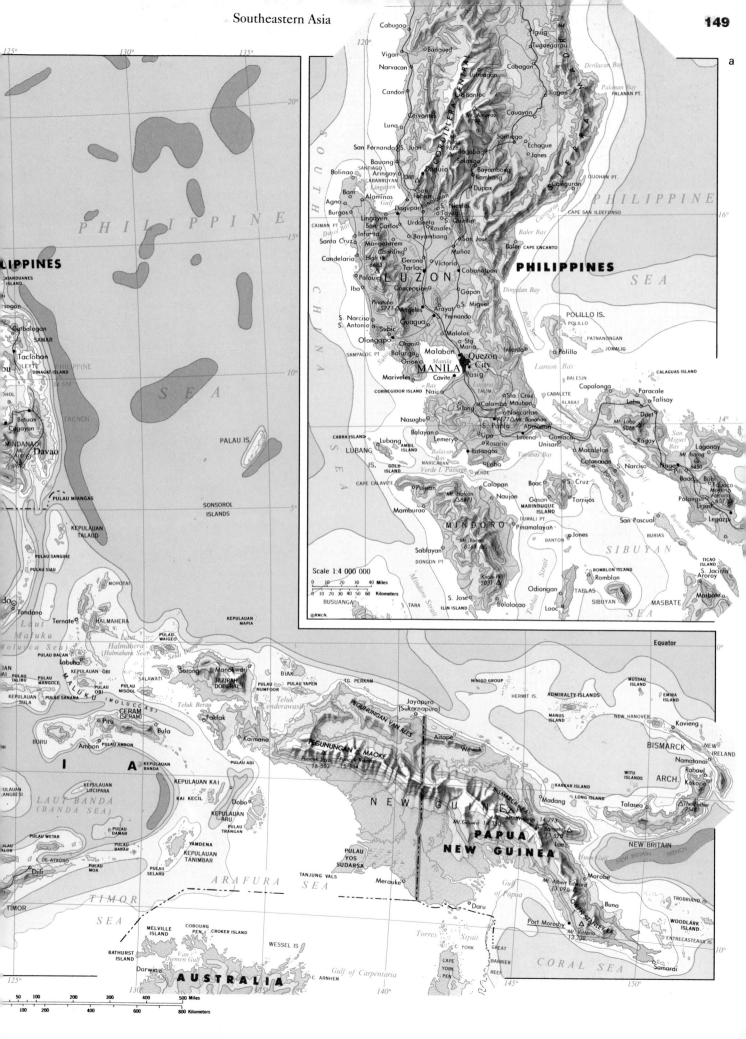

a

PHILIPPINES

PHILIPPINE SEA

PHILIPPINES

SAMAR

Tacloban

LEYTE

DINAGAT ISLAND

PHILIPPINE TRENCH

MINDANAO

Davao

PULAU MIANGAS

PALAU IS.

SONSOROL ISLANDS

SOUTH CHINA SEA

LUZON

Pinatubo
5771

Angeles

MANILA

Quezon City

Pasig

Manila Bay

Mariveles

CORREGIDOR ISLAND

Naic

POLILLO IS.

POLILLO

Polillo

Lamon Bay

CALAGUAS ISLAND

Capalonga

Paracale
Labo
Daet

Talisay

Mt. Labo
5086

San Miguel Bay

Ragay

Lagonay

Mt. Isarog
6450

Naga
Pili

Baao
Buhi

Mayon Volcano
8077

Polangui
Ligao

Legazpi

Scale 1:4 000 000

0 10 20 30 40 Miles

0 10 20 30 40 50 60 Kilometers

©RMcN.

BUSUANGA

TARA

ILIN ISLAND

S. Jose

Bulalacao

Odiongan

TABLAS

LOOC

Romblon

ROMBLON ISLAND

TICAO ISLAND

S. Jacinto
Aroroy

Masbate

MASBATE

SIBUYAN SEA

LUBANG IS.

CABRA ISLAND

Lubang

AMBIL ISLAND

GOLD ISLAND

CAPE CALAVITE

Paluan

Mamburao

Sablayan

MINDORO

Mt. Baco
8163

Knob Pk.
3031

DONGON PT.

Mindoro Strait

Mt. Halcon
8471

Calapan

Naujan

Gasan

MARINDUQUE ISLAND

DUMALI PT.

Pinamalayan

Pola

S. Cruz

Boac

Torrijos

San Pascual

BANTON

Jones

BURIAS

SIBUYAN SEA

Equator

MALUKU (MOLUCCAS)

PULAU OBI

KEPULAUAN OBI

Labuha

PULAU BACAN

MOROTAI

HALMAHERA

Ternate

Tondano

PULAU SANGIHE

PULAU SIAU

KEPULAUAN TALAUD

KEPULAUAN MAPIA

PULAU WAIGEO

Sorong

Manokwari

JAZIRAH DOBERAI

BIAK

SALAWATI

PULAU MISOOL

PULAU NUMFOOR

PULAU YAPEN

Teluk Cenderawasih

PEGUNUNGAN VAN REES

Jayapura
(Sukarnapura)

NINIGO GROUP

HERMIT IS.

ADMIRALTY ISLANDS

MUSSAU ISLAND

EMIRA ISLAND

NEW HANOVER

Kavieng

NEW IRELAND

BISMARCK ARCH.

Namatanai

Rabaul

Kokopo

NEW BRITAIN

WITU ISLANDS

Talasea

The Father
7546

Fakfak

Kaimana

PULAU ADI

KEPULAUAN BANDA

KEPULAUAN KAI

KAI KECIL

Dobo

KEPULAUAN ARU

PULAU TRANGAN

YAMDENA

KEPULAUAN TANIMBAR

PULAU SELARU

PULAU YOS SUDARSA

Merauke

TANJUNG VALS

ARAFURA SEA

PEGUNUNGAN MAOKE

Puncak Jaya
16 503

Puncak Trikora
15 584

NEW GUINEA

BISMARCK RA.

Mt. Giluwe 14 330

Mt. Wilhelm 14 793

Mt. Bangeta
13 523

Lae

PAPUA NEW GUINEA

Madang

KARKAR ISLAND

LONG ISLAND

Wewak

Aitape

Sepik

Morobe

Huon Gulf

Mt. Albert Edward
13 090

Buna

OWEN STANLEY RA.

Mt. Victoria
13 238

Port Moresby

Gulf of Papua

Daru

TROBRIAND IS.

WOODLARK ISLAND

D'ENTRECASTEAUX IS.

Samarai

CORAL SEA

NEW BRITAIN TRENCH

TIMOR SEA

Dili

TIMOR

PULAU WETAR

PULAU DAMAR

PULAU MOA

I. DE ATAURO

PULAU BABAR

MELVILLE ISLAND

BATHURST ISLAND

COBOURG PEN.

CROKER ISLAND

WESSEL IS.

Van Diemen Gulf

Darwin

AUSTRALIA

C. ARNHEM

Gulf of Carpentaria

Torres Strait

C. YORK

CAPE YORK PEN.

GREAT BARRIER REEF

50 100 200 300 400 500 Miles

100 200 400 600 800 Kilometers

Oceania (including Australia and New Zealand)

Oceania is comprised of Australia, New Zealand, eastern New Guinea, and approximately 25,000 other islands in the South Pacific, most of which are uninhabited. Many of the islands are coral atolls, formed by microscopic creatures over scores of centuries, while others are the result of volcanic action.

Bay of Islands, North Island, New Zealand

Oceania's largest landmass is Australia, which at three million square miles (7.7 million sq km) is the world's smallest continent. In fact, it is smaller than five countries—Russia, Canada, China, Brazil, and the United States. Australia is generally flat and dry. The interior is sparsely populated, with most people living in coastal cities such as Sydney.

The next-largest part of Oceania is Papua New Guinea, the country occupying the eastern half of the island of New Guinea, which has some of the most forbidding and remote terrain in the world. New Zealand, Oceania's third-largest country, is known for its natural beauty and its huge herds of sheep.

Oceania at a glance

Land area: 3,300,000 square miles (8,500,000 sq km)

Estimated population (January 1, 1995): 28,400,000

Population density: 8.6/square mile (3.3/sq km)

Mean elevation: 1,000 feet (305 m)

Highest point: Mt. Wilhelm, Papua New Guinea, 14,793 feet (4,509 m)

Lowest point: Lake Eyre, South Australia, 52 feet (16 m) below sea level

Longest river: Murray-Darling, 2,330 mi (3,750 km)

Number of countries (incl. dependencies): 33

Largest independent country: Australia, 2,966,155 square miles (7,682,300 sq km)

Smallest independent country: Nauru, 8.1 square miles (21 sq km)

Most populous independent country: Australia, 18,205,000

Least populous independent country: Tuvalu, 10,000

Largest city: Brisbane, pop. 1,334,017 (1991)

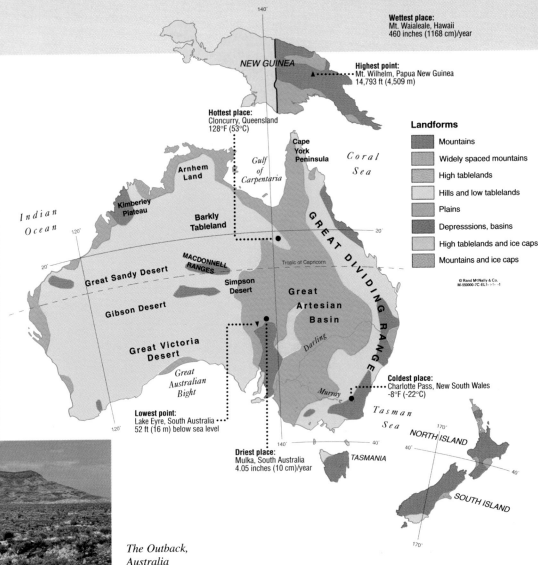

Wettest place:
Mt. Waialeale, Hawaii
460 inches (1168 cm)/year

Highest point:
Mt. Wilhelm, Papua New Guinea
14,793 ft (4,509 m)

Hottest place:
Cloncurry, Queensland
128°F (53°C)

Landforms

- Mountains
- Widely spaced mountains
- High tablelands
- Hills and low tablelands
- Plains
- Depresssions, basins
- High tablelands and ice caps
- Mountains and ice caps

© Rand McNally & Co.
M-550000-7C-EL1- :-1- -1

NEW GUINEA

Cape York Peninsula

Coral Sea

Gulf of Carpentaria

Arnhem Land

Indian Ocean

Kimberley Plateau

Barkly Tableland

GREAT DIVIDING RANGE

MACDONNELL RANGES

Great Sandy Desert

Tropic of Capricorn

Simpson Desert

Great Artesian Basin

Gibson Desert

Darling

Great Victoria Desert

Great Australian Bight

Lowest point:
Lake Eyre, South Australia
52 ft (16 m) below sea level

Coldest place:
Charlotte Pass, New South Wales
-8°F (-22°C)

Murray

Tasman Sea

NORTH ISLAND

Driest place:
Mulka, South Australia
4.05 inches (10 cm)/year

TASMANIA

SOUTH ISLAND

The Outback, Australia

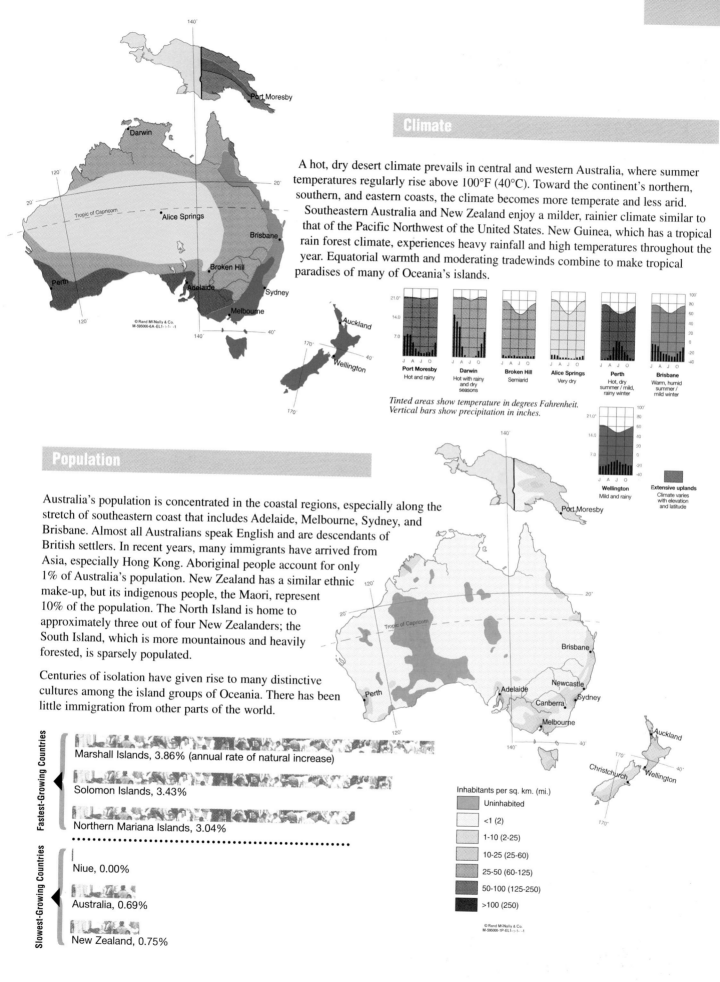

Climate

A hot, dry desert climate prevails in central and western Australia, where summer temperatures regularly rise above 100°F (40°C). Toward the continent's northern, southern, and eastern coasts, the climate becomes more temperate and less arid. Southeastern Australia and New Zealand enjoy a milder, rainier climate similar to that of the Pacific Northwest of the United States. New Guinea, which has a tropical rain forest climate, experiences heavy rainfall and high temperatures throughout the year. Equatorial warmth and moderating tradewinds combine to make tropical paradises of many of Oceania's islands.

Tinted areas show temperature in degrees Fahrenheit. Vertical bars show precipitation in inches.

Port Moresby — Hot and rainy
Darwin — Hot with rainy and dry seasons
Broken Hill — Semiarid
Alice Springs — Very dry
Perth — Hot, dry summer / mild, rainy winter
Brisbane — Warm, humid summer / mild winter
Wellington — Mild and rainy
Extensive uplands — Climate varies with elevation and latitude

Population

Australia's population is concentrated in the coastal regions, especially along the stretch of southeastern coast that includes Adelaide, Melbourne, Sydney, and Brisbane. Almost all Australians speak English and are descendants of British settlers. In recent years, many immigrants have arrived from Asia, especially Hong Kong. Aboriginal people account for only 1% of Australia's population. New Zealand has a similar ethnic make-up, but its indigenous people, the Maori, represent 10% of the population. The North Island is home to approximately three out of four New Zealanders; the South Island, which is more mountainous and heavily forested, is sparsely populated.

Centuries of isolation have given rise to many distinctive cultures among the island groups of Oceania. There has been little immigration from other parts of the world.

Fastest-Growing Countries
Marshall Islands, 3.86% (annual rate of natural increase)
Solomon Islands, 3.43%
Northern Mariana Islands, 3.04%

Slowest-Growing Countries
Niue, 0.00%
Australia, 0.69%
New Zealand, 0.75%

Inhabitants per sq. km. (mi.)
- Uninhabited
- <1 (2)
- 1-10 (2-25)
- 10-25 (25-60)
- 25-50 (60-125)
- 50-100 (125-250)
- >100 (250)

Environments and Land Use

Much of central and western Australia is a dry, inhospitable land of sand, rocks, and scrub vegetation. Surrounding this desert region is a broad band of semiarid grassland that covers more than half of the continent and supports a huge livestock industry. Australia has more sheep—132 million—than any other country in the world, as well as sizable herds of cattle. The dry climate and sparse plant life, however, mean that each animal requires a dozen or more acres to survive. Six percent of the continent is suitable for crops; most of the arable land is found on fertile plains in the southeast. Major crops include wheat, sugar cane, oats, barley, sorghum, and rice.

Farmland on North Island, New Zealand

Tourism plays an important role in Australia's economy. Among the continent's major attractions are its unusual wildlife, such as kangaroos, koalas, wombats, and platypuses; the Great Barrier Reef, which stretches for 1,250 miles (2,100 km) along the northeastern coast; and the ruggedly beautiful Outback, with its dramatic rock formations such as Ayers Rock (Uluru) and the Olga Rocks.

Thanks to its fertile land and temperate climate, New Zealand has a thriving livestock industry and is a leading world exporter of dairy products and lamb. Thinly populated and with little industry, it is one of the world's least polluted countries. Its pristine beauty encompasses a variety of scenery, including mountains, fjords, glaciers, rain forests, beaches and geysers. Only the country's relative isolation restrains its growing tourism industry.

Dense tropical rain forests blanket much of Papua New Guinea. These forests have thus far escaped the large-scale deforestation that is taking place in other tropical forests around the world.

Tourism is central to the economies of many of the islands throughout Oceania. Abundant sunshine, pleasant temperatures, and beautiful beaches draw millions of visitors each year to islands such as Tahiti and Fiji. For islands with little or no tourism, the economic scene is less promising: many islanders rely on subsistence fishing and foreign aid from former colonial powers.

Map labels:

NEW GUINEA

Darwin

Gulf of Carpentaria

Coral Sea

Indian Ocean

Great Sandy Desert

Gibson Desert

Great Victoria Desert

Great Artesian Basin

GREAT DIVIDING RANGE

Tropic of Capricorn

Brisbane

Perth

Great Australian Bight

Adelaide

Sydney

Tasman Sea

Melbourne

TASMANIA

NORTH ISLAND

Auckland

SOUTH ISLAND

Legend:

- Urban
- Cropland
- Cropland and woodland
- Cropland and grazing land
- Grassland, grazing land
- Forest, woodland
- Swamp, marsh
- Tundra
- Shrub, sparse grass, wasteland
- Barren land

0 100 200 300 400 500 Miles
0 200 400 600 800 Kilometers

© Rand McNally & Co.
M-590200-8L-EL1- ·1· -1

Herding sheep near Goulburn, New South Wales

The Original Australians and New Zealanders

Many anthropologists believe that Australia's Aborigines are the oldest race of people on Earth. During the 40,000 years since they migrated to the island continent from Asia, they have developed a rich culture with an intricate spiritual and social life.

The original New Zealanders, the Maoris, arrived from other Polynesian islands in the 10th century. At the beginning of large-scale immigration from Britain in the 1800s, the British government signed a treaty with the Maoris which granted them full rights as citizens. With the exception of some disputes over land, this agreement has paved the way for the historically harmonious relations between the races in New Zealand.

Aboriginal boy with elders, Western Australia

Relations between the Aborigines and whites in Australia have been less harmonious. The arrival of the first European colonists in 1788 set in motion a chain of events that decimated the Aborigines and threatened their unique culture. Disease and skirmishes killed Aborigines along the coast, and thousands of others were forced from their lands by settlers. Some sought refuge with Aborigines already living in Australia's interior, the Outback. Alcoholism and other social problems became common among the Aborigines as they found themselves confronted by a society they did not understand.

Australia was slow to recognize the rights of its first inhabitants. In the early 1960s, official attitudes began to change as public embarrassment grew over the decades of discrimination. A significant step occurred in 1962 when full rights of citizenship were extended to the Aborigines.

Questions of land ownership, however, remain problematic for both

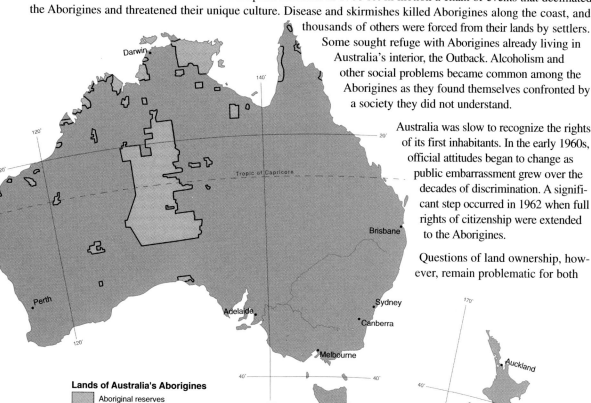

Lands of Australia's Aborigines

Aboriginal reserves

© Rand McNally & Co.
M-595000-3R-EL1-·-1- -1

sides. The government has set aside large reserves for the Aborigines, but much of the land is in the continent's hostile interior (see map above). Only in the past two decades has an agreement been reached allowing Aborigines to share in the vast mineral wealth of their northern lands. Recent court decisions have awarded individual Aborigines rights to ancestral lands which were seized by settlers, but many local governments continue to fight these decisions.

In the face of indifference and hostility, there has recently been an upsurge of interest in cultural traditions among the 240,000 Australians of aboriginal descent. Still, many of the traditions of the 500 different tribes that were present 200 years ago have been lost.

INDONESIA

Pasuruan
Singaraja
Rinjani
12 060
V.
G. Mahomeru
10 932
LOMBOK
SUMBAWA
Sumbawa Besar
Raboo
Bima
SUMBA
Waingapu
SAWU
FLORES
LOMBLEN PANTAR
ALOR
Dili
TIMOR
Kupang
ROTI
SAVU SEA

SUNDA ISLANDS

SUNDA TRENCH

SUNDA STRAIT

SELARU
TANJUNG VALS

ARAFURA SEA

TIMOR SEA

CAPE LONDONDERRY
Joseph Bonaparte Gulf

C. VAN DIEMEN
DUNDAS STR.
CROKER
COBURG PEN.
MELVILLE
Van Diemen Gulf
BATHURST
Clarence Str.
Darwin
WESSEL IS.
CAPE ARNHEM

ARNHEM LAND
Pine Creek
Blue Mud Bay
GROOTE EYLANDT
Katherine
Anson Bay
Daly
Roper
Limmen Bight
SIR EDWARD PELLEW GROUP
GULF
CARPENTA
WELLES

Wyndham
Mt. Hann 2600
KING LEOPOLD RANGES
BUCCANEER ARCH.
CAPE LEVEQUE
DAMPIER LAND
Broome
Derby
GEIKIE RANGES
Fitzroy Crossing
Halls Creek
Roebuck Bay
LaGrange

Victoria River Downs
Birdum
Borroloola
Newcastle Waters

NORTHERN
Burketown
BARKLY TABLELAND
Alexandria
Tanami
Tennant Creek
Camooweat
Mount Isc
Dai

TERRITORY
Barrow Creek

LARREY POINT
EIGHTY MILE BEACH
RIPON
DeGrey
DAMPIER
ARCH.
Port Hedland
MONTE BELLO IS.
BARROW
Roebourne
Marble Bar
Nullagine
GREAT SANDY DESERT
Mackay

Mt. Ziel 4955
MACDONNELL RANGES
Arltunga
Alice Springs
JAMES RANGE
SIMPSON
Hay

NORTH WEST CAPE
Onslow
Millstream
HAMERSLEY RANGE
Mt. Bruce 4052
Jiggalong
Disappointment
Macdonald

WESTERN
GIBSON DESERT

Ayers Rock 2844
L. Amadeus
Finke
Charlotte Waters
DESERT
Birdsville

POINT CLOATES
Tropic of Capricorn
CAPE FARQUHAR
Carnarvon
Peak Hill
Nabberu
Carnegie
Gillen
Wells

MUSGRAVE RANGES
Mt. Woodroffe 4724
EVERARD RANGES

BERNIER
DORRE
Shark Bay
DIRK HARTOG
STEEP POINT
Meekatharra
Nannine
Cue
Sandstone
Wiluna
Yeo

Oodnadatta

AUSTRALIA
Laverton
Mount Magnet

STUART RANGE
William Creek
Marree
Farina

HOUTMAN ROCKS
Ajana
Northampton
Menzies
Ballard
Carey
GREAT VICTORIA DESERT
SOUTH AUSTRALIA
FLINDERS RANGES

Geraldton
Mingenew
Moore
Barlee
Goddards Soak
Rawlinna
Oldea Station
Hughes
Penong
Ceduna
Woomera
Parac
Pimba
FLI
Port Aug
Pet

Dongara
Pithara
Miling
Moora
Lake Brown
Southern Cross
Coolgardie
Kalgoorlie-Boulder
Lefroy
Dundas
NULLARBOR PLAIN
Eucla
Eyre
Point Fowler
Penong
Whyalla
Port Pirie
Moonta
Glads
Port W

SWANLAND
DARLING RANGE
Cowan
Norseman
Salmon Gums
Eyre
Hughes

EYRE PENINSULA
Port Lincoln
Gulf St. Vincent

Perth
Fremantle
Northam
York
Narrogin
Ravensthorpe
Esperance
GREAT AUSTRALIAN BIGHT
Spencer Gulf

Collie
Bunbury
Katanning
Hopetoun
ARCHIPELAGO OF THE RECHERCHE
KANGAROO
CAPE JA

Geographe Bay
Busselton
CAPE NATURALISTE
CAPE LEEUWIN
Nornalup
Albany
PT. D'ENTRECASTEAUX
WEST CAPE HOWE
King George Sd.

INDIAN

OCEAN

INDIAN OCEAN

40,000 SQ MI AREA

0   100   200
Miles

A-590200-26
COPYRIGHT BY
RAND McNALLY & COMPANY
MADE IN U.S.A.

Longitude East of Greenwich

Scale 1:16 000 000; one inch to 250 miles. Lambert's Azimuthal, Equal Area Projec
Elevations and depressions are given in feet

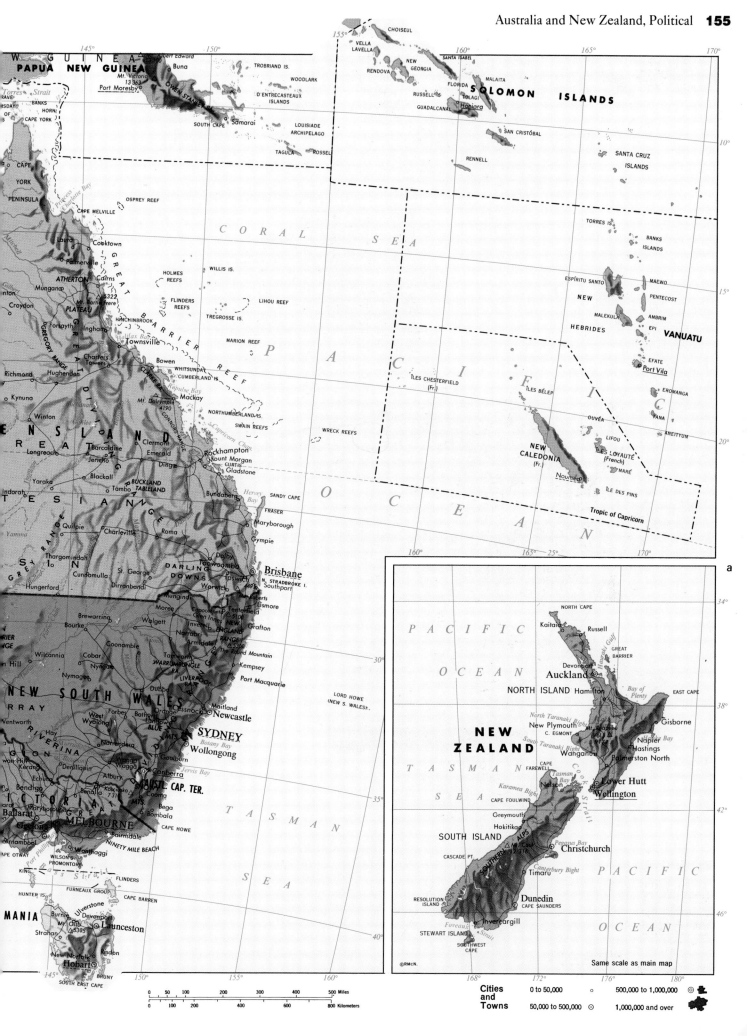

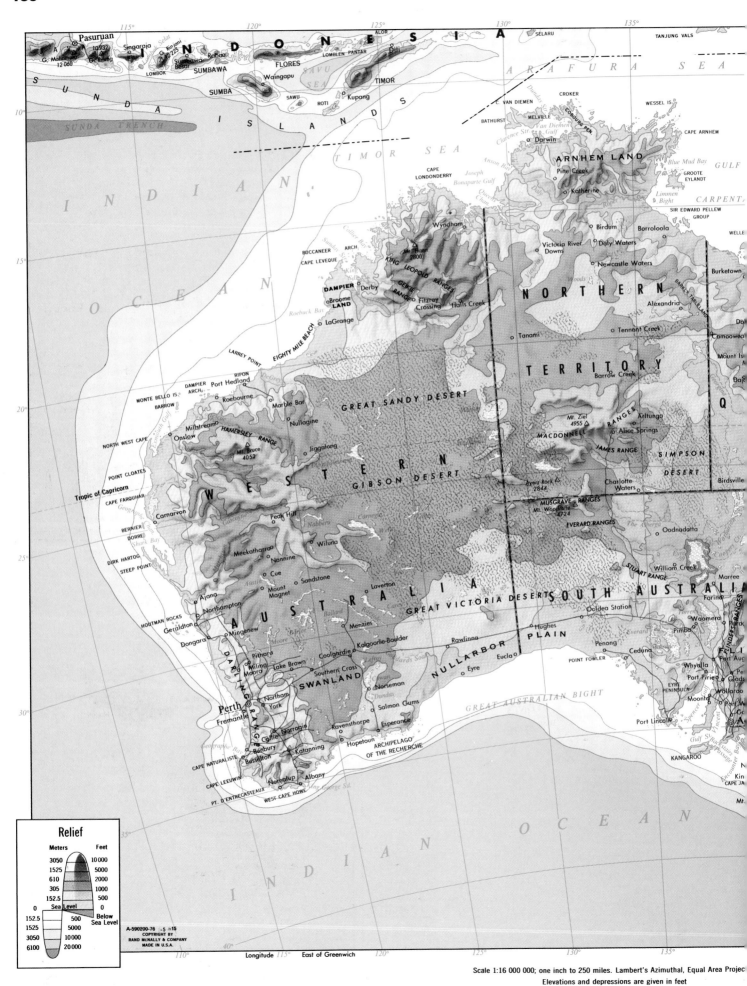

Relief

Meters		Feet
3050		10 000
1525		5000
610		2000
305		1000
152.5		500
0	Sea Level	0
		Below
152.5		500 Sea Level
1525		5000
3050		10 000
6100		20 000

A-590200-76 -5 -15
COPYRIGHT BY
RAND McNALLY & COMPANY
MADE IN U.S.A.

Longitude   115°   East of Greenwich   120°   125°   130°   135°

Scale 1:16 000 000; one inch to 250 miles. Lambert's Azimuthal, Equal Area Proje

Elevations and depressions are given in feet

PAPUA NEW GUINEA
NEW GUINEA
Mt. Albert Edward 13100
Buna
Mt. Victoria 13 363
Port Moresby
OWEN STANLEY RA.
SOUTH CAPE
Samarai
D'ENTRECASTEAUX ISLANDS
TROBRIAND IS.
WOODLARK
LOUISIADE ARCHIPELAGO
TAGULA
ROSSEL
Torres Strait
BANKS
HORN
CAPE YORK
CAPE YORK PENINSULA

CHOISEUL
VELLA LAVELLA
NEW GEORGIA
RENDOVA
RUSSELL IS.
FLORIDA
TULAGI
Honiara
GUADALCANAL
SANTA ISABEL
MALAITA
SOLOMON ISLANDS
SAN CRISTÓBAL
RENNELL

SANTA CRUZ ISLANDS

CORAL SEA

OSPREY REEF
CAPE MELVILLE
Cooktown
Laura
HOLMES REEFS
WILLIS IS.
Palmerville
ATHERTON PLATEAU
Mungana
Cairns
Mt. Bartle Frere 5322
FLINDERS REEFS
TREGROSSE IS.
Croydon
Forsayth
Ingham
HINCHINBROOK I.
Halifax Bay
MARION REEF
Townsville
Richmond
Hughenden
GREGORY RANGE
Charters Towers
Bowen
WHITSUNDAY
CUMBERLAND IS.
Kynuna
Winton
Mt. Dalrymple 4190
Mackay
Repulse Bay
NORTHUMBERLAND IS.
SWAIN REEFS
Longreach
Barcaldine
Jericho
Clermont
Emerald
Dingo
Rockhampton
Mount Morgan
CURTIS
Gladstone
Yaraka
Blackall
Tambo
BUCKLAND TABLELAND
Bundaberg
Hervey Bay
SANDY CAPE
FRASER
Quilpie
Charleville
Roma
Maryborough
GREAT DIVIDING RANGE
QUEENSLAND
Thargomindah
Cunnamulla
St. George
Dirranbandi
Dalby
Toowoomba
Ipswich
Warwick
Brisbane
Southport
N. STRADBROKE I.
Hungerford
DARLING DOWNS
Mungindi
Lismore
Brewarrina
Moree
Grafton
Bourke
Walgett
Narrabri
Armidale
NEW ENGLAND RANGE
Round Mountain
Coonamble
Cobar
Nyngan
Tamworth
Kempsey
Wilcannia
Coonabarabran
WARRUMBUNGLE RA.
Port Macquarie
NEW SOUTH WALES
Dubbo
LIVERPOOL RA.
Forbes
Orange
Maitland
Cessnock
Newcastle
West Wyalong
Bathurst
BLUE MTS.
SYDNEY
Narrandera
Wagga Wagga
Goulburn
Wollongong
Albury
Canberra
AUST. CAP. TER.
Cooma
Mt. Kosciusko 7316
SNOWY MTS.
Bega
Bombala
CAPE HOWE
VICTORIA
GREAT DIVIDING RANGE
Ballarat
Bendigo
Geelong
MELBOURNE
Bairnsdale
NINETY MILE BEACH
WILSON'S PROMONTORY
Wonthaggi
RIVERINA REGION
Kerang
Echuca
Deniliquin
Wentworth
MURRAY

PACIFIC OCEAN
Tropic of Capricorn

ÎLES CHESTERFIELD (Fr.)
ÎLES BÉLEP
WRECK REEFS
NEW CALEDONIA (Fr.)
OUVÉA
LIFOU
ÎLES LOYAUTÉ (French)
Nouméa
MARE
ÎLE DES PINS

ESPÍRITU SANTO
MAEWO
NEW HEBRIDES
MALEKULA
AMBRIM
PENTECOST
EPI
AMBRYM
EFATE
Port Vila
VANUATU
EROMANGA
TANA
ANEITYUM
TORRES IS.
BANKS ISLANDS

LORD HOWE
(NEW S. WALES)

TASMAN SEA

BASS STRAIT
FLINDERS
FURNEAUX GROUP
CAPE BARREN
HUNTER IS.
KING
TASMANIA
Burnie
Ulverstone
Devonport
Mt. Ossa 5305
Launceston
Strahan
New Norfolk
Hobart
BRUNY
SOUTH EAST CAPE

a

NORTH CAPE
Kaitaia
Russell
GREAT BARRIER
Devonport
Auckland
Hauraki Gulf
NORTH ISLAND
Hamilton
Bay of Plenty
EAST CAPE
North Taranaki Bight
New Plymouth
C. EGMONT
Mt. Egmont
Gisborne
South Taranaki Bight
Wanganui
Napier
Hastings
Palmerston North
NEW ZEALAND
CAPE FAREWELL
Tasman Bay
Nelson
Cook Strait
Lower Hutt
Wellington
Karamea Bight
CAPE FOULWIND
Greymouth
Hokitika
SOUTHERN ALPS
Mt. Cook
SOUTH ISLAND
Pegasus Bay
Christchurch
CASCADE PT.
Canterbury Bight
Timaru
RESOLUTION ISLAND
Dunedin
CAPE SAUNDERS
Foveaux Strait
Invercargill
STEWART ISLAND
SOUTHWEST CAPE

PACIFIC OCEAN
TASMAN SEA

PACIFIC OCEAN

Same scale as main map

0   50   100   200   300   400   500 Miles
0   100   200   400   600   800 Kilometers

Cities and Towns

0 to 50,000	500,000 to 1,000,000
50,000 to 500,000	1,000,000 and over

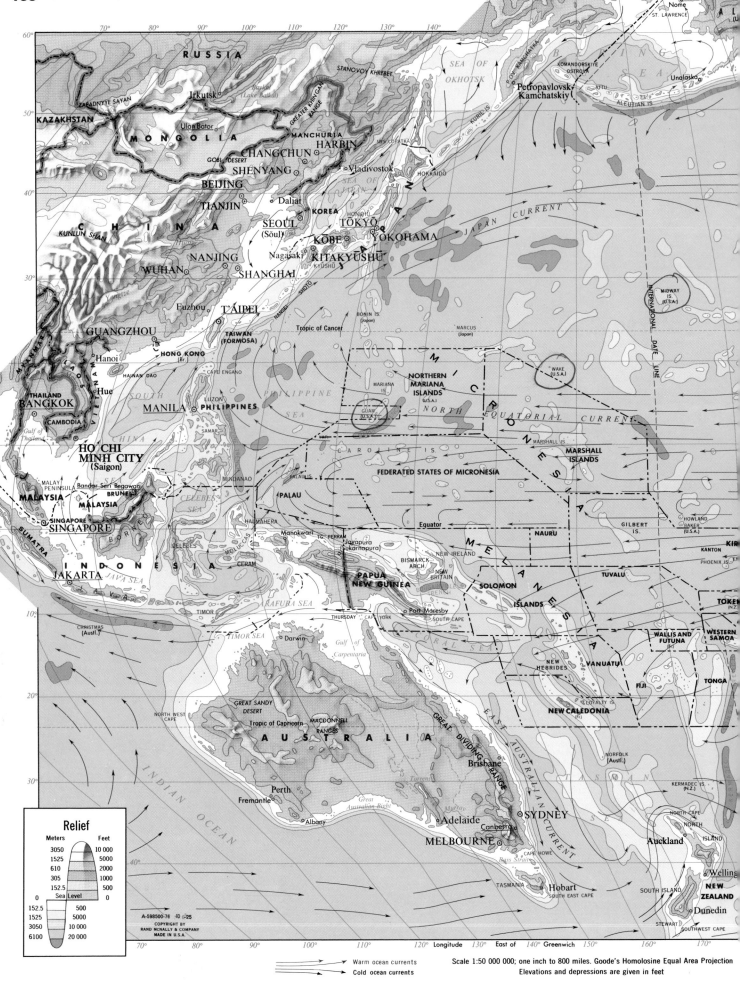

Relief

Meters		Feet
3050		10 000
1525		5000
610		2000
305		1000
152.5		500
0	Sea Level	0
152.5		500
1525		5000
3050		10 000
6100		20 000

A-598500-76   40   25
COPYRIGHT BY
RAND McNALLY & COMPANY
MADE IN U.S.A.

Warm ocean currents
Cold ocean currents

Scale 1:50 000 000; one inch to 800 miles. Goode's Homolosine Equal Area Projection
Elevations and depressions are given in feet

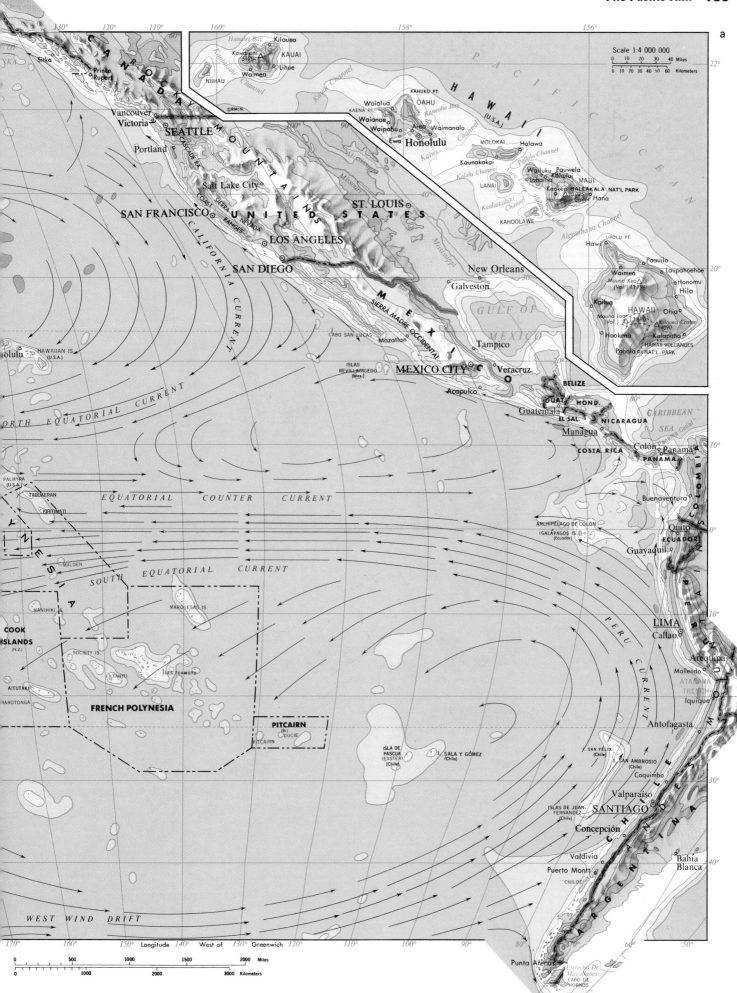

a

Scale 1:4 000 000

0   10   20   30   40 Miles
0 10 20 30 40 50 60 Kilometers

PACIFIC OCEAN

HAWAII
(U.S.A.)

Hanalei Bay   Kilauea
Kawaikini   KAUAI
5170   Lihue
Waimea
NIIHAU   Kaumakahi Channel

KAHUKU PT.
Waialua   OAHU
Waianae   Kaneohe Bay
Waipahu   Aiea   Waimanalo
Ewa   **Honolulu**   Kaiwi

MOLOKAI   Halawa
Kaunakakai   Pailolo Channel
Wailuku   Pauwela
Kalohi Channel   LANAI   Lahaina   Kahului
Keokea   HALEAKALA   MAUI
Aupu Chan   NAT'L PARK
Kealaikahiki   Hoolehua Crater   Hana
Channel   KAHOOLAWE
Alenuihaha Channel

UPOLU PT.
Hawi   Paauilo
Waimea   Laupahoehoe
Mauna Kea   Honomu
(Vol.) 13,796   Hilo
Kailua   **HAWAII**   Ohia
Mauna Loa   Kilauea Crater
(Vol.) 13,680   4090
Hookena   Kalapana
Pahala   HAWAII VOLCANOES
Kapapala   NAT'L. PARK

CAN   ADA
ROCKY   MOUNTAINS
Sitka
Prince
Rupert
Vancouver
Victoria
SEATTLE
Portland   CASCADE RA.
Salt Lake City
COAST   SIERRA
SAN FRANCISCO   RANGES   NEVADA   **UNITED   STATES**   ST. LOUIS
CALIFORNIA CURRENT
LOS ANGELES
SAN DIEGO   M   E   X   I   C   O   New Orleans
Galveston
SIERRA MADRE OCCIDENTAL   GULF OF   MEXICO
CABO SAN LUCAS   Mazatlan   Tampico
ISLAS   **MEXICO CITY**   Veracruz
REVILLAGIGEDO   **BELIZE**
(Mex.)   Acapulco   GUAT   HOND   CARIBBEAN
Guatemala   HOND   SEA
EL SAL.   NICARAGUA
Managua
COSTA RICA   Colón   Panama
PANAMA

ORTH   EQUATORIAL   CURRENT

Honolulu   HAWAIIAN IS.
(U.S.A.)

PALMYRA
(U.S.A.)
TABUAERAN
KIRITIMATI

Buenaventura

EQUATORIAL   COUNTER   CURRENT

ARCHIPIELAGO DE COLÓN
(GALÁPAGOS IS.)   Quito
(Ecuador)   **ECUADOR**
Guayaquil

MALDEN   SOUTH   EQUATORIAL   CURRENT

COOK
ISLANDS   MANIHIKI IS.
(N.Z.)   MARQUESAS IS.   PERU
LIMA
Callao

AITUTAKI   SOCIETY IS.   Arequipa
RAROTONGA   TAHITI   ÎLES TUAMOTU   Mollendo
ATACAMA
TRENCH   Iquique

FRENCH POLYNESIA
PITCAIRN
(&
DUCIE)   Antofagasta
PITCAIRN

ISLA DE
PASCUA   I. SALA Y GÓMEZ
(EASTER)   (Chile)   I. SAN FÉLIX
(Chile)   (Chile)   I. SAN AMBROSIO
(Chile)
Coquimbo

Valparaíso
ISLAS DE JUAN   **SANTIAGO**
FERNÁNDEZ
(Chile)   Concepción

Valdivia   **ARGENTINA**
Puerto Montt
CHILOE   Bahía
Blanca

WEST   WIND   DRIFT

Punta Arenas
Estrecho De
Magallanes
CABO DE
HORNOS

170°   160°   150°   140°   Longitude   130°   West of   120°   Greenwich   110°   100°   90°   80°   70°   60°   50°

0   500   1000   1500   2000 Miles
0   1000   2000   3000 Kilometers

POLYNESIA

Relief

Meters		Feet
3050		10 000
1525		5000
610		2000
305		1000
	Sea Level	
0		0
152.5	500	Below
1525	5000	Sea Level
3050	10 000	
6100	20 000	

A-594000-76
COPYRIGHT BY
RAND McNALLY & COMPANY
MADE IN U.S.A.

ANTARCTICA IN PROFILE

SECTION ALONG LINE AB

Scale 1: 60 000 000; (approximate)
Lambert's Azimuthal, Equal Area Projection
Elevations and depressions are given in feet

Glossary

Foreign Geographical Terms

Afk.	Afrikaans
Ara.	Arabic
Ber.	Berber
Blg.	Bulgarian
Bur.	Burmese
Cbd.	Cambodian
Ch.	Chinese
Czech	Czech
Dan.	Danish
Du.	Dutch
Est.	Estonian
Finn.	Finnish
Fr.	French
Gae.	Gaelic
Ger.	German
Gr.	Greek
Heb.	Hebrew
Ice.	Icelandic
Indon.	Indonesian
It.	Italian
Jpn.	Japanese
Kor.	Korean
Lao.	Laotian
Lapp.	Lappish
Mal.	Malay
Mong.	Mongolian
Nor.	Norwegian
Pas.	Pashto
Per.	Persian
Pol.	Polish
Port.	Portuguese
Rom.	mountains
Rus.	Russian
S./C.	Serbo-Croatian
Slo.	Slovak
Sp.	Spanish
Swe.	Swedish
Thai	Thai
Tib.	Tibetan
Tur.	Turkish
Ukr.	Ukranian
Viet.	Vietnamese
Viet.	Vietnamese

-å, Dan., Nor., Swe. ..... river
āb, Per. ..... river
ada(lar), Tur. ..... island(s)
adrar, Ber. ..... mountains
ákra, akrotírion, Gr. ..... cape
altos, Sp. ..... mountains, hills
-älv,-älven, Swe. ..... river
-ån, Swe. ..... river
archipel, Fr. ..... archipelago
archipiélago, Sp. ..... archipelago
arquipélago, Port. ..... archipelago
arroyo, Sp. ..... brook
-ås,-åsen, Swe. ..... hills
baai, Du. ..... bay
bab, Ara. ..... strait
Bach, Ger. ..... brook, creek
-backen, Swe. ..... hill
bælt, Dan. ..... strait
bahía, Sp. ..... bay
bahr, baḥr, Ara. ..... river, sea
baía, Port. ..... bay
baie, Fr. ..... bay
-bana, Jpn. ..... cape
banco, Sp. ..... bank
bandao, Ch. ..... peninsula
bassin, Fr. ..... basin
batang, Indon. ..... river
bātlāq, Per. ..... marsh
ben, Gae. ..... mountain
Berg, Ger. ..... mountain, hill
-berg, Afk. ..... mountains
Berge, Ger. ..... mountains
bi'r, Ara. ..... well
birkat, Ara. ..... lake
bocca, It. ..... river mouth, pass
boğazı, Tur. ..... strait
bogd, Mong. ..... range
bolsón, Sp. ..... enclosed basin
-breen, Nor. ..... glacier
Brücke, Ger. ..... bridge
Bucht, Ger. ..... bay

bugt, Dan. ..... bay
bukit, Indon., Mal. ..... mountain, hill
-bukten, Swe. ..... bay
bulu, Indon. ..... mountain
Burg, Ger. ..... castle
burn, Gae. ..... brook
burnu, burun, Tur. ..... cape
cabezas, Sp. ..... peaks
cabo, Port., Sp. ..... cape
campo, It. ..... plain
cap, Fr., Cat. ..... cape
capo, It. ..... cape
catena, Sp. ..... range
cayo(s), Sp. ..... cay(s), islet(s)
cerro(s), Sp. ..... mountain(s), hill(s)
chaîne, Fr. ..... range
château, Fr. ..... castle
chiang, Ch. ..... harbor, harbour
chott, Ara. ..... intermittent lake, salt marsh
cima, It., Sp. ..... peak
città, It. ..... city
ciudad, Sp. ..... city
co, Tib. ..... lake
co., cerro, Sp. ..... mountain, hill
col, Fr. ..... pass
colina(s), Sp. ..... hill(s)
colline, It. ..... hills
collines, Fr. ..... hills
con, Viet. ..... islands
cord., cordillera, Sp. ..... range
costa, Sp. ..... coast
côte, Fr. ..... coast, hills
cuchilla, Sp. ..... hills, ridge
dağ, dağı, Tur. ..... mountain
dāgh, Per. ..... mountains
-dake, Jpn. ..... mountain
-dal, -dalen, Nor., Swe. ..... valley
danau, Indon. ..... lake
dao, Ch., Viet. ..... island
daryācheh, Per. ..... lake
dasht, Per. ..... desert
deniz, denizi, Tur. ..... sea
desierto, Sp. ..... desert
détroit, Fr. ..... strait
dijk, Du. ..... dike
distrito, Sp. ..... district
djebel, Ara. ..... mountain(s)
-do, Kor. ..... island
-elv,-elva, Nor. ..... river
embalse, Sp. ..... reservoir
erg, Ara. ..... sand desert
estrecho, Sp. ..... strait
étang, Fr. ..... pond
-ey, Ice. ..... island
fjäll(en), Swe. ..... mountain(s)
fjället, Swe. ..... mountain
fjärden, Swe. ..... fjord
-fjell, -fjellet, Nor. ..... mountain
-fjord, Nor. ..... fjord
-fjorden, Nor., Swe. ..... fjord, lake
-fjörur, Ice. ..... fjord, bay
-flói, Ice. ..... bay
foce, It. ..... river mouth, pass
forêt, Fr. ..... forest
-forsen, Swe. ..... waterfall
Forst, Ger. ..... forest
-foss, Ice. ..... waterfall
-fossen, Nor. ..... waterfall
g., gora, Rus. ..... mountain, hill
g., gunong, Mal. ..... mountain
gang, Ch. ..... bay
-gang, Kor. ..... river
gave, Fr. ..... mountain torrent
gebergte, Du. ..... range
Gebirge, Ger. ..... range
Gipfel, Ger. ..... peak
göl, Tur. ..... lake
golfe, Fr. ..... gulf
golfete, Sp. ..... bay
golfo, It., Sp. ..... gulf
gölü, Tur. ..... lake
gora, Rus. ..... mountain, hill
gora, S./C. ..... mountains
góra, Pol. ..... mountain
gory, Rus. ..... mountains, hills

góry, Pol. ..... mountains
gr'ada, Rus. ..... ridge
guba, Rus. ..... bay
gunong, Mal. ..... mountain
gunung, Indon. ..... mountain
-guntō, Jpn. ..... islands
Haff, Ger. ..... lagoon
hai, Ch. ..... sea, lake
-hama, Jpn. ..... beach
hamada, Ara. ..... desert
hāmūn, Per. ..... lake, marsh
-hantō, Jpn. ..... peninsula
hare, Heb. ..... mountains, hills
-hav, Swe. ..... sea, bay
havre, Fr. ..... harbor, harbour
he, Ch. ..... river
ho, Ch. ..... river
-ho, Kor. ..... reservoir
-holm, Dan. ..... island
hora, Czech, Slo. ..... mountain
Horn, Ger. ..... point, peak
hu, Ch. ..... lake, reservoir
Hügel, Ger. ..... hill
-huk, Swe. ..... cape
ig., igarapé, Port. ..... river
île(s), Fr. ..... island(s)
îlet(s), Fr. ..... islet(s)
ilha(s), Port. ..... island(s)
ilhéu(s), Port. ..... islet(s)
Insel(n), Ger. ..... island(s)
isla(s), Sp. ..... island(s)
isola, It. ..... island
isole, It. ..... islands
istmo, Sp. ..... isthmus
jabal, Ara. ..... mountain(s)
järv, Est. ..... lake
-järvi, Finn. ..... lake
jazā'ir, Ara. ..... islands
jazirah, Indon. ..... peninsula
jiang, Ch. ..... river
-jima, Jpn. ..... island
-joki, Finn. ..... river
-jökull, Ice. ..... glacier
-kai, Jpn. ..... sea
-kaikyō, Jpn. ..... strait
-kaise, Lapp. ..... mountain
kali, Indon. ..... brook
kandao, Pas. ..... pass
-kang, Kor. ..... river
-kapp, Nor. ..... cape
kepulauan, Indon. ..... islands
khalīj, Ara. ..... gulf
khrebet, Russ., Ukr. ..... range
-ko, Jpn. ..... lake, lagoon
-kō, Jpn. ..... harbor, harbour
kólpos, Gr. ..... bay
Kopf, Ger. ..... peak
körfezi, Tur. ..... gulf, bay
kosa, Rus., Ukr. ..... spit
kou, Ch. ..... bay, pass
kuala, Mal. ..... bay
kūh(ha), Per. ..... mountain(s)
la, Tib. ..... pass
lac(s), Fr. ..... lake(s)
lag., laguna, Sp. ..... lagoon, lake
lago, It., Port., Sp. ..... lake
lagoa, Port. ..... lake, lagoon
laguna, Sp. ..... lagoon, lake
lagune, Fr. ..... lagoon
laht, Est. ..... bay
-lahti, Finn. ..... gulf
län, Swe. ..... county
laut, Indon. ..... sea
liedao, Ch. ..... islands
liman, Rus. ..... estuary
ling, Ch. ..... mountain(s), peak
llano(s), Sp. ..... plain(s)
loch, Gae. ..... lake, inlet
lomas, Sp. ..... hills
lough, Gae. ..... lake
lyman, Ukr. ..... estuary
-maa, Est. ..... island
-man, Kor. ..... bay
mar, Sp., It. ..... sea
marais, Fr. ..... marsh
mare, It. ..... sea
massif, Eng., Fr. ..... massif

Meer, Ger. ..... sea, lake
mer, Fr. ..... sea
mesa, Sp. ..... mesa
meseta, Sp. ..... plateau
-misaki, Jpn. ..... cape
mont, Fr. ..... mount
montagna, It. ..... mountain
montagne(s), Fr. ..... mountain(s)
montaña(s), Sp. ..... mountain(s)
monte, It., Port., Sp. ..... mount
montes, Port., Sp. ..... mountains
monti, It. ..... mountains
monts, Fr. ..... mountains
more, Rus., Ukr. ..... sea
morne, Fr. ..... mountain
morro, Port., Sp. ..... hill, mountain
mui, Viet. ..... point
munkhafad, Ara. ..... depression
munṭii, Rom. ..... mountains
-nada, Jpn. ..... sea, gulf
nafūd, Ara. ..... desert
nagor'ye, Rus. ..... plateau, mountains
-näs, Swe. ..... peninsula
ness, Gae. ..... promontory
nos, Blg. ..... cape
nuruu, Mong. ..... mountains
nuur, Mong. ..... lake
-ø, Dan., Nor. ..... island
-ö, Swe. ..... island
o., ostrov, Rus. ..... island
óros, Gr. ..... mountain(s)
ostriv, Ukr. ..... island
ostrov(a), Rus. ..... island(s)
otok, S./C. ..... island
ouadi, Ara. ..... wadi
oued, Ara. ..... wadi
-øy, -øya, Nor. ..... island
oz., ozero, Rus., Ukr. ..... lake
pampa, Sp. ..... plain
pas, Fr. ..... strait
paso, Sp. ..... pass
Pass, Ger. ..... pass
passe, Fr. ..... passage
passo, It. ..... pass
peg., pegunungan, Indon. ..... mountains
pélagos, Gr. ..... sea
peña, Sp. ..... peak, rock
península, Sp. ..... peninsula
pertuis, Fr. ..... strait
peski, Rus. ..... sand desert
phnum, Cbd. ..... mountain
phou, Lao. ..... mountain
pic, Fr. ..... peak
pico(s), Port., Sp. ..... peak(s)
-piggen, Nor. ..... mountain
pik, Rus. ..... peak
pique, Fr. ..... peak
piton(s), Fr. ..... peak(s)
pivostriv, Ukr. ..... peninsula
planalto, Port. ..... plateau
planina, S./C. ..... mountain, range
plato, Afk., Blg., Rus. ..... plateau
playa, Sp. ..... beach
pointe, Fr. ..... point
polje, S./C. ..... plain, basin
poluostrov, Rus. ..... peninsula
pont, Fr. ..... bridge
ponta, pontal, Port. ..... point
porto, It. ..... port
presa, Sp. ..... reservoir, dam
presqu'île, Fr. ..... peninsula
proliv, Rus. ..... strait
puerto, Sp. ..... port
pulau, Indon., Mal. ..... island
puncak, Indon. ..... peak
punta, It., Sp. ..... point, peak
qundao, Ch. ..... islands
rão, ribeirão, Port. ..... river
ras, ra's, Ara. ..... cape
rās, Ara. ..... cape
récif, Fr. ..... reef
represa, Port. ..... dam, reservoir
-retto, Jpn. ..... islands
ría, Sp. ..... ria (inlet)

rib., ribeira, Port. ..... brook
ribeirão, Port. ..... river
rio, Port. ..... river
río, Sp. ..... river
riviera, It. ..... coast
rivière, Fr. ..... river
roca, Sp. ..... rock
rocca, It. ..... rock, mountain
rt, S./C. ..... cape
sa., serra, Port. ..... range
sahrā', Ara. ..... desert
-saki, Jpn. ..... cape
salar, Sp. ..... salt flat
salina(s), Sp. ..... salt marsh, salt flat
salto(s), Port., Sp. ..... waterfall
-sammyaku, Jpn. ..... range
-san, Jpn., Kor. ..... mountain
-sanmaek, Kor. ..... mountains
Schloss, Ger. ..... castle
sebkha, Ara. ..... salt flat
See(n), Ger. ..... lake(s)
selat, Indon. ..... strait
seno, Sp. ..... sound
serra, Port. ..... range, mountain
serranía(s), Sp. ..... ridge(s)
shan, Ch. ..... mountain(s), island
shanmo, Ch. ..... mountains
-shima, Jpn. ..... island
-shotō, Jpn. ..... islands
sierra, Sp. ..... range, ridge
-sjø, Nor. ..... lake
-sjön, Swe. ..... lake, bay
-sø, Dan. ..... lake
Spitze, Ger. ..... peak
sta., santa, Port., Sp. ..... saint
ste., sainte, Fr. ..... saint
step', Rus. ..... steppe
štít, Slo. ..... peak
sto., santo, Port., Sp. ..... saint
stretto, It. ..... strait
Strom, Ger. ..... stream
-ström, -strömmen, Swe. ..... stream
-su, Kor. ..... river
-suidō, Jpn. ..... channel
Sund, Ger. ..... sound
-sund, Swe. ..... sound
-take, Jpn. ..... mountain
Tal, Ger. ..... valley
tanjong, Mal. ..... cape
tanjung, Indon. ..... cape
tao, Ch. ..... island
teluk, Indon. ..... bay
thale, Thai ..... lagoon
-tō, Jpn. ..... island
tônlé, Cbd. ..... lake
-tunturi, Finn. ..... hill, mountain
ujung, Indon. ..... cape
-umi, Jpn. ..... lagoon
-ura, Jpn. ..... bay
valle, It., Sp. ..... valley
vallée, Fr. ..... valley
vârful, Rom. ..... mountain
-vatn, Ice., Nor. ..... lake
vdkhr., vodokhranilishche, Rus. ..... reservoir
-vesi, Finn. ..... lake
-viken, Swe. ..... gulf
vodokhranilishche, Rus. ..... reservoir
vodoskhovyshche, Ukr. ..... reservoir
vol., volcán, Sp. ..... volcano
wādī, Ara. ..... wadi
wāhat, wāhāt, Ara. ..... oasis
wan, Ch., Jpn. ..... bay
-yama, Jpn. ..... mountain
yarımadası, Tur. ..... peninsula
yoma, Bur. ..... mountains
yumco, Tib. ..... lake
yunhe, Ch. ..... canal
-zaki, Jpn. ..... point
zaliv, Rus. ..... gulf, bay
zatoka, Ukr. ..... gulf, bay
zee, Du. ..... sea, lake

Abbreviations of Geographical Names and Terms

Ab., Can..... Alberta, Can.
Afg. .... Afghanistan
Afr. .... Africa
Ak., U.S. ..... Alaska, U.S.
Al., U.S. .....Alabama, U.S.
Alb. .... Albania
Alg. .... Algeria
Ang. .... Angola
Ant. .... Antarctica
Ar., U.S.... Arkansas, U.S.
Arg. .... Argentina
Arm. .... Armenia
Aus. .... Austria
Austl. .... Australia
Az., U.S. ....Arizona, U.S.
Azer. .... Azerbaijan
B. .... Bay
Bah. .... Bahamas
Bahr. .... Bahrain
Barb. .... Barbados
B.C., Can. .... British
     Columbia, Can.
Bdi. .... Burundi
Bel. .... Belgium
Bela. ....Belarus
Bhu. .... Bhutan
Bngl. .... Bangladesh
Bol. .... Bolivia
Bos. .... Bosnia
     and Hercegovina
Bots. .... Botswana
Braz. .... Brazil
Bul. .... Bulgaria
Burkina ...... Burkina Faso
C. .... Cape
Ca., U.S. ... California, U.S.
Camb. .... Cambodia
Can. .... Canada
C.A.R. .... Central
     African Republic
Cay. Is..... Cayman Islands
C. Iv. .... Cote d'Ivoire
Co., U.S. ... Colorado, U.S.
Col. .... Colombia
C.R. .... Costa Rica
Cro. .... Croatia
Ct., U.S. ....
     Connecticut, U.S.

Ctry. .... Country
C.V. .... Cape Verde
Cyp. .... Cyprus
Czech Rep......... Czech
     Republic
D.C., U.S. ......District of
     Columbia, U.S.
De., U.S. .. Delaware, U.S.
Den. .... Denmark
Dep. .... Dependency
Des. .... Desert
Dji. .... Djibouti
Ec. .... Ecuador
El Sal. .... El Salvador
Eng., U.K. .England, U.K.
Eq. Gui......... Equatorial
     Guinea
Erit. .... Eritrea
Est. .... Estonia
Eth. .... Ethiopia
Eur. .... Europe
Falk. Is....Falkland Islands
Fin. .... Finland
Fl., U.S. ......Florida, U.S.
Fr. .... France
Fr. Gu. ...... French Guiana
G. .... Gulf
Ga., U.S. ....Georgia, U.S.
Gam. .... Gambia
Gaza Str. .... Gaza Strip
Geor. .... Georgia
Ger. .... Germany
Grc. .... Greece
Guad. .... Guadeloupe
Guat. .... Guatemala
Gui. .... Guinea
Gui.-B. ...... Guinea-Bissau
Guy. .... Guyana
Hi., U.S. ......Hawaii, U.S.
H.K. ....Hong Kong
Hond. .... Honduras
Hung. .... Hungary
I. .... Island
Ia., U.S. .... Iowa, U.S.
Ice. .... Iceland
Id., U.S. ...... Idaho, U.S.
Il., U.S. ..... Illinois, U.S.

In., U.S. ..... Indiana, U.S.
Indon. .... Indonesia
Ire...................... Ireland
Is. .... Islands
Isr. .... Israel
Jam. .... Jamaica
Jord. .... Jordan
Kaz. .... Kazakhstan
Ks., U.S. ...... Kansas, U.S.
Kuw. .... Kuwait
Ky., U.S. ..Kentucky, U.S.
Kyrg............. Kyrgyzstan
L. .... Lake
La., U.S. ....Louisiana, U.S.
Lat. .... Latvia
Leb. .... Lebanon
Leso. .... Lesotho
Lib. .... Liberia
Lith. .... Lithuania
Lux. .... Luxembourg
Ma., U.S. .. Massachusetts,
     U.S.
Mac. .... Macedonia
Madag. .... Madagascar
Malay. .... Malaysia
Mart............ Martinique
Maur. .... Mauritania
Mb., Can.................
     Manitoba, Can.
Md., U.S... Maryland, U.S.
Me., U.S......Maine, U.S.
Mex. .... Mexico
Mi., U.S. ..Michigan, U.S.
Mn., U.S..Minnesota, U.S.
Mo., U.S.... Missouri, U.S.
Mol. .... Moldova
Mong. .... Mongolia
Monts. .... Montserrat
Mor. .... Morocco
Moz. .... Mozambique
Ms., U.S.................
     Mississippi, U.S.
Mt. .... Mountain
Mt., U.S. .. Montana, U.S.
Mts. .... Mountains
Mwi. .... Malawi
Myan............. Myanmar

N.A..........North America
N.B., Can............ New
     Brunswick, Can.
N.C., U.S. .... North
     Carolina, U.S.
N. Cal. .....New Caledonia
N.D., U.S. .... North
     Dakota, U.S.
Ne., U.S. .. Nebraska, U.S.
Neth. ....Netherlands
Neth. Ant. ...Netherlands
     Antilles
Nf, Can... Newfoundland,
     Can.
N.H., U.S. ....New
     Hampshire, U.S.
Nic. .... Nicaragua
Nig. .... Nigeria
N. Ire., U.K....Northern
     Ireland, U.K.
N.J., U.S..................
     New Jersey, U.S.
N. Kor. ..... Korea, North
N.M., U.S. ....New
     Mexico, U.S.
Nmb................. Namibia
Nor. .... Norway
N.S., Can. .... Nova
     Scotia, Can.
N.T., Can. ......Northwest
     Territories, Can.
Nv., U.S. .... Nevada, U.S.
N.Y., U.S. ....
     New York, U.S.
N.Z. .... New Zealand
Oc................... Oceania
Oh., U.S. .... Ohio, U.S.
Ok., U.S. .Oklahoma, U.S.
On., Can.... Ontario, Can.
Or., U.S..... Oregon, U.S.
Pa., U.S..................
     Pennsylvania, U.S.
Pak. .... Pakistan
Pan. .... Panama
Pap. N. Gui....... Papua
     New Guinea

Para. .... Paraguay
P.E., Can. .Prince Edward
     Island, Can.
Pen. .... Peninsula
Phil............. Philippines
Pk. .... Peak
Plat. .... Plateau
Pol. .... Poland
Polit. Reg...Political Region
Port. .... Portugal
P.Q., Can. ..Quebec, Can.
P.R. ....Puerto Rico
Prov. .... Province
R. .... River
Ra. .... Range
Region .... Reg.
Res. .... Reservoir
R.I., U.S. ....Rhode
     Island, U.S.
Rom. .... Romania
Rw................... Rwanda
S.A. .... South America
S. Afr. ....South Africa
Sau. Ar.......Saudi Arabia
S.C., U.S. .... South
     Carolina, U.S.
Scot., U.K. ....
     Scotland, U.K.
S.D., U.S. .... South
     Dakota, U.S.
Sen. .... Senegal
Sk., Can.... Saskatchewan,
     Can.
S. Kor. ...... Korea, South
S.L. .... Sierra Leone
Slvk. .... Slovakia
Slvn. .... Slovenia
Som. .... Somalia
Sp. N. Afr. .... Spanish
     North Africa
Sri L. .... Sri Lanka
Str. .... Strait
St. Vin. .... St. Vincent
     and the Grenadines
Sur. .... Suriname
Swaz. .... Swaziland

Swe. .... Sweden
Switz. .... Switzerland
Tai. .... Taiwan
Taj. .... Tajikistan
Tan. .... Tanzania
Ter. .... Territory
Thai. .... Thailand
Tn., U.S. . Tennessee, U.S.
Trin. .... Trinidad
     and Tobago
Tun. .... Tunisia
Tur. .... Turkey
Turk. .... Turkmenistan
Tx., U.S. ...... Texas, U.S.
U.A.E. .... United
     Arab Emirates
Ug. .... Uganda
U.K......United Kingdom
Ukr. .... Ukraine
Ur. .... Uruguay
U.S. .... United States
Ut., U.S. ...... Utah, U.S.
Uzb. .... Uzbekistan
Va., U.S..... Virginia, U.S.
Ven. .... Venezuela
Viet. .... Vietnam
V.I.U.S. .... Virgin
     Islands (U.S.)
Vol. .... Volcano
Vt., U.S. .....Vermont, U.S.
Wa., U.S. ....
     Washington, U.S.
Wales, U.K. . Wales, U.K.
Wal./F..Wallis and Futuna
W.B. .... West Bank
Wi., U.S. .Wisconsin, U.S.
W. Sah. ... Western Sahara
W. Sam. .. Western Samoa
W.V., U.S........... West
     Virginia, U.S.
Wy., U.S...Wyoming, U.S.
Yk., Can. ....Yukon
     Territory, Can.
Yugo. ....Yugoslavia
Zam. .... Zambia
Zimb.............Zimbabwe

Index

This universal index includes in a single alphabetical list approximately 4,100 names of features that appear on the reference maps. Each name is followed by geographical coordinates and a page reference.

Abbreviation and Capitalization

Abbreviations of names on the maps have been standardized as much as possible. Names that are abbreviated on the maps are generally spelled out in full in the index. Periods are used after all abbreviations regardless of local practice. The abbreviation "St." is used only for "Saint." "Sankt" and other forms of this term are spelled out.

Most initial letters of names are capitalized, except for a few Dutch names, such as "'s-Gravenhage." Capitalization of non-initial words in a name generally follows local practice.

Alphabetization

Names are alphabetized in the order of the letters of the English alphabet. Spanish ll and ch, for example, are not treated as distinct letters. Furthermore, diacritical marks are disregarded

in alphabetization. German or Scandinavian ä or ö are treated as a or o.

The names of physical features may appear inverted, since they are always alphabetized under the proper, not the generic, part of the name, thus: "Gibraltar, Strait of." Otherwise every entry, whether consisting of one word or more, is alphabetized as a single continuous entity. "Lakeland," for example, appears after "Lake Forest" and before "La Línea." Names beginning with articles (Le Havre, Al Manāmah, Ad Dawhah) are not inverted. Names beginning "St.," "Ste." and "Sainte" are alphabetized as though spelled "Saint."

In the case of identical names, towns are listed first, then political divisions, then physical features.

Generic Terms

Except for cities, the names of all features are followed by terms that represent broad classes of features, for example, Mississippi, R. or Alabama, State.

Country names and names of features that extend beyond the boundaries of one country are followed by the name of the continent in which each is located. Country designations follow the names of all other places in the index. The locations of places in the United States and the United Kingdom are further defined by abbreviations that indicate the state or political division in which each is located.

Page References and Geographical Coordinates

The geographical coordinates and page references are found in the last columns of each entry.

Latitude and longitude coordinates for point features, such as cities and mountain peaks, indicate the locations of the symbols. For extensive areal features, such as countries or mountain ranges, or linear features, such as canals and rivers, locations are given for the position of the type as it appears on the map.

Index